Killing Joke: A Prophecy Fulfilled

By CHRIS BRYANS

www.thisdayinmusicbooks.com

A catalogue record for this book is available from the British Library.

ISBN: 978-1838078324

The author and publisher gratefully acknowledge the permission granted to reproduce the copyright material in this book. Every effort has been made to trace the copyright holders of the photographs in this book but one or two were unreachable. We would be grateful if the photographers concerned would contact us.

Production Liz Sánchez and Neil Cossar
Design and layout by Gary Bishop
Front cover design by Mike Coles
Album and singles images & additional artwork/photography by Ian T. Cossar
Thanks to Dave Evely and all at Sound Performance. Printed in Italy

This Day In Music Books Bishopswood Road, Prestatyn, LL199PL

Email: editor@thisdayinmusic.com

Exclusive Distributors: Music Sales Limited 14/15 Berners St London W1T 3JL

FOREWORD

I've noticed this with other musical revelations I've had: often, the ones that have made the greatest personal impact have taken a while to digest before I can fully appreciate them. Killing Joke was one of those bands. The first track I heard was 'Requiem'. I was 17-years-old, heavily into punk and at work with a friend. He played it on the boombox. First thought was: what the hell is this? I loved loud, distorted guitars, but these weren't Steve Jones-style power chords on his Les Paul. It had a sinister, discordant vibe to it, and I can remember my first impression as clear as day – it reminded me of Rush or King Crimson. I rejected it immediately.

It wasn't until about a week or so later… I was over at Chuck Mosley's house and he put on 'Change'. I thought: "Wow, this is some serious hard funk. It is so wrong and so right, so badass." It was then that I learned that this was in fact the same Killing Joke – and that's when the gravity of it hit me, because I somehow had a way to conceptualise 'Requiem'. This wasn't Neil Peart playing 'Tom Sawyer'; it was Sly Dunbar playing a dub from hell. And I understood now – it wasn't that I previously didn't like it; it was that I had lacked the ability to fully process it. But once I got it, that was it. There were all types of completely disparate influences going on, and at full power. It was something really different – not afraid to be heavy, not afraid to groove, not afraid to have its voice.

What makes KJ authentic to me is more than just the music. There is something synchronous with the life of the band and the vibe of the music. Completely and always unapologetic, maybe sometimes to its own detriment. Primal. Feral. And completely detached from a mainstream that seeks reassuring comfort and traditional norms.

I cannot think of a single band that has released records for four decades where I'm just as interested in hearing what they are doing now as I was 40 or so years ago. The vibe is still completely there – they continue to pleasantly surprise me. Put into perspective, 40 years is the time period between 1960 and 2000.

Who else has done something like this?

Bill Gould ***(bass, Faith No More)***

INTRODUCTION

What were the odds? The first meeting between editor and publisher for a proposed 'people's history' of a band cancelled on account of an unfolding virus pandemic. And what band would that be? A band that for 40 years has surrounded us, backed us all into a corner and enveloped us with music brutal, beautiful and bleak about all manner of existential threats...

I had to laugh. But then it stopped being funny.

Most of the planet – and the lives being lived on it – ground to a halt; appalling loss of life became our daily diet of news; the political leaders we suspected would be useless – or, even worse, legally culpable – didn't disappoint. "See! I told you!" – you can almost hear the words, spat out at close quarters, by the band's harlequin, eyes sparkling.

I was introduced to Killing Joke through a door that seemed always to be locked to me. This was the door to my older brother's bedroom. As so often happens with these things, it was a sibling who would hold the key to opening up new music. And Killing Joke weren't going to let a little thing like a door come between us.

Martin 'Youth' Glover, Big Paul Ferguson, Geordie Walker and Jaz Coleman © Frank Jenkinson

My brother's mate tipped up with the debut album in late 1980. Most folk recall their first reaction being shock and awe at that cover, the repurposed Don McCullin photo. It opened up to a gatefold image of staggering audacity. As this remained unseen for me for some time, I had only the music with which to form an impression. I say 'only', but we know what we are talking about here.

My brother being a hi-fi nut at the time – "A thousand quid? For a fucking needle?" – the message coming out of his room was very loud, very clear and, even to a 13-year-old, SOUNDED RIGHT. Teenagers are famous for knowing everything and nothing simultaneously, but this was INCONTROVERTIBLE.

My brother got to see Joke at Preston Poly on the *Revelations* tour. I recall his shell-shocked expression when he got home (could have been the beer, but I doubt it). I still listen to the cassette bootleg of that night from time to time, loving Jaz's intro to 'Empire Song' – "Is this a college or what?"

I had to wait until early 1985 in Blackburn to see them, a warm-up show for *The Tube*. Thirty-five years later, my mate swears his shins still give him grief from the kicking they received at the front.

I remember expecting sounds along the same lines of the debut for the second album. *What's THIS for...?* taught me that this was a band that would not be sticking to a template of diminishing returns. And so it has proved ever since. Whatever life is, it isn't boring around Joke. It's like staring into the abyss, but with like-minded friends for company in those final moments. What other band can, one minute, explore the primitive urges of our species and then pivot to a defence of the European Ideal?

Sprinkled liberally around this book are quotes from musical peers who turn into fans for a few moments. Their testimonies are a measure of the depth of feeling that the band's intensity and innovation have inspired. Their influence runs deep but too often unacknowledged.

Killing Joke have been characterised as a band for the end times. For me, they are a band for *all* times. But that's not quite true. In 1996, largely reductive Britpop held court and most us actually believed that PM-apparent Tony Blair would be a force for good. Well, didn't that work out well? At the same time, the Joke went AWOL.

In 2003, with the world going up in flames, millions marching against an illegal war and oil prized more than lives, it was the ideal time for a Joke resurrection. *KJ 2003* stands as an unforgettable hour of boiling, burning, righteous rage. With that, the band enjoyed the last laugh.

The pendulum swings. Look at the back-to-back nature of *Outside the Gate* and *Extremities...*; same with *Democracy* and *KJ* 2003. It's as if the band take time away until they are needed the most, until they can contain their fury no longer. Then they blow up in society's face.

Iraq War. There's a band for that. Surveillance society. There's a band for that. Brexit. There's a band for that as well.

So here we are. You have already marvelled at Mike Coles' majestic cover design and read the wise words of Faith No More's Bill Gould. You have even managed to make it this far through my two penn'orth. In the pages that follow, you will find the fruits of new interviews with all the band, plus producers, engineers, remixers, artists, video directors, film directors, former members, industry peers, designers, magazine editors, photographers, studio owners, journalists, friends, an astrologer and even a Professor of Condensed Matter Physics Theory. At the end of it all, you have Jaz signing off (and sounding off) on the meaning of the title he gave to this project.

For a goodly portion of the book, though, the floor is handed over to you, to find out how important this singular band has been in guiding the courses of lives. Not just musical lives. Lives in general. As I collected stories from right around the world, several themes emerged. Principally that Killing Joke is more than music. People have had alternative ways of life revealed to them, different ways of critical thinking, ways to stay sane in an increasingly insane world. People who saw themselves as outsiders found some sort of safe haven within the Killing Joke community. Outsiders who connected with other outsiders discovered they were no longer alone with their thoughts.

At times during this project, I confess that I have felt more priest than editor, and I say that as someone who has no religious component to his life. Some of the memories of youthful loss and confusion are nakedly intimate. I was honoured to be entrusted with them. Now I entrust them to you. Pretentious, moi?

What we have are four radically different, lavishly talented, fiercely intelligent individuals. Bring them together and they attain what they would probably call a higher level of consciousness. I'm not totally sure if I know exactly what that means, aside from the fact they make music that stirs something deep inside that almost nothing else can bring to the surface. These four people can make you dance, laugh, love and, perhaps most important of all, THINK.

Who knows – we may never all achieve that higher state of consciousness. We might never save the planet from ourselves. But we should still keep trying, right?

As we have all recognised, this is not a band to invite indifference. And, to my knowledge, they never wear sunglasses on stage. I interpret that as a statement – we will never try to hide from you. That's got to be a good thing, yes? It's all about connecting. Especially in times like these.

CHRIS BRYANS

© Frank Jenkinson

1979

"Every direction leading to the same place"

© Frank Jenkinson

YOUTH

The thing to remember is that we're all very, very different. Part of the magic of Killing Joke is the extreme juxtaposition of opposites in both our personalities and our tastes.

JAZ

We are a dysfunctional family. Youth did this amazing cartoon. I have gotta get it off him. It shows this mixing engineer with his head in his hands. There's me on one side of the mixing desk and Youth on the other side. I'm going "Up" and Youth's going "Down".

GEORDIE

1973. I was after an electric guitar. My Mum and Dad took me up to Northampton. I'm in the market for a Zenta Les Paul, like 90 quid, something like that. It was a Saturday morning in the shop, all the local muso heads are there. My Mum spots this Les Paul Deluxe Sunburst on the wall. "Let's try that."

I could only play about three chords. I'm sitting there with it, all these hip kids staring evils at me. But the fucking thing just played itself.

Anyway, my Dad was looking a bit pale, so we went down the café round the corner. And she talked him into buying it.

That's hanging on the wall. £318. I found the receipt.

YOUTH

Geordie had never been in a band. But his Mum bought him a Les Paul at 13. Only child. He was pretty good, but he'd never actually been in a band.

© *Frank Jenkinson*

GEORDIE

The radio was always on from when I was born. I think Youth had the same upbringing in that there was always music in the house.

BIG PAUL

I was born in Ilford, Essex. My Dad was in the Royal Air Force, so we moved a lot. Every three or four years, a different place, different school, different friends. I learned from an early age to never be too attached to anyone.

I went to school in High Wycombe when I was 13 and then, when my folks left to live in Saudi Arabia, I was left there as a boarder. After A-levels, I stayed in Wycombe for a Foundation Course in Art.

GEORDIE

I've got the guitar and I've blagged the school music teacher to get a Marshall amp from a music shop in Bletchley, a really loud Marshall combo. She let me rehearse in the music room, which was quite a big room with a high ceiling. I'm in there at lunchtime, cranking this fucking thing. I look up and see all the bad boys in detention hanging out the window, banging their heads.

There was a girl there – Linda – at the door. Barbie on fucking steroids.

Well, that was my career choice decided there and then.

JAZ

There *was* an epiphany. I knew exactly what rock music and pop music was. Brian Jones was a regular visitor to our house. I wasn't remotely interested. It wasn't until puberty kicked in. I was on a big orchestral course. This viola player said to me: "Don't you listen to anything other than classical music, choral music?"

That's when they introduced me to weed and the music of Can, *Tago Mago*. This experience changed my life. The next day, I was different. It was an epiphany. I realised what I wanted to do – rock music. It was liberating. And it still is. It's a liberating force. There's only one song – it's freedom.

Great rock music is loud, rebellious and, as my colleague Youth points out, it's got a fuck-off attitude to it.

Big Paul: "Backstage at The Nashville with Andy, bass player with the Mat Stagger Band" © Frank Jenkinson

BIG PAUL

London was a short bus ride or thumbing a lift [away], so I got used to going there. My oldest sister was there and I'd visit when I could. I would go to London and see bands like The Pirates, Wayne County, Motörhead.

I was in an art-school band called Pink Parts, which played locally, and also at the usual punk venues like The Hope and Anchor. The band supported Adam and the Ants at the 100 Club, although that was after they threw me out.

As for the London scene, I was never part of it, but I did go to gigs. High Wycombe was on the London pub circuit, so I was lucky to see great bands at The Nag's Head – The Jam, XTC, Elvis Costello, Gen X, Dr. Feelgood, among others. I would hang out in a dub-reggae record shop off Oxford Street hoping to score weed and listening to *Two Sevens Clash* [by Culture].

Although I had a flat in Battersea, I stayed in Portland Road with my girlfriend and that was where I was introduced to Jaz. I was playing in a band at the time. Jaz was brought round to the house by Carlos, a Bhagwan Rajneesh disciple (there were a couple in the house) after they met at the dole office and he thought we'd get along. I guess he was right.

YOUTH

They didn't get on at all from the beginning.

BIG PAUL

I think he [Jaz] would like to say it was immediate and mutual loathing. But not really. We had and have different and opposing personalities but enough common interest to spend a lot of time in each other's company. And, yes, the occult was certainly one of them. He soon moved into the Battersea flat with me, but we spent most of our time at Portland Road. A very long walk when you have no money. Jaz and I jammed with some guys he was in a band with. They all left the room and we carried on, so, yes, we had a connection. I then got him into the Mat Stagger Band.

© Frank Jenkinson

YOUTH

Mat Stagger was like a wine bar reggae band. The reason Jaz and Paul never go on about it is because it was so bad. Mat was a lovely guy, but the band was terrible.

BIG PAUL

We both quit before Jaz's first gig. Not something I'm too proud of. We both had day jobs for a while. He worked at a garage and I worked in the warehouse of a clothing company, but we both knew that work was interfering with our dreams. I took some time off sick and painted our flat in some crazy black and white dartboard thing with a magic circle on the floor hidden by the carpet. That was where we did our subsequent rituals. Who knows how the universe works, but strong intent manifests itself in unseen ways. We had intent and the unseen manifested.

JAZ
Straight after the ritual, we put an advert in *Melody Maker*. We had about 200 applicants.

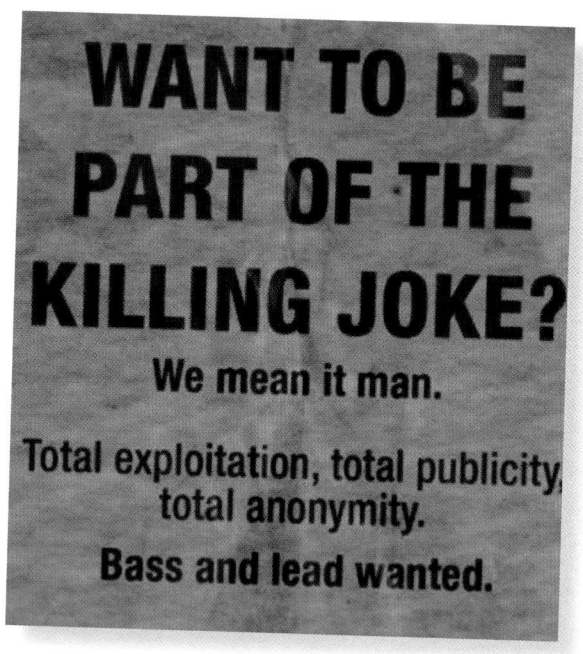

WANT TO BE
PART OF THE
KILLING JOKE?
We mean it man.
Total exploitation, total publicity, total anonymity.
Bass and lead wanted.

YOUTH
Paul and Jaz put the band together, put an ad out. Geordie picked up on that.

GEORDIE
It was a bit of a slog to get hooked up to Jaz. I only got one of my three A-levels. My girlfriend from up Bletchley – Cockney girl, Peckham family, fucking lovely. She got into teacher-training college up in Trent Park Polytechnic, up by Cockfosters. I was up there when the ad appeared.

No way to treat footwear of quality, Geordie © Frank Jenkinson

BIG PAUL
Geordie showed up in his donkey jacket and brothel creepers, a Gibson and an attitude.

GEORDIE
It was grey and grimy back then. Get down to the address and there's this swarthy-looking geezer digging through bin bags. "Oi, you looking for your breakfast?"

Up we went to the top floor. We didn't really hit it off but the one thing we had in common was fishing.

I headed out. I'm not sure if I wanna do this. Paul was away but his bedroom door was ajar. On the floor, under the telly, I spotted a pair of blue suede brothel creepers. "All right, I'm in. He's gonna be all right."

YOUTH
Then I picked up on the ad.

GEORDIE
We still didn't have a bass player. We had this other guy. Luckily, when [Big Paul] Ferguson came back to his burned-down flat, he didn't like this bass player.

BIG PAUL
The flat burning down robbed the old lady who lived next door of her home.

YOUTH

Geordie invited me up to Cheltenham, although he refused to play my three-stringed, six-string acoustic in my bedsit. He wouldn't touch it.

GEORDIE

I ain't fucking playing that.

YOUTH

I sort of took a chance on him. I thought: "He sounds serious."

GEORDIE

I just had a feeling about him [Youth].

JAZ

The two people we tried to get rid of all the time was Youth and Geordie.

YOUTH

I ended up going to Cheltenham for this audition, rehearsal. Even though I was the youngest, I'd actually been in two or three bands [including The Rage, right]. And I'd made a record. And I'd toured. I was probably the most experienced.

And, of course, it went really badly. Jaz and Paul were: "He can't play." They went down the pub to get some Rizla or something. There were a load of friends asking: "How's the new bass player?" Out of sheer front, they went: "Oh yeah, he's really good."

JAZ

Big Paul and myself went into town.

YOUTH

They came back from the pub. Geordie – only because I was Geordie's idea – stuck with me and we ended up while they were in the pub doing this one-note riff and building up this great intensity... They [Jaz and Paul] walked in and went straight to their instruments and that was 'Are You Receiving', our first single. That was it. Fait accompli. That track kicked off. We all celebrated. And that was it. I was in the band.

A rare image of Youth, then strictly Martin Glover, in The Rage, supporting The Adverts at Newcastle University in November 1977. Youth: "I've hardly ever seen a Rage pic! I used to look and dress a bit like elves then. Love it"

JAZ

We're gonna structure future rehearsals on the very first rehearsal – leave Geordie and fucking Youth together and we'll come later. They have an understanding, those two. Geordie speaks Youth's language.

YOUTH

Maybe it did have something to do with their botched ceremony that resulted in Paul's flat being burned down. But I suspect it's a much older and ancient magick at play there. Our karmas had brought us into that circle in a weird, abstract and obtuse way. But, once we were there, we knew we were supposed to be there.

GEORDIE

Cheltenham – nice. Boring as hell. Lovely architecture.

YOUTH

I was hitchhiking back to London every week to sign on. We spent 10 months rehearsing. I say that to kids now. We spent a lot of time writing and rehearsing. I was hitchhiking every week to go back to Fulham to sign on. The rest of the week, we were staying in Jaz's little bungalow [in Cheltenham] behind his Mum's and rehearsing.

GEORDIE

Micky Clark owned the rehearsal studio in that lovely little square as you come into Cheltenham. There was a couple of ladies and we were hanging around their place. They went on holiday and left us the keys. We pulled all the gear out of the rehearsal studio two doors down and set it up in their yard garden. The cops got called for the noise, but we wrote 'Pssyche' that afternoon.

YOUTH

Out of that 10 months, we just about got a 20-minute set together. That's a lot of work. We threw a lot of stuff away. But what remained I think gave us an edge and gave us a bit of an advantage. So, by the time we did our first gig, we were kinda up to speed.

WHITCOMBE LODGE
4 August 1979,
Brockworth, UK

GARY BOON

I have no idea if they were a late addition or just not worthy of a mention. I would suggest that it was a late inclusion. I say this as I went to this venue almost every week and all the support bands were usually on the posters. Usually, the first band on stage was a local band. These were bands like The Dead Airmen, Protein Pigs.

GEORDIE

Micky Clark was a mover and a shaker in the locality. He was probably mates of the promoter and stuck us on.

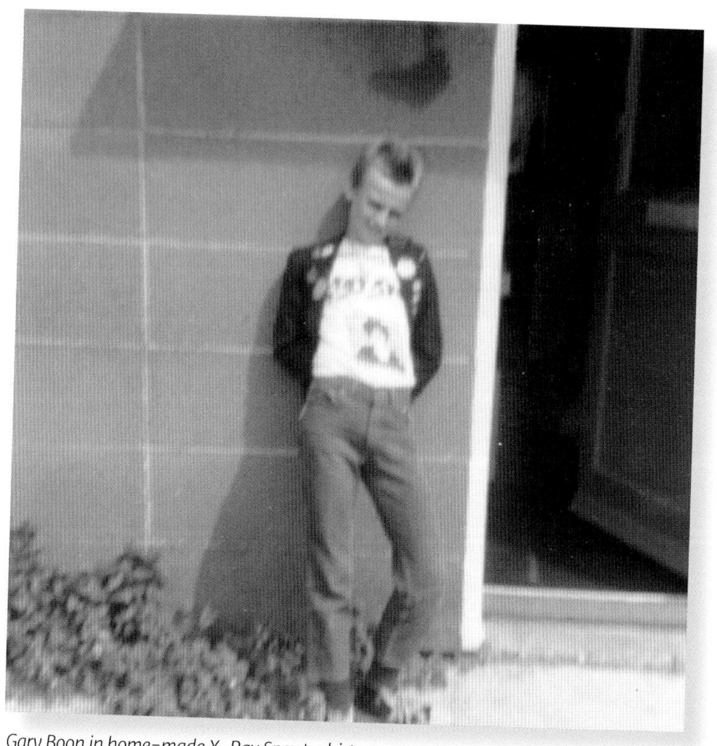

Gary Boon in home-made X-Ray Spex t-shirt

GARY BOON

I was a massive fan of The Ruts and all the gigs each week at Whitcombe Lodge. Me and my mates were young (14 or 15) and would actually have to cycle to the venue (not very cool, eh?) in the early afternoon and usually got there about 1pm.

The events were run by a promoter called Chris Garland. He used to let us in the venue, even though it was over-18s only (like so many venues back then).

The idea of us going early was manyfold. We wanted to meet the bands when they arrived, try and get in for the soundcheck (we always did) and sometimes get on the guest-list.

Anyway, this day we were there for The Ruts. We'd seen them loads before and we loved 'em.

The Selecter were okay, but we had already seen them, too, supporting The Special AKA.

We were inside the venue early (as always) and these people (punks who were older than us) came in who we didn't know. They were giving Chris Garland a 'talking to'. We knew they were obviously a band as Jaz (we had no idea who he was then) was asking about soundcheck stuff and stage-time stuff, etc.

We were stood right next to them whilst this chat was taking place. It was by the mixing desk.

The main thing I noticed was this other guy. He had very black spiky hair (cool, like Sid Vicious hair but longer spikes) and also a VERY NOTICEABLE red Sid Vicious swastika t-shirt on. He looked cool as fuck! It was Youth. I had no idea who he was either, of course.

We knew all the Cheltenham and Gloucester punks, but didn't know them, even though Jaz Coleman is from Cheltenham and his mum taught at the local comprehensive (Bournside School, by my house).

They didn't hang around in Cheltenham or go to the gigs I went to...

We asked Chris who they were and were told they were Killing Joke. "Never heard of 'em."

Killing Joke were on first. They were a cacophony of fucking noise and were loud. I remember them because I thought, "Who's this big-headed c**t singing and acting like some fucking star? They're only the support band."

I thought it was just a fucking noise. It was like nothing I had heard before really. Very heavy bass and a screaming big head shouting.

The only song I think I remember was 'Wardance', because, when it came out on single, I thought, "I already know that song."

'Nervous System' came out a few months after this gig. I wasn't convinced, so didn't buy it, even though they were a local band and I'd seen them.

(Got it now, though.)

Of course, in retrospect they were WAY ahead of their time and were unique. The nearest at that time would have been PiL, I would think.

For years, I mentioned to people that Killing Joke played at Whitcombe Lodge and they didn't believe me because they weren't mentioned on the poster.

I was proved right when The Ruts book came out and it's mentioned in that book. I remember the gigs vividly and treasure so many memories of that time. All the bands were friendly – Ruts, UK Subs, The Cramps (on their first UK visit). Guess who weren't friendly to us – U2! He was a pompous sod even then.

HONEY BANE
(Fatal Microbes)

I think it was their first gig. They were just amazing. Everyone took to them immediately. Their music really knew how to stir up a crowd. Youth's just a great bass player. They built a following very quickly.

I was 15, I think, if that, when I met Youth in London. He took me out to Cheltenham, where I met Jaz and the others. There were a few nights when nobody really slept. We all just got very stoned and played *Risk*. I would quite often stay at their squats.

SEGS
(The Ruts)

I still see Youth to this day and we talk about it! He always says: "I did my first ever gig with you!" I believe the promoter's name was Chris – a nice chap, as I recall.

KJ were not on the bill but just turned up and asked if they could play — we kinda shrugged and said: "Yeah, why not." It was kinda the spirit of the times. The Ruts and KJ became friends.

BIG PAUL
The gig in Cheltenham I remember clearly, supporting The Ruts.

© Gary Boon

YOUTH
[When they came to see us] they could have all walked out. I think eventually it [success] would have happened because we were a very different band from anything else out there.

GEORDIE
I remember being so fucking terrified. I couldn't stand still. My fucking legs would shake. So I was walking around the whole gig. It was only a half-hour set.

Youth, Geordie and Big Paul at 11 Portland Road, headquarters for the embryonic Killing Joke and Malicious Damage operations © Frank Jenkinson

BIG PAUL
I get more nervous now. The crowds are bigger, and festivals and support slots aren't our crowd.

JAZ
You have to remember there's factors as a young band that put us way ahead of our contemporaries. Firstly, the house that I met Big Paul in [11 Portland Road] was a house full of psychiatrists, actually industrial psychiatrists, who were working at the Tavistock Institute of Human Relations, which is, of course, behaviour control. So we had a kind of savage awakening there. It all happened there. It all happened in that place there. 11 Portland Road.

BIG PAUL

I have many memories of Portland Road. I can't actually believe we were so privileged to stay there, as it's a beautiful part of London and now completely unaffordable. The building was owned by Quakers and there was a communal way of living. It was there that we met Brian Taylor and all the people who would invest their time and effort into creating the Malicious Damage label and getting KJ off the ground.

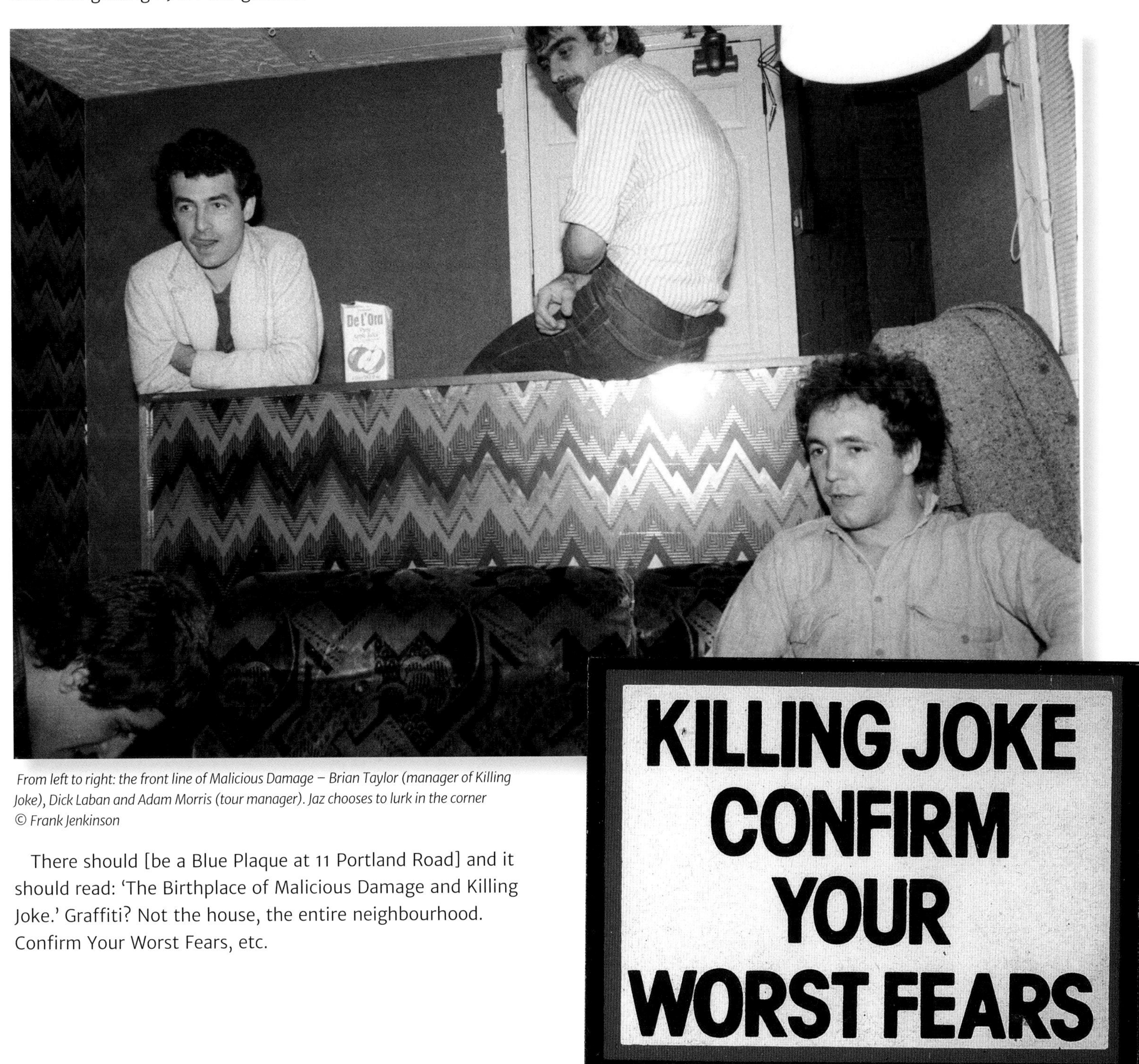

From left to right: the front line of Malicious Damage – Brian Taylor (manager of Killing Joke), Dick Laban and Adam Morris (tour manager). Jaz chooses to lurk in the corner
© Frank Jenkinson

There should [be a Blue Plaque at 11 Portland Road] and it should read: 'The Birthplace of Malicious Damage and Killing Joke.' Graffiti? Not the house, the entire neighbourhood. Confirm Your Worst Fears, etc.

© Mike Coles

JAZ
It was only until I learned how to fight – mentally, physically, intellectually, on every level – that I was prepared for Killing Joke really. The thing that made me like that was being an Anglo-Asian born in a very white town. I had to get used to being physically assaulted on a regular basis. I don't mind a fucking fight. I don't mind it at all.

BIG PAUL
I knew it would be special.

YOUTH
I think it was only about 15 gigs before we were headlining the Lyceum.

BIG PAUL
Our first gigs in London were epic.

1979 – 1982

"I'm getting out of this system"

GEORDIE
Dick Laban's girlfriend was a nurse named Bindi [below]. She just kind blew out this sentence: "What? You mean like a killing joke?" Everyone was like: "Aaarrgghhh. Fucking genius. That's it." The name came from a nurse called Bindi.

© Frank Jenkinson

YOUTH
I was amazed anybody got it [the music] at the time, even though we had rehearsed and rehearsed. It was so different and so particular to us. I just thought it's gonna be too weird for everybody. If we wanted to, we could rock like the Pistols, we could groove with some funk-disco bass-lines as well as anyone else. I thought at least we'll get them dancing. If they're punks and they really want some noise, we can pull that out of the bag as well.

But I did think what we were doing was a little bit too progressive, even though you listen to 'Wardance' and it's basic, isn't it? It's as basic as the Ramones in a way. I loved that.

But there's a weird sort of almost prog-ness to it that makes it a little bit more sophisticated than just straightforward punk and I didn't think people would really get it. It was hard for them to relate it to other things. Some of it was like Alex Harvey, some of it was Ramones, some of it was AC/DC, some of it was just noise. Can was a big unifying influence and not a lot of people got Can that I knew at the time.

I thought we might end up on the fringes.

MARK LUSARDI

(engineer 'Turn to Red'/'Nervous System')

I did do a lot of reggae and I did a lot of punk stuff. I worked with the Sex Pistols. I think the combination – I was doing reggae stuff and doing punk stuff – sort of interested people.

Gooseberry Studio, right in the middle of London, in Soho.

One of the things about 'Turn to Red' was that we wanted a sort of sequenced keyboard going through it and nobody could play it tight apart from me. It was a one-finger keyboard part. We had to play that bang in time; it's through the whole track. Even though I wasn't much of a keyboard player, I could keep time like a machine.

Jaz is a great bloke. Very creative. He's such a great, creative musician; tremendous-sounding voice. He made you want to hear what he was gonna do. He's got Alpha Male-itis.

There were occasions where things got so disorganised that we weren't quite sure if it was a musical event or a psychiatric one.

I liked the band. A good band. Good musicians. Couldn't keep time as well as me, though.

JOHN DORAN

(co-founder The Quietus)

Killing Joke doing 'Turn to Red' is more of an authentic connection with dub-reggae culture and sound-system culture to my ears than, say, most of the crappy punk/reggae crossovers that were going on at the time.

FRANK JENKINSON
(early band photographer)

Frank Jenkinson

I fancied myself as a photographer. I lived in the same house [11 Portland Road, London W11] with the then manager Brian Taylor. And the house was owned by the Tavistock. To live there, you had to be in therapy, but my mate was caretaker there and we got rooms. We pretended we went to therapy. We should have done.

There was a whole group of connected people living in the house. All kinds of creative people.

We had really good fun. From '79 to '81, me and Malicious Damage were all living in the house.

They [Killing Joke] blew me away. I had that emotional connection anyway [but] I thought they were amazing. They were the best thing around at the time.

MIKE COLES
(graphic artist)

I used to drink in The Prince of Wales in Holland Park, where I met Brian Taylor, a friend of Jaz and Paul. They wanted to form a band and Brian wanted to start a label, so I jumped in with the idea that, if you ran your own record label, you could design everything yourself.

I loved Aubrey Beardsley's stuff in my teens. I really enjoyed the Beardsley exhibition [In London in early 2020]. I also loved all the hippy posters and artwork – Hapshash and the Coloured Coat, American West Coast stuff, *OZ* magazine, *International Times*, etc. Then I discovered John Heartfield, George Grosz, Gilbert & George and Francis Bacon, plus lots of Victorian freak-show stuff. I was fascinated by Robert Rauschenberg's work, and that influenced me a lot – the idea that you could make art from anything.

Mike Coles © Frank Jenkinson

The first track I heard was 'Are You Receiving' and I knew then that they had something special. It was a cocktail of band, music, me, Brian and a shared sick sense of humour.

Originally, the idea was that the band members remained anonymous: no photos, only unsettling and intriguing imagery. I used to make my own sleeves for my singles, but it was many years before I actually got to do real ones.

MIK RAVEN

It started before I had ever heard them. Back in the late Seventies, a religious-indoctrinated teenager with a love of punk rock was taken into care. The religion was very quickly beaten out of me, I'm glad to say! There was a certain freedom that he'd never had before, which allowed him to discover a DJ called John Peel. Does that sound familiar?

So JP played a song by Killing Joke. It was probably 'Wardance'. I cannot remember exactly but I thought it was great. Then I think he played 'Pssyche'.

Frank Jenkinson: "When I was taking photographs, the band could be less than cooperative. I tried to be as inconspicuous as possible, it was best to catch them at gigs"

ART COLLEGE
c.1979
Canterbury, Kent

MARTYN SEARS

I got into Killing Joke via John Peel. Saw them a few times in the early days.

The gig I will always remember was in Canterbury, Kent. Peel announced it on his radio show, so I went along. I think it was the art college. Got there early and had the chance to meet the band in the bar, talking to Youth. He brought me a drink – rum and pineapple in a half-pint glass.

I think Ski Patrol supported. Not a big crowd, but great gig. I will always remember Youth buying that drink – got me hooked on it for a while.

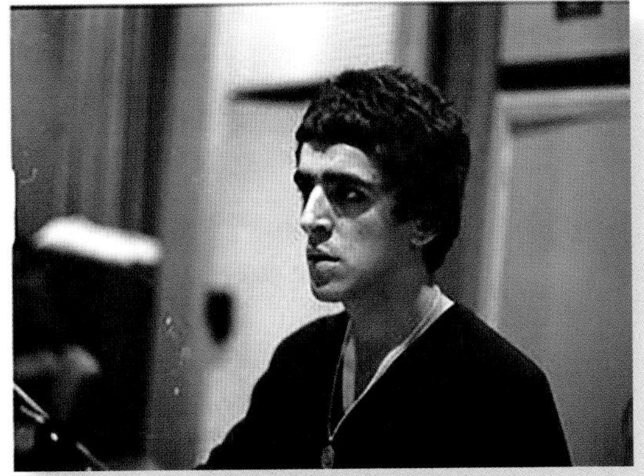

Maida Vale – 17 October 1979. Frank Jenkinson: "The night of the first Peel session was long. You can see that from the pictures of the clocks that I took at the time. It ended around, I think, six in the morning"

MIXMASTER MORRIS (DJ)

I think I saw them three times in the Seventies...

CHRIS KIDGER TOOLE

October 1979: I was 13 and in the habit of listening to John Peel's show while doing my homework. I would listen on my ghetto blaster at the kitchen table with a C90 [tape] in position, ready to record anything interesting.

"Killing Joke" the great man announced. "Interesting name," I thought. "Let's press record. I can always rewind the tape if it's no good."

Minutes later, I was hooked. And, of course, on the last track (can't remember the playing order) my cassette ran out, leaving me to listen avidly for the repeat of the session in December, when I got the lot on tape.

Although KJ had made their mark, I can't say that they immediately became my favourite band. That would take time.

After all, in late '79, they had significant competition, not least from Public Image Limited and their seminal *Metal Box* album. My tastes were quite broad, from Crass to The Fall to The Cure. Killing Joke slotted nicely into the middle of all this.

HONEY BANE

They were really intense on stage. The riffs and the bass. The power. They sounded massive. They managed to sound massive. One of my favourite bands from back in the early days. A bit larger than life. Jaz – very cool, very into his magick.

TIM FOSTER

I went to two KJ gigs at the Moonlight in West Hampstead in winter 1979 [13 November/18 December]. Also the Rock Garden [26 November 1979], where I recall propping up the bar with Paul Cook and Steve Jones. KJ were supporting and everyone left after their excellent set – we felt sorry for the headlining band and stayed for them, although I can't remember their name.

Big Paul: "LX Orb [Alex Paterson] giving it some with 'Bodies'." Rock Garden, 26 November 1979
© Frank Jenkinson

RUSTY EGAN

(drummer Rich Kids, Visage/DJ @ Blitz Club, Camden Palace/music producer)

'Turn to Red'/'Nervous System' – first single, 12-inch – was the first time I had heard from Killing Joke. At that time, I was just setting up Billy's Club in Soho after the demise of Rich Kids and I was seriously into Kraftwerk and also loved dub since the *Two Sevens Clash* album [by Culture] and had some Joe Gibbs records. I was going to Rough Trade in Portobello, which had all the indie records I needed for my DJ sets. Obviously, I had everything we all loved and all the stuff no one knew, but the reason I took up a DJ position was I hated DJs who only played DJ music. So I was looking for current 12-inch extended records that you wanted to dance to but were not disco or funk – and were a bit off the wall. I went to see Marco [Pirroni] in The Models and Rema-Rema at the Screen on the Green and I had the records that these guys all split into different bands. During my DJ sets from Billy's to Blitz to Camden Palace, I ended up playing the massive sound system where 'Turn to Red' and 'Requiem' were massive tracks on the Tuesday TRASH night.

Hope & Anchor, London, 9 December 1979 © Frank Jenkinson

ROBERT PAYES

It all started with 'Wardance'. I don't remember if I first heard it on a college radio station or received a review copy (I was writing for *Trouser Press* magazine at the time). I do remember listening to it and saying: "The mix is COMPLETELY wrong. The bass is too clanky, the guitar has waaay too much flanger on it, the drums sound like oil cans. But, dammit, this is a cool song."

By the time 'Follow the Leaders'/'Tension' came out, I was hooked.

MIKE COLES

I wanted to put dead bodies on it [the cover of 'Wardance'], as that was what war was all about, but it was missing the 'joke'. I played around with various dancing images, but they weren't quite right. My friend Stinky Miller had lent me a book on Hollywood musicals and the Fred Astaire image was in there. It worked perfectly. The typeface on 'Wardance', that became pretty standard. There's never been an actual logo as such. [It] was all down to finding a sheet of Letraset with two Ks and a J.

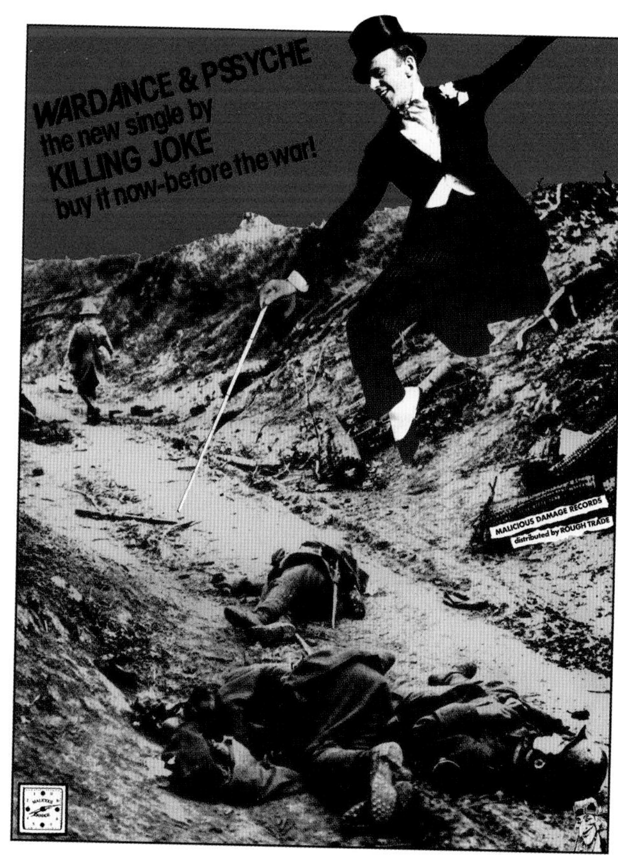

DAVID LADWIG

My first exposure to Killing Joke was when I was 13–14 years old and purchased the 'Wardance'/'Pssyche' single at Vintage Vinyl in Evanston, IL (a suburb of Chicago). This was 1980–81. The art aesthetic is what drew me in. Mike Coles' artwork perfectly matches the music. Killing Joke is my favourite band – and the only band I collect.

RICHARD FARRELL

Seven-inch singles were a special currency at school, swapped between classmates (to 'educate') or used as ice-breakers to cement new friendships – and, naturally, carried in plain sight to casually advertise your musical awareness. One record which regularly did the rounds featured a curious image of Fred Astaire dancing across a trench full of corpses. Probably an anti-war record, I suspected. The name on that record sleeve was one which was increasingly being mentioned, with talk of Peel sessions and call-up papers: Killing Joke. The name itself sounded uncompromising.

SEAN RILEY

My best mate in secondary school, Russ, always got into new bands before anyone else. One day in class, he wrote Killing Joke on my exercise book. He was tapping his pen to the drum beat and singing 'Wardance'.

Apart from the fact I was now in trouble with school property defaced, the name of this latest 'new band' he had stumbled across appealed to me. It made me want to look into it a bit further...

So, on the Saturday morning, in all our punk gear, me and my mates jumped on the bus into town (Manchester) for our weekly visit to the Underground Market, where two shops sold punk music. One of them had all the single covers (with a 99p price tag on most of them) on the wall. There must have been 100 different sleeves, a rainbow of colours.

I wanted to own them all, but usually had either a quid or two to my name, so I had to choose carefully. As I surveyed the wall intently, I spotted a cover with a famous-looking dancer. Fred Astaire, no less – my Mam told me when I asked her who it was when I got home! Tap-dancing on the bodies of injured and dead soldiers lying face down in their trenches, with a backdrop of a blood-red sky and a small white box in the top right-hand corner, with KILLING JOKE in black type face, which looked really good, the smooth G and J without the stroke across the top of it.

Well, I'd heard my pal sing it, I liked the look of the cover and the strange spelling of the B-side song 'Pssyche'. So I took the plunge and bought it. Later that afternoon, I took it out of the brown paper bag, intrigued by the label, a broken clock, with the words Malicious Damage. It all felt mysterious and appealing, even the fact the record was on black vinyl (no coloured vinyl required here to help induce you into buying it). This very much had the feel of dark art and a take-it-or-leave-it offer on the table. The drum beat by Paul Ferguson was so smooth, effortless, timing impeccable, before I heard Youth's jagged bass for the first time. A hint of keyboards followed (didn't realise it was Jaz playing them) and then a guitar sound which was punchy, in very short but exact bursts, before I heard Jaz's voice (and not my pal's) sing that opening line – "The atmosphere's strange, out on the town."

I'd heard enough after 45 seconds to tell me I'd found my latest new 'best band' – and it just got better and better. No sooner had it finished, I flipped it over to the B-side and what I heard next completely blew me away. It was such a powerful tune. This wasn't music for daytime listening. This sounded like four young, angry, disillusioned young men who were telling it as it was and gave me the impression they didn't give a toss whether you enjoyed it or not.

CHRIS KIDGER TOOLE

The 'Wardance' single emerged and, having heard both 'Wardance' and 'Pssyche' on the Peel session, the music didn't have as much impact as the brilliant Mike Coles sleeve and call-up-papers insert did.

Somehow, I thought 'Wardance' was KJ's first release, until the guy in the record shop (Jumbo Records, Leeds, I think) asked if I had the 'Turn to Red' 12-inch – which I thought for years was actually called the 'Nervous System' 12-inch – so I was back a week or two later, when funds allowed, to pick that up too.

That iconic bright red sleeve with the Centre Point tower continued to reinforce the combination of completely original imagery and music that continues to be a vital part of the Killing Joke experience.

UNIVERSITY OF LONDON UNION
2 February 1980,
London, UK

ADAM MORRIS

(tour manager and Malicious Damage operative)

In February 1980, Joy Division played three shows with Killing Joke. I still remember ULU as being a brilliant gig. I was a massive fan of *Unknown Pleasures*. I thought it was one of the best albums I'd ever heard in my life, made by one of the best bands that have ever existed. I still think that. So hearing it live, plus 'Love Will Tear Us Apart' for the first time, was a privilege.

BILLY'S
5 February 1980,
London, UK

TIM FOSTER

My favourite of these early gigs was in a Soho basement on the corner of Meard Street, which was a typical sleazy club with worn, red-velvet seating. I recall a fire-eater also performing – definitely no Health and Safety.

We knew a rather annoying Irishman called Brian who claimed to be KJ's manager – I suppose he must have been as he gave us tickets to their very early shows. And also a copy of the first single in a plastic bag! He used to come round to score as we had a connection with Frestonia – the commune in Freston Road. I remember him once being "very disappointed" at the failure of a transaction due to the non-arrival of the desired commodity. He couldn't understand that it was unreliable cargo.

I did meet KJ a couple of times in Portobello Road and also The Prince of Wales, which was our local.

THE VENUE
10 February 1980,
London, UK

HONEY BANE

At the Music Machine, they played there and called me up on stage to basically jam. We kinda ended up with this song ['What's the Matter?'] that came together more at The Venue when we both played there.

TOWN HALL
20 February 1980,
High Wycombe, UK

ADAM MORRIS

Joy Division eventually released their set from that gig, plus some of the soundcheck, on the deluxe edition 2CD set of *Still*. I have to tell you, when I put that High Wycombe CD on and the soundcheck recordings played, almost 20 years after the show, I had the most vivid flashback. I was there in the hall again. I could almost smell the stale beer from the previous evening's entertainment.

We were in the dressing room, when Ian [Curtis] appeared. He was carrying a six-pack of lager. Lager was what the promoter had put on the rider. He looked at me and asked, very politely, "Can I swap this for some stout?" I shook my head. "Nah, mate. You are down south now. They don't do stout." I probably added something like "The soppy southern jessies" as I was prone to do back then. Ian looked sad, grunted and disappeared again. That was it, my one and only conversation with the legend and, at that point, the biggest hero in my universe.

DAVID HARDAKER

Being a couple of years older than John Kelly [see page 59], I was lucky enough to see KJ earlier at Wycombe Town Hall when they supported Joy Division.

I had been to quite a few gigs at the town hall. We were really lucky that the promoter of most Wycombe gigs was Ron Watts, who ran the gigs at the 100 Club. [He] put on the punk festival there with the Pistols, The Clash and the first Banshees gig with [Sid] Vicious on drums. Ron also ran gigs at the Nag's Head, a pub in Wycombe, which also saw all those bands.

I had heard of Killing Joke on Peel. I remember where I stood at the Town Hall. I was on the left-hand side, halfway down the hall. Luckily enough, I was stood on a seat so could see a lot.

KJ were different – threatening but entertaining. Youth looked more like Sid Vicious than Sid did. Band were mesmerising.

From where I stood on my seat, I could see in the middle of the audience a guy who looked like a Red Indian. Topless maybe. He had a small headdress on and a big fuckin' stick in his hands dancing/swirling around. He had his own space. No one went near him. Wycombe was a tough crowd back then, but this guy had the bollocks and dominated it.

Then KJ kicked into 'Wardance'.

This guy set alight both ends of his stick, carried on his dance and was then blowing fire from his mouth into the air.

Ha. The crowd stepped even further away. As a kid, I had never seen nothing like this and to be honest never since.

BIG PAUL

We found a building to squat on Elgin Crescent and that was where we met Dave the Wizard and his dog Helldom. He blew fire. How could we say no? Mind you, there were a few moments where it looked like it'd all go up in smoke. Dodgy business.

DAVID HARDAKER

The other memories of this [Wycombe] gig – they played 'Pssyche' and Big Paul sung it. He is from Wycombe, as it goes. They also played 'Bodies' by the Pistols with, I believe, Alex Paterson – who was a roadie at the time – on vocals. I'm sure that Youth was also dressed in all white.

Maddest thing is I cannot remember much about the Joy Division set. Love Joy Division, but obviously KJ left the biggest impression.

LYCEUM BALLROOM
29 February 1980,
London, UK

ADAM MORRIS

Joy Division at the Lyceum on a double bill with Killing Joke © Frank Jenkinson

The Lyceum was the primary show to do in London at that time. It had been a big band venue around wartime and Bob Marley recorded his incredible *Live!* LP there. The one with the live version of 'No Woman, No Cry' on it that busted the singles chart when Island cut it on a 7-inch. It was a brilliant venue to play: nice big stage, big payday, full house, streams of sweat running down the walls. Killing Joke followed by Joy Division – my Lord, what a show. We broke the box-office record that night: the most tickets ever sold for a Lyceum show, or so the promoter claimed. The fool. That just meant that he had to pay us more, didn't it?

EG Records came to that gig. They had been sniffing around Killing Joke for a few months and that night was the final piece in the jigsaw that convinced them to sign the band. We (the management) didn't really want to sign to them, to be honest, but we were so broke and Killing Joke got so popular so quickly, we had to do it.

CHRIS KIDGER TOOLE

Come March 1980, things moved on a leap. The second Peel session, featuring 'Change', 'Tomorrow's World' and 'Complications', showed a new, more focused direction. The earlier music had been unique, but this was unique with glaring purpose and intent.

I managed to miss the April 1980 gig at the Fan/F Club at Brannigans, Leeds. Still only 14 years old at this time, I'm pretty sure that was down to lack of funds.

✦ ✦ ✦

MUSIC MACHINE
31 March 1980,
London, UK

ADAM MORRIS

I don't think any band could match them. Their live shows in particular were incredible. [Paul] Cook and [Steve] Jones came to see them once, *ZigZag* [magazine] party at the Music Machine in Camden. I remember Cook smiling at me and giving us a thumbs-up.

Joke play at the ZigZag party to mark the magazine's 100th issue © Frank Jenkinson

JAZ

Jonesy and Cook. In the early part of our career, Cookie and Jones were at every single gig, cheering us on. And, of course, John Lydon supported us in the press. And, of course, John Peel.

YOUTH

It happened really fast. And the reason that really, really accelerated it was eternal thanks to John Lydon, citing us as a good band. The first interview he did after the Pistols had split up – there'd been a year gap – and he had a cover in the *NME*. At the end they said: "What are you listening to?" "Fatal Microbes and Killing Joke." And that was it. We had single of the week in two mags, every gig sold out instantly. You can't underestimate the value of someone's approval like that.

HONEY BANE

I used to stay at John Lydon's. I wanted to introduce him to Youth. I arranged for Youth to come to John's. John almost passed out when he saw him, thinking it was a ghost. Youth looked so much like Sid Vicious. John was still grieving at that time. It made him take a double-take. They got on really well.

GERMANY
June 1980

ADAM MORRIS

That summer, KJ and Basement 5 went on tour together. That was a formative tour in many ways, certainly for me. I had become KJ's tour manager by then and, I have to say, I wasn't very good at it. I'd never even been on a plane before I got involved with those guys, so let's say I had a lot to learn. We used to say I was most famous for my U-turns, because it took me a while to realise even the most basic of things. Like it is a good idea for a tour manager to carry with them, when going on tour to somewhere they had never been before, a few maps.

That tour was a great education for me (and everyone else, I'd wager).

Alex Paterson at the SO36 venue in Berlin on the 1980 German tour © Brian Taylor

Geordie on tour in England during October 1980. "When you're young, you think living on a tour bus is glamorous" © Frank Jenkinson

KJ turned in some epic performances on that tour; both bands did. They seemed to push each other to new heights. It was on that tour that KJ wrote the basis of '$.O.36'.

That tour really made the first KJ album so brilliant. When it ended, we got off the ferry, drove back to London, went straight into the studio. We laid down the first album. Bosh! Most of it in one take. That was where Geordie earned his nickname, 'One Take Wonder'. I say 'we' laid down the first album. It was mostly the band, of course, but we all got recorded making noises, handclaps, whistles and so on. I am proud to say that a little bit of me appears on the first two Killing Joke LPs.

Thanks to Adam Morris and Louder Than War for permission to use Adam's extracts

Big Paul: "Firstly, how much time did I spend on the hair? And how? Secondly, how did we all spend so much time in that Volky? I mean, the band and the guitars? Must have been keen. Thirdly, the two German promoters. Volker, whom I'll never forget from Dennis Morris, the Basement 5 singer, frequently screaming his name. Where are these guys now?" © Brian Taylor

LES BAINS DOUCHES
25 June 1980,
Paris, France

ALAIN WOJIEK

I had the chance to see them at their first concert in Paris. The place was called Les Bains Douches. I was at the front of the stage.

MIXMASTER MORRIS (DJ)

I missed half the set at Camden Palace [Music Machine] because I was playing pinball with Lemmy...

MARQUEE STUDIOS
August 1980,
London, UK

PHIL HARDING
(engineer of debut album)

Phil Harding © Stan Shaffer

I started at The Marquee Studios in 1973 as a tea boy/tape jockey/runner/assistant engineer. It was an unofficial apprenticeship where you learned on the job, observed what the engineer on the session was doing (when you had time) and hustled the management for spare available time to practise engineering yourself when possible – often weekends – often with the other assistants, recording friends' bands etc. There was very little official training, but, after three or four years, assistants would be let loose on paying clients to see how we got on.

After spending all those years training, the norm was to see a producer alongside the engineer in the control room with the band in the studio recording area, communicating via a talk-back system to the musician's headphones.

But the punk revolution brought with it the rebellious attitude from bands that they did not want to work with old/established corporate-rock producers. In fact, initially, many punk bands refused to work with producers and that was the case with The Clash on the sessions I worked on with them. I mixed '(White Man) in Hammersmith Palais' with Joe and Mick in the room but no producer. Paul popped in at one point and wasn't particularly happy with what he was hearing. That was an early indication to me of having no producer there and the problem that can cause between band members and their differing views.

I got on well with Mick and Joe and that led to a recording session where they came back into the Marquee to record four songs for the *Black Market Clash* mini-album. Those sessions really geared me up as an engineer to getting used to the idea of being on my own in the control room without a producer by my side – just an empty chair. It was very good practice for the Killing Joke sessions.

I was only ever the engineer for the [Killing Joke] album – the band were the producers and that was made clear from day one. The Killing Joke sessions were a baptism of fire because it wasn't just a few tracks – it was a whole album. The label were very generous at the start of the sessions, bringing in a crates of beer and champagne on day one, which was very celebratory and set everyone off in a very good mood.

Playing together in the same room with good sight of each other was very important to the band. We had a good studio layout at the Marquee and were able to accommodate getting all four members seeing each other and enough separation of the amps and sounds for me to record everything with an acceptable, minimal spillage between instruments.

© Frank Jenkinson

The control-room window looked out on to one end of the long, oblong studio recording space. So, we set up Paul closest to the control room with him facing into the long studio. There were a few low-level acoustic screens around the drums, but Paul could still see over them to have contact with the other guys. Youth was a third of the way along the studio to the right, with his bass amp in a booth and him sitting or standing outside of that and a long lead to the amp. Geordie was set up almost opposite Youth on the left-hand side of the studio (looking from Paul's end). His amp was behind him with heavy acoustic panels around it to give as much separation as possible.

Inevitably, there was some guitar spill on to the drum mics – especially the pair of Neumann '87s at the far end of the room that were there to pick up drum ambience. Jaz was then set up with his keyboard and a guide vocal (Shure '58) mic in the middle of the studio, facing Paul, with Youth to his left and Geordie to his right.

Jaz's keyboard was plugged into DI (direct injection) boxes for a stereo feed and I encouraged him not to sing too loudly.

Everyone had the same headphone balance, so that was tricky to get right, especially for Jaz to hear enough of his keyboard with no amp behind him. The great thing was, though, by taking one headphone slightly off, everyone could hear Paul because he thumped the drums so loudly! Geordie could hear a fair bit of his amp in the room behind him and Youth managed to cope. The whole album was recorded like that – almost like the band were live on stage or in a rehearsal room.

Drop-ins for mistakes or overdubs were fairly minimal. Paul's drum takes were always brilliant, once he was happy with the control-room playback. Obviously, we would then record the lead vocals separately and Jaz got better at that as the album went on.

It was pretty chaotic – especially the playbacks in the control room after recording a take out in the studio. It would go something like this.

The band would come back into the control room, generally buzzing from having played a good take and everything sounding loud in their headphones, backed up by the physical noise of the drums and Geordie's guitar amp in the studio.

I would therefore have to play back really loud on the main monitors for the band to get the kind of volume excitement they had just experienced in the studio.

Each band member, one at a time, would then appear in front of me from the other side of the mixing console and scream instructions at me, whilst the really loud playback was going on, generally demanding that their instrument be the loudest and heaviest-sounding in the balance. Especially Jaz, wanting more aggression and reverb added to his keyboard sounds.

When the tape stopped after the playback, generally everyone would congregate on the sofa at the back of the studio and say nothing about the balance – just whether or not to do another take or stick with what we had.

So it was very chaotic initially for me, but I soon got used to it. I would generally only comment on anything technically with regard to suggesting another take or not, usually based around how the drum performance sounded as we should generally drop-in and replace any bass/guitar or keyboard mistakes (there weren't many).

I think it was around a month, maybe less, to record. Then there was a break after the first attempts at mixing.

We did hit a crisis point at the mixing stage because I suggested we should mix in the upstairs mixing room – Studio 2 – a much smaller room, designed for mixing. This was something the studio management encouraged – record downstairs, mix upstairs. Unfortunately, it didn't work for the Killing Joke project. The room was too small for everyone to sit in comfortably, the lounge area was a bit too public as it was alongside the office with a lot of people passing by, which wasn't good for the band's privacy.

I thought the mixing was going okay, but I could tell the boys weren't happy with the logistics or the sound of the room compared to what they had become used to in the larger downstairs studio and control room.

So, the project came to a grinding halt at that stage, with the label cancelling the rest of the mixing sessions and suggesting the band wanted to mix elsewhere.

My feeling was that we should go back downstairs and mix in Studio 1, where the band were happy with the recording results, the more spacious control room and the sound of the speakers/acoustics there. I suggested to the studio management that we offer the label a free day to do an experimental mix downstairs to see if everyone felt happy about that. We managed to find a day of free studio time to offer that a week or so later. The band and the label graciously agreed to try it out. As I had hoped, it turned out really well. I can't remember which song we mixed, probably 'Requiem', as that was planned as the first single. Everyone was happy to carry on like that and, to my relief, the label agreed to book the studio time to complete the mixing of the album in the downstairs Studio 1.

Geordie wasn't keen on double-tracking or overdubbing guitars, but, when he did, it always sounded great to me. I noticed on the albums that followed, there was a lot more overdubbed guitar work and maybe the first album lacked that a bit. 'Primitive' is a great example of Geordie tracking his guitars and I like how that gives the track a better stereo balance and more power. Same goes for 'Change'.

Geordie and fire extinguishers... Does this image from the sessions for the first album point the finger in the right direction for who was responsible for ambushing Youth during recording of What's THIS for...! the following year? *© Frank Jenkinson*

Jaz was the strongest character at that time, but the rest of the band didn't let him get away with anything, so it balanced out quite well. Geordie and Paul were really great characters and masters of their instruments. They didn't need to say much as their instruments did the talking for them and they were determined to get great recording results. Youth was a bit younger and less experienced. The rest of the band gave him a lot of encouragement and I think he improved as a musician as the album progressed. He was and still is easy to get on with and we had a good chat a few years ago at the MPG [Music Producers Guild] Awards ceremony. I also did a few mixes with Youth after he left the band and was starting his career as a producer.

I liked all of them and felt they were a well-matched unit of characters and musicians. I think it goes without saying that Geordie is now and was at that time an accomplished musician that knew exactly what his sound was and what he wanted to achieve.

The standout musician to me, though, was Paul. His ability to step back into the studio after a 'relaxation' break or playback and play such powerful and tight drums really left an impression on me on how rock drummers need to play in the studio to achieve great results both creatively and technically. Jaz knew his limitations as a keyboard player but created some great parts and sounds that worked fantastically with the standard rock set-up of drums/bass and guitar. That's not always an easy thing to achieve as a keyboard player and often his keyboard parts were the backbone and start point of the songs. Youth progressed into being a great bass player throughout the album, I think, and it's a shame in many ways that he didn't stay with the band longer, but it's great to see the original line-up back together in recent times.

It was and still is annoying for engineers and producers like myself not to get credits and it can still happen. But, at the time, it was the norm for punk and post-punk bands not to credit engineers, studios and backroom staff. It was part of the attitude and rebellious punk revolution in the late Seventies/early Eighties. I wasn't credited on the engineering I did for The Clash, either. To the best of my knowledge, this has never been rectified.

[On the debut being a landmark album] I think as much as anything it was the power and attitude of the band and the fact that we managed to capture some of the live raw power in the studio, achieved largely by not doing many overdubs and making sure the individual sounds and performances were as spot on as possible. The band were very much in control of all of that. How they were marketed by the record label was dictated by them as well. www.philhardingmusic.com

YOUTH

We already knew what the arrangements were. There wasn't that much experimentation. The first album was simply a matter of recording it. It was simply a matter of execution. Phil Harding. So unassuming. You never knew what was going on with him. He was just a total professional. He was like a doctor. But he handled us really well and allowed us to do it the way we wanted to do it. But he would cover our arses technically and make sure it was recorded right.

GEORDIE

It was so easy in the beginning. A lot of that first album, we'd played that shit out live for nigh on a year and just walked in the studio and did it.

YOUTH

The Marquee was great because, five nights a week, we could just go down and watch the bands. There'd be Budgie one night, John Mayall, The Groundhogs. Me and Geordie loved that.

We'd recorded 'Wardance' twice. I think the best version we got was some John Peel session where we got it right. But trying to get that distorted vocal right, ugh. The album version came out the worst one. But then I go to America and meet all these hardcore bands and they are like: "That was the first record that allowed us to sing like that." It was so influential, and I was like: "Really?"

It's a simple recipe in its essence. I essentially am Geordie's seventh string. There are a few tracks where they are bass-line orientated and then Geordie is my seventh string, like 'Change'. Geordie is a bloody great bass player. He was Grade 7 cello when he was a kid. So he knows his chops as a bass player.

Luckily, he's a fan of my bass playing. But I had to fight to get my bass-lines in because he's so fucking good. If it didn't have a bass-line, I would just follow his guitar. I'd learned guitar before bass. I would just follow his hands. And then you put these tribal disco drums on it and some sort of moody synths and that's it really.

We had a lot of pop sensibilities. On the first album, every song has a really pop chorus. I have to remind the band of that sometimes. Whenever I bring a new poppy chorus, they say, "ugh, it's pop", but so's 'Wardance', so's 'Change'.

MIKE COLES

[Using Don McCullin's image for the cover of the first album] EG, the label at the time, wrote to him and he said it was fine, so long as the band didn't expect him to endorse the music. I suspect he thought it was just another bit of punk nonsense that would be dead and buried in a couple of years. Forty years on...

JEAN-CHRISTOPHE VAN THIENEN

As I did regularly back then, I went on holiday in the summer of 1980 from my home town Lille (France). That time, I went with a friend who was also into those weird sounds. We'd stay near Earl's Court in some dodgy youth hostel, where, incidentally, The Cure's Lol Tolhurst's sister also worked.

We saw many gigs that summer, including Wasted Youth (Fulham Greyhound).

My mate had seen an ad for KJ merch in the *NME* or *Sounds*. The address given was in Portland Road (or so I remember, near Ladbroke Grove, since we went to Rough Trade next). Anyway, when we got there one morning, it appeared to be your average, albeit slightly dilapidated, terrace house. We rang the bell, if there was one, and got to the first floor (left apartment) and knocked on the door.

And, lo and behold, none other than Jaz Coleman opened. We were rather gobsmacked and explained we'd come for merch and, most of all, their new single, which had recently been announced as 'Requiem'.

Jaz was holding three or four kittens in his arms and asked if we would take one or two with us. I replied that we were in London for a while and, since we came from France, that would have been impossible anyway due to quarantine.

He seemed quite happy some French blokes would be interested in his band and explained that the address was meant for mail-order only but, since we'd come all this way, he could sell us a copy of the newly pressed 'Requiem' but it would be unlabelled and in a white sleeve. We agreed and he then produced two copies, which he sold us dirt cheap and went to fetch a biro to write 'Requiem' on the right side.

I only saw them live much later, at On the Beach Festival in De Panne, Belgium [10 August 1985] alongside Anne Clark, The Sound.

✦ ✦ ✦

ACKLAM HALL
30 September 1980,
London, UK

PHIL HARDING

I went backstage to see the band after their London gig to launch the album. I was a bit nervous as that was an early experience of networking for me and I wasn't very good at that outside of my comfort zone of the studio. I often recount the experience to students in my guest lectures and masterclasses because we all have to start somewhere with our networking and mine was straight in at the deep end.

© Frank Jenkinson

I think it was good that the band went on to work with producers rather than just young engineers like myself with the band producing. The following two albums were a fantastic progression for the band in terms – great sounds and productions. I don't think they'd have achieved that if they'd tried to repeat the recording experience of the first album.

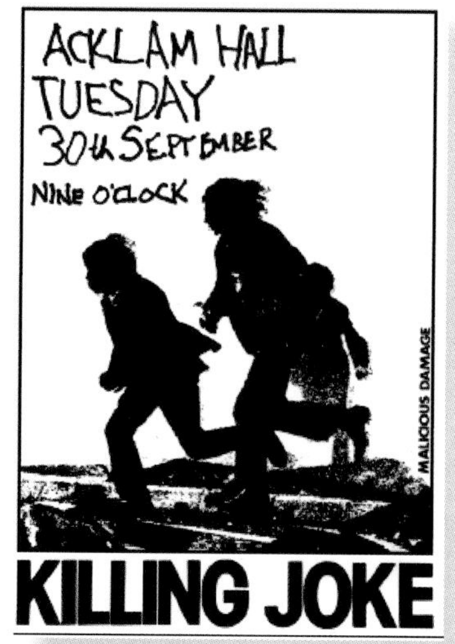

© Mike Coles

I do look back with fond memories and it's good to get the chance to reflect and note my memories of engineering the album. I went on to engineer and produce for Nitzer Ebb in the early Eighties. Working with Killing Joke was a good grounding experience to cope with that project and how to record loud, aggressive singers and bands with confident members. It probably helped and prepared me for Pete Burns and Dead or Alive as well! I spent quite a bit of time with Youth at PWL during the Brilliant sessions.

[On the contrast of working later on with Stock Aitken Waterman acts on the PWL label] Entirely different experiences. In many ways, I have missed that creative interaction between a fantastic set of musicians in the studio and a creative technician like myself. Working with bands like Killing Joke can be a very rewarding experience for an engineer. Working with drum machines and computers, by contrast, can be a very frustrating experience and takes a lot more time and effort to keep the energy flowing in a studio.

MIK RAVEN

Hearing that first album was brilliant! I had a combat jacket at the time and painted the boy from the wall from 'Change' on it.

So, in my school days, I lent this album to as many of my friends who would listen to it. I particularly remember a friend who said that this is how music should be! Do you remember those days when you took albums into school to share with mates?

Let me say at this point I left school at 16 with no ambition other than to be a musician. So I was very poor. Plus, living in Bradford, I did not get the opportunity like a lot of KJ fans to see them live in the early days. Does that make me less of a fan? I was walking around Bradford in 1979 with Killing Joke painted on my back even though I had never seen them live and would not until the Nineties.

SEAN RILEY

I had a poster promoting the 'Requiem'/'Change' single from the first album. This was, at the time, on the ceiling of an independent record store in Manchester, by the name of Record Peddler, on Swan Street (Northern Quarter nowadays). I knew the owners, Craig and Mark, as a regular customer and I tried everything I could to get them to part with this poster, but I had to have something tempting enough for them to do the deal. So, I only went and got my original copy of Joy Division *An Ideal for Living* EP gatefold – yes, that very, very rare one. Not surprisingly, they agreed! They even threw in a promo Killing Joke video for me. They must have known what a good deal they were on. Anyway, I've never regretted it. I still have it. As for that Joy Division EP, I don't know who owns it nowadays, but, when I checked recently, it sells for £1,700. But Killing Joke memorabilia is priceless in my eyes...

✦ ✦ ✦

LYCEUM BALLROOM
5 October 1980,
London UK

MATTHEW LAMBETH

So, as a few readers may remember, Sunday night at the Lyceum was a regular visit, it was like a showcase evening for every up-and-coming alternative band of the era, four or five bands, always someone good to see.

This particular Sunday was unusual, as we did not know the headline act [Pink Military] at all. We had not seen any of the bands on the bill, although we had heard the Killing Joke singles on John Peel and heard they were meant to be pretty good live.

Again, unusually, as we did not know the bands on the bill very well, rather than stand downstairs/in the mosh pit, we sat upstairs, front row of the balcony.

Wah! Heat and Comsat Angels were good, LiLiPUT were entertaining. John Peel had been playing their 'Split' single a lot, which we liked.

Then Killing Joke arrived on stage. They absolutely blew the place apart. I can remember the intensity and excitement of the show even now. It seemed like the entire audience

The famous Lyceum Ballroom on The Strand in London witnessed three savage Killing Joke sets during 1980 in the space of just nine months © Frank Jenkinson

downstairs started jumping up and down, from the opening track of 'Pssyche' to 'The Wait'. The set-list was brutal. When they finished, it was clear who the majority of the people had come to see as at least half the audience left the building, not bothering to see Pink Military.

We did stick around to watch them, but there was no way any band could follow what had just been heard and seen.

GARY HOWES

Killing Joke has been a large part of my life. Born in London at just the right time to enjoy the heyday of new wave. 'Turn to Red' was the start and 'Requiem' and 'The Wait' quickly followed.

Lyceum Ballroom in The Strand. Whole floor of sweaty masses shouting "THE WAIIIIIIIIIIIT" with Jaz – one foot on the monitor at the front of the stage.

Waiting after the show to see how many badges you could find on the floor that had dropped from leather jackets...

Saw KJ at various venues and later covered 'Chop-Chop' in my own band.

Every single and album was eagerly awaited and listened until the grooves wore down on the vinyl. Then the cassettes for the car and Walkman.

RUSTY EGAN

First album: October 1980. I am a track jumper when I DJ. I find the song that works. I have to say, if I had a car and I put this on, I would be a road-rager, so I never really listened to the whole album. My lifestyle was fast.

CHRIS KIDGER TOOLE

To say I could not wait for the first album is a complete understatement. I lived some way out of Leeds and would not be able to make it into Jumbo Records until the Saturday after release, so I took the unusual step of pre-ordering it from WH Smith in Dewsbury. I had to have it as soon as possible. I trotted down after school in my uniform to pick it up on Monday, 6 October 1980.

A school friend had a birthday the next Saturday, so I went along with the album under my arm, feeling like a missionary taking the good news to the natives. I waited patiently for my turn on the record player and, with some bravado, dropped the needle onto the first side of the album.

Everyone listened politely. Hmm, too overcome by the greatness to verbalise, I thought. But no. Come the end of the first side, it was requested that we listen to something else rather than the second side. Philistines! I could not believe it.

JAMES FRYER

In 1980, on the last day of the school term, we were allowed to bring records in and a lad in our class brought in a new album by a band called Killing Joke, who up to that point I had not heard of. As he cued up the first track, 'Requiem', I looked at the sleeve art – no vain pictures of the band, just a monochrome gatefold with the now famous Mike Coles creation of the KJ graffiti wall in a barren, riot-strewn landscape with the silhouettes of kids fleeing.

Add to this the eerie Jesus-like character in the centre of the gatefold flicking the Vs and the creepy, grinning bald guy with a fag in his mouth, and this 13-year-old was hooked on both the music and the accompanying mysterious and slightly sinister imagery.

I went out and bought all the band's output to date – the 'Turn to Red'/'Nervous System' and 'Requiem' singles, together with the album itself. From that moment on, they have been and will continue to be my favourite band.

✦ ✦ ✦

AJANTA THEATRE
18 October 1980,
Derby, UK

CHRISTINE RICHARDSON

At the tender age of 17, I had seen a few bands there during that year (The Slits, Joy Division, Magazine amongst many others) but the one that stuck in my head was Killing Joke. I found the music so dark and powerful. And to give it that edge they had a flamethrower on a raised platform. It made the hairs stand up on the back of my neck.

✦ ✦ ✦

F CLUB
19 October 1980,
Leeds, UK

AKI NAWAZ

(Southern Death Cult, Fun-Da-Mental, Nation Records)

I left school at 15 for punk. I recall stealing their [Killing Joke's] records from the local HMV shop in Bradford on Saturday afternoons. We had no money but had set up some kind of corruption practice with the employees where we would come back and get a refund for the record and share it amongst us. But KJ records never went back for refund. They would be put on my hi-tech Waltham hi-fi system and spun until the plastic grooves on the vinyl cried to be left to cool down.

I had been dancing to them in some weird form at clubs prior. They were unconventional. Probably my dancing complemented their music, the intensity and stiffness of my body almost gave the impression I was having an epileptic fit as you attempted to make footprints into the dancefloor.

It was in the sticky, sweaty, dingy atmosphere of the Leeds F Club [Fan Club] that I first came across them live. They were booked by my brother for a concert. We had for a few weeks been fly-posting their posters around Leeds, completely illegally and with a sense of fear as there was a pretty hardcore Nazi skinhead element in Leeds, unlike my home town of Bradford, which would have them running like the clappers.

At the time, I was pretending to be intellectual and have journalistic skills by writing for a small fanzine called *Apathy*. I managed to get the band to agree to an interview after soundcheck. I really did not know what I was dealing with. Naively, I asked stupid questions and got stupid answers from an irritated Jaz. I would have told me to go "f*** myself" if I was asked the same questions – and I think he did!

The eventual interview in the fanzine was probably totally made up and made myself interesting by making up answers to some new questions after realising my stupid ones.

But it was the actual concert that had me enlightened. It was a wall of sound, awesome and bewildering. The sheer power of Geordie's guitar and Paul's drumming was perfect for Youth's deep bass and the mesmerising, manic Jaz.

I knew that this was a creative venture in which the chemistry was in harmony and the thought processes unified. I had seen the Sex Pistols as my first-ever gig, but this was more important. This pulled on the deeper strings of the soul.

It does not matter how much I can rate Killing Joke – it will inevitably be less than it should be. I was taken aback and it was this juggernaut of sound that stayed with me every time I saw them. They were faultless.

✦ ✦ ✦

TRAFALGAR SQUARE
26 October 1980,
London, UK

KEVIN HAWES

A life-changing moment for me. I was just 18 and with a mate on the CND rally. As the march wandered into a packed Trafalgar Square, we became aware that there were some bands about to play.

Killing Joke started up and, within a few moments, my jaw was on the floor and all I could do was stare with a huge grin on my face. I was totally blown away by the power and intensity of it, like nothing I had ever experienced before. I loved every second of it.

I think I remember Jaz making some derogatory comment about CND, which upset a lot of people, but I was hooked from that moment and truly believe that it changed me and showed me the path that my life has subsequently followed. I have seen KJ many, many times since then and continue to love it all, although nothing will beat those first two albums.

MIXMASTER MORRIS

Trafalgar Square demo with The Pop Group and Tony Benn. It's not easy to remember drunken nights five decades ago! It was, oh, so many years ago.

LEE HOLFORD (NUCLEAR BOY)

Where to start? Late 1980 into 1981. I'm at school, I'm 12 going on 13, I like Adam and the Ants (*Kings of the Wild Frontier* era), Gary Numan and not much else...

I see an older, cooler kid walk across the grass with a teacher shouting "walk on the path, not the grass". He carries on across the grass. I see something painted on the back of his leather jacket – it says KILLING JOKE. I don't know what it means, but I like how it sounds.

Few weeks later, walking home across the railway bridge, I see something spray-painted on a wall – KILLING JOKE. I ask my mate what it means. "They're a punk group." "Okay," I say, none the wiser.

Later that year and after seeing PiL and The Exploited on *Top of the Pops*, I'm ready for a new obsession in music, because Numan and the Ants had failed to keep my interest.

Stumbling on a late-night radio show after listening to a European football game on a transistor radio under my bedsheets, a song INSTANTLY got my attention. "This is great." At the end, the DJ (it was John Peel, but I only found that out days later) announced "And that was Killing Joke with 'Requiem'." WHAAT! Wow. Okay, now I know what music is gonna be my new obsession.

© Neil Little

TOWNHOUSE STUDIOS
Late 1980,
London, UK

MICHAEL DENT

Now, Lydia Lunch may be my favourite artist, but Killing Joke are my favourite band. I've been a Killing Joke fan and friend for 39 years. I met the band in London, UK, just after they completed their second LP, *What's THIS for...!*

I had to go to the UK with Nash the Slash in October '80 so Nash could tour with Gary Numan, which lasted a month. We were picked up at Heathrow Airport and taken to our suite at the Townhouse Studios to settle in. Right beside the entrance on the wall, someone had written in black marker KILLING JOKE. As I looked at it, I had no idea what it was or meant. I THOUGHT it might be a band name but wasn't sure. But, if it was, it had to be one of the coolest band names ever. I was soon to find out.

The Dead Kennedys were staying on the floor below us, so I ran down and called out. "Hey, Dead Kennedys, where are you?" They all poured out of their rooms into the hall, where I introduced myself.

Jello had heard of Nash, which I thought très cool. The Dead Kennedys were about to start a UK tour with UK Decay supporting them. The DKs had to vacate their rooms when they went on tour. Jello asked if I'd look after his records while he was out. He'd been there a week and already had over 200 LPs. Wow, no flies on Jello.

When I started to flip through them, I came to the Killing Joke 'Requiem'/'Change' 12-inch. I put it on. It was like getting hit by a locomotive – I had NEVER heard anything like it before in my life. When Nash returned, I had to turn him on to this record. He had the same reaction. He was so impressed with them, he went out the next day and bought us each copies of it and the debut LP.

After the Numan tour was over, I saw an advert in one of the music papers that Killing Joke and UK Decay were playing. I got there early and hooked up with UK Decay and helped them load in.

As I watched KJ soundcheck, the band terrified me. The show was amazing but KJ scared me so much I thought them unapproachable.

AL JOURGENSEN
(Ministry)

My first encounter with Killing Joke was a seminal moment in my life. It was one of those occasions where you clearly remember what you were doing, where you were, who you were with — only a couple times in your lifetime do you get that emotion. 9/11 is certainly one, the Moon Landing. Fuck, I'm even old enough to remember JFK getting shot, but, either way, this first encounter too was like a lightning bolt to the senses.

Jaz with Ministry's Al Jourgensen © Liz Walton

I was at a party with a date and when we walked in somebody put on Killing Joke's first album, which had just come out. 'Requiem' started playing and I lost my shit.

I couldn't believe the intelligent rage coming out of the speakers. It was a visceral gut punch. I ignored the party and just sat there transfixed with what I was hearing. When the whole album was over, I took it upon myself to play it again and again until someone wrestled the turntable duties away from me. At that moment, I knew what I had to do with my life. Needless to say, the 'date' I was with split, never to see her again. I think I got the better end of that deal.

JUSTIN BROADRICK
(Godflesh/Jesu)

My first exposure was hearing the first album shortly after its release at a drummer's [house] who played in my stepdad and Mom's punk band Anti-Social. They were somewhat notorious for a year in '77. Ha ha! But they also made one of the allegedly most collectable 7-inch singles ['Traffic Lights'/'Teacher Teacher'] in punk rock from that era – it was in Peel's legendary box of 7-inches that were next to his front door in case of a house fire!

They had just enlisted a young drummer into their ranks and we were at his house as he put on the first Killing Joke album. I was only around 10, but already obsessed with The Stranglers, who I was exposed to through my stepdad and Mom's band and their love of punk rock in the Seventies, so I heard all these popular punk bands at a very young age.

When I heard the first album, initially it reminded me of The Stranglers, but I couldn't work how and why. I was also a 10-year-old with a council estate upbringing, not immediately educated, so to speak, but the album had that flavour of Birmingham in the Seventies – reggae/dub, which was already a part of Public Image Ltd at this period. I recall sitting, hearing it and poring over the album artwork, to this day one of my most favourite record artworks ever. It captures so, so much (especially Britain in the late Seventies).

Within a very short amount of time whilst listening to Peel, I heard 'Wardance', with that other recording of the song, which I found even more direct and punishing, so all that more appealing. I was hooked, and converted. KJ replaced The Stranglers as my favourite band. The Stranglers at that point were 'softening' up. KJ was so much harder, more dissonant, which is what was communicated to me more than anything – my first real exposure to dissonance and percussive reductionism.

I felt it was similar to what had come before from both Siouxsie and the Banshees and Public Image Ltd. But KJ went so much further – heavier, more alien, more challenging, more scary.

STEN SAWICZ

My love affair with KJ started way back with the first album, bought from my local record store for the princely sum of £3.99, which was a big sum of money back then, especially when your finances only came by way of pocket money and a couple of paper rounds.

I got the album by way of hearing 'Requiem' from a friend. Being a punk fan, I was intrigued at what I thought was a variation of the punk sound of the time. On playing the rest of the album, I was blown away by this unique aural landscape that no one had ever come up with before. Very prevalent keyboards, pulsing, dominating percussion and vocals which sounded very sinister in a lo-fi kind of way.

On top of all that was this singular, lurching, almost laidback guitar noise, which appeared here and there throughout the album, but whose presence you felt instantly when it happened.

Hence, I was instantly smitten.

NICOLA FROUDE

(EG Records)

It was a wonderful time in my life. I joined at the end of 1980 and was there until '86. I was as green as the grass. I ended up working at EG through a friend. My first job was at *Billboard* magazine in Carnaby Street. *NME* were above us and *Smash Hits* were opposite. I went for an interview [at EG]. They were looking for a receptionist. I thought: "I'll give it a go. I've been at *Billboard* for a year now, getting a bit bored." I liked the music business.

I got the job and suddenly realised this was a bit more what the music business was about. Working in the King's Road, you used to see all the punks wandering along. This is fab. I'm loving all this.

All these people started walking into the office. I remember Bryan Ferry came in on my first day. Then the likes of Robert Fripp, Adam Ant, Bill Bruford, Andy Summers, Johnny Black. And then, one day, I remember this motley crew rocked up. Who are these guys? My God, they're a bit scary, aren't they? Really quite menacing, angry. Youth was quite quiet. I think he had on his white suit. Geordie was a joker to start with and Big Paul was Big Paul.

Then they were gonna start doing some gigs.

I hadn't actually listened to the [first] album, so I did the day before [the gig]. "These guys are pretty good," I thought. "I'm quite liking this. It's different." I was listening to the likes of Blondie and The Clash and sounds like that. I thought Killing Joke were a bit more ruthless, had a bit more edge to them.

The gig. I ended up thinking: "Where do I go to say hello?" I'd never been backstage before. But I found my way to this stark white dressing room. It all seemed pretty busy but pretty intense. I wondered if I should really be there because they're like focusing on going on stage. At that time, I didn't really know them that well.

I remember the build up to the actual gig. This slow growl of an earthquake building and building. I thought: "Whoah, what is going on here?" This is intense and exciting, filled with anticipation.

All of a sudden, kapow, they're on stage. I think they jumped into 'The Wait'. Wow. Really, really fantastic. I was getting into the loudness of it. What really did stick in my mind was Jaz's dark make-up. And his quite manically staring wide eyes staring at you, which was kind of captivating.

I remember walking out of there in pain because it was so loud. They were the days when they really cranked it up. Your ears were ringing. It was just fantastic. I was hooked after that.

✦ ✦ ✦

LYCEUM BALLROOM
30 November 1980,
London, UK

IAN BYRNE

I was in awe of Killing Joke after hearing the first album. It was 1980 and I had to see them, but I was 16 at the time and they never played in Kent. My first bike was a moped, a sporty thing but not that reliable. I saw they were playing in London, 65 miles away. It was a winter gig and I decided to risk it. With a handful of spanners in my pocket and spark plugs in the other, off I went. Stopping every eight or nine miles to warm my gloved hands up on exhaust pipes, I finally made it! Going from the cold to a warmed-up, crammed venue, I made my way slowly to the front. I had to – I couldn't see that well through the large mohican hairstyles and thick leather jackets. Everyone seemed taller than me. I could smell some weird smoke/weed, but didn't understand that back then. Finally, standing in front of a Kool dude (Youth), I watched the entire show, loving every minute!

The journey back was eventful. I broke down – as expected – near Faversham, still 20 miles from home. Finally got back to Ashford 1.30am. Cold on the outside, but, man, found a new warmth in their music. Still do.

ST GEORGE'S HALL
4 December 1980,
Exeter, UK

DAVEID PHILLIPS

I was searching for a band that I could call my own. In 1978, my sister, who was two years older than me, played me the Sex Pistols album *Never Mind the Bollocks...* and the first Clash album.

I was 13. I felt blessed and fully initiated into punk rock, but my first thought after I heard them was – I needed a band of my own.

My childhood was fucked up and I needed escape. From that moment, which meant acceptance, my sister took over where my parents had given up on me. She told me about John Peel. I became an avid listener.

When I heard him play Killing Joke – 'Turn to Red' and, later, 'Pssyche' and 'Wardance', I knew I had found my band, my escape. My entire world started to (excuse the pun) CHANGE.

I bought the first album on a school trip to Bristol. The money was supposed to be for the coach, but I just had to have the record. I convinced my local youth club the artwork was exactly what we should paint on the huge back wall, and not the *Dark Side of the Moon* artwork the guy who ran the place was bidding for.

It felt like some kind of ritual involving black and white paint. The album was the only soundtrack as we painted.

I finally got to see them live in December 1980 at St George's Hall in Exeter. The support band was Theatre of Hate and, amazingly, the DJ in between the acts was John Peel. It was like a serious dream come true crossed with an exorcism of my difficult childhood and the start of a new life, where I finally felt like I actually belonged.

The following weekend, I bought a second-hand, long, white tuxedo that I had seen Youth wearing at the gig – and never washed it.

MIXMASTER MORRIS

I do remember Youth's suit, which started off brilliant white but soon became covered in disgusting stains of everything rank.

IAN ROBERTSON

Killing Joke had come to Aberdeen [11 December 1980], but, back then, there wasn't a snowball's chance in hell of getting into Ruffles as a spotty 15-year-old.

© Frank Jenkinson

In response to one contributor calling Youth "fashion-indifferent", the man himself said: "It's hard to be different, isn't it? I'll take that as a compliment. It's not like we're Duran Duran" © Frank Jenkinson

ALAIN WOJIEK

I was 15. I was about to meet a friend at his place. My friend opened the door with a hangover. He was a musician at this time, bassist in a punk rock band called Fucking Mods. They played the night before in an old foundry factory that was a big underground place where all the punk scene gathered at the time. He was still in a kind of fog from the concert.

He invited me in, told me to sit on his old faux-leather couch and offered me a coffee. I sat on the sofa next to some dirty clothes from the previous night. My friend goes to his turntable, vinyl in his hand. As I was about to drink my coffee, the music begun. It was 'Requiem'. I put the coffee down – the song put me in some kind of trance, I felt something I never felt before. I was stunned by this – like something in me opened up.

RUSTY EGAN

'Requiem'/'Change' and 'Wardance'/'Pssyche' was such a sound and I have to say influenced me in my heavy, bass-laden 'The Anvil' [by Visage]. We hit some metal and made some hard instrumental mixes and made it in German, later, to be covered by Die Krupps/Client and, in German, as 'Der Amboss'. That was influenced by that sound I would try to get when mixing 'Requiem'/'Change' and 'Wardance'/'Pssyche'.

My hard set may have had 'Change' into Siouxsie and the Banshees' 'Spellbound' 12-inch, ToH's 'Do You Believe in the Westworld', 'Alice' by Sisters of Mercy. After the demise of the Camden Palace, I had a club at the Lyceum in The Strand.

COLIN BAMFORD

My first encounter with Killing Joke was when I was 10-years-old – 1980 – watching the TV at home in Swinton, near Rotherham. My older brother was in the room talking to a friend of his and exchanging vinyl. My brother had strange taste in music, listening to Mike Oldfield and Yes, which I hated. I was into Thin Lizzy at the time. His friend was a typical record collector, with the three-quarter raincoat and long hair.

During their exchanges, he pulled out a record and invited my brother to listen to it. I was attracted straight away to the cover – black and white with kids causing riots and a figure of Jesus Christ. They put the first track on, and my music senses changed for ever – 'Requiem', with the hypnotic synths. My brother hated anyone to touch his record player and was even more guarded about his record collection. I played that Killing Joke album to death whenever he was out and did so for nearly three years.

TOBY O'REILLY (APPLE)

I was walking to the school library. Opposite was the sixth-form common room. On this day, they were playing this song. I had never heard anything like it before – it was like a single note being repeated, then heavy, thumping drums, then the vocals came in. It was like the bloke was shouting but also not shouting at the same time. All of a sudden, the guitar came in. Wow, I needed to find out what this song was. I got back to class and told my mate Rob about this song I had just heard. I asked if he could ask his sister, who was in the sixth form, if she could find out who it was. It's Saturday night and I'm round at Rob's house and he says to me: "Our Linda just got this new album. Shall we have a listen?" What joy it brought me as the needle dropped and the opening note of 'Requiem' blasted out. I started shouting, "This is the song I've been talking to you about, to ask your sister about."

MATTHIAS RICH

My love affair with all that is Killing Joke is a reasonably quirky tale. It started in 1981. I would have been nine years old. Post-nuclear-family dynamics had plonked me in a situation where I temporarily had a stepbrother who was 17 and identified himself as a punk. We found ourselves stuck together on a holiday and I think he was babysitting me. He played a record that really got under my skin, left me feeling a bit creeped out. I didn't know it at the time, but it was Killing Joke's 'Tomorrow's World'. I never forgot the vibe or tune, which hung around in my memory for another 30-plus years without a home.

TOWNHOUSE STUDIOS
London, UK

NICK LAUNAY

('co-producer' What's THIS for...!)

I was young. I was very geeky. I looked a bit punk rock but not very. I was 17 in 1977. I had spiky hair, brothel creepers.

I came from a very arty upbringing. I grew up in the south of Spain. It was all very bohemian. My whole schooling was in Spanish. By the time I came to England, the main connection with the English language was through music. I went to every gig I could.

I wanted to make records from when I was quite young. I got a job as an assistant engineer at the Townhouse Studios on Goldhawk Road. Townhouse belonged to Virgin, to Richard Branson.

So, *The Flowers of Romance* came out, did very well. It was pretty experimental and had some pretty cool drum sounds. There's no credit on the record – engineering, producer or where it was made. John [Lydon] was asked in the press who

© Frank Jenkinson

produced it. He said it's this young kid called Nick Launay. He did a good job. That completely started my career off.

The Gang of Four rang me up, so did The Birthday Party, so did The Slits... and Killing Joke. It wasn't mentioned but they had clearly heard that album and liked it.

The other reason I got asked was because Killing Joke started the record with Hugh Padgham, one of the chief engineers at Townhouse. I worked with him, which included albums produced by Steve Lillywhite, producer on Peter Gabriel's third album, an extraordinary album, a great-sounding record. I really learnt from them.

Hugh had recorded two songs, but he didn't finish them. 'Tension' and 'Follow the Leaders' were both started by Hugh, but it was drums and guitars. I don't think he got on very well with the band. He found them a bit... abrasive, verbally abrasive. There was quite a lot of verbal stuff. I think he recommended me. I'm pretty sure.

YOUTH

We liked the vibe in the Townhouse. It was west London, near where we were living. We got quite a few weeks there to experiment. We were playing around with Hugh Padgham. I think we were testing the water with him as a co-producer. He did a couple of things with Nick assisting. And then there was a bit of an altercation. I was getting a bit stroppy and I was taking a lot of acid. Apparently, I threw a pizza in his face because the bass was too low in the mix or something. Management made me go and apologise, which I did, as graciously as I could. He forgave us but he never worked with us again [laughs].

GEORDIE

There was always the reputation that we were just hard to deal with as a collective. I'm not gonna go any further than that.

NICK LAUNAY

I get on with difficult people. I remember enjoying the sessions with KJ. They're all really strong characters. There was almost a comedy duo in Jaz and Geordie. They were really, really obnoxious, hell bent on upsetting me and annoying me with comments, constantly taking the piss. You couldn't win because there were two of them. Jaz would always instigate something and then Geordie would always back it up. I was still living at home with my Mum. I didn't have a life outside the studio.

These are bullies that are very interesting bullies. They make great music and it's all part of the whole vibe of the band to be like that. I mean, look at the name of the band.

Both my parents were very humorous people. My dad was a writer. Both my parents were very sarcastic in that English/French way. So I think I was brought up to be able to handle a lot of verbal abuse from amusing people. If I had any ideas, I had to be really strong.

Paul was the sane one. He is a really, really cool guy and a phenomenal drummer. I remember thinking: "Thank God Paul is sane." Paul clearly has an understanding of what KJ is and always has from the very beginning. And he is sane. I would strongly suspect that if Paul had left the band in those early days, the band would not have survived. You need one person to call out the bullshit and Paul was that person. Thank God for Paul. He can stand his ground. Very patient guy, very calm.

Jaz was intense as fuck, scary. He's like an Egyptian pharaoh, risen from the pyramid, a kind of zombie character. There's definitely a lot of black magic going on. Just such an interesting character. I really love Jaz. I find him very intriguing. As far as he is concerned, he rules the world. He certainly ruled the darkness of all music.

I'd been to see KJ many times live. I was a big fan. I'd seen the gigs. They were wild, quite scary. I was very familiar with their first record.

YOUTH

By the second album, it was dissipating into a little bit more experimental. Second album's one of my favourite albums. We still had some great songs on it. We started it with only a few ideas. Some of it, we were writing in the studio. We'd gone up to Wales to write it. Done a lot of mushrooms but came up with some more abstract ideas. But we were also experimenting on the sound. We wanted a bigger drum sound. Self-producing again. Townhouse was a little more funky a studio than the Marquee.

NICK LAUNAY

Studio 2 at the Townhouse has this unusual room. It's not that big. The ceiling is very high. It has a stone floor and all the walls are stone and rock. It sounds extremely loud. You put the drums in there, you can get these killer drum sounds. Studio 2 – one of my favourite rooms ever.

Nick Launay: "I get on with difficult people" © Frank Jenkinson

BIG PAUL

I've always been impressed by the rhythmic pulsing-of-hand percussion, and repetitive pulsating beats are at the root of the communal spiritual trance experience.

NICK LAUNAY

[Paul is] one of the most killer drummers. They're riffs, they're like drum riffs. It's not all kick and snare, all hi-hat.

Killing Joke arrived at the studio. There was only three of

© Frank Jenkinson

© Frank Jenkinson

them. Youth wasn't there. I don't think Youth even turned up the second day. We got this phone call from reception. The receptionist, Penny, had this very strong Cockney accent: "Oi, Nick, can you come up here? I think it's one of your musicians. He's been delivered here by the police."

Sure enough, there's Youth, in a straitjacket. He'd obviously been in a hospital. He was very drowsy, looked very tired. So one of the band had to sign for him that he'd been delivered. "Here's your bass player. Can you sign for him?"

We brought him down to the studio. He immediately laid down on one of the couches and fell asleep.

YOUTH

I was doing so much acid, I was really getting into a Syd Barrett thing. It was super psychedelic as well. People forget Killing Joke were a very psychedelic band. You go to a gig in those days, outside the toilets people were going: "Acid, acid, acid."

NICK LAUNAY

We continued recording. But it got to night-time and the band really wanted to hear bass on the songs. So they tried to wake him up, but he just wouldn't.

I can't remember if it was Jaz or Geordie. One of them got the fire extinguisher, the ones with the sort of dry ice. They just sprayed him. It was freezing cold. It really woke him up. "Fuckin' 'ell, what's going on?" Of course, Jaz and Geordie are pissing themselves laughing. But it worked. He was awake. They put a bass on him.

And he played really well. I think it was 'Follow the Leaders', which is a great bass-line, a killer bass-line. I was surprised. He was pretty out to lunch. He did a couple of takes. It worked.

Then he went back to sleep again.

YOUTH

I had acquired this bass from going to see The Damned. Sensible had smashed it and thrown the bass into the audience. This girl grabbed it. I ran over. I said: "Look, I'm a bass player. I want the body and you have the neck." I found a fretless neck for it, stuck it on, and, hey presto, I had a Fender Precision fretless. This, of course, completely freaked the band out. There was massive amounts of hair-pulling, screaming abuse but I resolutely refused to budge.

Youth playing the cannibalised bass. "Sounded fucking amazing" © Frank Jenkinson

NICK LAUNAY

He's basically playing dub reggae. Most of his bass-lines are dubby, low end.

YOUTH

That fretless is part of the sound of the album, this subby, dub thing. It's just an amazing feel. Incredible.

NICK LAUNAY

I honestly think we went home that night and just let him sleep on the couch and then came back the next day, when he was more awake.

YOUTH

It's the same drum room Phil Collins used for 'In the Air Tonight'. Although Paul would never admit to liking that, I love it.

BIG PAUL

It had a stone drum room made famous by that Phil Collins drum fill. How could I not do something tribal?

YOUTH

We were really getting into the rhythms, getting this great drum sound. Things like 'Who Told You How?' and 'The Fall of Because'. Those rhythms are like African voodoo rhythms. [We were] getting them sounding great.

NICK LAUNAY

Studio 2 – you have to compromise a little bit on your playing. You couldn't play cymbals. You'd have to do them as overdubs. The cymbals were so loud in that room. All the cymbals were overdubbed later. There's quite a lot of layering of drums. 'Butcher' has got probably two drum kits on it.

YOUTH

'Butcher' – that was kind of a Kraftwerky industrial pulse, with the voodoo drums and then that thin, spidery, chordal chorus. When we do that live now, it's so heavy. The chorus has a sub-moog bass under my bass when I go high. It shakes the whole theatre.

NICK LAUNAY

Geordie had this... basically, a wardrobe, the type that you would put clothes in. It had holes cut in it for the speakers. It was about six foot tall, maybe taller. It was fantastic. I'd seen things like this in Notting Hill. It rattled a lot. It wasn't built to have a crazy amount of volume in it.

Jaz has that intensity in his vocals. When he was doing his vocals, he was quite aggressive and pissed off. When you're working with someone who's angry, when the anger is channelled through the microphone into the vocals that are going to tape, that's not upsetting at all. That's just really fantastic.

I just did an album with Idles. Joe [Talbot] is a really sweet guy, but, when he gets behind the mic, he's angry. He's phenomenal. He's aggressive as fuck.

There's certain singers who can shout while singing notes. It's really cool-sounding. Jaz is one of those singers who's shouting but it's not annoying.

He's picking really unusual notes to go to. He's the real deal. He might be batshit crazy, but it's a very good batshit crazy.

© Frank Jenkinson

NICK LAUNAY

Underneath the drum room [at Townhouse], the Stone Room, there was this trapdoor. Jaz said: "What's down there?" The building used to be a film studio. There was a swimming pool under the Stone Room. It never got used. It echoed really well. There was a little ladder. It had microphones down there and a speaker. Jaz was fascinated by it.

There was a group of friends who turned up while we were doing the album. I do remember a dwarf. He was quite a character. He looked like someone out of *Oliver Twist*. He had a suit and a top hat. It was a great look. I think he even had a waistcoat and pocket watch.

Jaz tells him to come have a look. So the guy climbed down and Jaz shut the trapdoor. There's no fucking lights there. It's dark and feels damp and, of course, he starts shouting and screaming. "Let me out."

Jaz got really excited and said: "Push 'Record', push fucking 'Record' right now." There's him screaming: "Let me out, let me out."

Jaz and Geordie were pissing themselves laughing. They eventually let him out.

We took the recording and slowed the tape down to half speed so the moaning and screaming sounded more like a demented monk or Satan. It's like a David Lynch movie.

That is on 'Madness', in the background.

YOUTH

Nick disappeared on his bike for a few days after eating some birthday cake that was spiked with hash.

NICK LAUNAY

We'd finished recording. We were mixing. While mixing, the band are just hanging around. Their friends came down. The Wizard, the dwarf, a lot of goth-looking girls that looked like Siouxsie. One night, it was Jaz's birthday. There was like 15 people in the studio.

I was just concentrating on mixing. I didn't drink. I'd never done any drugs in my life. Geordie comes up to me with this huge birthday cake. "Do you want a piece of cake?" And then Jaz comes up. "Yeah, Nick, do you want a piece of cake? It's really good cake. Have a big piece." I was so young and naive.

I start eating and I'm mixing. I look at the speaker and the speaker starts popping out of its chassis. It's coming right at me. I look at the other speaker and it starts to do the same.

What the fuck is going on?

I look down at the knob on the equaliser and it turns into a snake and comes out of the desk and starts dancing at me. Things start moving.

I start reaching for things in a weird way. I hear all this laughter. I'm obviously acting a bit weird.

Jaz said: "Are you all right, Nick?" And it sounded like this: "Are you all right, Nick? Are you all right, Nick? Are you all right, Nick? Are you all right, Nick?"

I turn around and the whole room spins around me. It's like I'm in a kind of tornado. I'm in some crazy Fellini circus. The whole place is going WHOOSH! WHOOSH!

I just couldn't work it out. I thought they had put something weird in my drink. It didn't occur to me at all that it was the cake. But I was hungry. So what do you think I do? I eat more of the cake.

After a while, I sat on the couch. It seemed more stable. I sat there for quite a while. I thought: "I can't do this."

I left the studio and went down the corridor. At the end of the corridor, I see Cousin Itt from *The Addams Family*, all hair, right the way down to the ground. I'm really curious about this, so I start walking faster to try and catch up with Cousin Itt. I go round the corner – GONE.

I go to the kitchen. All I can see to eat is cheese so I grab it and put it in my mouth. My God, this cheese tasted great but it also totally consumed my mouth. It was so over the top. So I spat that out. "I've just got to go and lie down. Sleep it off."

Little did Killing Joke know, there are apartments above the studio. I found an empty bedroom and fell asleep.

Apparently, although some people could say that Killing Joke are nasty, mean people, they actually got very concerned, went looking for me and couldn't find me anywhere in the building.

They started a search party around the streets of Goldhawk Road and Shepherd's Bush. They were very worried I might have walked into the street and got hit by a car. SERVES THEM RIGHT.

I wake up the next morning. Go down to the canteen, made myself some breakfast. In walks Steve Howe, from Yes. Yes were in the other studio. He walks in. His wife walks in. His wife has very, very long hair that goes all the way down to the ground. That's Cousin Itt. That makes sense.

I go down to the studio. Eventually, the band turned up. "Thank fuck. We thought you might be dead." For the first time, they were actually really nice, concerned about my health.

YOUTH

I thought that album had sonics and had something else.

NICK LAUNAY

A lot of the character of that album is Studio 2, Townhouse. I got the sounds that I wanted to, that I liked, from my taste.

It's one of my favourite, favourite records that I've ever been involved with. I was so happy to be making this great record with one of my favourite bands. That was my main concern, getting it right. I'd only been making records for about a year, a year at most. That was just me doing what I did. I got the sounds that I knew how to get in that room. It was great. It was really great. I couldn't have been happier. I think we were only in the studio for three weeks.

And it's influenced a lot of other bands. A lot of other bands have found me and worked with me because they know I did that record, even though I wasn't credited. It's an important record.

I was very proud of the record. I was so squeaky clean. I didn't drink. I didn't do drugs. Jaz nicknamed me The Padre. Right towards the end of mixing, he says: "Here, Padre, you're really proud of this record, aren't ya? You think you done a really good job? We're gonna call the record *Padre's Pride.*" I said: "That's very nice. Do you mean the record's gonna be called that?" He says: "Nah, we're not gonna fackin' call it that. In fact, we're not even gonna credit ya."

I thought he was joking. I thought he was just winding me up. I had no contract. I was just the house engineer, but I had put a lot of ideas into it. I felt I had at least co-produced it with them. I was a little bit concerned about it.

When it came to mastering the record, I attended the session. Ian Cooper mastered at the Townhouse Cutting Room. With vinyl, it was the mastering engineer's job to write on the inner groove – that gap of about an inch. In that space, you write the code for the record. But you could also write other things. Very often, the mastering engineer would write their names.

I thought it would be really funny to write my name in there. If I didn't get credited, at least I'm in there on the vinyl. If you look on the early pressings, it actually says 'Padre's Pride'.

The record comes out. It just says produced by Killing Joke. No one's credited. I was a little bit miffed.

The review for it, I think it was in *NME*. Right at the beginning, "Killing Joke's new album, produced by wunderkid Nick Launay, Public Image's record producer." That's what it says. I was pissing myself. Such is karma. Revenge.

GEORDIE

It was a group effort – with the fabulous assistance of Nick Launay. And thanks for setting the desk up a bit beforehand.

NICK LAUNAY

I knew that studio really well by this point. An absolutely extraordinary recording studio. There's no other studio in the world that was like it. Unfortunately, it doesn't exist anymore. It's now some rich person's apartment, which makes me wanna puke. I have this image of this rich banker guy sitting in his living room, which was Townhouse Studio 2 drum room. They're having people over for cocktails and he's saying: "This is where 'In the Air Tonight' was recorded." Boasting about that. Fucking wanker.

✦ ✦ ✦

TOWNHOUSE STUDIOS
Early 1981,
London, UK

MICHAEL DENT

One day, I'm sitting around our suite when Nash comes in: "You'll never guess who I just met – Killing Joke." I was immediately blown away. "Where?" "Right here – they recorded their second LP here and we're invited to sit in and hear the final mix."

We went downstairs and up the block to the recording studios and piled in. I met all the band and saw that all my fear was inside my head.

Don't get me wrong – they are a volatile lot, but they were very nice. I took up a spot on a stool against the back wall.

Nick Launay hit 'PLAY'. I nearly jumped out of my skin. First off, it was on 11. I actually jumped out of my seat and yelled out in surprise. I then proceeded to be blown away by the album. My favourite to this day.

MIK RAVEN

The second album came out and I did not like it. It was nothing like the first one, something I had to come to terms with about KJ. It took a good few listens before I grew to love it and subconsciously got into the KJ thing.

SEGS (THE RUTS)

We both, for a while at least, used to get records cut at Townhouse Cutting Room in Goldhawk Road by Ian Cooper. Ian was cool and the cutting sessions sometimes might turn into a bit of a celebration. Some of us (certainly me) attended KJ cuts and vice versa – certainly Youth and Geordie. I remember rum and weed.

MICHAEL DENT

Portobello Road is a walk from the studio and there was a Sunday market where stalls sold all sorts. Nash and I would go on occasion and buy some tapes. One afternoon, out of the blue, Youth comes bounding up with a huge grin on his face and says "Nash" as he wrapped his arms around him.

Youth was wearing that filthy white jacket. Filthy is an understatement – it was disgusting – probably never washed even once. Club stamps, spilled drinks, food and other filth. He still wears the same type of jacket but now it gets laundered. I always called it THAT jacket.

Health hazard? © Frank Jenkinson

✦ ✦ ✦

TIFFANY'S
26 April 1981,
Leeds, UK

AKI NAWAZ

They came back to Leeds to a bigger concert hall. I managed to lie to the promoter (John Keenan, I think) that I was commissioned to write a piece for the fanzine again 'cos the first one was great and needed to get them after the soundcheck. It worked.

After soundcheck, I, with all arrogance, just walked up to the security guard and told him I had an interview with the band and to let me go backstage. It was a big concert and the dressing rooms were a guessing game. I forcefully opened up a door which appeared to be jammed. To my shock, all I saw was this white arse, with pants halfway around the knees, going like a rabbit on the floor. It was live porn!

I said, "Excuse me, I am looking for Killing Joke" and all I saw was Youth's head turn around and just say, "Why don't you fuck off?"

I think I ended up writing another interview totally made up. I think I did share a room where Youth might have seen my brown arse also going like Usain Bolt!

CHRIS KIDGER TOOLE

So to the first gig – 26 April 1981 at Tiffany's in Leeds. By now, my school friend John was deeply into KJ too, so we went together. Turning up before the doors opened because we didn't want to miss a moment, we were allowed in just as Expelaires were coming off stage following their soundcheck.

Much to our surprise, we found Jaz and Youth hanging out by the mixing desk. Even more to our surprise, we found them chatty and welcoming, maybe because we were only 15-years-old, maybe because they reserved their reputed unfriendliness for those who deserved it. We got probably two minutes of their time, Youth signed my ticket – I still have it – and it made our day.

The performance was full-on. From the fire-blessed introduction by the Wizard to the end of the second encore, here was a band that had meaning and meant everything. They reach inside you and make a connection.

Dave the Wizard sends temperatures soaring © Frank Jenkinson

So there we have it. The approximately 18-month process from October 1979 to April 1981 that turned me into a true Killing Joke obsessive. I now had all the pieces: the music, the visuals and the performance. Laugh, I nearly did...

JASON MILLS

I remember the moment like it was yesterday. It was between the hours of 10pm and midnight on 27 April 1981. I was 13. As per normal, I was listening to John Peel under my duvet on my little red, battery-powered transistor radio via my headphones so my parents wouldn't detect that I was still awake. Little was I to know this wasn't going to be a 'normal' night.

A sound came pounding through the airwaves, up into my headphones, brutally attacking my eardrums with an energy and force I had never experienced before. It threw me into an immediate panic!

There was no record button on my transistor so I had to find pen and paper quick before the song finished so I could scribble down who in God's name was making this incredible noise!

I ended up frantically scribbling 'The Fall of Because' and Killing Joke. This was the start of a lifelong relationship, one incredible journey of sound, influence, learning and extreme pleasure and fulfilment.

TOP RANK SUITE
27 April 1981,
Reading, UK

GRAHAM ELSTONE

Probably my first proper gig. Got three other mates up for it. I was 14! First odd thing was they made everyone take off their boots: Docs, army boots, etc. No reason. So most people were in socks! No support, but firebreather ranting incantations. There were metal crowd-control barriers round the stage. As soon as Joke came on, they disintegrated and ended up in a big metal pile at back. The stage was pretty much invaded – loudest, most intense gig ever. Firebreather came back on – fire above our heads! It was extreme – the sound, the atmosphere, everything.

It was all of the first LP, but also first time hearing work that would go onto *What's THIS for...!* It was like shellshock. After the gig, it was like we had been to an awakening. I've seen Joke too many times to count, but that first time was a drug, a huge rush – and has been ever since.

Down the front since '81.

YOUTH

I had this new bass rig. We'd been making a little bit of money. It was half a PA. Took four roadies to carry it live. That, with the fretless, gave me my own little sound system on stage.

With that rig and that bass, I made that house rock, man. So much so that one night in Kilburn [National Ballroom, 28 April 1981], the stack was on the tiered stage and the rig toppled over and I literally had to kick Jaz out the way from being crushed by it. That tour – best tour we've ever done.

JOHN DORAN

For me, there are definitely two tiers of post-punk bands. There were the bands that were dead easy to get into: Bauhaus, New Order, Joy Division, Echo & the Bunnymen, early U2, Simple Minds. But there was this other layer of bands – The Pop Group, Killing Joke, Wire, definitely The Fall.

IAN LIDGETT

I first heard Killing Joke in the Roxy nightclub in Sheffield when 'Follow the Leaders' was released. It was the menacing vocals and the rhythm to the song that sounded different from anything else at the time. It was the year I first saw them live also – 40 years on and the music still sounds fresh. Having seen them live at least 60 times up and down the country, the music is still relevant.

MICHE MARCISZ

I started hearing their name and music approximately 1981. I was an active pen-friend, and new wave and punk were new to me. My pals and I exchanged music mix cassettes on a regular basis. I think I had seen a home-made video of 'Follow the Leaders' (made by who? KJ?) on a punk VHS tape around this time. The company that put out these video compilations may have been named Target Video, but I don't remember.

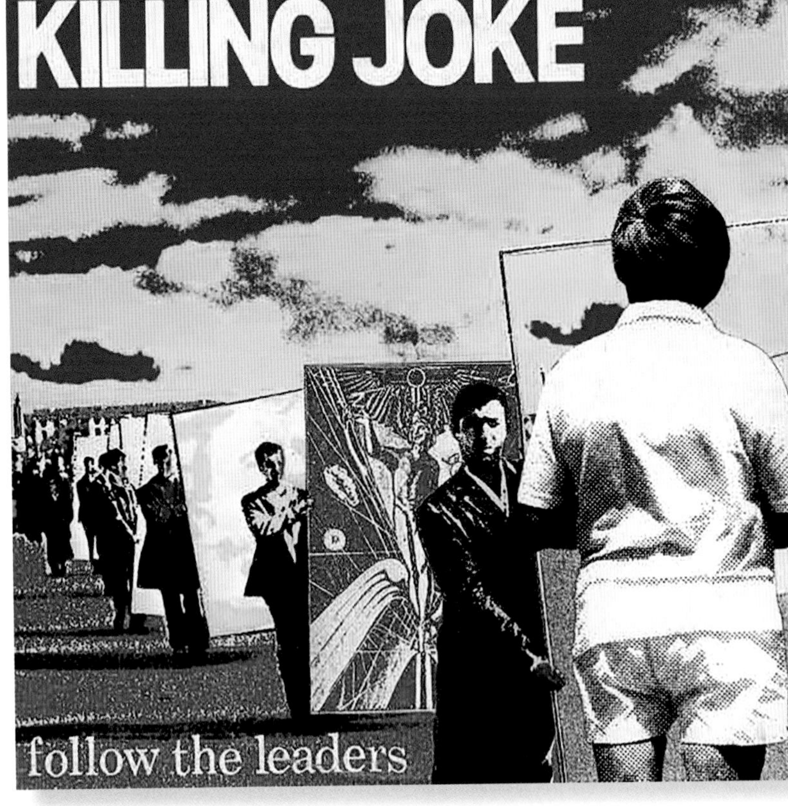

✦ ✦ ✦

POLYTECHNIC
20 June 1981,
Manchester, UK

SEAN RILEY

Well, whatever impact they were looking to make, it certainly made it on me. I had to find out more.

Then the interviews appeared in all the weekly music papers. I bought them all and saved the cuttings (still have every one that I could find from then up to the present day in large scrapbooks).

I got to see them for the first time – a sold-out gig at Cavendish House, Manchester Polytechnic. One of my pals didn't get in. It was over-18s only. We looked older than 16 and had facial hair so passed the test, but he didn't and got the bus back home (absolutely gutted for you, Fiddler).

That night, in June 1981, was one neither I, nor anyone else there, will ever forget. It wasn't a gig; it was a ritual. They were promoting their new album, *What's THIS for...!* Having heard some of the tracks via John Peel, I had an idea what to expect. But the noise level was absolutely deafening! So many highlights that evening, but 'The Fall of Because' became my own signature tune for the band. It oozed power from the start, tribal drumming, always in time, and Jaz lurching from behind his keyboards, contorting his face as he screamed out the chorus, he looked like someone who was rallying the nation to go to war. It was so hot and sweaty in there it was untrue. The set felt short, too short, but, as I was to learn in the four decades that have followed, Killing Joke have a habit of leaving you desperate and begging for more.

NIGEL WALLBANK

I had heard KJ on the [John] Peel show, bought 'Wardance' and the first album, but didn't get to see them. A bit later – June 1981 – I bumped into two friends, who I hadn't seen for a while, in the local pub. I hadn't been to many gigs for a while as

I'd got a bit bored with punk, etc. I asked them what they were up to and they said they were off to see KJ the night after at Manchester Polytechnic. I was instantly animated and asked if I could join them. I went to the gig. My memories are very blurred due to alcohol and the best Moss Side skunk. Jaz was ultra scary, KJ were amazing and left a lifelong impression on me as a 21-year-old. There is no one like Killing Joke.

LEISURE CENTRE
27 June 1981,
Stroud, UK

TIM MCLELLAN

When my youngest daughter was born, 30 years ago, her mother wanted to give her a name beginning with letter J and suggested Jemima. I said she would be teased and called Puddle Duck, so suggested Jasmin, but spelt Jazmine, after Jaz Coleman. I won. She's been going to festivals and gigs with me from when she could walk. It was her idea to try and see Killing Joke this year.

I first saw Killing Joke on 27 June 1981 at Stroud Leisure Centre when I was 17. There was a lot of glue sniffing and fighting going on outside at the start. The venue was odd – in fact, it was a leisure centre, so you had access to nearly all of it: viewing galleries, bars (no ID required then). The sound was powerful enough to keep me moshing it at the front all the way through.

FRIARS
25 July 1981,
Aylesbury, UK

JOHN KELLY

Killing Joke at Friars was my third-ever gig, my first at Friars and first Killing Joke. The first was The Jam at The Rainbow in November 1980 and the second was local High Wycombe punk band Xtraverts.

I had to lie about my age (only by one year) to attend Friars as I was only 15. I went on the train from High Wycombe to Aylesbury with two school friends, Neil Shorter and Chris Post, who were terrified I wouldn't get in and scupper their chances of seeing the band (they looked older for their age and had been visiting Friars since the previous year).

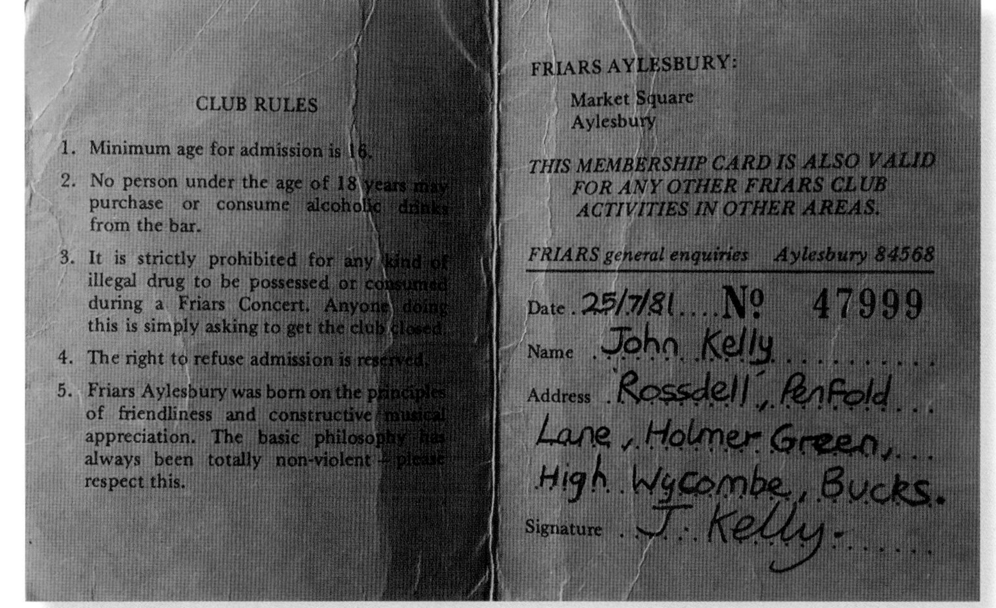

CLUB RULES

1. Minimum age for admission is 16.
2. No person under the age of 18 years may purchase or consume alcoholic drinks from the bar.
3. It is strictly prohibited for any kind of illegal drug to be possessed or consumed during a Friars Concert. Anyone doing this is simply asking to get the club closed.
4. The right to refuse admission is reserved.
5. Friars Aylesbury was born on the principles of friendliness and constructive musical appreciation. The basic philosophy has always been totally non-violent – please respect this.

FRIARS AYLESBURY:
Market Square
Aylesbury

THIS MEMBERSHIP CARD IS ALSO VALID FOR ANY OTHER FRIARS CLUB ACTIVITIES IN OTHER AREAS.

FRIARS general enquiries Aylesbury 84568

Date 25/7/81 № 47999
Name John Kelly
Address Rossdell, Penfold Lane, Holmer Green, High Wycombe, Bucks.
Signature J. Kelly.

Friars membership card belonging to John Kelly

Well, of course I got in and ensured life membership for Friars, as you can see from my card.

Killing Joke had come to my attention from my fascination with the display of 7-inch singles on the wall of Virgin Records at Oxford Circus.

I purchased 'Nervous System'/'Turn to Red' based purely on the cover art, which was common for me and usually spot on (see also 'Realities of War' by Discharge!). Obviously, schoolboy chatter with friends also confirmed suspicions about the credibility of bands with word-of-mouth recommendations.

I didn't think much of UK Decay as we waited in anticipation for the great ones with one of my first-ever pints.

My memory of the gig is how black everyone's clothing was and the horrific display of gobbing that was going on, which clung and dripped from the band's black clothing. Yuck. Eventually, I think I did a gob as it seemed to be the thing to do.

Among this blackness, a feeling of togetherness was apparent, almost tribal. This was the first time I'd danced in the pit (The Jam was seated and Xtraverts far too violent) with that feeling of camaraderie. As you fell into a crushing crowd of Doc Marten-booted feet, somebody would pull you back up.

'Wardance' was so awesome, I was hooked. I was (am) a massive Pistols fan and Youth looked more like Sid Vicious than Sid Vicious did, so I was probably staring at him most of the time! A lot of the songs were anthems and just BIG songs: 'Wardance', 'Follow the Leaders', 'Requiem', 'The Fall of...' So lucky to have witnessed these masterpieces.

Shortly after the gig, I purchased their debut LP to relive 'Wardance'.

IAN RABJOHN

I wanted to go and see them live after I bought the single 'Follow the Leaders', which I'd heard on John Peel one evening.

Having got the 7-inch single, I was also impressed with 'Tension', the so-called B-side and so I went to discover their back catalogue. Both 'Requiem' and 'Wardance' were quickly purchased (I couldn't afford the LP and didn't know about 'Turn to Red' for some reason). Amazingly, all three had great B-sides, really double-A sides. They had a real raw power and energy that appealed to 15-year-old me, so this had to be a group worth seeing live if I could manage it, as I now knew that they had at least six good songs.

Sure enough, they were touring to support the new single. Even better, I saw that they were playing quite locally to me, at Aylesbury Friars, and were due to be supported by UK Decay, who were from Luton, near to where we lived at the time and who I had also just started getting into, so this was not a gig that I was going to miss if at all possible.

Tickets were bought (£3) and we even managed to persuade my mate Jim to come along. This sticks in my mind for two reasons: firstly, as his favourite group at the time were Level 42, so I'm not sure why I thought he'd want to come, or why he agreed to, and, secondly, I recall him having to take his leather cowboy hat down to the local second-hand store to sell to raise the required funds. The joys of being at school without a job to fund our music addiction.

To be honest, it was going to be my third gig. Still being under-age always presented problems getting into venues and getting a drink once inside, making things even more exciting when you succeeded, of course.

The previous two were The Stranglers (still good at the time, especially as my first-ever gig, but in hindsight I'd missed them at their prime) and Bauhaus, who were on the up and very good indeed. The good news was that you had to be a member to get into Friars, so, once you were a member, getting in and getting served was never an issue. I'd seen Bauhaus there, so these bases were well and truly covered (I guess I must have made a mistake when I filled in my DoB on the membership form!).

As I've just confessed, at the time I hadn't seen that many gigs, so I wasn't familiar with the usual headline-act ploy of giving the support act a crappy sound and no lights. So I wasn't aware of how rare it was for KJ to give UK Decay full use of everything and they took full advantage of the smoke, lighting and strobes to put on a great show – what a group and what a set, and this was only the support act. I went on to see UK Decay many times, but this first time still sits in my mind as a cracking gig. So I have to thank KJ for introducing me to this as well.

And then came KJ. The start was a tad weird with the group coming on stage and Jaz abusing the part of the audience who were still at the bar at the back of the hall, but, after a few seconds of silence, KJ let rip and the show began.

Another stutter happened after maybe the second or third song, when Geordie broke a string during the intro to 'Requiem', so the band stopped, but a drone of feedback soon announced that he was back up and running and they re-started the song, with added gusto this time. To be honest, this all made it even more special, as I soon realised that KJ live weren't just a rehash of the records but were all slightly different, even more aggressive than on vinyl: louder, fiercer, better. I was buzzing and loved it.

They played both sides of the three singles that I owned, plus the best bits of the first two LPs – what's not to like about a set-list like that?

What a night, what a set, what a group. In those days, a set was usually 45 minutes, maybe 60 minutes at most, and we went home happy. Nothing like the two-hour-plus sets that we all get and expect these days. Luckily, they used to fit on one side of a C90 cassette perfectly, which this one did. I know as I bought a bootleg tape of it a year or so later, and it sounded really good, a sign of how great it was and how good the four musicians are. I've still got the cassette, but nothing to play it on these days.

The night didn't end there. On the way home, we broke down with about 10 miles to go and had to drive the last part of the journey at about 5–10 miles per hour, but nothing was going to take a shine off this night, even a very late arrival back home.

It's weird. I can't remember what I had for breakfast this morning, but I remember that gig (and how I talked my mate into coming along) like it was on the TV now.

Oh, and for the record, Jim probably still loves Level 42, but I recall that he had a great night anyway.

RICHARD FARRELL

Fast-forward slightly to summer 1981 and I'm idling around after doing my O-levels. Lying on my bed on a sunny Saturday afternoon, not really watching the tennis on our old portable black-and-white television. In walks my brother, two years younger, holding a pair of newly borrowed singles.

"Put this on."

He rarely wasted words. I looked at the stark monochrome sleeve of 'Requiem' and took it out of its sleeve.

"There's no label."

This was unexpected after all the colourful printing and sharp logos on United Artists sleeves for The Stranglers, 999 and Buzzcocks. No band photo, either – was this part of their design ethos or were EG just cheapskates? It gave little hint about the actual music. And how do I describe what came out of the speakers as needle met vinyl? A lot of music sounds new when you're 16 but rarely does it sound so different. The opening note, repeated, sounded like some kind of warning or a call to attention – stop listening to that and listen to this. Then the guitar came in. The power of the song was crushing, mesmerising. It didn't gallop like so much stuff of the time. The almost walking-pace tempo exuded much more threat – like a sinister juggernaut. I couldn't make out all the lyrics but that didn't matter. I sensed a feeling of rage, even disgust, from the delivery of the vocals. Not having yet discovered Krautrock, I couldn't believe anyone would have the balls to chug away on the same riff for the whole song. Couldn't they have come up with a chorus?

Yet, after a few plays, it sounded like an inspired idea. This hypnotic song had changed the direction of the musical path I'd started out on a few years earlier.

I bought the first LP soon after. Once, having had to walk home after being ejected from a club (my trousers deemed unacceptable), I was soothed by repeated listens to 'The Wait' and 'Complications'. The sound of the LP was, like 'Requiem', angry but coherent, raw yet in a strange way melodic. 'Requiem' always takes me back to that summer afternoon – and, no, I've totally forgotten what the other record was.

© Simon Reeves

MONT SHERAR
(author of the book Twilight of the Mortals)

It was 1981 when, by complete chance, I wandered into a ballroom-size 'alternative music' nightclub in New York City called The Ritz. The theme of the evening was FUTURIST NIGHT. Despite being in my late teens, I had never been to any club before, let alone one as completely alien to me as this. There must have been a thousand people inside, mostly dressed up like new romantics while I stood in the corner with my bell-bottom jeans and moustache, looking like an early version of porn star John C Holmes.

I had no idea what the punk or new wave scene was about, either, but that night I got a crash course in all that I'd been missing. Imagine the jaw-dropping experience it was to suddenly be immersed in everything from The Specials to OMD to Joy Division to Bauhaus. And, to cap it all off, they had the world's largest video screen above the dancefloor, projecting bands like Siouxsie and the Banshees at 30 feet tall. All of this alone made for a great awakening, but the real life-changer was when I got hit by a cattle-prodder just as I was about to leave the venue – in the form of the song 'Are You Receiving' by Killing Joke.

From that day on, I was hooked. I even became a full-time club DJ myself – not for the girls and the rest of it, but to simply promote Killing Joke's music. I wanted the whole world to hear it. Not that I didn't appreciate the rest of it, though.

✦ ✦ ✦

LYCEUM BALLROOM
26 July 1981,
London, UK

SCOTT FORD

Back in early 1981, I was at a boarding school – aged 16 – in West Sussex. It was a very sporty school and I was more into art and music and, as such, didn't really fit in, I guess.

Earlier that year, I had been to my first concert. Duran Duran at Hammersmith Odeon. I'd also seen [John] Otway and [Wild Willy] Barrett in Guildford. I had come late to the punk thing and was opening my ears to more and more different stuff. My albums of choice whilst revising for my O-levels were *Overkill* by Motörhead and *Welcome to the Cruise* by Judie Tzuke.

Anyway, one day I'm having a chat with one of my mates, James Perring, and he asks had I heard this band called Killing Joke. He said they weren't his thing, but he had the first album on tape and did I want to listen. I remember him saying "it's music to slit your wrists to", which was nice.

I had a very basic Walkman-type personal stereo and it was a Saturday, which meant we could take the school coach into Chichester. I was sitting at the back (as you do) and still remember putting on the headphones and hearing for the first time those first notes of 'Requiem'. What was this? I had never heard anything like this. Then 'Wardance', with that cough at the beginning.

This... was... amazing! I listened to the whole album and had been in that moment transported to another place. This was otherworldly.

After the trip to Chichester that day, I had to give the cassette back to James. However, the next day I borrowed it again – and again.

Eventually, [I had] a weekend home so I was able to get my very own copy of that first album, with the gatefold sleeve designed by Mike Coles. It was like a gift from God. From then on, I would cut out anything about Killing Joke in the music papers. I found a single in a shop on Island Records by Killing Joke called 'Nervous System' that wasn't on the album. Again amazing, but a difference, with a sort of reggae-influenced B-side, 'Turn to Red'.

They were my band. Nobody else really knew them. To me, they were so special, unique.

I hear they are going to play live in London. I buy a ticket – Killing Joke at the Lyceum Ballroom, supported by The Meteors and a reggae band, Talisman. Their new album was out – *What's THIS for ...!*

I went up to London that day in the school holidays and stayed with a mate called Tim Burton, who assured me that I could jump over the gates at Finsbury Park [tube station] and not have to pay. Unfortunately, that advice wasn't correct. I had an on-the-spot fine, which was in fact all the money I had for a drink or a t-shirt. I finally get to the gig and remember the atmosphere being dark and menacing, and here's me – not scared, more in awe. This was my band, my KILLING JOKE.

Talisman play... Meteors do their rough, tough, punky-rockabilly stuff, then KILLING JOKE. I really can't remember much of the gig, apart from being in absolute awe!

✦ ✦ ✦

BATH PAVILION
28 July 1981,
Bath, UK

STU BIRD

This was not my first Killing Joke gig. In fact, I think 'first gigs' are not really a useful barometer of a fan's relationship with any band. After all, many people see lots of bands for the first time following radio exposure, recommendations, media etc... A lot of first gigs result from a first record release, new and fresh, taking it out to the masses for the first time away from their home town. It's always the 'second times' with bands that relate with me. Can they follow up on that great first gig, album, or will they get stuck in their own quicksand?

There's no doubt that my first encounter with Killing Joke at Bristol Berkeley in December 1980 was a superb show. Following lots of airplay from John Peel, the unique sound and energy left me wanting more.

Six months later and second album *What's THIS for...!* is released and lives up to everything the recent 'Follow the Leaders' single had promised. I have to see them live again. Nothing in Bristol, but a show in neighbouring Bath at the end of July. The fact that this is at the Pavilion shows just how big the interest in the band had become in just a few months. Tickets bought, it's an easy bus journey from where I live. There's lots of familiar faces mingling outside, along with many from other areas. Support is provided by Bristol multicultural reggae band Talisman; a great choice, and a band I am already familiar with. They go down well to an open and enthusiastic crowd.

The first thing I remember about Killing Joke is just how comfortable they filled this much bigger stage. Like the stage, the sound is big – loud and punchy. Bass and drums fill the hall, with scything guitar and vocals only Jaz can deliver. The new songs dovetail seamlessly with the older ones. The groove becomes almost tribal, especially with songs like 'Tension' and 'Follow the Leaders'. Even songs like 'Wardance' seemed to become more urgent, polished and vital. They totally mesmerised me. I left the gig with a sense of euphoria, something only a very small handful of bands have managed since. There was nothing around that compared to this.

TIM MCLELLAN

My usual venue, Bath Pavilion, never had a bar back then. At the end of gigs, they opened the ticket collection box for you to help yourself. I got some really pristine ones. My mate and I then went round outside the back of the building and climbed into the backstage area. Normally, the bouncers don't mind a few people going back. I've met The Undertones, The Photos, Dead Kennedys and Toyah there, as well as seeing loads more. I think only about 10 people made it before the window got closed. Somebody was passing around a bottle of rum, I remember. I asked if I could get my ticket signed and they did. Not knowing what all the band looked like, I asked this one guy with them for an autograph, to be replied with "I'm the roadie." Only just researched the gig dates to discover that it could have been Dr Alex Paterson (big fan of The Orb, but that's a longer story).

FRANK JENKINSON

The house [11 Portland Road] came to an end in 1981. I got married at the end of 1981. Summer, the time of the first American tour, everybody was gone. I was the last person of the residents' group to leave the house. We all went our separate ways. We were expecting a child, so I moved out to Ealing where I was working as a social worker.

✦ ✦ ✦

THE CHANNEL
15 August 1981,
Boston, USA

MICHAEL GRECCO
(photographer)

© Tim McClellan

I remember having to shoot Killing Joke for *Boston Rock* magazine. I usually shot the show and then hung out with the band after the show to do some portraits. When the band came on, I was really surprised at the power and animation of their lead, Jaz. Not a very big guy, but he was big when he performed, really big. The band created a wall of sound that was ridiculous. It was powerful and layered with dense and subtle sounds of the electronica of the day. Jaz was animated, flashing his hands and screaming into the microphone in a way most comatose Eighties bands just did not do.

Afterwards, I hung out and made some pictures of all four members, totally drenched backstage at The Channel. It was an unexpected evening for sure.

Michael Grecco's images and Killing Joke photos can be seen in his new book from Abrams: *Punk, Post Punk, New Wave: Onstage, Backstage, In Your Face, 1978–1991*

✦ ✦ ✦

EAST SIDE CLUB
17 August 1981,
Philadelphia, USA

MICHAEL DENT

Here's another example of just how cool Killing Joke are. Caroline Robbie (Nash the Slash's new light person) and I decided to bus it to Philly to see Killing Joke and we would be there a day early and waiting for Nash, who was playing the next day. The band were surprised to see us, but treated us like royalty, as they usually do with friends.

I asked if we could crash on the floor for the night as Nash was playing the same club the next day. Killing Joke had decided to drive to their next gig that night and sleep on their tour bus, so they gave us two of their rooms. Such stand-up guys.

So many gigs, so long ago and my memory's not as good as it was – the passage of time, drink and drugs.

Really decent and down-to-earth folks, but a volatile bunch at the same time. I just love them to death.

POLICE PICNIC FESTIVAL
23 August 1981,
Oakville, Canada

GEORGE WASYLENKO

It was an outdoor festival with a large number of new-wave bands, headlined by The Police. I was 21. I didn't care for most of the other bands, but had to see Killing Joke. The first album ripped through my soul like a love affair. It was Cleopatra, Joan of Arc, Aphrodite, harmonised through the sound of Geordie Walker's guitar. It was a new, meaningful, dangerous type of music, unlike anything that was previously released.

Killing Joke hit the stage around 5pm. Geordie Walker's guitar filled the ambient background as Jaz Coleman punched through with a chant above the bass and drums. 'Wardance'! In the heat of the moment, I was lifted on to a spiritual plane, transformed and taken to a higher level of consciousness. Brighter than a thousand suns, Killing Joke covered the stage in pure daylight. No stage lighting or special effects, just raw power. From that moment on, I was hooked. I left the concert during the headliner's performance. After Killing Joke, no one else seemed relevant.

MICHAEL DENT

The first time Killing Joke played Toronto was at the first Police Picnic, put on by the 2 Garys [promoters Gary Topp and Gary Cormier]. It was an all-day outdoor event featuring The Go-Gos, Nash [the Slash], Iggy Pop, Killing Joke and, closing the day, The Police.

Trailers were rented and used as dressing rooms. Bands shared. The show was in midsummer, so it was very hot. It seems that Killing Joke had to share a trailer with The Police. We all had a hate on for The Police for various reasons, but mostly Sting. I fucking hated them because they were all assholes when I did a number of dates with them when I worked for Tom Robinson's Sector 27 on a North American tour earlier that year.

So, after Killing Joke's set, we finished off all the booze in the trailer and all of us pissed all over the seat cushions in the trailer and I killed the air conditioning. After that, I dropped some green pyramid acid with Youth. Youth and I spent the rest of the day stealing golf carts and bombing around, causing complete mayhem. It was a glorious day and we were in hysterics at what The Police were going to encounter in their trailer. Good times. Yes, real good times. I got to watch Killing Joke from onstage.

MARK COWLING

It was a big concert just north of the city. Iggy Pop was there, I think The Specials, a few other bands and, of course, The Police were the headliner. I had camped out and was actually the very first person allowed in as we knew the guy at the gate, so my arms were literally on the front fence at the very front of the stage. I had never heard of Killing Joke at the time, but I gotta tell ya, I was blown away! They became my favourite band and still are today almost 40 years later. Cool, huh?

Jaz at The Police Picnic, watched from the side of the stage by Michael Dent © Paul Tozer

UNIVERSITY OF EAST ANGLIA
7 November 1981,
Norwich, UK

ROGER MOSEDALE

I was 15 and had been to a handful of gigs: The Cure, Stiff Little Fingers, some local bands.

I'd heard a couple of KJ bits on John Peel (of course) and had picked up the 'Follow the Leaders' 10-inch. Pored over the album covers in the local record shops too, of course. There was something about the band that made them stand out from the hordes of punk noisemakers of the time.

Now, I'd say it was Youth's monstrous bass sound as a foundation for what the rest of the band were doing. Then, I just thought they sounded interesting, like a lot of bands had stopped doing. I do remember a quite hostile feature in (I think) *NME* of the time; perhaps written by Paul Morley? That, and a quote from Jaz explaining the band name – something concerning a First World War soldier about to go over the top and thinking about the fucker in Whitehall who'd put him there. Certainly enough to hook in a history-obsessed teenager.

Looking back at the set-list, I wouldn't have known many of the songs at the time. 'Requiem' and 'Tension' at the end maybe. I do remember them coming on and Jaz cackling away: "1982? Good times on the way, haha." Then that noise! The bass was a physical pressure (it's probably no accident that I ended up obsessing on dub for years after this). Jaz again: "Is that some students out there not dancing? This is 'Change'."

I went backstage after, but, as a shy 15-year-old, I didn't hang around; the atmosphere felt kind of intimidating (not in the physical sense).

✦ ✦ ✦

FRIARS
6 December 1981,
Aylesbury, UK

DAVID HARDAKER

After the gig, me, my brother and a mate were walking towards Aylesbury train station car park. As we were walking across a grassed area, I was singing the lyrics "See the sun turn green, from a penthouse window" from 'Complications'.

And there were three guys in front of us, soul boys who thought I was taking the piss. So they turned on me.

My mate and brother stepped back and didn't help. I don't [fight] and am not a fighter, believe me, but I managed to get the better of one of them and sit on top of him. Anyway, one of the other guys was hitting me with a four-pack of beer in the back. Every time he hit me, I punched his mate in the face and said I'm gonna keep on doing this. Luckily enough, a car pulled up with a bunch of

punks in and asked if I was all right, did I need help, which was when they scarpered towards the train station.

One plus was that they shot off in such a hurry that they left their four-pack of beer behind (one of the cans had a big dent in it). So I took them all home with me and didn't share with my brother or my mate for not helping me out.

The only reason I think these guys picked on me is because they misheard what I was singing.

Maybe they heard "See the soul boy grin, from a penthouse window".

Who knows?

Killing Joke were as awesome as ever. I remember seeing Jaz on stage, mesmerising and manic-staring at the crowd, flexing his hands, opening and closing them to the music, just fucking staring through everyone.

Brilliant.

✦ ✦ ✦

MAIDA VALE STUDIOS
11 December 1981,
London, UK

JOHN OWEN WILLIAMS

(producer of the fourth John Peel session)

They're really an unbelievable band. Some sessions stand out in the memory of recordings there. Generally, the ones that stand out are usually the ones that get released on CD or album. This was one of those sessions.

It was the first live Radio 1 session for me. Stuart Grundy [BBC producer] asked if I would like to do some sessions. The BBC would have the studio producer as a freelancer.

In the allotted time, you would start it at 2.30[pm] and finish at 11 and you would record and mix four songs. You would have a break for dinner between seven and eight. You would have to have all the recording done by seven.

It's a really tight turnaround. Then you've got three hours to mix.

It's all about time-management, getting the confidence of the band, to make them play as well as they could in an alien environment.

So you spend the first hour setting the gear up, getting a drum sound, getting a bass sound, getting a guitar sound. And then working out what overdubs besides vocals and whatever the band wanted to do.

Jaz wanted to put on a keyboard opening on one track, I think it's on 'The Hum'. I think he had got this new keyboard that no one seemed to know how it worked, so

© John Owen Williams

you had to program it to get the sounds. I think we spent about an hour fiddling about with this keyboard, to get the right sound Jaz wanted, which we eventually got.

We recorded it. In those days, it was on 24-track, two-inch tape. You would probably use eight, 10 tracks [for] drums, couple of tracks [for] guitar. We used all the tracks and recorded his part and then he turned the keyboard off and we went on to the next thing.

The very next overdub we did, we went over his overdub, erased it. To say Jaz was not best pleased was an understatement.

He was absolutely furious. I don't know how it happened. It's an easy mistake when you're in the heat of the moment, the time pressure as well. So we had to record it again.

I was listening to the session this morning. You wouldn't know it [about the mistake]. The session sounds amazing.

This session really blew my mind. When they started playing the opening riff of 'Chop-Chop' or 'We Have Joy' or 'Empire Song' – just amazing. To have the vision to create something so powerful was not something I was used to. But I thoroughly enjoyed it.

I can't say I know the band, and our paths haven't crossed since, but to start my Radio 1 session-producer career with Killing Joke was an honour and a really exciting experience.

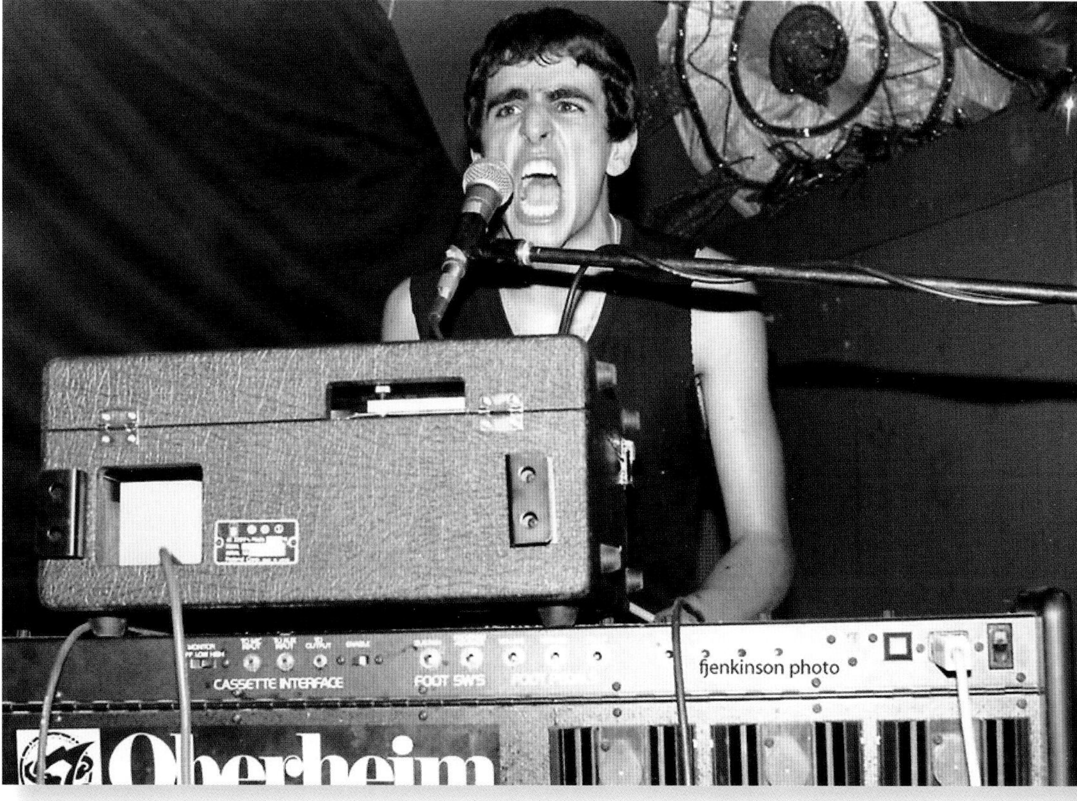

© Frank Jenkinson

They were just a fantastic rock band. They made this extraordinary racket. They're great players.

I can't remember many other sessions having that kind of intensity.

GEORDIE

Revelations. Neunkirchen-Seelscheid. Ancient farmhouse, courtyard and a little bit of land.

He [Conny Plank] had seen us live on the tag-team tour we did with Basement 5 [in 1980]. Basically, he went for a live recording, all in the same room, overspill. The thing is, what I did on that album… It was my mistake. Rather than use the piano, I tuned by ear and mistakenly tuned a whole semitone below. By accident.

I loved Conny's fucking cymbals. Just the sheen. I found out what that is. If you mic the cymbals sideways on, you get that sheen. Stick it on the top and you get the dustbin lid.

It [the album] is what it is. I think the first recordings [with the famous Gibson ES-295] were still with Conny Plank. 'Birds of a Feather'/'Sun Goes Down'. 'Sun Goes Down' was the one that turned out right. "I'm on the right track here," I thought.

Conny said to me: "When I was a young boy during the war, I used to listen to the classical music on the radio, like full volume – your sound is that sound." Probably the biggest compliment I ever got paid. A lovely, lovely man. Lovely, gentle, big bear of a man.

YOUTH

And then the third album – that just became a dirge, with no choruses. That was shocking because we had Conny producing and he was our hero: he'd done Can, Kraftwerk. But I was on the substitutes' bench from my acid meltdown and I think Conny just saw us as a kind of noisy rock band. He got a vacuum-cleaner hose and swung it around. I remember him doing a couple of weird things.

If he'd done what he did with Ultravox and just replaced us with Linn Drums and synths, I would have been into that. But he recorded us traditionally like a rock band.

Nevertheless, the experience of hanging out with him and Holger [Czukay] was incredible, that was life-changing.

BIG PAUL

We rehearsed in Can's studio nearby. Recording with Conny was a fantastic experience.

YOUTH

It was just so disappointing that album came out so moody. I remember doing these endless German tours where we'd start with 'The Hum'. This bleak, dirgy march, East European glumness. I was like: "Why do you wanna do that?" 'Dregs' – another one. It just felt like you were in the bottom of a bin. They love that.

I'm the only one who feels like that. A lot of the fans love it. The band love it. The band are always going, "Let's do 'The Hum'." And I'm like, "Oh, fuck off."

GEORDIE

['The Hum' riff] came up on magic mushrooms. "What the fuck is this?" I thought.

YOUTH

I thought that whatever ground we had gained with that *[What's THIS for...!]*, we lost with the third album.

ROTTERS CLUB
21 February 1982,
Manchester, UK

MARK WHITELEY
(The Folk Devils)

It was a cold February morning when me and my friend Graham J started on our mission to Manchester. We were off to see Killing Joke. As enthusiastic 16-year-olds, we were determined to enjoy it. We hitched from our Snowdonia home and made it to Oxford Street in Manchester by mid-afternoon. The venue, Rotters, was easy to find and, fortuitously, we arrived as Killing Joke pulled up in their van.

We said "Hi" to the guys and I ended up in a conversation with Dave the Wizard, who would read *The Book of the Law* [a key Aleister Crowley text] to introduce the band and then perform his fire dance during the set. He was worried there might be too much glass on the floor, a very ordinary concern held by an extraordinary man.

He invited us both into the venue, and so I stepped into the world of Killing Joke. Alongside a dozen or so others – Si, Weasel, Medicine Dog, to name a few – we represented the embryonic Gatherers. For the rest of that tour, we'd hitch from city to city, crash where we could, attend the nightly gatherings and were lucky enough to get to know the band and their inner circle. Dave the Wizard became a firm friend, Brian the manager, Danny the tour manager, Alex Paterson – the then drum tech – and, of course, Geordie, Paul, Youth and Jaz – they all treated me well. I became Paul's spliff-roller.

Getting to know the band: Geordie showed me riffs and gave me strings. He also introduced me to Gematria [numerological system in which letters correspond to numbers]. Youth let me hang out with him, often at Risk [clothes shop and general hangout] on Portobello Road. He sold me his Ricki cheap and encouraged me to play, even lending me his bass rig when I rehearsed with Hack Hack in Risk basement in '83. He showed me the first-ever sampler.

For a 16-year-old, I was already living the dream and my desire to become a musician was fuelled when the Wizard turned to me after a stunning gig at York University [22 February] and handed me a copy of his version of *The Book of the Law* and his address. His dreadlocks and facial tattoos gave him an exotic, otherworldly look; his warm, unique personality made him instantly likeable. So when he said, "Come to London and we'll start a band", I said, "Yes! Fuckin' right." I told Jaz and he said, "Fuckin' right" too. It's hard to communicate what this meant to me.

They were, for me, the perfect blend of music and ideas. The early gigs I went to, when the Wizard did the fire, were life-changing. The effect was, well, fucking awesome.

I'd always try to get a spot in front of Geordie's guitar rig. Later in life, doing a gong bath has a similarly profound effect on my mind, body and soul.

© Nigel Wallbank

I'd listened to the band since 'Turn to Red' and 'Are You Receiving'. I'd seen them in Bath [28 July] the night before Charles and Diana's wedding in 1981 – and here I was, a year or so later, making a decision, for better or worse, to follow the band and Dave Wizard to London. It was pretty crazy, but things were not too good between me and my Dad. Mum gave me her blessing to go. Her mother's heart knew I had to follow my own heart. At 16, I was already riding with a biker crew, living in a caravan in a field or crashing here and there. I had to go. Nothing would've stopped me.

I left home as a precocious adolescent, always plagued by a god-shaped hole in my heart and soul. Just as Jaz was compelled to travel to Iceland to continue his individuation process, I was compelled to seek out individuals or groups to hold inner gold I was unable to carry for myself.

Robert A Johnson, the Jungian scholar, is instructive on this. I projected on to Killing Joke what I aspired to for myself. The archetype of the jester is truly powerful, for the jester is the only one present who can mock the king. I had a little way to go before I resolved that complex, sublimating the archetype and harnessing the anima and animus of my Self.

✦ ✦ ✦

HAMMERSMITH PALAIS
23 February 1982,
London, UK

MATT TIBBITS

My first KJ memory is the buzzsaw synth of 'Requiem' piercing my bedroom wall from my sister's turntable. First gig was the infamous Hammersmith Palais before Jaz fled to Iceland. All I can remember is it being absolutely rammed and an air of violence and menace. Loved it at that age! I got very drunk indeed.

✦ ✦ ✦

TOP RANK SUITE
24 February 1982,
Brighton, UK

MARC JONES

Just want to tell you a little story about me and Jaz Coleman. My love for Killing Joke began when, on 5 October 1980, they released *Killing Joke*. After purchasing this album in our local record store, Max Records in Eastbourne, I was hooked.

I played it over and over again for the next few days. Killing Joke were now my new favourite band, so out came the Airfix model paint so I could paint the album cover on the back of my leather bikers' jacket.

Now, for some unknown reason, the first time I was to see them live was 24 February 1982 at Brighton's Top Rank Suite.

After queuing outside for what seemed an age, the doors opened and, after a quick ticket check, in we went. I managed to secure a decent spot down the front. After watching the support acts, Peter and the Test Tube Babies from Peacehaven, and Aztec Camera (which I thought a strange support), excitement grew: I was about to see my favourite band for the first time.

On came the band. I was in awe. During the time they were on stage, there was a lot of spitting going on, which made it unpleasant being at the front.

Jaz was on stage above me, covered in his black-and-white face make-up, when all of a sudden I was aware of him picking up his microphone stand and swinging it towards the crowd. I had to back away, as it skimmed just in front of my face. It was at this point he leaped from the stage, grabbing hold of me and attacking me. I can only assume that he thought I was one of the ones spitting at him. After bouncers pulled him off me, they went off. I was in shock to be honest: the vocalist of my favourite band had just been beating and punching me.

Then, the following week, I read in *Sounds* music paper that Killing Joke had split up due to persistent gobbing at a recent Brighton gig.

I was gutted. My favourite band had split up. Even though I was not to blame, I still felt guilty for some reason.

MIK RAVEN

This was my favourite band, without a doubt. But then came the rub. Jaz went missing and my favourite band was no more. Am I remembering this right? I think it was front-page headlines on the *NME*.

CHRIS BRYANS

Soon after the Brighton show, Jaz left the country and travelled to Iceland. The music press reported that you, Youth and Geordie were "stunned". Just four weeks later, you appeared on Top of the Pops with the first single from Revelations, 'Empire Song'. Did you draw straws for who 'sang' in Jaz's absence?

BIG PAUL

No, it was obvious that I'd do it. It was always a toss-up between Jaz and myself as to who'd be the singer in the band, but singing drummers are a bit naff and Jaz always had the ego for the job. So I won and he got the job! There's a fair bit of miming going on in these shows anyway.

✦ ✦ ✦

TOP OF THE POPS
25 March 1982,
London, UK

MARK WHITELEY

Paul was particularly cool with me. When I arrived at the *Top of the Pops* studio ('Empire Song') with Dave Wizard, he looked up and looked pleasantly surprised. "How the hell did you turn up?" he said, smiling. Again, he encouraged me to make my own music. We talked music, magick, karma and nukes all night in the BBC bar. I remember Kenny Everett was there… vaguely.

LEE HOLFORD

Fast-forward to '82 and I'm becoming a (young and naive) punk rocker. I buy records almost every weekend with my paper-round and pocket money. I walk into Revolver Records in Leicester and see a Killing Joke record at the front of a rack. I buy it without even knowing what it is (it was the 'Turn to Red' 12-inch). I obsess over all four tracks.

Then comes 'Empire Song'. Also see it on *Top of the Pops*. The first time I see what they look like. Very cool. Singing drummer! But who is THAT in the space suit? Haha.

ROB HAYNES

I was 17 and bored with all the bands who had got me into music a few years earlier. The Stranglers, Motörhead and The Damned had all released their classic albums and were variously drifting into what I saw as less interesting directions. I needed something new.

I picked up a magazine, looking for someone offering something different. There, standing out amid a glut of unimaginative second-wave punks, were Killing Joke. Like The Stranglers, they kind of looked fairly normal, with none of the needy desperation of many bands with 'images' – and yet they also looked distinctly dangerous. It may even have been the interview where they said they wanted to sound like nature throwing up – anyway, I was intrigued.

I went out and took a punt (no internet in those days) on the 'Follow the Leaders' 10-inch and the 'Requiem' and 'Nervous System' 12-inch singles. These were quite a diverse bunch of songs, not all of which hit home straight away, but there was definitely enough to keep my interest, especially the tribal rhythms of 'Leaders'/'Tension'. A few weeks after that, 'Empire Song' came out, with the spaceman replacing the absent Jaz on *Top of the Pops*. That was very much that – I was down for life.

MICHE MARCISZ

Being a regular customer at Wax Trax! Records (Chicago), I was able to keep Killing Joke in mind when shopping. One day (approx. 1982), the 7-inch single 'Empire Song', in all its colourful glory, caught my eye. I took it home. I also loved the jester image. After that, I was after anything I could get my hands on.

ANDY MAXWELL

I was brought up in a medium-sized town called Dumfries in south-west Scotland. There wasn't a lot happening here back in the late Seventies. We had the usual chains of stores that stocked the usual chart singles and albums, nothing else – apart from one very small shop that catered for the punk, new-wave and independent scene. One of my friends bought 'Empire Song' on 7-inch, then a few weeks later gave it to me after I pestered the shit out of him to part with it. That was the start of my Killing Joke journey back in '82.

CHRIS BRYANS

There was a lot of confusion in 1982. How did you see it from your perspective?

BIG PAUL

Very distressing. I learned first-hand how one person's actions can immediately turn other people's lives upside down. I've had to forget the hurt and betrayal in order to forgive and be forgiven.

GEORDIE

It was a difficult time.

1982–1988

"Push, push, struggle"

YOUTH

When Jaz fucked off to Iceland and he left me and his girlfriend in the flat without telling us, she was so furious she burned all his clothes.

He came back a couple of weeks later, then Geordie left with him and then Paul. It was like betrayal, betrayal, betrayal. It was the end of the line, I thought.

And then Jaz knocked on the door of the flat. "Come on, we got a German tour next week."

"I dunno if I can handle it. You take Raven. I'm gonna get into production and do some other weird things."

GEORDIE

Youth had spun out. I didn't realise until years later that they'd given him ECT. He was just a shell of his former self, which I found very sad. I was quietly heartbroken. Where's the Youth gone?

YOUTH

I was very lucky to come through it. One of the reasons I had to leave the band was I was so fragile. I stopped taking acid for about seven, eight years.

MARK WHITELEY
(The Folk Devils)

While Jaz and then Geordie were away, me and the Wizard went to Avebury stone circle to conduct a fire ritual. That's another story, but I believe it's one of the elements that brought the Killing Joke core back together. Of course, to some this may seem insane but, as in Euler's Formula, it's a universe of waves; energetic and flowing, constantly. Quantum entanglement, as a theory, indicates that a ritual could indeed tap into the energetic connectivity between two or more human beings. And, even if it doesn't, it's a darn fine and rather elegant idea.

RUSTY EGAN

I went to Youth's flat on Ladbroke Grove when he left KJ. He was down. That place [was] wrecked. I asked had he been robbed. "No," he said. "I am just too fucked to deal with anything." "How about coming to Trident, my studio? If you have a project, I am here to offer you studio time. I know it will be amazing."

Jaz, Münster, Germany, 18 February 1984 © Larry Bate

YOUTH

I wanted to experiment. I felt like we'd already put ourselves in a straitjacket. If I'd known that they were gonna come up with 'Love Like Blood' and 'Eighties', I'd never have left. But, after the third album, I thought it was gonna be another load of dirge. I couldn't face it. I thought we'd worked ourselves into this dingy, cold, dirty cul-de-sac and morose dirge. I think Jaz is quite happy with that. And I wasn't. I wanted to go for a more punk/funk thing, experiment with dance music. It allowed me to sharpen my skill set as a producer.

RUSTY EGAN

I had signed Specimen and created Batcave Club and I had Paul Cook and Matthew Ashman, Chiefs of Relief. Youth met Roz, our session booker, who said she could get him producer work. We had [producer] Flood. I was in touch with U2, Spear of Destiny. We had Foetus, The The, [label] Some Bizarre and [promoter] Final Solution, who were in touch with New Order – it was really a well-connected place and Youth plugged right back in, made Brilliant with [vocalist] June [Montana]. Roz had calls and, boom, he became a hit record producer. I lost Trident and everything. By 1990, I was fucking homeless.

MARK WHITELEY

I first met Raven at Youth's basement flat. I think I was there with Kris Needs, Luca (Brilliant's second bass player) and Youth getting ready to catch a 52 [bus] to the Churchill at Notting Hill Gate. Youth and Kris introduced me to so much music. It's not an exaggeration to say they were probably responsible for the fledgling rave scene; they sourced cassettes of Kiss FM in New York and played a lot of funk, disco, dub and house music loud. Youth threw parties from time to time that were epic both musically and guest-wise. Youth always seemed to know everyone! You could hear the impact of those parties on music that was emerging within the London scene in the early and mid-Eighties.

As for the Churchill, you'd find a herd of musicians, scoundrels and vagabonds there most nights of the week. Raven was a friendly, humorous and engaging personality. I spent many evenings with him at the Churchill with a cast of many characters – Ray McVeigh, Dave Barbarossa, Guy Pratt, all the Folk Devils, and even Lemmy from time to time. Sadly, though, the era of the Grove and its music and squat scene was coming to an end. Where once lived skint and not-so-skint musicians, the area was becoming the playground of the accountants, lawyers and bankers.

HONEY BANE

(Fatal Microbes)

Youth later formed Brilliant. Andy Anderson was playing drums. I had already worked with Andy. He played on the 'Turn Me On, Turn Me Off' single. I did a TV show. There was a club scene. I was fronting a live band on stage and I used Brilliant as my backing band. We played two songs.

MARK WHITELEY

I wasn't hugely surprised that Raven got the gig with Killing Joke once Jaz and Geordie had returned from their Icelandic adventure. Youth had decided to work on Brilliant. He had Andy Anderson, a great drummer and really good bloke, and Marcus [Myers] as a front man who could deliver the goods, so it was a solid unit. I saw them play The Ace in Brixton with Cocteau Twins and Sisters of Mercy supporting. Brilliant, with the two-bass line-up, were bloody brilliant, pardon the unavoidable pun. You could see Youth was pushing into new musical terrain. It's not a surprise that he's ended up as a world-renowned producer. Through all the time I knew him, he simply lived and breathed music.

NICOLA FROUDE

It was awesome over the years starting to get to know them and what they were about. Going through the trials and tribulations, the changes. Youth leaving and going on to do great things. The intensity of Jaz.

MARK WHITELEY

A few weeks after first meeting Raven, Dave the Wizard announces to me that we're off to Camden to see Killing Joke rehearsing their new bass player in. I don't know to this day how he knew. Dave just seemed to intuit things and they would invariably come to pass... that or he had the world's first mobile phone!

Things always seemed to move quickly. One week I'm at a BBC bar getting hammered on Southern Comfort talking to Big Paul about Jaz fucking off and karma and replacements. Then, a matter of weeks later, we rock up to a rehearsal studio in Camden and there's Paul, Jaz, Geordie and Raven blasting their way through 'The Hum'.

Jaz was oozing enthusiasm and energy [at the rehearsal]. He said Raven had learnt the set in a week. It was quite something to get to see this second line-up of the Joke. They sounded ferocious.

Once they'd wound down the rehearsal, Geordie entertained us with a spot of shredding, then got behind the drums. I picked up his guitar. Just turning the volume up on his rig created a tone that literally flowed through my bones. So, for a one-off, Geordie on drums said to me "play something", so I struck up a riff – a song called 'Energy' that I'd done with the Wizard in [the band] Last Rites. Raven picked up the bass and the Wizard took to the mic. I can't express what a joy this was for a 17- or 18-year-old fan to now be privileged enough to be allowed in rehearsals and then to jam with some of the guys. To add even more to this particular evening, Jaz played us the opening phrases of the symphony he'd composed on his Icelandic trip. It was quite an experience.

Even Helldom, the dog always with the Wizard back then, seemed to appreciate the importance of what was coming to pass.

BIG PAUL

Raven was a great bass player and solid. I loved playing with him and his character is very much missed. Youth has an uncommon magic. Different breed and not to be compared.

IAN ROBERTSON

Even at school, Keith Legge looked like Jaz Coleman. Killing Joke had suffused my ps(s)yche from the get-go – I saw them every time I looked at Keith. But they were Keith's band: he saw them first, schoolyard rules.

Keith left school; he was gone. Except for Saturday nights at Ritzy's, when he was most certainly there; otherwise, he was mostly gone.

Around this time, I heard 'Chop-Chop' on the radio. Not long afterwards, the LP *Revelations* came out. Apparently, at the behest of Conny Plank, Kevin "Geordie" Walker had found his beloved hollow-bodied Gibson ES-295, and that was it – sorry, Keith, but Killing Joke were now officially mine.

BIG PAUL

[Designer] Mike [Coles] was part of the early Malicious Damage record label and it was difficult for us to continue with him when we had gone to another label and management. I did my best to fill in with artwork and ideas and Rob O'Connor brought those to fruition with layout, etc. 'Chop-Chop', 'Empire Song' and 'A New Day' were my creations and, more recently, *Down by the River*, although with assistance.

JASON MILLS

I was living in England at the time, Daventry, a small market town in Northamptonshire, with no record shop. I used to read the *NME* and *Sounds* in the local newsagents and discreetly attempt to rip out any KJ articles.

It didn't work. I was soon banned from all the newsagents in town, apart from the one that employed me as a paper boy. The only other way of finding out more about KJ was to jump in the car with my Mum when she went food shopping in Northampton. She went shopping; I ran to the nearest record shop.

By the time I heard 'The Fall of Because' on JP, the first two albums had been released. On the release of *Revelations*, I cycled from Daventry to John Lever Records, Gold Street, Northampton, and back – a two-hour round trip. It was Saturday, July 10 1982, the first weekend of its release. I remember getting close to home and an articulated lorry came flying past me and pushed the carrier bag that the record was in into my spokes. I thought, "That's it – record smashed!!" To my relief, it was only a bent sleeve.

TROY GREGORY

(bass, European tour, 1996)

A guy made a tape for me. He put on 'Chop-Chop', 'We Have Joy', 'The Pandys Are Coming' and I just fucking loved it.

MIK RAVEN

They came back with Raven on bass. I loved them just as much. It took me a while to warm to Raven, as his bass-lines were not the same as Youth's, but it was still KJ.

✦ ✦ ✦

EAGLES HIPPODROME
13 July 1982,
Seattle, USA

SHIRLEY WONG

I would like to share my meeting with Jaz. As a former punk rocker (I guess we never lose the punk with age), I have been to numerous concerts. My friend Rose was so excited about her favourite band, Killing Joke, coming to Seattle in 1982. I did not know anything about KJ, but was excited to see my friends – Rose, Brian and John from Tacoma, Washington.

The venue was filling up and, after the opening band, I went to the front of the stage and, since I'm only 5ft 1in and the stage was about eight feet high, I grabbed a chair and stood on the chair throughout Killing Joke's performance.

© Shirley Wong

I was mesmerised from the first beat: the heavy drums from Paul, Raven standing and sneering at us, Geordie cool as a cucumber and Jaz a maniac with his black-smeared face war paint. I just locked eyes with Jaz throughout the whole concert and, afterwards, felt like I was in a deep trance state.

After the show, I was a bit light-headed, famished and energised (strange combination) and was ready to leave. But Rose was so excited and wanted to wait and meet the band. I personally don't like hanging out and waiting for band members. I just quietly stood against a wall.

Rose was getting really emotional that her favourite band just played and didn't know what to do. I said, "Isn't that the bass player? Why don't you take your record to have it autographed?" So Rose, Brian and John go up to Raven and chat and I stood against a wall.

Next thing, Jaz comes up to me and says, "What can a person do in this town?" I replied, "Go out for a drink." He told me to stay there and he will be right back. Then my friends rushed to me and asked me what he said. "I guess we are going out for drinks!"

We ended going to a placed called The Vogue and everyone was looking at us. I had no idea what the night would entail.

Jaz talked about living in Iceland, working on a symphony and he was only 22 years old at that time. I felt he was so worldly and here I was, a student at University of Washington majoring in Dance and Art! He kept asking me if I would like to go to Iceland!

After we left the bar, I thought we would be just driving Jaz back to his hotel, but he wanted to continue his evening and we all piled into John's car and drove to my apartment in Seattle in the Eastlake area (just north of downtown Seattle, about a 10-minute drive). My apartment at the time had NO furniture except a stereo and a futon! We all sat on the floor and Jaz looked through my record collection. Jaz asked if he could take a bath, so I drew him a bath with bath gel and I recall that I had a soap that was shaped like a fish. (Jaz is a Pisces.)

My friends and I were looking at each other in the living room thinking, "Oh my God!" Afterwards, Jaz just crashed out on my living-room floor and we all kind of nodded off.

In the morning, Jaz asked me if I had a piece of paper and pen and he jotted down a note for me. I had to get to work. I worked downtown, close to Pike Place Market, and we all hopped into John's car and went to the market. Rose took our picture.

Jaz walked me to my place of work, a retail shop called All That Jazz, where he took a postcard of our business and crossed off (with black sharpie) the last Z on Jazz.

I gave Jaz my hand to say goodbye and he gently kissed it. My friends ended up taking Jaz back to his hotel. I was completely high and sleep-deprived.

When I got home that night, I found the note that Jaz wrote.

Till this day, anytime KJ is in town, I try to see their performances and, of course, Jaz and I laugh about our meeting back in 1982.

I wonder what would have happened if I took up his offer to go to Iceland?

To Shirley

I see the earth rising a second time

Out of the foam, – Fair and green

Down from the fells fish to capture,

Wings the eagle, waters flow

Love Jaz

The note that Jaz wrote for Shirley Wong. It is taken from the poem Völuspá and features on several occasions in Shaun Pettigrew's Death and Resurrection Show documentary film © Shirley Wong

THE HOT KLUB
31 July 1982,
Dallas, USA

COLIN MARSH

A 250-ish venue that I frequently played at with my own band. It was not necessarily in the hip part of town. But it was the place to be. Many great bands played there. The Stranglers, Black Uhuru, REM...

I knew little of KJ before attending other than a few tunes I heard previously. It truly was an awakening!

They took command of the stage. The lighting. The aura. The industrial... sooty, almost griminess, of it.

Totally new.

Totally fresh.

Jaz had me transfixed. At that point, he was playing keyboards dead centre. With that coalminer look of his. I was in. For life.

© Colin Marsh

LARRY'S HIDEAWAY
9/10 August 1982,
Toronto, Canada

MICHAEL DENT

When *Revelations* came out, the 2 Garys announced a Killing Joke show at Larry's Hideaway. They were coming for two days. I was in seventh heaven. On the day of the first show, I was beside myself with anticipation. I lived two blocks away on Church Street. Being the fanboy that I am, I went down to the gig early to wait for them. When the van finally pulled up and Killing Joke piled out, it was all smiles. I was thrilled to death they had remembered me.

They introduced new member Raven. I was very upset that Martin (Youth) wasn't with them. As far as I was concerned, Raven had to pass MY audition before I accepted him.

That took all of three songs.

They told me they were recording the two nights for a live record, which became *HA*. They also introduced me to Conny Plank. Very cool.

Jaz was classically trained. You play a piano hard. In Killing Joke, Jaz played an Oberheim synth. His Obie. Synths are light-touch keys, but that didn't stop Jaz playing them like a piano. This caused the 'J' strings inside to break. These are what make contact to complete the circuit to make the sound. Jaz's Obie was in very sad shape and needed some love.

Nash loaned Jaz his Pro 1 synth for the night (thank God for that) and called in an emergency repair. I picked it up the next day before the second show.

That Obie sure took a beating.

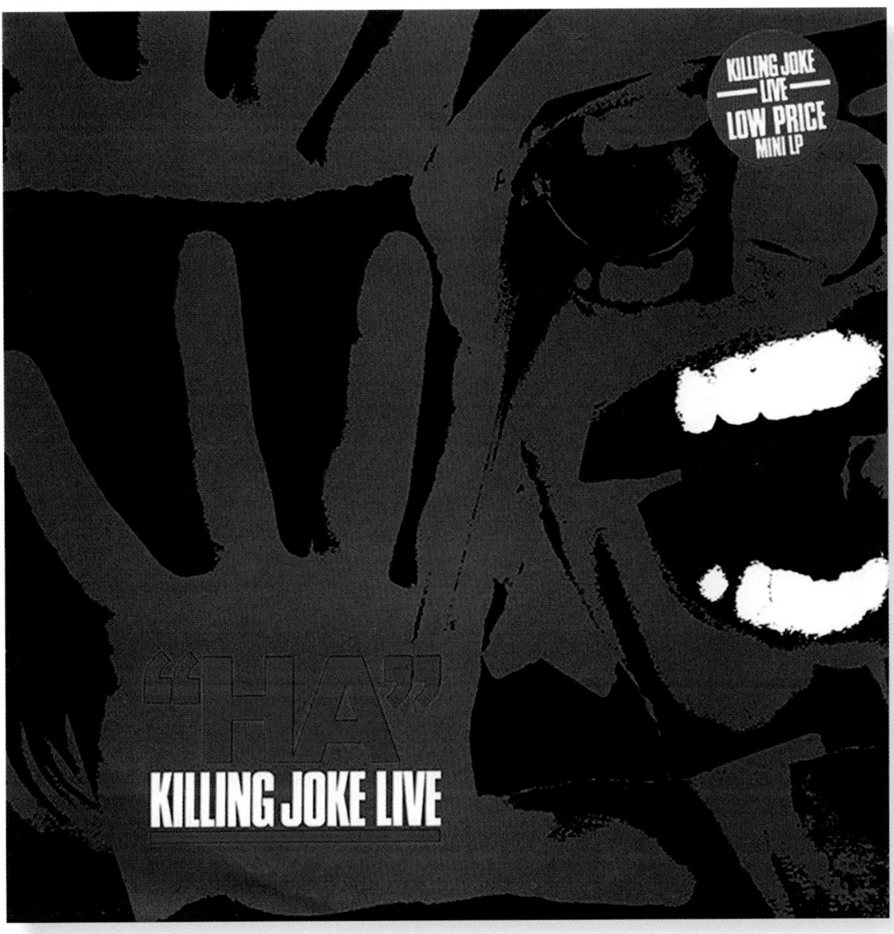

It was a glorious two days with Killing Joke. Raven and I even went for a swim in the outdoor pool.

MARK COWLING

Music was my life. I took it very seriously, so Killing Joke were very special to me.

They were playing a club where they recorded *HA*. It was my second time seeing them and I totally idolised this band. We got there early and were at the front of the line to get in.

It was great being at the front of the line at the entrance as we got there early enough to hear their soundcheck. Afterwards, Jaz came out the front door and looked down the line we were in. Okay, this is embarrassing. I, of course, recognised him, ran up to him, stuck my hand out to shake his and overexcitedly said: "Youth!" Okay, now this was the Eighties, remember, and to be totally honest I was, let's just say, under the influence of some psychedelics of the day and was impaired to say the least. Hence calling him Youth. Sigh.

Jaz took one look at me and said very loudly (there must have been 50 to 60 people within earshot): "Fuck off, I'm Jaz." I was left standing there, hand held out. My knickers may as well been on the ground. I was so embarrassed. Here was my hero, my idol, my influence, telling me to fuck off!

Well, I didn't let it ruin my night. I still jammed my way to the mosh to the front of the stage and took it all in, having a sheer blast and amazement at this new, incredible sound. I never forgot it, and never really got over the embarrassment – until...

Over 30 years later [24 April 2013], Killing Joke is playing at yet another small venue here in Toronto, a place called Lee's Palace. It was The Singles tour, and, yet again, I found myself at the very front and centre of the stage. Jaz was very ill. He sang maybe six or seven songs and walked off stage.

As we were all screaming and clamouring for more, Jaz came back out on stage alone, looked out to the crowd and very sadly touched his heart and pointed to his throat. He could not go on. His voice was quite obviously, for lack of a better term, toast. You could tell he was very sincere and had apologised to us all. As he stood looking out apologetically to the disappointed crowd, we were grateful and let a rip-roaring cheer.

Well, here is my musical idol literally standing a foot or two away from me. I started screaming with all I had left – "Jaz! Jaz!" and was flashing my huge Killing Joke tattoo. "Jaz! Jaz!"

Jaz stopped everything, looked down at me, smiled – and shook my hand.

It was the last thing he did. He walked off stage. Nevertheless, I got my handshake.

They are and I suppose always will be my favourite band. It meant a lot to me. Jaz – I'm sure – wouldn't remember some wanker calling him Youth 30 years later, but it meant a lot to get my handshake from a truly talented man. I'll always love their music. As a matter of fact, I missed out on a lot of great music throughout the years. To me, nobody came close to Killing Joke.

CAESAR'S
21 October 1982,
Bradford, UK

MICK HEAD

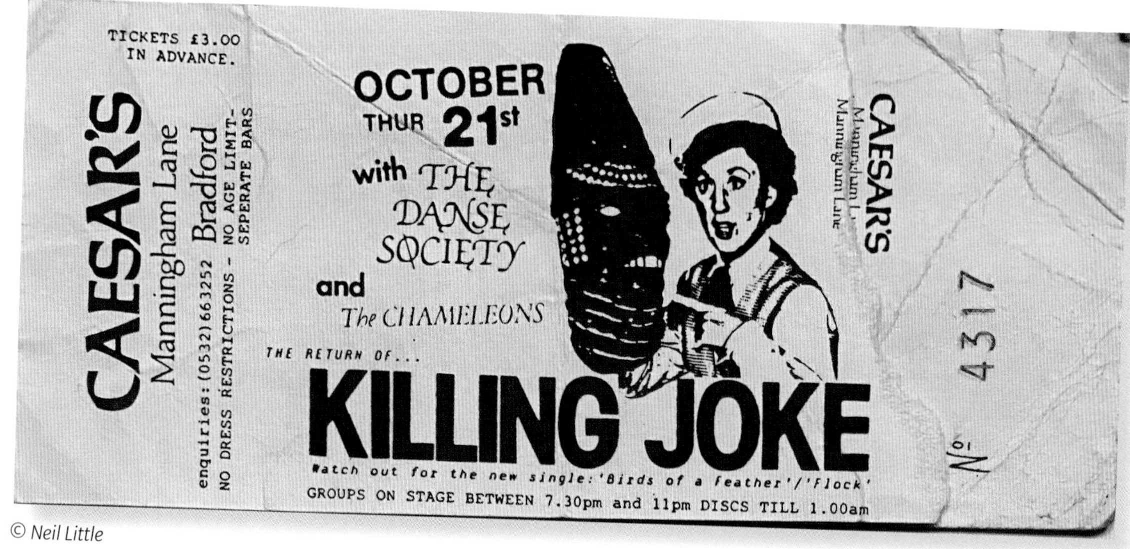

© Neil Little

I'd seen my number one band around a half-dozen times, always trying to check them out when they'd ventured north to God's Own County. My contact as a punter with the band members was limited to fleeting salutations at venues including – but not limited to – Leeds Tiffany's, Sheffield Limit Club, Bradford Rio's and York University.

And then, 21st October 1982, came the gig that changed it all.

Bradford Caesar's on the notorious Manningham Lane. A bill that also included The Danse Society and The Chameleons! Unbelievable line-up and so it proved – an unforgettable show.

After three blistering, huge and unique sets – and as I was wont to do – I found myself hanging stage front for a plectrum, smashed drumstick, set-list or the like. Looking between the various stage crew for said prize, imagine my surprise and elation when the newly joined, gangly, sweat-soaked bass player came over to speak to me.

"Oi, oi, what's that?" he asked, pointing to my left bicep at the crude Killing Joke tattoo I'd had done on a boozy seaside trip. "Let me look," he insisted.

"Come on!" the singer ordered him, "we're off."

"No, no – hang on a minute. He's a proper fan," the bassist exclaimed. "Are you coming tomorrow?" he asked me in connection to the next gig at Sheffield Lyceum. "Yes" I blustered, in reverence and awe, so pleased that I was able to answer truthfully. "Well, you're on the guest-list. Come see me after the show. What's your name?"

And so began a lifetime friendship with Paul Vincent Raven.

Raven was, of course, the perfect host and so the next night I had my first real interactions with Jaz, Geordie and Big Paul. Friendship with Youth, who I'd only spoken to whilst he was DJing at York in '81, was to follow when he rejoined the band *Pandemonium* era.

Being allowed into the inner sanctum at not only the next show but any I cared to turn up for following that has taken me to venues all over Europe and across to the States in pursuit of the magick that is Killing Joke.

✦ ✦ ✦

LYCEUM BALLROOM
24 October 1982,
London, UK

DAVID GRIEVE

The first I heard of them was a rerun of the late-1981 session, repeated in spring 1982. I enjoyed it and bought 'Empire Song' followed by *Revelations* (followed by everything else over the years).

In September 1982, I went to university in London and one of the first gigs I went to was Killing Joke at the Lyceum. As the intro music came to an end, four spotlights came on from the back of the stage pointing towards the audience and the band members were between the lights. They immediately launched into 'The Hum'. It was utterly astonishing and – 38 years on – I can remember it as clear as day. I must have enjoyed it as I went to see them two months later at the somewhat smaller Clarendon Hotel Ballroom (Klub Foot) in December [14th].

✦ ✦ ✦

TIFFANY'S
26 October 1982,
Glasgow, UK

DEREK S – FALKIRK

My friend John and I decided to go and see Killing Joke again, having loved their first two albums. *Revelations* really smacked us in the mouth, especially 'Empire Song', which was to be as relevant today as it was back then.

The set-list consisted mostly of the new album, beginning with 'The Hum' and ending with 'Birds of a Feather'. *Revelations* was produced by Conny Plank. This had told us the band were going to be huge.

On stage, Jaz was adorned in his trademark blanked-out face, black-and-green war paint and Big Paul Ferguson noticeably using his drumsticks upside down for maximum boom. Raven had just recently joined the band and he stood staring into the crowd in a menacing non-blink mode for the whole set, playing with fire and passion.

Geordie was in his familiar stance, facing away from the crowd as he strummed, back-strummed and caressed his guitar to deliver that swarm-of-bees hum we all know and love.

John and I hung around after the gig, trying our best to sneak backstage. To our surprise, we were led into a small green room by a bouncer we'd tried to befriend earlier. We were going to meet Killing Joke.

There was around 10 people sitting with Paul, Raven and Geordie. Everyone was taking part in the puffing of funny-looking long cigarette-type things and drinking shots.

The three band members stood up and introduced themselves, also thanking us for coming to the gig.

They were incredibly cool looking. Tight jeans, flat-top hairstyles (Geordie had slicked-back blond hair), obligatory sleeveless t-shirts and the most cracking suede pointed low-soled Doc Marten shoes.

They certainly didn't buy them in Falkirk, where we came from!

Paul was very inquisitive as to where I had got my KJ t-shirt – white with navy-blue print of the first album cover. I had purchased it for £3 at Ingliston Market, Edinburgh.

He gave me a large smile – it certainly wasn't on the official merch counter that evening!

The three then invited us to partake in the art of taking tequila. Paul was the orchestrator supreme – salt, shot, then bite the lemon. I've never forgotten. How could I?

We were having a ball, but where was Jaz? We didn't ask as not to appear rude. Was meeting the three and being taught tequila drinking not good enough?

After around 45 minutes, we said our goodbyes and walked back out through the hall, and that's when we set eyes on him.

Jaz was hard at work helping the roadies lift gear from the stage. Dressed in a black, three-quarter-length coat, black denims and the most over-used pair of Doc Marten shoes I've ever seen in my life.

I shouted "Hi, Jaz" and he turned around to grunt a "Hello, lads."

We were more than happy with that!

That evening is etched on my memory – so vivid and crystal clear.

Sadly, I lost my friend John to cancer five years ago.

✦ ✦ ✦

POLYTECHNIC
27 October 1982,
Manchester, UK

DAVE FLETCHER

1980. Was on a family holiday in Staithes of all places. Bloke in a leather jacket emblazoned with Killing Joke artwork. Bought 'Requiem' 12-inch same month. Hooked. Bought everything in next couple of years. Saw them at Manchester Poly in 1982. £3 ticket! Very violent but incredibly powerful and moving. Still got the tinnitus, thanks guys!

FRANK JENKINSON

I think I went to a couple of gigs in '81, '82 and some others occasionally after that. I became more distant from the band. They had also parted with the original Malicious Damage management. I kept in touch with Brian Taylor and sometimes the other Malicious Damage crew, and on occasion with Youth (usually through Brian).

You have to remember KJ were very young at the time. You're totally immortal at that age. They really didn't do themselves any favours with the media, but we knew they were the business.

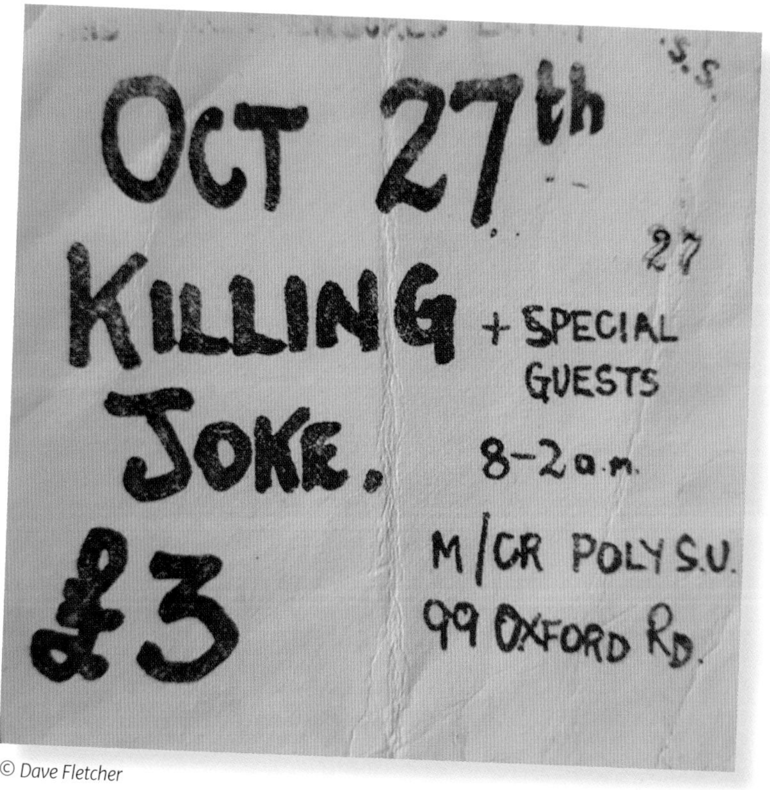

© Dave Fletcher

MARK WHITELEY

Although I was living with Dave the Wizard in our Archway squat, I spent most of my time, when we weren't rehearsing, over in Ladbroke Grove. Either at Youth's flat, at Risk or the Blenheim Crescent squat at No. 90. It was in the orbit of Killing Joke I got to meet all the musicians I befriended or ended up working with. The Folk Devils – me, Al Cole, Ian Lowery and Kris Jozajtis – were all part of the itinerant population of London W10, drifting between parties and squats and rehearsal spaces. All of us, it seemed, on a mission to create. It was a very particular lifestyle, one that would in fact now be criminal. Jaz touches on that in 'Ghosts of Ladbroke Grove' and 'War on Freedom'.

NICOLA FROUDE

Youth had left the band and Raven arrived. Cheeky, cheeky chappie.

After some time, I changed my role [at EG] and started to work with Alec [Byrn], doing more on the project side of the business. Working on the album, making sure the band were okay, going to interviews, to Radio 1.

I remember one time taking Jaz to a radio station in Reading to do an interview. The poor DJ said: "It's great to have your new single that's coming out." Jaz grabbed it, snarled and proceeded to snap 'Birds of a Feather' in half over his knee. 'Birds of a Feather' wasn't quite perhaps a record that sums up who they were as a band. It wasn't quite a weighty sound.

I was quite mortified when Jaz snapped it. I tried to be really cool and calm and said: "Don't worry, I'll send you another one." The poor guy was just sitting there, pale faced. Jaz used to freak some of these journalists out.

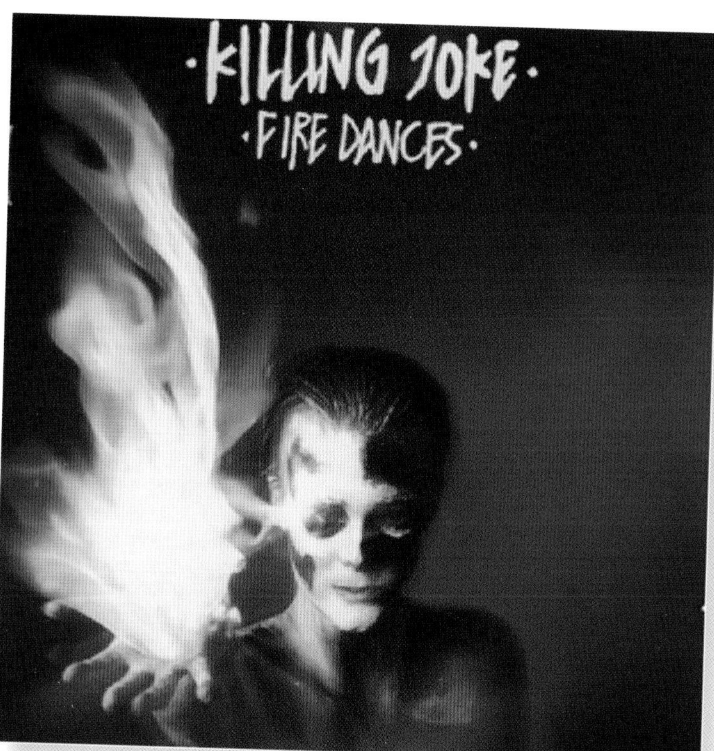

✦ ✦ ✦

BASING STREET STUDIOS
14 February 1983,
London, UK

NIGEL MILLS
(engineer, Fire Dances)

Recording started on *Fire Dances* in Studio One.

This was the start of 26 continuous (and intense) days of recording and mixing, starting at midday to four or five in the morning.

This was to be the last complete album recorded at Basing Street under the ownership of Chris Blackwell of Island Records. During this time, Trevor Horn bought the studio and renamed it Sarm West. An interesting time of various post-punk artists, with *Fire Dances* bookended with sessions from Aswad and The Associates.

Studio One was originally the nave of the church, with enough space for an orchestra. The history of the building, combined with what was then state-of-the-art equipment, gave the place a vibe that was soon to disappear under the remodelled digital, clinical face of Sarm and ZTT Records. Recently, it hosted a diverse range of band [and artists] including The Clash, Joe Jackson, Mick Fleetwood, The Slits and Madness.

Although the dawn of the digital revolution, the equipment in Studio One was an analogue Neve Desk recording on to a Studer A800 24-track tape machine.

The drums and amps were screened off to get as much separation as possible. Not easy with a massive sound made from Geordie's famous gold Gibson ES-295 and Raven's bass stack.

Recording the backing tracks was all about the energy. Each song was played as a performance, usually hitting a peak at take three or four.

After each song, the band would run up the stairs into the elevated control room for playback. The drums and bass were key, with guitar and vocal overdubs.

The sound was always big and loud. The studio was equipped with Urei 813 monitors that had lightbulbs as fuses to protect the cones when over-cranked. These were always glowing and often blowing. I do remember some poor victim, who had fallen asleep, being gaffer-taped to a control-room chair, with the monitors left at full volume.

There were of course 'refreshments' to keep us all going through the night, including the band's favourite studio tipple, hot saké.

The backing tracks and most overdubs were recorded in Studio One before moving down to the crypt to Studio Two for mixing. Although much smaller, this studio had its own unique atmosphere, recently used for mixes from Bob Marley, Bryan Ferry and John Martyn. The desk was an SSL, mixing on to a Studer half-inch two-track.

I remember a friend of the band coming in who had a spiderweb tattoo over his face. Initially disturbing but a really nice guy.

To get some daylight, we would go to Mike's Café on Portobello Road. At this time, Notting Hill was the pre-sanitised-by-Richard-Curtis version, with a great mix of artists and ethnic characters. In the evening, 'Lucky' Gordon (the jazz singer caught up in the Profumo Affair) would come in to cook the most amazing Jamaican food.

On 11 March, the last day of the mix, we staggered out at 6am, after a 19-hour session!

Basing Street closed its doors on 26 March for a total refurb.

Mastering took place at the Master Room on 16 May. Based in Riding House Street near the BBC. At the time, this was the place to go to get the maximum dynamics on to vinyl.

An amazing experience, which at the time was hard to fully appreciate, but my kids tell me it's cool!

Nigel Mills: "The test pressing which I'd forgotten I had" © Nigel Mills

BIG PAUL

Raven had [design] input, especially the graphics on *Fire Dances*.

MIKE COLES

I photocopied Raven's hand-drawn font for the *Fire Dances* sleeve.

JUSTIN BROADRICK

I remember when I first heard the opening song, 'The Gathering'. I was astounded at the beauty, there being such a minimal, primitive and reduced aesthetic at play – utterly brutalist, tribal and almost amusical/atonal. The production somehow amplified this. It felt so militant, too, like the sound of marching, terrifying. Jaz's vocals sounded like a call to arms. Such a dissonant album. Incredible tones and textures. That album alone inspired me to wish to make a form of heavy punk music which was so reduced that the musical content almost doesn't exist anymore. We're just left with the almighty rhythm, and everything locked into that to create this hypnotic, transcendental, celebratory state.

AKI NAWAZ

(Southern Death Cult, Fun-Da-Mental, Nation Records)

Many concerts and shared stages with Killing Joke, inspiration for intensity came from that band for me in all my skill-less drumming techniques.

During the Southern Death Cult days, I was always honoured to have Brilliant play with us, especially at the epic Heaven gig [21 February 1983]. Many times, we would meet Youth at clubs or gigs. I think he was tickled by our northern accents and straight-up Yorkshire lifestyle. Buzz [David Burrows], the guitarist, was quietly jealous of Geordie, as he was the only other guitarist who Buzz thought was cooler than him on stage. I do think as musicians Southern Death Cult definitely were inspired to some degree by KJ.

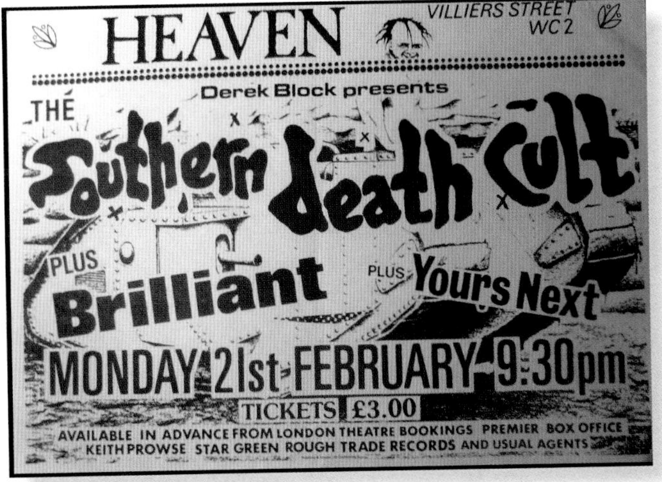

TROY GREGORY

Whenever I went to a record store, I just didn't know what the fuck to get. I would always see the [debut] Killing Joke record. I didn't know what it sounded like. It wasn't like they were getting played on the radio. [But] I always saw them in the record store because they were right before King Crimson.

But it wasn't until *Fire Dances*. I was just getting out of high school. I was in a band. There was this other group, kinda older guys. One guy was really into Killing Joke. I saw the record and I was kinda like: "I wanna hear this."

Right away, 'The Gathering' came in. It hit me at the right time. Peter Gabriel was doing the whole Africa thing. I thought: "I really like this."

LUC TIRONNEAU

I knew Killing Joke from when I was 13 in the bedroom of a 17-year-old punk boy, my best friend's neighbour in college. He had previously made known to us – who only listened to The Clash, Sex Pistols, The Cure and Depeche Mode – the famous Dead Kennedys' *Fresh Fruits for Rotting Vegetables*!

With Killing Joke, the shock was just as brutal because the first song he wanted to play was 'Frenzy', his favourite from the new album KJ had just released: *Fire Dances*.

It was during the song that he played just after 'Frenzy' that I became a Gatherer, with 'The Gathering'.

In less than two weeks, he made us listen to the album *Killing Joke* (aaah, 'Requiem' and 'The Wait'), the sumptuous *What's THIS for...!* ('Unspeakable') and the very inventive *Revelations* ('We Have Joy' in particular). I, of course, bought these second-hand records, including the live record *HA*, at a time when record stores still existed.

TONY VAN DEN ENDE
(video director)

I'd seen a lot of bands. My girlfriend at the time worked for Virgin publishers, up at Vernon Yard. And we were out every night. There was never a night when we didn't go out. Roundhouse, Camden, Shepherd's Bush. You name it. Support acts. Main events.

I worked in drama at the BBC as a director and I made a few short films. When the music-video thing began, sort of before MTV, I got a job with a band on A&M called Nine Below Zero and got hired on another one, 'Brass in Pocket', with Chrissie Hynde and The Pretenders.

I was on contract to the BBC. I'd do a drama and then I wouldn't have a job. I got a job as assistant director on Shakespeare's *A Winter's Tale*, which was gonna be shot by the BBC. I then got a phone call from EG Records. I don't know quite what Jaz might have seen [of my work] but I remember going down to EG Records in the evening and sat in reception, and Jaz was also sat in reception. And then he said something to me: "I've seen your work. You're all right."

I think I was given the track ['Let's All Go (to the Fire Dances)'].

I met them on the King's Road at EG Management, an office above a shop on a corner. They were sort of a combination of terrifying and worrying. I do remember thinking: "Have they ever killed anybody?" I could see Jaz was quite serious, quite tough. There's no band to compare them with these days. Disturbing boys.

I had to resign from the BBC because I wanted to do the job. The guy said to me: "If you leave now, you won't be coming back." I said: "I'm sorry, but I need to leave."

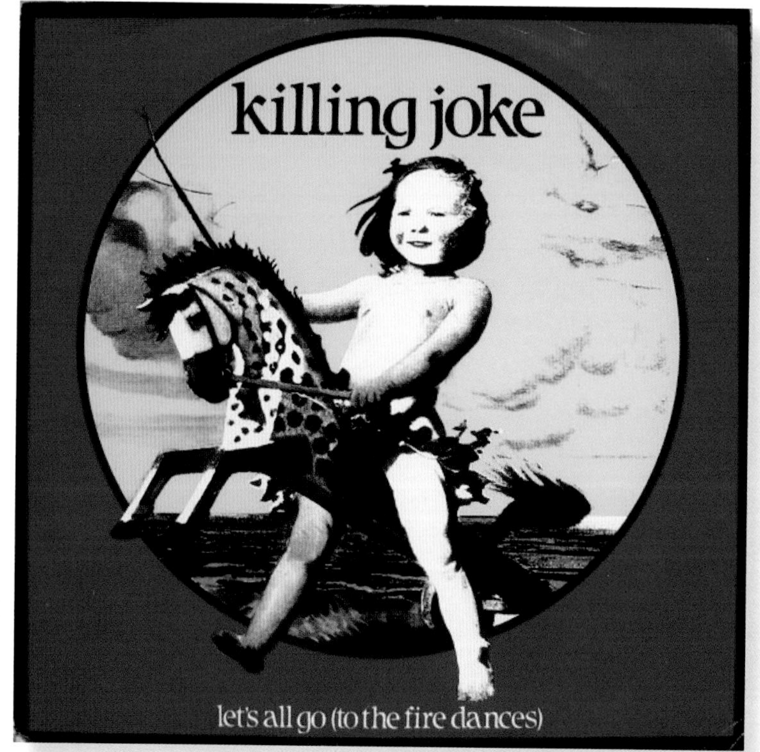

'LET'S ALL GO (TO THE FIRE DANCES)'

When you direct a music video, there's so much going on. Time is whipping by. I seem to remember getting them around 11-ish in the morning and we filmed right through the night. You just shoot the hell out of it, man. It was my concept. I developed it. One day and a very long night.

You really have to deliver. You gotta make it look good, gotta make it look sexy.

I grew up in Warwickshire and I was very aware of the Rollright Stones and the stone circles just outside Long Compton. Jaz knew about that, the occult and Lovecraft.

When we went up to book the stone circle, which was privately owned, the two ladies... I don't think they knew what they were letting themselves in for.

That set was built right next door to the stone circle. We built it outdoors. It's lit really nice, capturing the energy of the band. Some of the childlike behaviour [in the video] with [Big Paul playing with] the spinning top and the kids in it... I know it's quite old but it's pretty good, isn't it?

They would have all talked privately about how they wanted to portray themselves. They would have dressed how they wanted and behaved how they wanted. Paul Raven's girlfriend was a make-up artist. She would definitely have done the prosthetic nose [seen very briefly in the video].

I had a daughter at the same time and Paul [Raven] had a daughter. I think that both daughters slept under the make-up table.

Kind of makes me happy/sad reliving it. Once you get those videos done, whichever production company you've been working for use those videos to attract more work, via a showreel and so forth. That one got left off the showreel.

GEORDIE

Shooting the 'Fire Dances' video at the Rollright Stones. Went up to just downstream from Bourton-on-the-Water. Pulled a few trout out and got catering to cook it.

TONY VAN DEN ENDE

Geordie and I used to go trout fishing illegally on rivers and ponds, especially near Steve Winwood's [place]. I absolutely hated trout, then and now. I have never eaten it. We got back to my studio apartment and rested. Geordie fiddled with a drum machine that I bought in New York whilst shooting the Flock of Seagulls music video. Geordie was fascinated by this little drum machine...

A little Sunday rendezvous of fishing together. I actually can't believe it, but it happened, truly.

Trout fishing... yuck.

ANDY BOTT

I went to see Roy Harper in Leicester in 1983. I chatted with Roy before the gig. I was 17. The same age as his son, Nick. Roy enthusiastically told me of going to see Killing Joke with Nick. He clearly loved the energy. The following year, he brought Nick with him to play a gig I had arranged in Derby. I chatted with Nick over a game of pool. He was clearly wary of a kid his own age being so connected to the music of his old man (43 at the time, probably.) He pronounced that I should listen to Killing Joke. Young and broke, I was unsure. Aren't they a bit punk? I saw that Killing Joke were on *The Tube*. I'll give it a whirl. Bang. Sold. What a band, what an atmosphere they transmitted. More, please.

IAN LIDGETT

The picture with Killing Joke in tape on the wall was in Ibiza in 1983 – 'Wardance' on repeat in the apartment. We took the ghetto blaster and plenty of BASF tapes. They [other Beefa visitors whose music inclinations probably didn't include KJ] all came round to it in the end. We were right above the bars on the busiest street and the tunes were blasting out over the balcony. Vivid, brilliant memories. Amazing days.

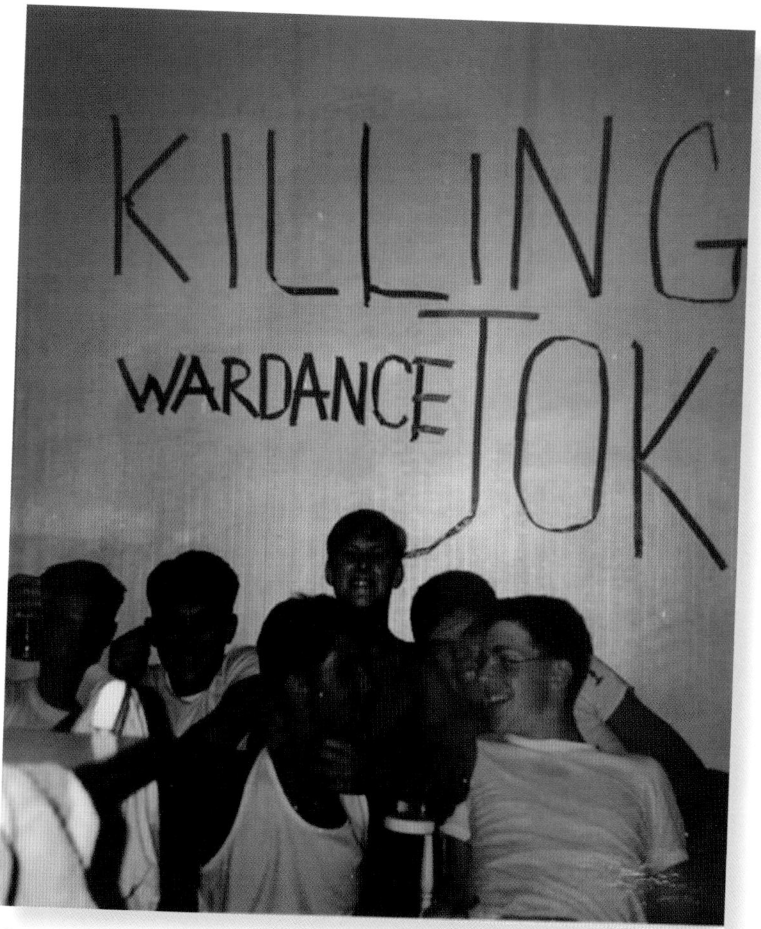

© Ian Lidgett

BOB CAMPBELL

It was so long ago, I do not remember which Killing Joke album I discovered first. In the US, bands like Killing Joke didn't receive much press in the late Seventies/early Eighties, so I am sure I probably saw one of the earlier albums, thought the cover was cool and bought it. What I do remember is that I bought whatever else they released as soon as I could find it. While I still love the first three records, as a guitarist I do distinctly remember having my mind blown with the guitar sound on *Fire Dances*. It was one of those times where I just couldn't wrap my mind around what Geordie was doing.

Since then, KJ has been a constant companion, with each new exposure deepening my appreciation. I remember seeing a clip of them playing 'Eighties' on some late-night music show, the first I actually saw them perform and not just stills.

Here was Geordie, playing a full-size hollow body with single-coil pickups and getting this roar of tone that just didn't seem possible.

METRO
24 July 1983,
Ashton-under-Lyne, UK,

NIGEL WALLBANK

It was during the *Fire Dances* tour. We were hanging around outside the venue when the band turned up. There were a few people waiting, including some Welsh punks who had hitched it to the gig. Raven knew the Welsh lads and asked them if they'd had anything to eat. They said they hadn't eaten in a couple of days as they had no money. Raven instantly responded and said: "Right, come with me." He took them to the chippy across the road, a really kind gesture. Jaz got out of the van and looked at my mate's Theatre of Hate t-shirt and said: "That's a very bad t-shirt." We were too scared to say anything else!

SPRING STREET THEATRE
28 July 1983,
Hull, UK

VAUGHAN SMITH

I met Tony Haggar, who was a roadie for KJ. A fantastic character, even with his shonky and dodgy deals. No matter what, even though he would rip you off, it was hard not to like him.

In my opinion, he was like the big brother for KJ and the followers. What a character, in and out of prison. I would have to say a good man. He stayed with me in Hessle, Hull. Had a good few laughs with him. He was about 10 years older than me, so I learned a bit from him. Everyone knew him. When he first heard the band, he wrote to them and got a job as a roadie, travelled everywhere, Britain and Europe. Tony was a great punk rocker. It suited him, he had great style. We would stay up for days on wiz, listening to and copying KJ.

One day, we went mushrooming and took 'em that night. What a scream. I think we all went through every emotion you can, powerful night (Gav 'n' Kev RIP).

Tony was sentenced to the local mental hospital – De la Pole. Not because he was mentally ill – we all was. Instead of prison. Then someone talked him into doing a runner. They said they would look after him. They didn't. Tony ended up at my place again, but moved around a lot and ended up in prison. We went to see him and I took him a little something to bend the bars and ease the pain.

That was all in a couple of years – '81–'83.

I'd never heard music like KJ before. It grabbed me like a spirit, a possession, in a good way. And it grew on and in me – the single 'Wardance' and the first album.

Then I met Fil [Legonidec, KJ roadie] – Tony's mate – tall, thin, spiky hair, and Penny, all punk rockers.

I think Tony had a lot to do with Hull having a massive KJ following.

So we all took speed and did gigs and went backstage at nearly every gig.

The sounds of KJ entered my head and stayed there, running around all the time. [I] could not stop playing tracks one after another.

It was a takeover.

I did as many gigs as I could. I felt like I knew the band long before I met them. I remember doing five dates of the *Fire Dances* tour.

DIGBETH CIVIC HALL
30 July 1983,
Birmingham, UK

IAN ORGAN

I have been a Gatherer since 1982, when, as a 15-year-old, I saw them perform 'Empire Song' on *Top of the Pops*. Their sound immediately drew me in and, to this day, it remains my signature tune as I go by The Gathering name of EmpiremanKJ. The band are in my blood, part of my DNA. My life has been dedicated musically to Killing Joke – every year, every gig you can physically attend, and there have been so many!

I first saw KJ at Digbeth Civic Hall in July 1983 and was immediately spellbound by them.

MARK WHITE

The power, intensity and passion of both band and fans stuck with me from that moment on. Strangely, one of my most vivid memories was the treatment of the fans by the bouncers. But, hey, the Gatherers just kept going back for more until the bouncers just gave up!

HAMMERSMITH PALAIS
31 July 1983,
London, UK

JASON MILLS

My next KJ experience was most significant. My first KJ gig – 31 July 1983, Hammersmith Palais, *Fire Dances* tour, Raven on bass. I was 15.

My Dad drove from Daventry and waited until the gig had finished – legend – a three-hour round trip. When he dropped me at the venue, the scenes outside were amazing – a swarm of leather-clad punks and rockers (the same as the images I had seen in the mags – it was really happening).

I remember my Dad nervously saying, "Blimey, you're not going in there, are you, son?" By the time he had finished his sentence, the car door had slammed shut and I was in the queue!

What. A. Night! I stood on the balcony, front and centre. The excitement and anticipation inside me was nothing like I had felt before. The lights dimmed, the crowd below moving like an ocean to the intro music, then BANG – 'Dominator' was unleashed. My ribs shuddered to Raven's bass (I think they still are); I felt Big Paul's every pounding hit, Geordie's scything guitar was beautiful to the ears. Then experiencing Jaz's on-stage energy and antics, in full face paint, demanding more from the band, just topped it off. A night of utter sonic, visual and physical brutality and splendour on so many levels.

I left the venue feeling exhilarated, overwhelmed and hooked. A whole new world had been exposed to me.

JANE RICHMOND

The *Fire Dances* tour. This was my first-ever gig. As a 16-year-old who had just sat her O-levels, life was changing. My school friend Pauline had a few months before met some local punks, including Mark and Glenn. We all become friends and recently I'd been to the second-to-last Stonehenge Free Festival with them.

So, this was the end of the *Fire Dances* tour and the boys had followed the band around the UK. At some point, they had met KJ and been backstage after gigs on a few occasions.

Pauline and I met the boys in Hammersmith. We were waiting outside the venue for the doors to open and I was taking the opportunity to admire the sights, sounds and smells (!) of the punks assembling. Leather jackets and spiky, dyed hair, people greeting each other, mixed aromas of body odour, Imperial Leather soap and smoke. It was also the first time I saw Jennie, who became a lifelong friend.

I was standing talking to Mark on the pavement when a large black car pulled up and the band got out. As they walked past, they said hello to Mark and asked whether he and his 'friend' were planning on going backstage that night. Mark said yes, I said no. Don't know why I said that to this day!

Anyway, the doors opened. It was such a great venue. We all fought our way to the bar and, by the time I had a pint of cider in my hand, there was a thick layer of smoke hanging in the air. Everyone was really friendly. We made our way to just behind the mosh pit to await the beginnings of the evening's proceedings.

The lights went down and a man in a full, painted bodystocking came on stage and started to dance. This was great – I hadn't seen anything quite like it before. He moved about the whole stage – a piece of performance art. Then, after a few moments of silence, you could feel the levels of excitement growing in the crowd and Killing Joke came on with Jaz in full-face make-up. I don't remember everything they played but do remember songs that have become some of my all-time favourites – 'Pssyche', 'Wardance', 'Sun Goes Down', 'Requiem'.

I hadn't heard much by them before, but it hadn't taken much to persuade me to go. I loved it – it challenged and excited me. That was the beginning of my life as a KJ fan.

I lost contact with Mark and Glenn a few years later but, in November 2018, Jennie and I went to see KJ at the Roundhouse. I also took my son Harry. I bumped into Mark again. I am now in regular contact with him and Glenn again.

TOM PAYNE

I was first introduced to KJ as a band by a mate who took me to see them on the *Fire Dances* tour. They totally blew me away. Their command of the stage and sheer power was something to behold.

From that date, I was hooked.

From that gig in 1983, I went to every London concert and still do. I've lost count as to how many times I've seen them live, but I know it's in the hundreds.

NICOLA FROUDE

I recall one situation. They were about to start a European tour and I wasn't going. Chris [Kettle] was going on that one.

We get a phone call at the [EG] office. Raven had left his passport at home. Muggins here was tasked with going to where he lived to try and get into his flat and get his passport, otherwise he wouldn't have been able to leave the country.

I rang on a few buzzers and spoke to a few people, asking them to let me in. They said I had to speak to the concierge or the landlord. I spoke to the emergency services to see if they could break the door down. They couldn't because it wasn't an emergency.

It took me two hours to get hold of a keyholder. I got the passport.

That was a long, hot day. At least they got to where they were going in the end.

They were boys in rock 'n' roll, being forgetful because they could. They had people like me when it went wrong. "Nicky, go and get his passport." You did what you had to do. You found a way.

[But] sometimes, you know, you just wanted to give them a slap. Pay attention!

Wake up, Raven © Larry Bate

Jaz holding court at Liverpool Royal Court © Larry Bate

TIFFANY'S
18 December 1983,
Leeds, UK

JAMES FRYER

The Sunday night after their Friday appearance on *The Tube* on Channel 4. I have seen them in the UK on every tour since and several times in Europe in recent years. My only faux pas is that I missed seeing them on my doorstep (Hebden Bridge) in 2014, when I was on a family holiday in Florida. My mates (who did go) continue to rib me about that one!

ROYAL COURT
20 December 1983
Liverpool, UK

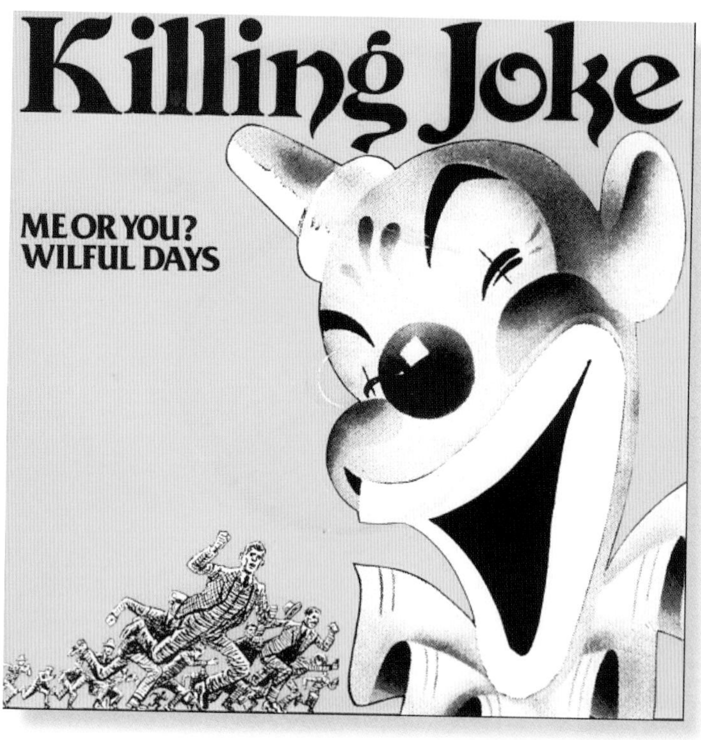

RICHARD FARRELL

I can't remember why it took so long to see the Joke in the flesh, so to speak, but it was just before Christmas 1983. We had an idea of what to expect as they'd been on *Whatever You Want* a few months previously. We were looking forward to a good night, but, at the time, it was one of several equally-anticipated gigs we had lined up. But, a few days before the gig, was the little matter of the Joke's first appearance on *The Tube*.

This was another Damascene moment, which sent expectations for the coming gig into orbit. The relentlessness of 'Dominator', the urgency and the menacing pulse of that cyclical riff. The drumming. The blond quiff. The face paint. How the intensity of that performance came across via the tinny mono speaker on our Eighties TV, I'll never know, but it's never lost its lustre in the interim (it's my go-to YouTube clip). What had we let ourselves in for in buying tickets for this gig?

The night – not so much a gig, more of an event – was everything I expected it to be, by turn strange, unnerving, mesmeric. It was the first of many, though memories are sometimes vague and mixed up. In 1985, Jaz jumped into the crowd and had his clothes shredded; in 1986, 'Chessboards' was the song on everyone's lips and featured a performance that just left me elated. In 1994, I was convinced my chest would collapse due to the drumming and Youth's bass. And so on.

BARRY INGS

The first time I was aware of Killing Joke was on *The Tube*, a live music show on Channel 4, when doing 'Frenzy' [in December 1983]. I was only about 15 at the time.

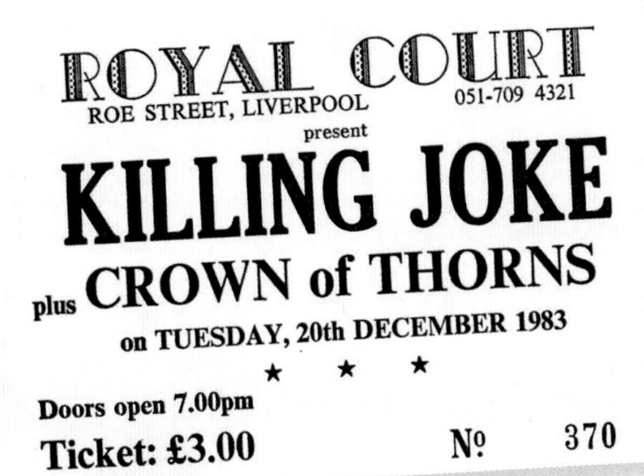

ROYAL COURT
ROE STREET, LIVERPOOL 051-709 4321
present
KILLING JOKE
plus CROWN of THORNS
on TUESDAY, 20th DECEMBER 1983
★ ★ ★
Doors open 7.00pm
Ticket: £3.00 № 370

JAMES VARLEY

The first time I saw KJ was on *The Tube* on Channel 4 in 1983. It was odd. I thought they were from the USA and they had some rockabilly-looking guitar player and a raccoon-faced clown as a singer (sorry, Jaz – it gets better). It was extremely interesting but very odd – I could not fathom it. I put it to the back of my mind, but it festered away in the background...

LARRY BATE

My addiction to KJ started in 1980, listening to John Peel on an old wireless radio. I was 12 and a big Ants fan, but the Ants had started to go pop so I was looking for something else. Peel played 'Requiem' and it was a life-changing experience!

I was first allowed, by my Mum, to see KJ live in December 1983 at the Royal Court in Liverpool. Amazing gig, and I got battered in the pit!

The intro of 'Booids' [by The Sensational Alex Harvey Band], then opening with 'The Fall of Because' – still makes the hairs on the back of my neck stand on end now, just thinking about it. Managed to get backstage afterwards to watch Geordie and Raven nicking money off the manager to go out clubbing in Liverpool.

Amazing evening that will never be forgotten. Managed to take only three pictures, as the pit was wild, but it was an experience.

© Larry Bate

TONY VAN DEN ENDE
(video director)

'Eighties'. That was an interesting video. Extreme imagery. Was there any imagery that was too extreme to make it in? Yes, we had a clip of someone having sex with a goat.

MIKE COLES
(graphic artist)

I wanted to use a photo of a two-headed baby once – that didn't go down too well...

TONY VAN DEN ENDE

All that stock footage, library footage [for the 'Eighties' video] – it was like putting your hand in a barrel of newsworthy incidents and ramming it into the video, like John DeLorean and Geordie looking like him with the suitcase, which is supposed to be a suitcase full of cocaine. Then there's all the book-burning references to Nazi Germany...

It was bonkers. At one point in the original version, until somebody chopped it out, he [Geordie] turns his body to the camera and you see these whip marks on his back. His back was naked and he wanted whip marks printed on by make-up.

And Jaz in the pulpit, going hell for leather. It was quite hard-hitting. I'm not sure if it was afternoon BBC Radio 1 [material]. I think he [Jaz] would probably have made it as a politician, don't you?

AKI NAWAZ

Always wondered why KJ music was never used in the film *1984*. It would have been ideal and far better than the Eurythmics.

ALEX SMITH

Technically, I was late to the table with Killing Joke, comparatively speaking. While I'd certainly read their name while thumbing through LPs in the bins of my favourite New York City record shops — sadly, all vanished here in 2020 — it wasn't until a chance viewing of the video for the then-recently-released single 'Eighties' in the spring of 1984 that I was properly indoctrinated. Infatuated as I was, at the time, with American hardcore bands like the Circle Jerks and Dead Kennedys, I was immediately captivated by the singular sound of Killing Joke, particularly Geordie's chiming guitar.

The visuals hooked me right in, as well — a vexed Jaz exhorting from behind a bushel of microphones, the black-clad Raven in full stomping mode, Geordie with his stylish blond quiff and priest's frock, and Big Paul Ferguson hammering out the rhythm, interspersed with stock footage, both ominous and absurd. To my mind, every possible box was checked for me. It was perfect. At that moment, I was at a friend's apartment in Greenwich Village and was completely captivated. Upon the song's completion, I literally walked right out to the door and across Cornelia Street to a favourite basement-level record shop and bought the 12-inch single on the spot.

It's hard to accurately put into words the effect Killing Joke had on me. Their inimitable music, the enigmatic iconography, their messaging – it was all so much more than just discovering another band. Based on my immersion of the 'Eighties' single, I immediately went out in search of more, my next find being the 12-inch single of 'Let's All Go (to the Fire Dances)', which I snatched up on sight at Second Coming Records on Sullivan Street. While I thrilled to the rousing A-side, it was the live B-side of 'The Fall of Because' that really embedded its hooks in me. With its pounding, tribal groove and strangely elliptical riff, 'The Fall of Because' gave full sway to Killing Joke's inexorable roots in mysticism, taking its cryptic title from the writings of Aleister Crowley. From there, it all led back to the first album, wherein I found arguably the band's ultimate manifestation. As they say, life was never quite the same again.

RUSTY EGAN

I produced and remixed Spear of Destiny's 'Liberator' 12-inch and tried to get that hard drum sound and anthemic sound that KJ somehow managed. But I failed.

✦ ✦ ✦

ROSKILDE FESTIVAL
29 June 1984,
Darupvej, Denmark

TOMAS KARLSBJEG

You know what it's like when you're young and at a festival – memories get fragmented, but KJ was, and still is, an important band in my life.

It was my second year at Roskilde Festival. I was 17 and money was tight, so I had been working my butt off as a summertime mailman to afford the ticket and the drugs and beer money. Besides Killing Joke, there were only about 10 bands worth listening to on the whole festival. Topping the bill was Lou Reed and New Order.

© Larry Bate

A year earlier, I left school, moved from the suburbs to Copenhagen and got sucked into the punk and squatter side of life. A friend of mine played *What's THIS for...!* for me one day and there was no turning back. Back then, before the internet, you could dial a phone number and listen to a recorded message announcing which bands were to play at Roskilde, months before the programme was final. When they announced KJ, I went through the roof – this was as huge as it could get.

I had been tripping on mushrooms all that day, always a bad idea on a wet festival, so things are a bit blurry, but I remember I was wearing a long, grey, woolly, army-surplus cape with a huge hood on it (due to the wet Danish summer) and, at some point during my trip, I had found a dry crate to sit on and a tree to sit under to the left of the stage. I sat down wrapped in my hood and cape (must have looked like a hobbit), several hours too early for the gig.

I don't remember anything until the music started. Then I flew up like a jack-in-the-box and jumped and danced my way through the crowd, until I hit a pocket full of dancing punks and squatters, and we all just went mad during the whole concert.

I didn't get closer than 20m from the stage so missed out on some of the intensity and magic that is Killing Joke when you're up close in a club or venue.

But the whole thing was epic for me. I had only been to a handful of big concerts with international bands in my life, so KJ and New Order on the same weekend made a huge impact on the younger me.

Here we are, 36 years on, and those two bands are still spinning on my turntable on a daily basis. I didn't get to see KJ live again until I went to the Roundhouse in '15 and then the Great Gathering at Brixton Academy in '16, and later they played in my home town, Copenhagen, and in '19 my wife and I went to Amsterdam to see them at Melkweg. It won't be the last time either.

ANDREW BLUNT

(record collector)

Spent most weekends going around all the record markets trying to find rare KJ records: test-pressings, acetates, etc. Was very interesting as an 18-year-old doing it. We were interviewed at Camden Market by a team from Phil Redmond [the writer/producer who created the TV series *Grange Hill* and *Brookside*], who was going to make a show about record collecting. It didn't end up happening.

It seemed like just wearing KJ t-shirts was enough to get yourself threatened. One time, my friend was jumped on for no reason by about six blokes in a car. He was wearing a leather jacket with Killing Joke on it.

Most gigs, we got there mega-early to get to the front. We usually beat everyone by several hours. Quite a few times, everybody else got there half an hour before as they went to the pub. We just tried to get to the front at all costs and stay there bruised and battered and hearing nothing for the next week – just buzzing noise.

TONY VAN DEN ENDE

(video director)

'A NEW DAY'

Jaz with the Nazca beetle [poncho]. They were always into ley lines. We built this mountain out of Styrofoam, and there's Jaz holding the Rosetta Stone. Man, that video's bonkers. Jaz in that tunic.

For 'Love Like Blood', they went elsewhere, and I seem to remember being hurt about that. I think they definitely wanted success.

People tend to go with the magic of success. I did a video for Texas, 'I Don't Want a Lover'. When that showed on *The Chart Show*, the next week I was offered 20 jobs.

I made videos with the band Youth had, Brilliant. That was always really cool that happened, because I didn't meet Youth when I was doing the Killing Joke videos, as Raven was playing bass by then.

I worked with a lot of other bands. I worked with The Cult, with Billy [Duffy], with Ian [Astbury]. That was a more fun day and a bit more of a rock 'n' roll day. With Killing Joke, they didn't suffer any fools.

I was grateful that I made it through. I really had to be sharp and be in there with them, otherwise they would have stamped all over me. They were humane, they were fun, they had great stories. Completely professional, boundless energy, take after take after take.

You never felt like they had much cash. I think they'd steal stuff from your fridge really. Once they knew where you lived, they would just arrive at any point in time. Jaz, in particular, was quite a handful. One time, I climbed out of the window and left him with my girlfriend of the time to talk to. If he got you on the wrong day, he could be there for hours.

Labels or management tried to tell bands what to wear. With Killing Joke, it was a lost cause.

If Killing Joke knew I worked with Tight Fit...

AUGUSTINE RODRIGUEZ III

My first impression of the greatness that is Killing Joke came from a video for the song 'A New Day' when I was a 13-year-old kid. I was blown away. Shortly thereafter, I saw this other video in 1984, 'Eighties'. Most people in the States used this as a party anthem and failed to realise the message. Here in the States, that's not surprising.

DIMITRI LORINGETT

I first learned about KJ in the summer of '84 when 'A New Day' was aired regularly on the Music Box channel. I was in my early teens and remember how I thought the band was laughable. Months later, I heard KJ on the radio – not sure whether it was 'Eighties', 'A New Day' or even 'Love Like Blood' – but something clicked in my head and suddenly I was hooked to that sound. In the summer of '85, while in the UK for a holiday, I grabbed a copy of the 'A New Day' 12-inch single – that was the point of no return.

MARK COWLING

They influenced me no end. I was touring with a band called No Flies on Frank and we covered probably six or seven Killing Joke songs from those earliest days. Naturally, nobody had heard of them. I guess it was '83–'85-ish. But I remember we did 'Complications'. After our set, half of the crowd were still singing the chorus – "Complications, Complications". Very cool indeed.

DAN PARKER

I was 16 and had recently seen – and was very intrigued by – the 'Eighties' promotional video being played by a still-nascent MTV. A friend's father took us to Wax Trax! Records in Chicago, where I stumbled upon the 'Eighties' 12-inch single. Looking at that cover art and its brash primary colours, United States and Soviet Union flags, and a menacing court jester, I recall feeling intimidated by the look and politics of it. I had not a clue what it all meant then. But I wore a deep groove in that song. It was propulsive, that infamous main riff dark and chunky, pulled along by a singer who seemed unhinged.

LUC TIRONNEAU

I went for a spin in the record stores and came across the maxi single 'A New Day', just released. What new Geordie sound had he invented? The one that would foreshadow *Night Time.*

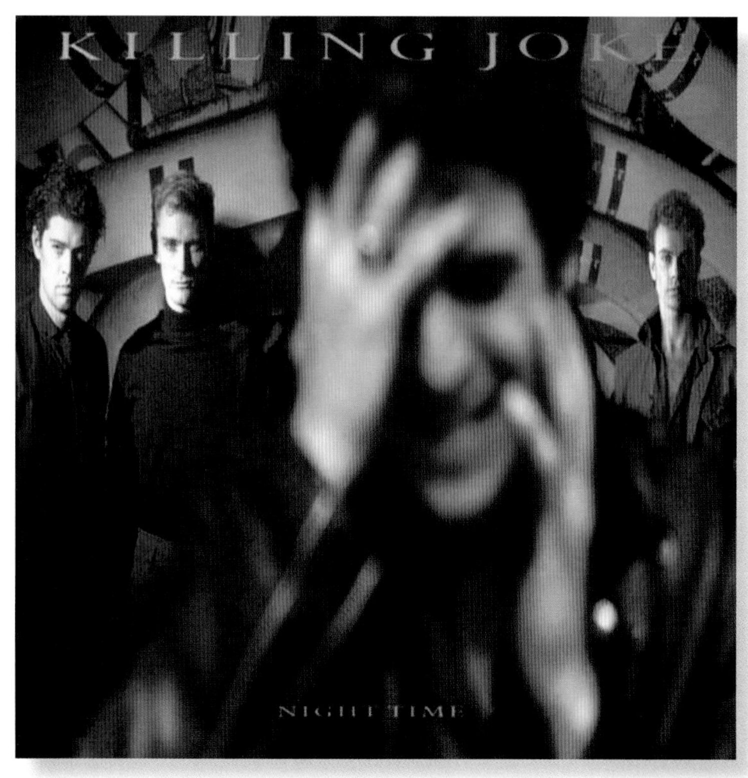

BIG PAUL

Recording in Berlin was with Chris Kimsey at Hansa [Tonstudio], right next to the Wall. David Bowie, Iggy Pop, Depeche Mode also recorded there.

When we were there, it was a single building in the midst of a derelict site, the Wall built across the tramlines running in front of it.

I've since been back and the area is now unrecognisable, with so many buildings and businesses surrounding it. I was, of course, delighted that the absurd and cruel Wall was brought down and that the people of Berlin were reunited. However, before it came down, Berlin had a vibe that was special, an island of freedom surrounded by restriction. Nightclubs and hedonism in the midst of gloom.

New York had a similar aspect when I moved there in the Eighties. Hedonism and danger, poverty and exuberance. I have to say, New York was a much more dangerous place to be. It's been sanitised now, relatively. Back then, it was the first time I'd had a gun pointed at me or seen dead bodies in the street.

Back to Berlin. We drank a fair bit. Starting late in the day or maybe Geords and I jamming in the morning after an all-nighter. Breakfast at some time in the bar downstairs and then LX Orb ferrying shots of vodka up and down between the bar and the recording room.

Check out the documentary about Hansa. Killing Joke is glaringly omitted from its history, as I'm afraid there was an incident involving a fire extinguisher inappropriately set off and causing massive problems. That's a long story.

JAZ

The recording of *Night Time* was terrible and wonderful. The sessions started on the first day with Geordie causing over a million pounds of damage. It was insured, thank God. Hansa Tonstudio – you can't mention our name there anymore. They allowed us to finish the session in one of the other studios we didn't destroy.

There was a lot of violence. Opening the windows of Studio 2, the guards in East Germany on the towers would wave at us. They could hear the music going right over the Wall. Hansa was right next to the Wall. It was an incredible place to capture that Cold War feeling.

Berlin at that time was probably the capital of subculture. Germans who wanted to escape conscription would go to West Berlin. It had a massive population. People who wanted to avoid the army. It was an amazing time. It was an amazing time to be living in Berlin. Very exciting.

BIG PAUL

Like most studios in those days, there was a pool table, so we all got fairly proficient. I clearly remember the joy of building our songs. The glory of guitars and bass parts being laid down, keyboards added, vocal tracks struggled over, and the constant repetition.

We could see East German guards standing in their towers staring back at us through binoculars. We could see over the Wall, the barbed wire, the tank traps, all to the sound of *Night Time*, 'Love Like Blood', 'Tabazan'. We did two albums there. Very intense periods of creativity.

CHRIS BRYANS

What do you recall of climbing the Berlin Wall in your birthday suit?

BIG PAUL

I confess, I was tequila-ed up! My room at the top of the building was too hot and I couldn't get the window open, so I staggered down and out on to the street. I was, at least at that point, wearing a robe. There were tramlines on the street. I followed them. It was dark, there's a wall. What's that doing there?

I woke up sitting in the road naked, the guards on the other side in their tower grinning at me.

✦ ✦ ✦

UNIVERSITY
21 January 1985,
Leicester, UK

LEE HOLFORD

For reasons I don't want to remember, I missed them the first time I should have seen them, late '83 [9 December] in Leicester. But finally got to see them live in January '85, and again in '86, although by this time my obsession had moved elsewhere. I hated the *Brighter.../Outside...* period.

✦ ✦ ✦

KING GEORGE'S HALL
22 January 1985,
Blackburn, UK

GILES SIBBALD

I was 16 at the time, went on my own. It was snowing heavily, so the tension for the gig built up when I got the bus from home, sliding through the snowy roads, giving it a strong Cold War vibe. The venue was about 700 capacity. Brutally loud. Probably about the fifth gig of my life. Can't remember the set-list and have looked online for it but no luck.

I'd got into Killing Joke when I'd heard them played by Peel and the sessions they'd done for his show. I was obsessed with the album covers of *What's THIS for...!* and *Revelations* and what lay beneath them. They were one of a handful of bands who had this incredible, mystical aura.

Night Time was much more commercial but I hadn't seen them live and needed to hear that aural assault. It was only years later that I got to meet the band. I'm involved with an Arts Lab with Youth (who, of course, wasn't playing on that 1985 tour).

THE TUBE
25 January 1985

MATT TIBBITS

Still think their *Tube* performances are uniquely brilliant and powerful. The excitement of seeing them on *The Tube* in '83. What was Jaz on in '85?! Never seen him quite so exuberant and expressive before or since!

GUILDHALL
7 February 1985,
Southampton, UK

BARRY INGS

I first got to see them live in February '85 on the *Night Time* tour with three of my mates. One of them, Paddy, had his 18th birthday the same day. As I went into Southampton Guildhall to see them for the first time, I bought a t-shirt from the merch stand and put it straight on, not realising that, after around 90 minutes of screaming and moshing, the dye had soaked out of the garment and dyed me a greyish mush. I also remember many punks moshing so hard that part of the floor of the Guildhall had given way and a hole had appeared. A lifelong love affair had been set in stone.

Killing Joke owning the stage for their performance on The Tube – 25 January 1985 © Shutterstock

ST GEORGE'S HALL
8 February 1985,
Exeter, UK

ANGELA WARD
(astrologer, funeral celebrant and druid)

It was just five weeks before my Dad died that I first saw KJ on *The Tube*. It was in the front room, Friday, early evening. Dad was in his chair struggling for every breath as the quiet hiss of his oxygen machine was drowned out by the chugging sonic wash of Geordie's guitar, the insistency of Paul's tribal rhythms and Raven's pounding bass. But it was Jaz – possessed... grimacing... twisting leer – as if exorcising some visceral demon from himself and the crowd, that transfixed me. This was my pain. Right there on the screen.

It was not the first encounter with the mighty Killing Joke. Their music was a part of our young teenage experience, a back pulse for those of us who were not drawn to the lighter side of pop. We who found a home in the shadowlands of the early Eighties after punk had melted away and its gaudy and less political sister – new romantic – had taken its place.

Angela Ward at the line-up reunion double-header in Kentish Town in early October 2008

But KJ were never about the darkness as secret and shame, nor ignorance, nor knotty, tight, shrivelled half-lives of the snivelling creatures of the sewer. Theirs is a darkness full and rich with the potent radiances of the Black Madonna, Kali and Lilith, of Kuk, Erebus and Dionysus – ecstatic, revelatory and glorious. The music was for me then, and still is for me now, the sound of what it is to be fully human in the temple of the gods, to embrace everything we are in an orgiastic triumph of the energy of life, in spite of, and because of, the very pain of existence, the wild edge of sorrow in which we can know most acutely "I am!"

It was just six weeks later, one week after my father had died, that I went to St George's Hall in Exeter to see KJ live. There began a relationship which has woven deeply through the fabric of my life – and still continues to this day, not just with the band, but with the fellow Gatherers. Too many to mention here, but all fellow travellers who just get what the song is all about, because it's in their heart too.

I found myself on the bus at the end of the night and I was gone, just like that. We went on to Bristol, and then around England in a snowy winter. Then a few weeks and on to Europe.

It was quite an initiation for a 16-year-old, but, to be honest, that summer saved my life. The deaths of both my parents in quick succession so that I was homeless and adrift – these were body blows that had left me inwardly screaming and outwardly numb. The boys never really asked about it, we never talked about it, but they let me be there, and the music did its cathartic work. Every dingy hall became a fetid hot-with-breath cauldron of magic that purged and transmuted the rage and stench of death from me and the fires burned on it. They still do.

THE STUDIO
10 February 1985,
Bristol, UK

CHRISTOPHER MAW

I'd been into KJ for a couple of years, since falling in love with 'Wilful Days'. The second time I saw them was at The Studio in Bristol. I was 15 (I'm 51 now). I was right at the front in the middle, happily crunched up to my chest into the stage.

They were about 10 songs in. It was a triumph, as usual. Jaz turned, big smile on his face, to say something to Big Paul. I turned to look at the crowd behind me, just as some halfwit threw an empty plastic pint glass at Jaz. I watched it arc over me and hit Jaz on the back of the head.

He turned, the smile replaced by pure fury. How he knew who'd done it, I'll never know, but he did. He flew off the stage, those magnificent patent leather Doc Martens several feet above my head, landing on top of said halfwit. A couple of blows later, we helped Jaz back onto the stage, and that was that. Straight into the next song.

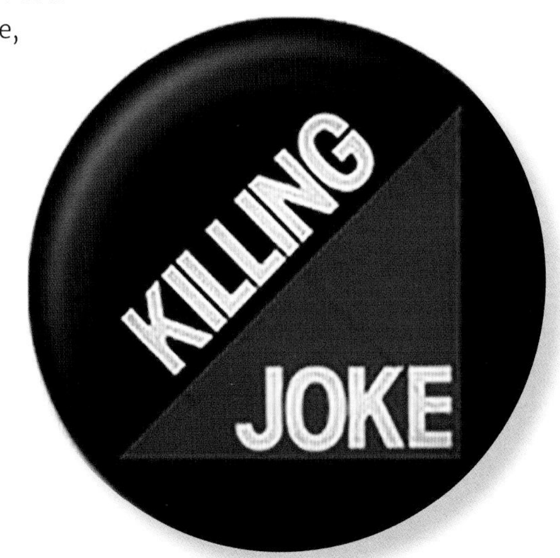

INGIMAR BJARNASON

I became aware of Killing Joke as a tween in Iceland. I read about Jaz and Geordie in Icelandic newspapers when the two lived there and how their involvement with my favourite Icelandic band, Þeyr, broke them up in the end. I first heard them at age 14 when a friend gave me a cassette with a mix of music he thought I needed to hear. The first song was a Killing Joke song that supposedly was pressed in an infinite groove. I never knew the name of that song and still don't. Needless to say, I loved that song. Around that time, *Night Time* came out and 'Eighties' and 'Love Like Blood' got airplay. I loved those songs as well. Then the band kinda faded away. I came back to listening to them in my early 40s and they've been a growing obsession since.

LEEDS UNIVERSITY
19 February 1985,
Leeds, UK

JAMES VARLEY

The Tube in 1985. It was a powerhouse of a performance that seemingly would break out of my TV screen and bash its way into my family home. It was scarily great. Good grief! This was what I was searching for all my teen years! It was power but had sophistication. "See you at Hammersmith"? Isn't that a Motörhead album? Well, they'd just blown Motörhead straight out of the water!

A couple of weeks later, I find myself at Leeds University, witnessing the thermonuclear device of sound and precision that is Killing Joke live on the *Night Time* tour. They start straight off the blocks and are creating the fusion of suns, superheat and light pouring out of their furnace. I am in awe and disbelief. The audience are hitting each other in a wild frenzy. They are in total reverie.

This gathering of metallurgists onstage are indeed alchemists and have somehow turned base metal into shining gold and silver. I'm in total shock at this blitzkrieg. Big Paul's drums pounding like carpet-bombing. Master of ceremonies Jaz is alight with mystical power channelled from civilisations that I have yet to encounter. Geordie's guitar is some form of weaponised aural device. He coolly brings it forth. This is not the usual plain cock-rock. I walk away afterwards – my life changed and Geordie's final guitar flourish still ringing hypnotically through my mind. It stays there for the rest of my life.

✦ ✦ ✦

CALEY PALAIS
21 February 1985,
Edinburgh, UK

IAN ROBERTSON

Agonisingly, it wasn't until the *Night Time* tour that my live Faustian Pact with the band was finally sealed.

QUEEN MARGARET UNION
22 February 1985,
Glasgow, UK

ANDY MACPHERSON

I was 13 or 14 when a school friend, who had an older sister with a good attitude, first alerted us to John Peel and the whole alternative music scene. Amazing anti-system music. What an impact that had on me.

One day, I heard Killing Joke! I froze. My heart hammering in my chest. I had never heard anything like this before. I was in awe. The sound! Fuck! I cannot describe the connection I felt to this thing! My main band ever since.

Anyway, big memory for me was an early-ish gig at the QMU (Glasgow University). After the gig, a friend and I climbed on to the roof of the venue over seriously high drops, pished, then upward circles before dropping down a floor or two to get to the level where KJ had their space. Someone opened the window for us from inside (Geordie?) and we clambered in, helped eat the band's food rider with them, had a chat then felt a bit embarrassed about it all and fucked off again!

Killing Joke are immense.

✦ ✦ ✦

SELECTADISC
1985, Nottingham

PHIL BARTON

Thought I'd get in touch. Left it for a week, then got hit by a cyclist on Oxford Street whilst listening to a live version of 'European Super State' on my headphones. A week later, my arm is in a cast, typing isn't fun – but stories need to be told.

After my O-levels, my mother promised to buy me an LP. I'd already bought the 'Requiem' 7-inch and was hooked by how different Killing Joke sounded.

We took a trip to Canterbury and scoured the record shops. No joy. As a last resort, I had a look in Woolworths, and there it was – £5.29.

Mum didn't like the look of the sleeve, the name of the band, the track titles – in fact, she had objections to everything about it. "Are you sure this is what you want?"

She kept saying it, but my heart, my head and my will were set in stone. I still have it. Still love it.

Fast-forward to Nottingham 1984. I was working in the singles department of Selectadisc (RIP) on Bridlesmith Gate. The shop had a chart machine. Data entered into it was used to compile the UK Top 40 charts. We were one of hundreds of shops that had these machines. Our Polydor rep, Lee, came in with white labels of new KJ song 'Eighties'.

We played it, was sure it was a hit and took copies for every indie DJ we knew. This was going to be a hit. No joy – it stalled outside the Top 40. 'A New Day' didn't have the same potential but fared a little better chart-wise.

Lee continued peddling the other Polydor acts that he was responsible for and, after what seemed like an eternity, turned up with some more KJ white labels. 'Love Like Blood' had to be a hit, surely?

Everyone we knew was talking about it. There was a big demand. I ordered loads of stock and we were ready to launch KJ into the Top 40. The single entered the charts at No.46. We were so disappointed. Lee and I had convinced each other this was the one. We'd sold a huge amount of singles. It was easily outselling Tears for Fears, Bruce Springsteen and Madonna in our shop. How could it not have cracked the 40? We just had to hype harder.

Galvanised by the fact it had got to No.46, Polydor made the record its No.1 priority. The following week, we waited for the chart announcement – No.32 (with a slow bullet). Lee brought in champagne and cans to celebrate.

The charts meant a lot more back then, still important to artists now, but having a Top 40 hit led to *Top of the Pops* (Janice Long introduced, Geordie in menacing white polo neck, Jaz's menacing stare and Raven just full-bore menacing).

The single peaked at 16, there was a remix, the album sold well and the band were established, but the thrill of being part of getting 'Love Like Blood' into the charts has never left me.

I own Sister Ray Records on Berwick Street in Soho. I saw the band last year: still punishingly powerful, still playing *Pylon*. It is a colossus of a record.

MANFRED ROLEF

I discovered Killing Joke in 1985 when my older brother bought the 12-inch single of 'Love Like Blood'. I thought it was absolutely brilliant and to me still sounds timeless and has a power that makes it standalone in the Eighties. A TV-broadcasted Rockpalast live gig from Loreley brought me more into older stuff of the band.

SIMON BARRINGTON

I would've been 12 in 1985. I wasn't into music at all really at this stage, although I do recall hearing a slightly weird song about a year before on the radio on the drive back from my Grandma's house which I liked, and was nothing like the stuff you usually heard on the radio (I later discovered that to be 'Blue Monday' by New Order). I seem to recall there was a bit of a thing at school about taping the charts on Radio 1 on Sunday night and, at the time, I particularly liked 'You Spin Me Round (Like a Record)' by Dead or Alive. So I remember one Sunday night sitting by the stereo and recording the chart songs I liked on C90 cassette. I did get the Dead or Alive song down, but that week recall being very drawn to a slightly eerie-sounding rock track with a sensational and unique guitar sound. I taped it. The DJ said it was 'Love Like Blood' by Killing Joke. I played it back a few times over the next few days and the song remained in the back of my mind from then on but I wasn't much into music at that stage so I thought not too much more of it.

LUC TIRONNEAU

Regardless of the 'Love Like Blood' riff (after 30 years playing guitar I still can't reproduce it correctly, the particular tuning of Geordie's guitars having a lot to answer for), it is the musical chorus of 'Darkness Before Dawn' that I keep in mind, the sound barrier.

ALAN MUSTAFA

It's 1985, I am nine years old. 'Love Like Blood' floats from my oldest brother's bedroom like some stately hymn. It sounds alien, ancient and very important. It feels like something unfolding for the future, kicking at the past, burying childish things. Scary but necessary. Later, the tribal drums of *Fire Dances* hook my ears again. Different now, channelling into something more primeval, tugging the heart. "Oh, you like them? Check this out." He [my brother] plays the yelp and kick of 'Pssyche'. Forever etched as the scary, real and true fury of punk. The path is set...

ANDY MAXWELL

'Love Like Blood' blew everyone away, even those that knew very little about the band.

MATTHIAS RICH

Moving through time, at the age of 15, with bumfluff appearing on my chin, my father bought me an electric razor, which had a free compilation cassette bundled in with it as part of a sales promo. Various bands prominent during the mid-Eighties featured on the tape, including Killing Joke with 'Love Like Blood'. How could I not fall in love with it?

BRIAN RICHARDSON

My first true exposure to Killing Joke was 'Love Like Blood'. Probably like a whole ton of other fans. I was about 12 when my brother bought me a double-tape compilation for my birthday. It opened me up to a whole new world as I was just starting to experience music properly. The tape had been vaguely sectioned out into genres: AOR, hair metal, but also, tucked in between The Damned and Siouxsie and the Banshees, was 'Love Like Blood'.

I was hooked from the opening riff. It was outstanding and completely different to everything else on there. It got played until my Walkman killed the cassette when it chewed the tape up. 'Love Like Blood' helped establish my appreciation of rock and metal and set me on my way. This is the thing with KJ – I don't think they should be forced into a genre because, in truth, they have their own. In retrospect, sticking them between new romantic tracks did them an injustice.

✦ ✦ ✦

THE POWERHOUSE
24 February 1985,
Birmingham, UK

NIGEL CLARKE

(Professor of Condensed Matter Physics Theory)

I'd been indifferent to music until I was 15. To keep up with friends, I'd bought some Top 40 singles by bands I've long forgotten. I guess I was looking for some late-night entertainment among the four channels when I stumbled across *The Old Grey Whistle Test* and watched with indifference until they showed the video of 'Eighties'.

Emotionally, it was like being hit by a freight train. I had never felt such a raw connection with music. My Dad thought it was the start of a slippery slope. My Mum was less concerned, dismissing it as a teenager's passing rebel phase – 36 years on and the phase has yet to pass. KJ's music – past and present – remains among my most frequently played.

I first saw them a few months later on the *Night Time* tour at the Birmingham Powerhouse, a venue that, sadly, no longer exists. I remember being surprised to see Jaz amble past us as we queued outside – and I'll never forget the intensity, the heat and the sweat of my first live KJ experience.

I can draw a very tenuous line musically to KJ. I played in a band, purely for fun rather than money, for many years, with John Cockburn, a bass player who was in a band – The Mynd – with Martin Atkins before he left to join PiL. They were good friends; Martin was the best man at his wedding. I only found out about three years ago despite knowing the bass player for nearly 30 years. I've lost track of the number of times I've asked, "You didn't think to mention this earlier because...?"

The band I was in with John was called Spontaneous Emissions, which is the phenomena behind how lasers work, which I guess gives an indication of physicists' humour.

MARK GEMINI THWAITE

(Spear of Destiny, Tricky, The Mission, Gary Numan)

Killing Joke first hit my radar not on early seminal and genre-groundbreaking releases such as *What's THIS for...!* or their first album, but when the *Night Time* album hit the record stores back in 1985. The band's chartbusting single 'Love Like Blood' was on heavy radio rotation. I went down to see the band live at that time – fellow Midlander Paul Raven was on bass, Youth having jumped ship a couple of years before, and I was impressed how loud they were, and how immense Geordie's guitar sound was through his Burmans and Golden Lyre ES-295. They immediately became one of my favourite bands and I eagerly picked up and digested their back-catalogue, loving the gothic majesty of the *Night Time* material and the post-punk ferocity of the early albums. Geordie became a massive influence on my guitar playing during the Eighties and on, and Big Paul quickly became one of my favourite drummers – an omen of things to come...

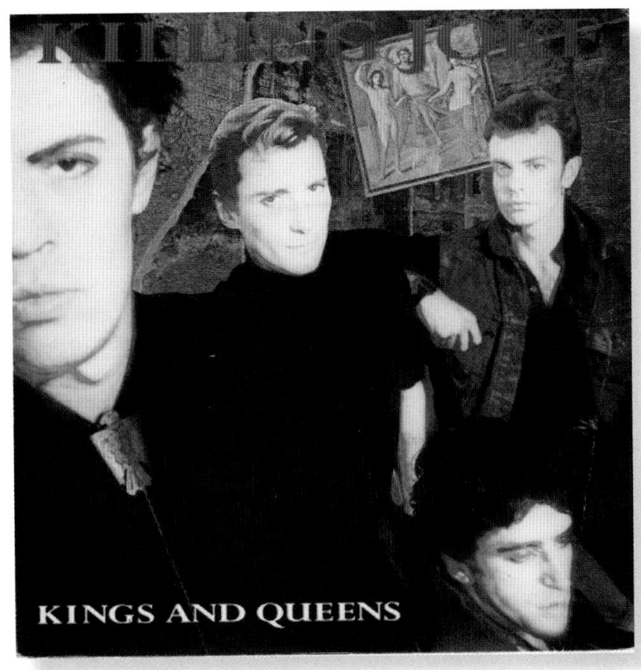

DAN PARKER

Flash-forward to spring 1985, sitting outside after lunch during junior year of high school. My pal Bob is going on and on about his new tape. It's *Night Time* by Killing Joke. He gives me his Walkman headphones and insists I listen to a few choice cuts - 'Love Like Blood', 'Kings and Queens' and my old friend 'Eighties'. And 35 years on, it remains one of my favourite albums. Yes, it was the songs, but it was as much the sound, that amazing end-times production.

MARK WHITELEY

I'm round at Raven's flat. He's showing me the bassline to 'Love Like Blood' that's just charted. I bought a Tokai bass off him, too, that night and then the Joke were gone. Off on tour. Aside from seeing Raven once in passing at the '89 Carnival, I never saw Raven again.

By this time, I was pretty busy with Folk Devils and with something of a family life. My daughter Danielle was born in 1984, a significant, life-affirming day. She was actually born the day after a Folk Devils gig down in Soho. Her mum is convinced it was either me playing Killing Joke loud at home or the volume of that gig on 18 May 1984 that led to her going into labour. I guess we'll never know for sure... Was it 'Pssyche' or [FD track] 'Hank Turns Blue' that triggered her labour?

✦ ✦ ✦

GRAND PARC
9 March 1985,
Bordeaux, France

FLORENCE CHARO

Teenagerhood is a time of recklessness and craziness. A teenage girl's life is full of parties and music. With my friends, we were in bedrooms and garages of one another with our vinyl to listen to: The Damned, Buzzcocks, The Clash, Ramones, and many more. Among them were KJ. Some of my friends tried to play guitar to imitate their favourite band's musical styles.

We were only 16, 17 when we were moving from concert to concert. Unforgettable memories – the best of them being KJ's concerts.

All your body, soul and mind were shaken. It was a shock of so much intensity, like an earth tremor. Such feelings are embodied in you all your life.

I saw a concert of KJ for the first time in 1985 in Bordeaux at the Grand Parc venue. Huge! A tiny girl of 17, her hands clinked to the barrier at the front of the stage, taken by waves of decibels, mainly boys' bodies all around jumping on the sound of 'Wardance', 'Follow the Leaders' and 'Requiem'.

UNIVERSITY
28 April 1985,
Melbourne, Australia

STAN MANIATIS

I've grown up with Killing Joke and seen them perform in Melbourne in 1985 as a 19-year-old uni student, in 2003 as a 37-year-old parent of two toddlers, and in 2013 as a 47-year-old middle-aged man.

I was initially introduced to The Clash in 1982, at Saturday Greek School by a friend who is now an emergency-department doctor. Then his brother gave me *What's THIS for...!* in 1983 to listen to and I was hooked by that wall of sound. They made The Clash sound like the Bay City Rollers. The Clash seemed contrived like The Exploited, with their funny hair. Killing Joke seemed more genuine and threatening.

I went back to the first album and the others at the time and was amazed how they can sound familiar yet sound unique with each recording. First album is more metal; the second more tribal with a different, less metallic, guitar.

I went to university in 1984, as The Clash were imploding and running out of ideas. I saw that crazy clown on the 'Eighties' single at the La Trobe University record shop. Another great memory – my first Killing Joke single – followed by 'A New Day'.

Hard to obtain Killing Joke releases back then. Had to get import releases from independent record stores in the inner city. I lived further out in the suburbs where the record stores had just Top 40 crap!

I only had to wait a year before seeing them live in 1985.

Great performance, though the university crowd was subdued and stunned by the Killing Joke onslaught and the wall of sound. I should have gone to the Prince of Wales hotel gig [27 April 1985]. A more loyal and energetic audience, I heard.

BRIAN JAMES

(guitarist/songwriter The Damned, The Lords of the New Church)

Raven and I during the Eighties became good drinking buddies at a pub called Portobello Gold on Portobello Road. Jaz and Geordie also used to pop in from time to time as Jaz had a flat around the corner. After a while of meeting each other, usually lunch times, we figured it might be a good idea to recruit a drummer – which was usually Rat [Scabies] – and go and jam and mess around on some songs after a few pints. Usually in the company of a couple of bottles of wine and a lump of hash. This, of course, was when Killing Joke or The Lords of the New Church were not gigging.

© Barry Pitman

Both Raven and I used the pub not only as a watering hole and social club, but also as a kind of office, where people knew how to get hold of us and would phone and leave messages with bar staff. In fact, me and my wife Minna never bothered with a landline phone, and mobiles were a thing of the future (until our son was born, when we figured it was a good idea to get a phone).

Raven was one of the funniest fuckers I ever met. Totally amoral, this was a man who didn't give a fuck but also happened to be one of the toughest bass players I have ever worked with. I miss that devil very, very much.

MICHE MARCISZ

I don't think I actually saw a photo of the band until around 1985, when I was at a friend's house and she had the *Night Time* album. I demanded to hear it! I think my friends were annoyed. They wanted to listen to U2 all night. What?!

NICO PLEIMLING

The first contact I had with Killing Joke goes back to when they had their major commercial success with 'Love Like Blood' and the accompanying album *Night Time*. I was a high-school student then and had my puberty kick in around that time. This means that I started to go out with a few like-minded lads from school and from our suburb near Luxembourg City.

We were 15 or 16, so going out for us meant hanging out at events organised by the Party Team (we're not going to discuss their choice of a less creative albeit successful name). And mostly what we did was literally hang out at those parties, complaining about the musical choices of the Party Team's DJs – mid-Eighties pop music that we could not stand. We waited and stood around on the dancefloor until finally they'd put on a couple of songs we enjoyed, including New Order's 'Blue Monday', 'Don't You (Forget About Me)' from Simple Minds and, of course 'Love Like Blood', after which they went back to their commercial routine and us to our silent protest on the floor.

Thanks to the album *Night Time*, I got hooked to Killing Joke and never lost my interest, even though it took many years and a bit of a listening effort to finally halfway appreciate *Outside the Gate*.

DEREK FORBES

(Simple Minds – when they were really good)

Derek Forbes and Raven © Ray McVeigh

I was first made aware of Killing Joke by way of long-time friend Ray McVeigh, guitar player of The Professionals. I was introduced to Geordie Walker on the occasion of my 'should they keep me or not' invitation from Virgin Records to record demos, which would seal my fate. I'd been removed from Simple Minds that March, whilst at number one in the music charts worldwide with a film-track song… they certainly had forgotten about me!

I, with the help of Ray, got together with a few friends, new and old. The track was written by myself and Ray, and the band recording it was Geordie Walker, Billy Currie (Ultravox), Ray McVeigh, Ray Weston on drums (too many bands to mention), and myself on bass.

This was my first experience of meeting and working with Geordie. A meeting that to this day is still a great friendship. I have been to Killing Joke gigs over the years. After getting to know the band better, I wouldn't miss them for the world. The songs are genius, the performance is, to me, reminiscent of early Alex Harvey – theatrical but with more menace, mysticism and magick!

I was invited to a party with the band in London. It was one of the best nights of my life.

There was a bona fide wizard doing the rounds of the guests, twirling a stunning wand with glass balls on each end that seemed to light up like two small Van de Graaff generators with strokes of what looked like violet lightning. Yes, I was not adverse to the odd 'mood enhancer' in those days, but I swear to Amduscias, that is what I recall!

I spent a lot of time with Raven over the years and we could be seen going in and out of the pubs in Notting Hill Gate on many an occasion. We also worked on Japanese albums in A&M Studios in Los Angeles – Raven with a huge Japanese star Hide (pronounced Hid-eh) and me with Japanese band Oblivion Dust.

ARENES DU PLUMACON
11 August 1985,
Mont-de-Marsan, France

FLORENCE CHARO

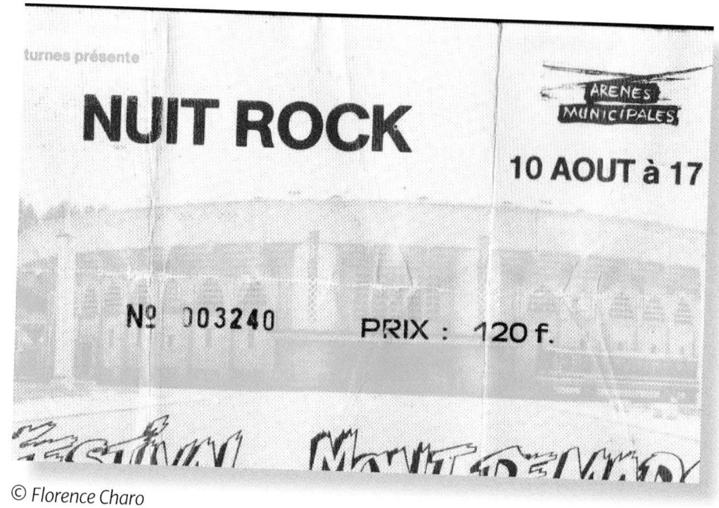

© Florence Charo

The festival was held in the arenas of the city. This famous festival saw The Damned and The Clash fighting in 1977 with stinkbombs and it was also the beginning of The Police. In 1984, the festival restarted. I was at that festival with a broken arm following a car accident.

The next year. It was August, a very hot day and we'd been waiting hours outside the venue with my friends.

There, a few paces from us, I could see the figure of Paul Raven. My eyes couldn't believe it. He was walking towards us then sat down next to me. He said hello, asked if everything was okay and if I would be at the concert that evening. My English was dreadful and shyness sky high. I was petrified. I stuttered a shaky yes, laughed and told him we were there for him. I added that we'd already seen his band five months before in Bordeaux.

Paul was an exquisite and charming man. I remember he talked about his girlfriend, who was in Brazil at the time if I am not mistaken. He was missing her very much and thinking of her all the time.

With his extreme kindness, he invited my boyfriend and I to visit him after the concert, backstage and offered to add the names of my friends on the guest-list.

He took all my friends' names, told us to enjoy our evening and went back to Geordie and Jaz. He kept his word, although my friends had been refused entry by overzealous staff. My boyfriend and I were able to see the band in their dressing rooms, although after-concerts are not easy for musicians; they are very often taken over by people, not to mention that their minds are in another dimension. We congratulated them and walked away with an extraordinary feeling of happiness. With my 40-odd-years' friends, we still talk about that day.

CARSTEN DOIG

In 1985, I was 10-years-old and watching a crazy film called *Weird Science* about two nerdy boys who make the woman of their dreams. There is a party scene in that film with this crazy, energetic music, which I loved so much that I paused the video during the credits to make sure I got the name of the song and the band. It was 'Eighties' by Killing Joke.

It stuck in my head. A couple of years later, when I started getting serious about music, I went back to that song and bought the *Night Time* cassette and its successor, *Brighter Than a Thousand Suns*.

HANSA TONSTUDIO
Summer 1986,
West Berlin

MARION SCHULT
(photographer)

Killing Joke cover shoot for *Brighter Than a Thousand Suns*.

In the summer of 1986, I met Jaz Coleman in the restaurant of Hansa. At that time, I had my photo studio in the house of Hansa, the legendary music studio in Köthenerstrasse, Berlin Kreuzberg.

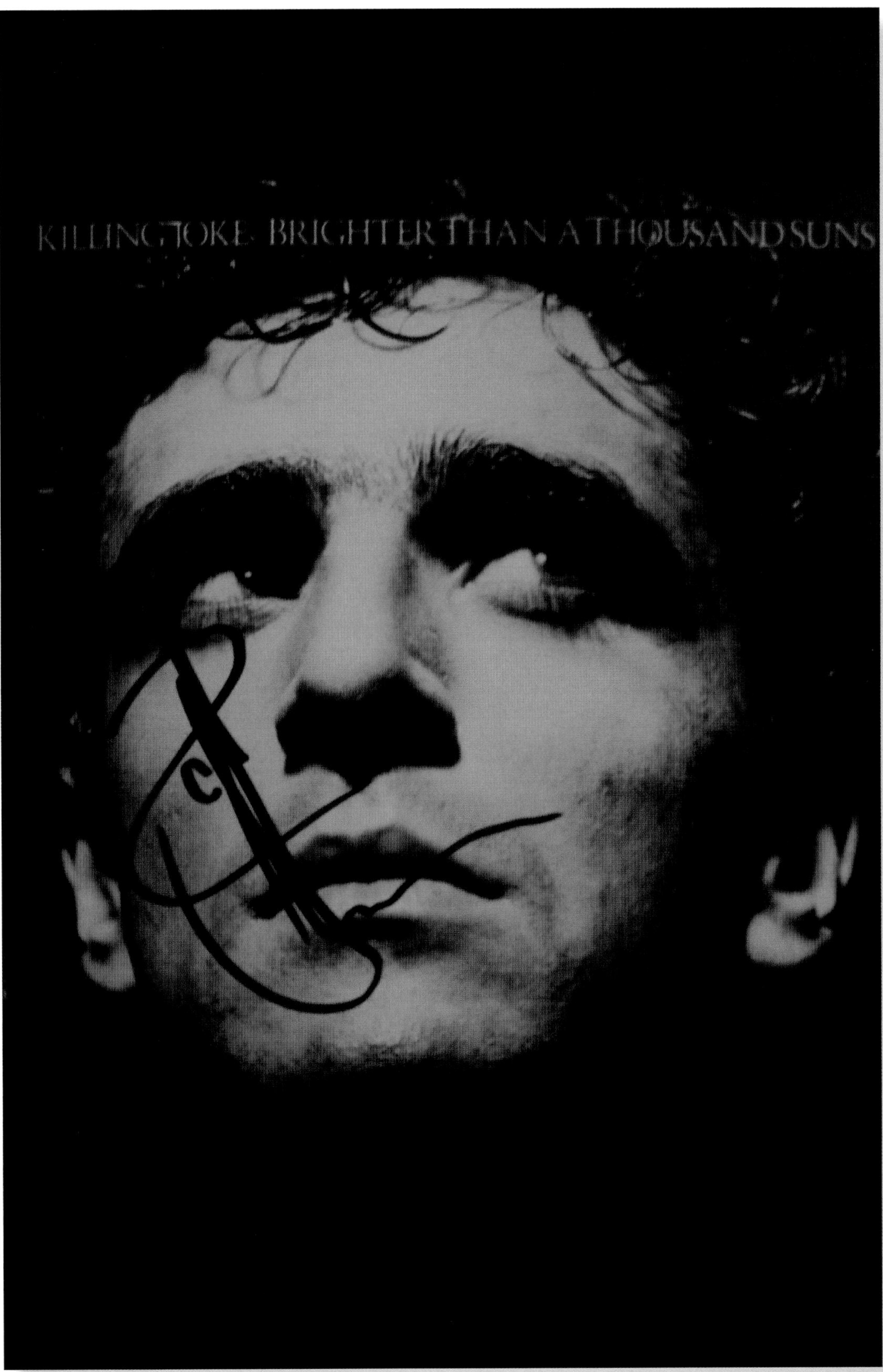

© Marion Schult/Daz Brown

He caught my attention with his charismatic face and cool look. We immediately got into conversation and he showed me a little book in which he'd written down his song lyrics. I was very impressed by the demanding lyrics, thought that was great.

I asked if I could do a portrait of him if he had time. "Why not?" We made an appointment.

After our conversation, I thought about how I would like to do the shooting. Inspired by his lyrics, I wanted to portray him mystically and reduce everything to his personality.

During our photo session, he was very surprised it took only 30 minutes. When he saw the results of the portraits as black-and-white prints, he was so impressed that he wanted to take one of the close-ups for the cover of *Brighter Than a Thousand Suns*, which they were just working on in the studio. Jaz spoke with his producer, Chris Kimsey, saying I should photograph the complete cover of the band in the same style as his portrait.

The producer came from London to Berlin especially. We had a great time with different photo settings.

JAZ

We were right next to the Philharmonia, where the Berlin Philharmonic play. The band would regularly go over and listen to Herbert von Karajan conducting the Philharmonic. That's where I heard the *Prague Symphony* by Mozart for the first time, which led me and Geordie to Prague.

STEVEN BORG

It started when my nephew gave me a cassette which included 'Adorations' and 'Eighties' in the summer of 1987.

Of course, I already knew 'Love Like Blood' (who doesn't!). I was impressed with 'Adorations'. Not much later, I bought *Brighter Than a Thousand Suns* on cassette. After that, it all went rapidly, collecting Killing Joke albums. No more tapes, but albums on CDs, and I went to record fairs to buy vinyl – 7-inch, 10-inch or 12-inch. I was unstoppable in collecting Killing Joke releases.

In my room were two posters – the one with the faces of the band members in black and white from *Brighter Than a Thousand Suns*, and the infamous Nazi poster from Malicious Damage.

TOM PAYNE

In 1986, I met Paul Raven as, purely by chance, he started seeing the sister of my then girlfriend. Super-nice guy with a huge personality in every respect. It was difficult at the time to try and hold back how much I loved the band, so as not to embarrass myself.

Raven split with my girlfriend's sister and I lost any connection. The next bizarre episode in my KJ relationship had to wait until 1990...

ZEUS B. HELD

(remixes – 'Sanity (The Insane Mix)', 'Adorations (The Supernatural Mix)', 'Love Like Blood (The '86 Remix)')

When I was contacted about a contribution to the KJ book, I re-listened to those KJ mixes I made back in 1986, and also to the original 'Love Like Blood', the first track I ever heard from KJ. It immediately caught me with its cold atmosphere, the shimmering sound of the synth chords next to those razor-sharp guitar riffs and rhythm – I felt at home.

So, when I got asked by Island Records to work on a few 12-inches and remixes for some club releases, I really felt privileged and loved the challenging task.

I went to work on the multi-tracks at Eastcote Studios off Ladbroke Grove and at Eden Studios in Chiswick. The brief by the record company was pretty open (make it better, extend the dynamics and frequencies, help to reach more people's ears) and it gave me a lot of freedom.

But, eventually, the moment came when I had a surprise visit by the band during my last days of mixing at Eden. Well, there they were, out of the blue, like arriving from some time travel. Geordie, [Big] Paul and Raven, three-quarters of KJ, demanding to listen to the mixes and remixes. Obviously, I had added sounds, sequences, FX and played around with the arrangement, which is always a very delicate and dangerous procedure: you interfere and fiddle around with the creativity of a dynamic, spirited and rehearsed team.

Well, here came the moment of truth – I play them my mixes – and I survived the stress test. Obviously, there were various requests for alterations. I clearly remember how certain sounds from the Roland TR-808 [drum machine] were disliked by the guys. After some discussions, I took most of them out, particularly the 'handclaps'.

I met Paul Raven a few years later (around 1994) in Golborne Road, where he then lived, just 'round the corner from my house and Eastcote Studios. For a while, we managed to hook up – like neighbours do – and have the occasional cup of coffee and inspired talk at the Lisboa [Patisserie].

READING FESTIVAL
22 August 1986,
Reading, UK

LEON LANGFORD

My first exposure to Killing Joke was Channel 4's *Whatever You Want* and/or *Whatever You Didn't Get*. I recorded the brilliant version of 'The Pandys Are Coming' with two mics taped to my black-and-white portable TV, connected to my Seventies music centre. I had to use cotton wool to stop the buzzing where the TV speaker was affecting the mic. Hi-fi it wasn't, or even stereo!

My most vivid memory of the band live was Friday's headline slot at the Reading Festival, 1986. It wasn't the gig or the set-list – it was the piercing, primeval, Banshee-like thunderous scream that Jaz did some time before they came on. Maybe he was testing the mic – or warming up his voice!

CENTRAL PARK
27 September 1986,
Burton-on-Trent, UK

MARK GEMINI THWAITE

I caught the band live again during the *Brighter Than a Thousand Suns* tour. Again, they were magnificent, despite the new album's more commercial sound, but I could sense there was some tension (no pun intended) and Big Paul jumped ship sometime after that album. I didn't see the band again until the *Extremities...* tour around 1990/91.

WE'RE BACK!
READING ROCKS AGAIN
24th NATIONAL ROCK FESTIVAL
AUGUST 22 · 23 · 24
AT RICHFIELD AVENUE

FRIDAY: from 3pm	SATURDAY: from noon	SUNDAY: from noon
KILLING JOKE	SAXON	HAWKWIND
THE MISSION	RUBY TURNER	ZODIAC MINDWARP AND THE LOVE REACTION
BALAAM AND THE ANGEL	GRAHAM PARKER	CHIEFS OF RELIEF
MARCH VIOLETS	BUDDY CURTESS & THE GRASSHOPPERS	THE ENID
THE BOLSHOI	FM · IT BITES	CHERRY BOMBZ
TWENTY FLIGHT ROCKERS	OUTSIDE EDGE	THRASHING DOVES
	SKAGARACK	WELL WELL WELL
	Special Guests from the USA JOHN WAITE AND THE NO BRAKES BAND	DUMPY CARDIACS
Special Guests DOCTOR & THE MEDICS	THE OUTLAWS	Special Guests THE LORDS OF THE NEW CHURCH
	ROUGH CUTT	NEW MODEL ARMY

TRAVEL

ADMISSION AT GROUND

£17.95

Brazil

PAULO GONCALVES

I'd read about Killing Joke in various publications in the music press, but only got to listen to their music when I played a friend of mine's *Brighter Than a Thousand Suns*. Then I went back and forth through the discography and have been hooked for nearly 40 years!

TROY GREGORY

Later, I bought *Brighter Than a Thousand Suns*. I love that era. Jaz would probably vomit hearing me say this, but I think his voice on that record is the best he's sung on any album.

MELODY MAKER OFFICES
October 1986
London, UK

NEIL PERRY
(journalist)

I first heard Killing Joke on John Peel's show in late 1979. He played the 'Are You Receiving' single. I was 14-years-old and just starting to take music seriously. And while I'd grown up with punk – loud and fast music being the norm – I remember being electrified by this sound. It was different. Mike Coles' artwork on the records added to the mystery, this sci-fi dystopian Pop Art vibe complementing the music perfectly. I first saw Killing Joke a year later in 1980 at the Lyceum Ballroom in London. That solidified my obsession. The band had a presence that just pulled you in. I travelled home from that gig feeling like I'd been initiated into something special, my teenage brain boiling over with ideas and emotions.

I spent the next five years obsessing over Killing Joke, seeing them play whenever possible. I used to sit with the lyrics and cross-reference with quotes from their press interviews to try and unravel their mysterious world and belief system. Music was my life and, after studying journalism at college, all I wanted to do was write for the music press.

I started writing for *Sounds* in the summer of '85. Killing Joke had released *Night Time* in early '85 so the next record, *Brighter Than a Thousand Suns*, wouldn't appear until late '86.

Early on, I let everyone in the office know that interview was mine!

It began at the record company office – me and the band sat in a tiny room. They were loud and boisterous, all shouting and talking at once. It was fairly intimidating – only Big Paul tried to inject some seriousness into proceedings. He was the only one trying to give considered answers to my questions. I was getting worried because the interview was really going nowhere. I didn't have enough for a feature, so I was relieved when Jaz took me aside and said he wanted to continue the interview elsewhere.

I heard him asking for a car to be ordered, then he said to me, "We're going to *Melody Maker*." We got into this big, black, chauffeur-driven car and headed off into central London, with Jaz smoking a hash pipe and looking increasingly agitated. He asked the driver to stop several times – at a butcher's and a fishing tackle shop – but I still had no idea what was going on, what he was planning, or if we were actually going to *Melody Maker* or somewhere else.

We arrived at the *Melody Maker* office and Jaz ran up the stairs, into the reception area, and gave the startled receptionist the names of several *MM* journalists he wanted to speak to. Apparently, something had been written about Jaz that had offended him – and he wanted an apology.

When he was told they wouldn't come out of the office, Jaz pulled out a bag and dumped some large pieces of liver on the receptionist's desk. Then he emptied a tub of maggots over the liver. The receptionist started screaming. Jaz picked up some scissors from her desk, held them up in an 'X' shape, muttered some words in what sounded like Latin and then thrust the scissors into the liver.

There was a security door into the office with a window. I could see the faces of various *MM* staffers looking through, open-mouthed, having been alerted by the sound of the receptionist's screams. But they weren't opening that door.

I was good friends with one of the journalists, Mat Smith, who was also a huge Killing Joke fan, and we made eye contact through the window, trying not to laugh.

Jaz grabbed me and we ran down the stairs, out into the street and into the waiting car, like we'd just pulled a bank job or something.

A few years later, I wrote for *Melody Maker* and got to know the receptionist, a great character called Marcia, and she did recall the day with a smile.

There were a lot of phone calls between *MM* and *Sounds* over the next few weeks. They didn't want us to mention Jaz's attack – as if! Whatever field they're in, not many journalists get handed a story on a plate like that. I was a music journalist for 13 years, but that was the most entertaining day of my career – and that's saying something. The music industry was a bubble in those days and word of the 'liver and maggots attack' spread quickly. Over the years, people have told me various exaggerated versions of what happened, without realising I was the journalist who was there. A few years later, I interviewed Jaz again and he joked about how he'd given me the best present a journalist could ask for. In those pre-internet days, the music press had a lot of power, and a lot of bands wanted the press on their side. Killing Joke and Jaz didn't give a shit. It was refreshing – and it's still being talked about, 35 years later.

Editor's note: in the interests of editorial balance, I emailed Steve Sutherland, *MM* deputy editor at the time, for his account of events. No reply was forthcoming.

JOHN DORAN

I think it's a lie about Killing Joke that they are universally despised among music journalists. For example, if you look back at the Eighties, I would say *Sounds* were fully in Killing Joke's corner. For the most part, *Melody Maker* had a foot in both camps. You had people like John Robb, who has always sung their praises.

Killing Joke came to prominence during the really brilliant age of music journalism in the Eighties, where a lot of cult, underground acts were given a lot of space, especially in the earlier part of the decade.

The negative side of it was that it was extremely trend-oriented. Somebody was of the opinion that KJ were no good and that was, by and large, an opinion that kind of stuck in the Eighties.

You can't just turn around and say KJ were spiky customers. It's true, they didn't do themselves many favours. The amazing incident that everyone knows about where they turned up with a bag of rotten offal at King's Reach Tower... I'm really, really torn about this. As a music journalist, I think isn't that a cruel way for bands to be acting when all someone's done is maybe given them a bit of a snide review. I kinda think that band should take it on the chin.

But I also think, "Wow, what an amazing thing to do." There's part of me that thinks – would today's underground rock climate be a bit more exciting if stuff like that still happened? I don't know. It's a tough one.

One – Killing Joke kinda asked for it a little in their antagonism with the press. Two – it was unfair in a way. They got it in the neck more than other bands. They got picked on in a way that, say, The Fall didn't get cancelled for using the n-word in 'The Classical'.

MATTHIAS RICH

I was ensconced in all things alternative to pop culture. My musical tastes were where this was most apparent. By this point, I had a few KJ releases, *Night Time* being a favourite. *Brighter Than a Thousand Suns* didn't move me as much, but 'Sanity' and 'Adorations' really cemented my admiration for the band.

APOLLO
21 November 1986,
Manchester, UK

JAMES VARLEY

Brighter Than a Thousand Suns raised my expectations beyond belief. I'd ventured to seek where these Gods would be revelling that night. I wanted to witness again this group of nuclear-fission explorers testing that thermonuclear device. I'd never been to Manchester before and, as a depressed and suicidal teen, had found my way through KJ to new ecstatic purpose. They lifted me to a newer higher purpose.

Here I am at 17 to worship. I bristle with excitement. Whoa! What's that door open at the side? Maybe I could just wander in for a look-see? No one stops me. I feel the thrill of the adventure unfolding. Not long and I'm backstage in the hallowed temple and I feel like Indiana Jones. I see light from a dressing-room door. A young man opens a lid to a case on a table and a golden light glows upwards. Laid down on the altar is Geordie's ES-295. I cannot believe my luck. I chat to the acolyte guitar tech (I think he may have been Simple Minds' guitar tech as well). Surprisingly, he lets me admire this religious icon I have come to worship. It's a moment I doubt many will understand or even get the opportunity to be this close to.

A soundcheck is mentioned. I venture further and into the auditorium. No one stops me. It seems I have some form of invisibility powers and cloak blessed upon me by Geordie's guitar. I sit in front of the sound-desk. The Gods stroll on in a relaxed manner on to the hallowed grounds. It's not long before critical mass is reached and the aural weapon is released. 'Chessboards' is unleashed and powers forth in full effect. They smash into an instrumental version of 'Night Time'. Geordie finds his way into the auditorium to get the full deal of what soundscape his weapon is creating. Now Jaz follows him and he's making his way in a determined attitude towards my position. He sits in front of me, perched on a seat back, but he's not come to see me but is transfixed as he dynamically counters the sound mixer. Jaz is incensed, but totally civil, as he wrestles this monster and a beast of a sound. Jaz is orchestrating and coercing the sound mix with the dexterity of a conductor. It's the mark of the Master – Karajan concentrating his precise sound and vision. I cannot believe I am witness to this.

As the soundcheck draws to a close with Geordie's cascading chords, a young man I recognise from the performance space offers me his tea. How kind. This is David Kovacevic, the keyboardsman. We chat and he rumbles I am an intruder but not here to steal anything but an audience with the Gods themselves. I must go thank that guitar tech. I encounter Geordie on stage and thank him for the performance. "That was just amazing. The *Brighter...* album is just phenomenal!" "Thank you. What tracks do you like?" "All of it! 'Victory' is really cool." At which point Geordie launches into the opening guitar lines. Big Paul says hi from his raised dais. Everyone I speak to is kind. This is not what I expected.

I walk away a changed person. That night, I am witness to the Temple of the Gods. Nuclear reaction is achieved once more. The power is also nuanced, bringing forth new joy. Chaos and yet mathematics to it. Raven is like the Muhammad Ali of bass – his lines are dancing around but anchoring the huge vessel on its pummelling journey. Jaz – all master and commander of this monster of a musical liner that ploughs through the night. I am happy and a lot delirious the whole day. There are moments in your life when you change and you take note of the process of that change – the reaction, the effect of it and what caused it. This is Killing Joke.

THEATRE DE VERDURE
7 December 1986,
Nice, France

LUC TIRONNEAU

I was extremely disappointed with the album *Brighter Than a Thousand Suns*. It was therefore with shiver and apprehension, during a Homeric thunderstorm, that I saw for the first time KJ in concert, with The Lords of the New Church supporting.

Jaz had a plastered arm after a jump in an audience perhaps too sparse during a previous concert. It did not change anything: the sound barrier was there, and we were breaking through it.

With my friend Albain, we had arrived early enough to be in the front row. No way to leave from there. The gig had started and the sound of KJ made The Lords of the New Church sound like a nice FM group like The Alarm.

Suddenly, I felt lifted from the ground. Were these magical Jaz incantations beginning to take effect? I landed from my short flight in the second row and found that, at the front row, a red-crested punk, smaller than me but at least twice as strong, had lifted me and just placed behind him.

My first reflex to challenge the assault was quickly calmed when he turned his head threateningly at me. At 16, my muscle mass being comparable to that of a flat, white fish, I didn't come up with any plan so cunning that you could have put a tail on it and called it weasel. So I swallowed my outraged pride, which did not change anything at this great concert.

After, Albain and me were hanging out under the marquee of the Green Theatre and who did we see, beckoning us to come – Paul Raven.

We weren't dreaming – he was taking us backstage. Jaz was not there but, as much as our poor English could allow, we exchanged admiration with Paul and Geordie, whose accent did not facilitate the fluidity of the conversation!

They very simply offered us a beer and soon we took leave of them, stars in our eyes, delighted with the experience and amazed at the extreme availability of these stars.

MIGUEL MEZA BUZETA

On an afternoon in 1987, when I was 13, my older brother give me a cassette that on side A was The Smiths' *The Queen Is Dead* – and side B Killing Joke's *What's THIS for...!*

I listened to The Smiths and was fascinated by the drums of Mike Joyce in the song 'The Queen Is Dead'. By the third song, I got bored (basically Morrissey and his way of filling in with his voice where silence is important). I decided to play the B-side, and that's where my story with KJ begins.

When I heard the drum beat of 'The Fall of Because', it was not only giving me love for that rhythm that accompanied the experiences of [Augusto] Pinochet's dictatorship very well – it was a light in the dark, a dance, a trance that made me unfold in this new reality musicalised by KJ. A parallel universe.

Then I became interested in the English language, in understanding very well what Jaz Coleman was saying, to discover that 'Tension' was also positive, 'Unspeakable' as a way to laugh at censorship.

'Butcher' and 'Follow the Leaders' encourage me to be a rebel on the street with barricades and throwing molotovs at the dictator's police (still today).

These sound and content experiences transformed me into a follower of KJ because they continuously accompanied my passage through this timeline. What will come next? I don't know. I just hope it's not Barry Manilow and his fucking 'Copacabana'.

Long live Killing Joke.

JAZ

Around 1987, I started going to East Germany to study classical music. From there to Minsk and from there to Cairo, and then I found a Hungarian master. I was going hell for leather.

THE COURTAULD INSTITUTE OF ART
19 September 1987,
London, UK

ANDY MACPHERSON

I was at Courtauld, which few can say – 30 or 40, if memory serves. Don't recall a great deal about it apart from feeling uncomfortable and out of place. I was unemployed but managed to get together enough for the return bus journey and the event. I had a good friend who had moved to Clapton, so I had an armchair to sleep on. Not a very comfy night but I had done a fair bit of sofa-surfing in my time, so no big deal. Got a wash at the sink in the morning (awful London water that doesn't leave you feeling clean) and my mate dropped me off near the flat where the event was.

It wasn't a home. It was some sort of business. Holistic or Chinese medicine or something – can't recall. You had to remove your shoes when entering, which I didn't like as I'd not had a shower. Then up the stairs and we sat in a room with rows of chairs and listened to Jaz talking of permaculture, Gematria and gods, if I recall correctly. And conscious/unconscious thought. Can't say that I got it, to be honest. Apart from the feeling, actually expectation, of impending societal collapse, which I think many of us shared.

At the end, we moved into a kitchen area and Jaz mingled and discussed what had been said. I listened but kept my mouth shut for fear of making a fool of myself. There were eastern-style fingerfoods wrapped in vine leaves, olives. Totally outwith the experience of a wee, unemployed Glasgow punk! I was starving but didn't eat much and shot off as soon as seemed reasonable! The main thing I took away was 'whit' – Glaswegian for WTF in a puzzled manner!

Oh, and I paid a fiver and signed up to something – ODIC [Order of the Distant Island Charter]? I think I got two typed letters and never heard anything again. Actually, I think I had to chase to even get those as they appeared to have 'lost' my details. Usual shambles!

NEIL BURKDOLL

When Metallica released their *Garage Days Re-Revisited* album, they covered 'The Wait' and I instantly recognised it and played it for my Dad. That made him get the original [Killing Joke] album out and I ended up recording it to a cassette tape for myself to listen to. I've always loved the production and performances of that first album, as there is a personality and atmosphere that is unique to that very album. I do enjoy and own almost everything KJ has released. Although 'A New Day' is my favourite song of theirs, the original S/T album is my favourite full length.

ERIC SOLIS

I crossed paths with Metallica's *$5.98 EP – Garage Days Re-Revisited*. Although it is a wonderfully curated collection of covers, it was 'The Wait' that immediately intrigued me. The music's frantic urgency felt like a missive from the future and the song quickly became my favourite track on the EP, though I'd yet to hear the original. It also didn't hurt that the song's original recording artists had a great handle – Killing Joke – and that the names listed in the liner notes sounded vaguely Droog-like and unapologetically English: Jaz Coleman. Geordie Walker. Martin Glover. Paul Ferguson.

Unfortunately, late-Eighties San Antonio, Texas, wasn't exactly the bleeding edge for alternative music. In short, mainstream radio was king. There were some independent record stores near downtown, but for a kid of limited means, living deep in the suburbs and too young to drive, those stores may as well have been on Mars.

CHRIS BRYANS

Released during the summer of 1988, Outside the Gate was the much-delayed, fan-dividing, critically savaged follow-up to Brighter Than a Thousand Suns. The music weeklies were not kind, dismissing it as "pompous melodrama", with Geordie's guitar "criminally muted".

GEORDIE

Oh, God. I knew it [*Outside the Gate*] was gonna be shit when I got involved. You just kinda knew.

We were nine months in that little studio. Well, it was a lovely walk down the King's Road. Stop at the deli, pork pies, baby beetroots, Worcester sauce. Then down Old Church Street, past the Manolo Blahnik shop and, tucked away, this really nice little studio. Think I went on holiday in the middle of it. I should have pulled the plug on it in retrospect.

BIG PAUL

This was to be his [Jaz's] solo project, but then Geordie got involved and then, when the budget went way over, they started calling it a KJ project, excluding Raven and myself. I recorded the drums with Geordie to the guitar only, no click, no keyboards, I just hated it. Sounded good to us until the keys got mixed back in and, of course, they were perfectly quantized, so the timing was all over the place. I'm told. I never listened to it again. I just left. You want this? You've got it. A very tough period in my life. Jaz and I were completely at odds.

YOUTH

They'd fallen out in a particularly violent way.

CHRIS BRYANS

In the aftermath, did you think you were done with Killing Joke, even done with music completely?

BIG PAUL

Music? No.
Killing Joke? For sure.

1988–1992

"The struggle is long
The struggle is hard
The struggle is beautiful"

The Extremities… line-up, snapped at Martin Atkins' Invisible Records studio in Bridgeport, Chicago, spring 1990 © Bobby Talamine

YOUTH

I went to Goa in '89. In '90/'91 I got a house there. I was living there six months of the year. Then I started experimenting with LSD again. I'd done the work, I'd studied shamanic traditions, mystery-school tradition and understood what I'd gone through. I'd done a lot of work on myself, built my ego into a stronger, more authentic person than I was before, for sure.

I got plugged into the mains of the cosmic machinery of the universe. I could do weird shit but didn't know really how to handle it, but it sent me on my path.

LUC TIRONNEAU

Never did I give up on KJ, even if I distanced myself a little more from the album *Outside the Gate* and gave up buying it (sorry, mates!).

MATTHIAS RICH

I liked *Outside the Gate* but felt a sense that maybe the best days of the band had already been heard. The razor edges seemed a bit blunted by synthesisers.

MANFRED ROLEF

Brighter Than a Thousand Suns became my most loved album of the time. In the next years, I discovered the whole catalogue and saw them regular play live in Bonn and Cologne. In 1988, I bought a two-day festival ticket in Bonn. On the first day, a billboard outside the venue announced, "Killing Joke gig is cancelled because the band split up." Quite a shock to me.

BIG PAUL

I left the country and pursued other projects... and day-jobs. I went to LA first, as any self-respecting British musician did in the Eighties. Didn't like it much. But I got a gig with Warrior Soul in NYC and that was a better fit, at least the place was. I put another band together with a mate who was once in the Banshees. We were called Crush. Then there was Murder Inc. and a brief stint with The Orb.

I worked in a junk shop for a couple of years before the serious business of sculpture restoration. That did give me focus on skills under-utilised.

That was also when I first learned welding and started a sculptural furnishings business. Blacksmithing was a by-product and, since I no longer have a place to do that, I've taken to Boneyard to get my pyrotechnic kick.

2013 – Mont Sherar and Big Paul in the latter's forge in New York © Mont Sherar

CLIFF MONK LIVINGSTON

How I became a fan of Killing Joke – I was listening to WRSU FM in New Brunswick, NJ, Rutgers College radio in the early Eighties. They were playing the 'Birds of a Feather' single and I loved it so much I bought the *Revelations* record. It hooked me.

Martin Atkins moved to my home town in New Brunswick when he left PiL. He used to come see our bands play at a rock club called the Court Tavern. We became friends. His band Lunar Bear Ensemble played at our wedding reception. On our honeymoon (October 1988), Ivy and I went to London, England. We were walking by a fish and chip shop. We decided to go in. Martin Atkins was sitting in the back, eating dinner. He invited us to a Killing Joke rehearsal the following day.

We got to hear them play *Extremities...* songs in their formative stages. They rehearsed in total darkness. No lights on.

On their tea break, we got to play for them. It was great.

They played 'The Pandys Are Coming' by my request and it was fucking brilliant. We got a few newsletters from the fan club called ODIC and autographed pictures from the guys and pictures of us from the London rehearsal, from Martin.

Right to left: Cliff, Ivy, Geordie and Jaz © Martin Atkins

BURBERRIES
18 December 1988,
Birmingham, UK

IAN ORGAN

Saw them frequently in the Eighties, notably a small gig in a nightclub – 200 fans max, no stage – an awesome close gig!

PORCHESTER HALL
22 December 1988,
London, UK

DAZ BROWN

Billed as a midwinter party with food and punch for members of the Order of the Distant Island Charter, this was for Killing Joke's then fan-base.

If memory serves, this was one of two private gigs, the other being held in Sheffield. They were the first gigs by the band since the *BTaTS* tour back in '86.

As I made my way to the venue, an eclectic mix of individuals were already queuing outside the front doors. Black leather was the order of the day and neither Santa nor his reindeers could be found. The Porchester Hall had indeed been taken over by a much more powerful, darker force...

Standing at the top of the grand staircase inside the main lobby was the man himself, dressed in a black pinstripe suit and gold lamé waistcoat. His black overcoat draped over his shoulders like a reluctant businessman. Jaz Coleman mingled with all the members of ODIC and greeted each one of us like we were old long-lost friends. That wide-eyed gaze and the sound of manic laughter blended in with the smell of incense that had already filled the air.

The majority of the punters seemed bemused that the band were so grateful and generous. Any thoughts of pretentiousness had been clearly left at home. A rock star world this was not.

As I made my way into the grand hall, it appeared that the place was about half-full. This, though, did not dampen my spirits, as something inside me knew that, even though it was not a sell out, THE RIGHT PEOPLE WERE THERE.

I made my way to the bar, which consisted mainly of cans of lager served by two girls – one dressed as a buxom wench and the other a jester who went by the name of Claudine.

A banquet of poppadoms, samosas and various Middle Eastern food was complimentary.

Dressed in a black roll-neck sweater and dark jeans, Geordie casually mingled with the guests. A packet of Rothmans in one hand and a bottle of Southern Comfort in the other. The other two members of the band I didn't recognise. I later found out that the new drummer was ex-PiL man Martin Atkins while the new bassist was a session man known as Taif Ball.

Our master of ceremonies for the night was Jaz, who went on to introduce the support acts, consisting of both Talvin Singh and The Voice of Morocco. Both artists may seem a strange choice when set in a post-punk environment. Believe me, it was. It felt like the end of the world was looming and was about to start in Marrakech via Bayswater.

Jaz had spent time chatting with a couple of young punks, one sporting an 'Empire Song' jester tattoo on his forearm. "Great detail," said Jaz and continued to examine the piece with intense admiration. He thanked them for coming out then casually turned around. I remember thinking this was my moment...

I hadn't met Jaz before. I'd read many things in the music press about him and thought most of it to be just plausible bollocks. As the late, great Lou Reed once said – believe half of what you see and none of what you hear.

I tapped him on the shoulder and cleared my throat. "When does your book come out?" I asked enthusiastically. He turned around and I can only describe the meeting as one of absolute sincerity. I knew I was talking to an individual that gives 150% into everything he does. His stare seemed to go right through me as if reading the very soul of this, then-19-year-old northern lad. I wasn't used to meeting any of my heroes and I really didn't know whether to get out my prayer mat and pray to the west or shit myself right there and then.

We chatted for a few minutes and he said he couldn't wait to get back on the live circuit and that the next album would be a far cry from the last one. Back to our roots, he said.

With that, he was off, and it was time for the intense spectacle known as Killing Joke to take to the stage.

When Jaz said "Back to our roots", he wasn't kidding. New tracks were showcased. 'Extremities', 'The Fanatic', 'Intravenous' and 'The Beautiful Dead' were played, alongside many tracks from their back-catalogue. Everything seemed fresh and angry. The members of ODIC were not disappointed. The levels of intensity were on the rise again and I remember thinking that the next album would be a corker. It was.

Outside the Gate seemed a distant memory.

Killing Joke was back. They were pissed off. Really pissed off. The following album, 1990's *Extremities, Dirt and Various Repressed Emotions*, proved this. I was fortunate enough to be at two further gigs during this period in the band's long history – Finsbury Park and Brixton Academy – and both gigs were just as intense.

22 December 1988 was indeed a very special, albeit bizarre, evening, one that only Killing Joke would do.

MARK BROWNE

Well, I've seen Killing Joke over the years too many times to count. But my standout memory was the fan-club gig they did at Porchester Hall in London, where Jaz was compère for the night. Me and my mates attended, and it was probably one of the poshest places I've ever seen a gig in. I remember we had food included and they were serving up a punch from big plastic dustbins from behind the bar, all included in the ticket price. It was very surreal seeing all these old punks sitting around drinking and eating pitta bread and dips, etc. If you look on YouTube, somebody has posted some footage – best Joke gig ever in my opinion.

DAVID GRIEVE

Buffet food and Middle Eastern music and, of course, the first we'd heard of *Extremities...* My clearest memory, however, was standing near the front of the queue in the cold beyond the time the doors should have opened. There was lots of good-natured grumbling going on. The next minute, Jaz and Geordie came out to apologise for the delay and to assure us we'd be in soon. They wandered down the queue for a few minutes chatting and then went back in, soon followed by the rest of us. It was a nice touch and a memorable event in what was a memorable evening anyway.

PAUL RANGECROFT

My obsession with Killing Joke began in the late Eighties – and the blame lies squarely with my younger brother's friend, James Farquharson, who lived down the street. He was a big fan and would inflict it upon us whenever he got the chance. Being into Nik Kershaw and Howard Jones, I would arrogantly maintain it was terrible, but some of Geordie's hooks must have penetrated my subconscious, because, after a while, I started playing a tape of *Night Time* that was lying around. It wasn't long before I revised my opinion somewhat and concluded this was the greatest music ever written.

The first album I bought was *Outside the Gate*, which I really loved at the time. Soon, the back-catalogue was purchased and, although it took me a while to acquire the taste for the darker earlier stuff, there was 'no way out but forward go'.

DREAM DIARY EXCERPTS
5 February 1989,
Chicago, USA

MICHE MARCISZ

I first met Killing Joke in a series of dreams! I was in a private room with Jaz and Geordie. Killing Joke were playing that night. They were talking and I watched and listened. They were moving pieces on a table. The room was the stage behind a heavy red curtain. The curtain was swaying into my back and I thought Jaz would get annoyed with me. I kept apologising. Jaz seemed as though he was very calm, but I was still expecting him to get violent. Whilst Jaz and Geordie were discussing, Jaz looked at a ring I had on. He took my hand and scratched at it and smiled (in a warm and friendly way). His staring eyes assured me we were friends. The curtain began swaying harder and the figures toppled a little. But none of this bothered Jaz. He kept the kind smile. The concert time was getting closer, so I looked for my camera. I couldn't find it.

BERKELEY SQUARE
18 April 1989,
California, USA

MICHAEL GARCIA

Years ago, I hosted a dance club at a now-gone club in Berkeley, CA, called The Berkeley Square. It was a very small venue, but many up-and-coming bands played there. My own band played there numerous times in the Eighties and early Nineties. I was there when Killing Joke did a small tour and played there. This is when Martin [Atkins] and Taif [Ball] were the rhythm section. Well, after the show, they were backstage and I wandered back towards the offices and decided to pop in and say hello. Jaz must have been doing something naughty because he popped up with a 'deer in the headlights' look. I made some small chat with them and then started talking to Geordie. "So, are you recording any new material?" I asked. "Yes, we're in the middle of something right now and it's going to be a blinder." Or something to that effect. At this point, I had forgot about how many drinks I had in me. My reply to him (with Jaz sitting next to him, listening intently) – "Well, that's good news because that last album [*Outside the Gate*] fucking sucked!" The look on Jaz's face was priceless and Geordie let out a massive laugh. To this day, my friend reminds me that I had the nerve to tell them that. We still get a good laugh out of it.

✦ ✦ ✦

RUTGERS COLLEGE
4 July 1989,
New Brunswick, USA

CLIFF MONK LIVINGSTON

The *Extremities...* tour, an outdoor concert by the river. Ivy and I and our long-haired German Shepherd Flash (we brought him to the concert). We walked up to the tour bus. Jaz invited us in. We brought Flash on to the bus. Geordie loved the dog and they made friends. We visited with Killing Joke on the tour bus while watching the opening act, the Red Hot Chili Peppers.

When Killing Joke played, it was epic. Fireworks going off and everything.

Mont Sherar and Geordie. Says Mont: "Martin is on the phone speaking to Al Jourgensen about joining Ministry!" © Mont Sherar

✦ ✦ ✦

THE KITCHEN CLUB
1989,
Miami Beach, USA

MONT SHERAR

I'd first meet the band on a personal level in 1989 during their *Extremities...* tour, providing them with free food and lodging in the hotel/nightclub I was DJing at, The Kitchen Club on Miami Beach. Skinny Puppy were staying on the same floor, and Martin Atkins turned down Blondie to play with Ministry on their upcoming tour.

Geordie has been quoted as saying, "One of my favourite gigs of all time was on Miami Beach [1 August 1989]. There weren't many people there, but they were the right people." All kinds of musical history that will never be repeated.

That marked the beginning of the close, personal bond with the band I've had to this very day. In fact, it was because of talks with Jaz during that time that I decided to pack it up and move to Europe at the end of

Killing Joke and members of Skinny Puppy at The Kitchen Club, 1989. Mont Sherar calls this image 'The Last Supper'. Left to right: Martin Atkins, Dwayne Goettel, cEvin Key, Mont Sherar, Jaz Coleman, Geordie Walker © Mont Sherar

that year – despite being at the height of my DJ career, both financially and in popularity. I guess you could call it my Iceland moment (!), except I never returned and have been living in Denmark ever since.

COLIN MURDY

I was first introduced to Killing Joke via a friend who was a lot older than myself. He had the band's name tattooed on his upper left arm, and that's how it began as I asked him who this Killing Joke band were. Moments later, we cracked open a Mexican beer and he proceeded to put on their seminal debut album...

The stinging opening synth chords of 'Requiem' rang in the air and, from that moment forward, I was absolutely hooked. It was 1989 and I was 15.

© *Mont Sherar*

✦ ✦ ✦

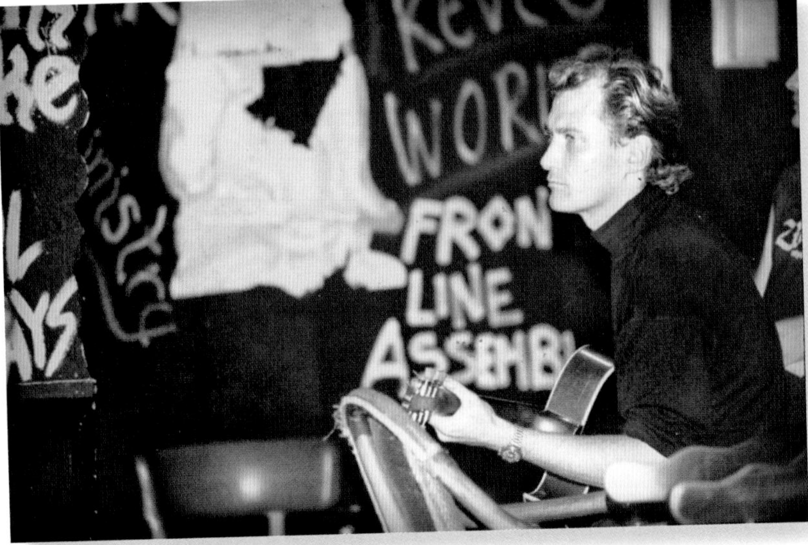

© *Mont Sherar*

THE CAT CLUB
15 August 1989,
New York, USA

ALEX SMITH

As it worked out, I didn't get to actually see Killing Joke in the flesh for several years. They did not tour the States for the latter half of the Eighties, during which time the band broadened its approach to embrace to a more stately, elegiac sound, only to give way during the recording of what had ostensibly been conceived as a Jaz Coleman solo album, *Outside the Gate*. While I, too, had been left puzzled by that record's abysmal detour, I dutifully kept the faith, so to speak.

In the summer of 1989, I finally got my chance, when the band returned to New York City in suitably feral form. Now boasting the kinetic Martin Atkins of Public Image Ltd/Brian Brain behind the kit and a Welsh bass player named simply Taif, Killing Joke were slated to play a comparatively intimate venue in Manhattan's East 13th Street dubbed The Cat Club, ostensibly a heavy-metal venue that normally played host to fledgling local bands like Circus of Power, Raging Slab and a bedraggled foursome called White Zombie.

Anticipation for the gig was high. Everybody who was anybody in New York's rock circles was in attendance. I remember spotting a couple of members of proto-New York hardcore stalwarts Kraut amid the throng, while in a booth behind my friend Rob and I sat Handsome Dick Manitoba of The Dictators alongside the inimitably towering personage of Joey Ramone. It was the event of the season.

The lights dimmed, and through the smoke — you could still smoke in New York City clubs back then — Jaz Coleman assumed the stage with his face wrapped in a keffiyeh scarf, not unlike the one famously sported by Yasser Arafat. Shortly joined by manfully louche Geordie, Martin and Taif, proceeding to launch into a suitably menacing airing of 'The Fall of Because'. All remaining doubts as to the mystique, majesty and staying power of Killing Joke were decimated in seconds.

In the ensuing decades, I went on to see Killing Joke perform multiple times in both New York and London, and — in my dubious capacity as an ersatz music journalist – was fortunate enough to interview Jaz, Geordie, Raven, Martin, Youth and Big Paul Ferguson. At some point in the very late Nineties, I joined an online cabal of similarly besotted KJ acolytes dubbed The Gathering and forged several lasting friendships. To this day, friends and family stare at me quizzically about my seeming unending passion for all things Killing Joke. I usually just have to rattle off some well-worn explainer that throws them off the scent, but the stark truth of the matter is that hold that Killing Joke established on my psyche one spring afternoon in 1984 has never relinquished. This is more than simple music fandom, and — much like the band itself — it suggests larger, tantalisingly intangible forces at work. I do not resist.

MARTIN PLÄTTNER

I started listening to Killing Joke in the late Eighties, as I'm a fan of Canadian progressive thrash metal band Voivod. Members of Voivod wore KJ t-shirts and were greatly influenced by Killing Joke in their music. So I started listening to *Fire Dances* and *What's THIS for...!* I love all their albums, including *Outside the Gate*. *Brighter Than a Thousand Suns* is a very good album when you have lovesickness.

YOUTH

That's the great thing with Killing Joke – you get a lot of metalheads love KJ. And then you get all the indie dance kids loving us. There's weird polarity in the fanbase.

MARTIN PLÄTTNER

I wish Killing Joke and Voivod would tour together one time.

✦ ✦ ✦

FESTIVAL FOR LIFE
30 March 1990,
Geneva, Switzerland

PAUL RANGECROFT

A little advert appeared in one of the music papers for some obscure anti-drugs event (is that ironic? I'll let you decide) called the Festival for Life in Geneva, Switzerland – and Killing Joke would be headlining.

Flight and hotel booked – off I went into the unknown. I managed to purchase a ticket at a record store and located the venue. I remember the organisers shaking my hand when they found out how far I travelled! The crowd was pretty small, but enthusiastic, and it was a great gig. I was delirious seeing my heroes perform all these amazing songs, which I already loved but sounded a thousand times better live.

I enjoyed building up my collection, scouring the record fairs and beating [fellow Gatherer] Jon Chapman to the latest rarities to be listed in *Record Collector* magazine (no internet back then). Killing Joke were really a great band to collect, because there were so many B-sides, remixes, non-album singles, live bootlegs, sessions and so on. Not to mention the posters, t-shirts and newspaper cuttings. I drove the staff at Cambridge University library nuts with constant requests for old copies of the *NME*, *Melody Maker* and *Sounds* to be retrieved from the archive.

SIMON BARRINGTON

Fast-forward to spring 1990. By now, music was just about the most important thing in my life. At this stage, I was regularly taking long walks around Billericay after A-level work/revision during half-term/holidays, listening to stuff on my not-so-trusty cassette Walkman. I recall wandering about one time listening to the Sisters [of Mercy] album, thinking it was pretty decent. My Walkman wasn't the best and a rewind of a whole side of C90 cassette would threaten a) battery life, but more importantly b) a complete spooling crisis. So I flipped it over. The cassette had no box, I recall, and no markings on the cassette itself to indicate what might be on there. It started up. Driving drums. Kinda funky bass. Sometimes soaring, sometimes chugging guitar. A bit eerie. "Hmm, sounds good. Sounds a bit like that 'Love like Blood' song from a few years back." Second track. Bit slower, atmospheric, quiet build-up. Wow! Awesome guitar in the chorus, kinda weirdly like a firework display. "This guitarist is amazing. Sounds a bit like that 'Love like Blood' song from a few years back." Third track. I was at the bottom of Horace Road and turned on to Stock Road, heading for the High Street. Highly strung minor-key hum from a synth; a few tumbling drums; HANG ON – THERE'S THAT GUITAR! IT IS 'LOVE LIKE BLOOD'!

The rest of the C90 side flew by. It was awesome. It must be whatever album 'Love Like Blood' was from. A bit of research later, I'd confirmed it was *Night Time*.

Well, that was it. The next week I was in Chelmsford market and picked up the 'Requiem'/'Change' 12-inch. Before the year was out, I'd got 'Money Is Not Our God', the *Extremities...* LP, the first album, and *Revelations* and *Brighter...* cassettes.

MATTHIAS BOSENICK

My first contact with Killing Joke was on the school bus in 1990. A friend had an older brother who was a little more culturally alternative than we were. On the friend's Walkman, we heard, each with a headphone in one ear, a tape that the older brother administered to him. For me, these were new worlds.

I still remember how surprised I was – as a pop listener – how great and exciting I found the non-pop music on the tape. Unfortunately, I remember only three songs: 'Los Niños del Parque' by Liaisons Dangereuses and two songs that initiated collections: 'Like a Hurricane' by The Mission and 'Love Like Blood' by Killing Joke. The classic and still the biggest hit that still works in clubs. Great, but, as I soon found out, not the best thing about Killing Joke.

The trigger for me from then on was to collect all the singles, albums, samplers and everything else from Killing Joke and celebrate them for the range of styles a band can have: post-punk, dub, pop, classical, metal, goa, ambient, NWoBHM, punk, avant-garde, Arabic folk.

✦ ✦ ✦

DREAM DIARY EXCERPTS
5 April 1990,
Chicago, USA

MICHE MARCISZ

I was in the lobby of an estate owned by Killing Joke. I was looking at objects, old, large books. I was really enjoying it. Jaz noticed me and came up behind me and asked if I was interested in astrology. Yes. And I became his friend. A 'part' of Killing Joke.

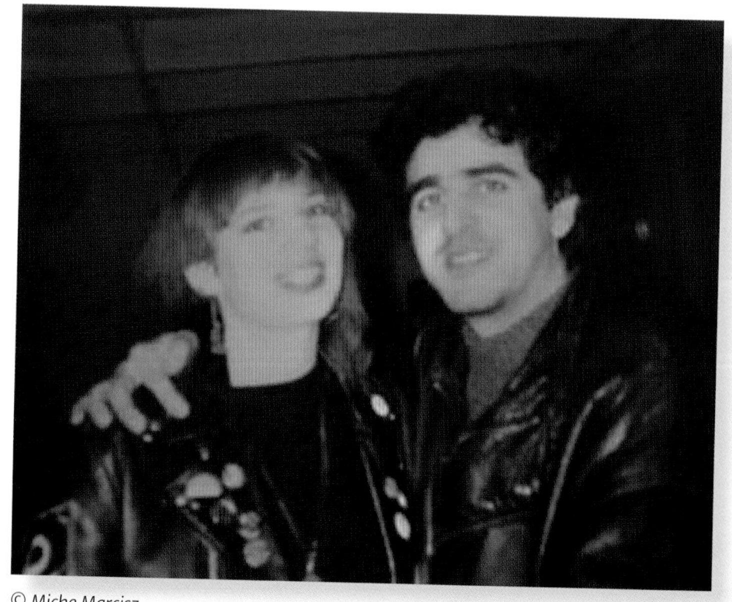

© Miche Marcisz

BOBBY TALAMINE

I'm a professional music photographer based out of Chicago, Illinois. I've been a Killing Joke fan for years and years, photographing the band since way back when. First got involved directly with Killing Joke back in 1990, courtesy of then Killing Joke drummer Martin Atkins. Martin needing pose photography and promo photography for their upcoming release, *Extremities, Dirt and Various Repressed Emotions*, at Invisible Records in Chicago.

We hit it off awesomely then and have been involved with Killing Joke off and on ever since.

I was the hired still photographer for the production of the video for 'Money Is Not Our God', when it was being filmed live at the Metro Chicago.

I consider Killing Joke one of my favourite bands of all time and have been honoured to be in their presence and contribute in some capacity over the past decades.

JOHN BECHDEL

(sound/technical support Extremities, Dirt and Various Repressed Emotions; live keyboards)

My time was kinda brief. Summer of '90 recording and we spent early '91 touring and summer touring. By Fall, the Murder Inc. thing was happening.

It was my first time in England. The first thing that struck me was how early everything closed. Being in New York – the city that never sleeps – by the time we were done with rehearsing and I was on my way home, all the shops were closed. The pubs were shutting down.

It was really hot that summer. When I first arrived, it was maybe late June. Shortly after that, it began to get very hot in London and I remember the city was just filled with pollution. I found it hard to even breathe at times.

New Killing Joker John Bechdel at the Townhouse Studios in London © John Bechdel

Was I a fan of Killing Joke beforehand? Absolutely, yes.

A small group of like-minded friends in high school, we travelled to the nearest cultural centre, State College, PA. As a college town, it had many record stores. One particular store, Record Revolution, had a guy following all this great music that was mostly coming out of England. Bands like OMD, Human League, Cabaret Voltaire, The Cure and Joy Division. One of the bands we discovered was Killing Joke.

I still remember the very first time I heard 'Requiem'. It altered my brain chemistry. It defined who I am. That pulsating synthesiser just resonated through my mind, and then, when the guitar came in, it just melted. In some ways, we had never really heard that modulation effect on the vocals. That alone made Killing Joke stand out.

They used synthesisers, but not in a melodic way. They had much more of an atmosphere-based style. I later found out that they were using the Oberheim OBX.

Much, much later, I was part of Brian Brain. The band wasn't really doing much and I hadn't talked to Martin [Atkins, front man in Brian Brain and former drummer in PiL] in a while. So I called our guitarist and asked: "What's going? Are we still a band?" And he said, "Martin joined Killing Joke." That blew my mind.

When Killing Joke came over to rehearse for the pre-*Extremities...* tour, they were rehearsing in Hoboken. Martin invited me over. I hopped on my bicycle and pedalled my way over. That's when I met the band. I'd never seen the band play.

In those days, there was so much mystique about Killing Joke. We didn't know anything. Those records just said KILLING JOKE. No pictures, no names, who does what. I didn't even really know what they looked like. I told Martin that, if these guys ever want or need a keyboard player, I would be totally down with that.

All the shows in the NY area I went to. One night [13 August 1989], I got a call from Martin, saying they were playing CBGBs that night. I was almost going to pass on that one. But I ended up going. It was a great show. I was so into it. I was front and centre.

Right before the song 'The Beautiful Dead', Jaz made a long speech about how drum machines and samplers were killing music, that it wasn't real, it was sterile and lacks soul.

[As a keyboardist/sampler] I started to get upset. After that concert, Martin said there was an after-show at the Mission.

Inside, Jaz said to me, "Let's go get some drinks." We pushed our way up to the bar. That was the moment I was going to tell him about my feelings about the stuff he was saying.

As he ordered the drinks, he said to me he was thinking he would like for me to be the touring keyboard player.

I shut my mouth.

I was kinda shocked. I never actually said: "Yes."

I walked out of there thinking: "I think I just joined Killing Joke."

A year went by. Jaz was doing the record with Anne Dudley [*Songs from the Victorious City*]. They were still putting a deal together to record the [*Extremities...*] album.

I got a call from Jaz.

I bought a one-way ticket to London. I was 25-years-old.

Really, it was all about the *Extremities...* material at that time. I thought: "This is do or die." At the same time, I couldn't think about being nervous. I didn't have time to be nervous. All I knew was that this was my chance. I took all the energy and focus that I had. Geordie and Martin started playing ['The Beautiful Dead'] and I stepped up. I didn't fully appreciate Geordie's genius until I was working with the band.

It was hard work. When we were working on 'Intravenous', Jaz said: "Throw away your notes. Just feel it, just feel it. Stop trying to count it." It was like one of those moments in *Star Wars*: "Use The Force, Luke. Switch off your targeting computer." And I did and that worked for me. Once I 'felt' it, I got it.

I learned a lot. I really came into it thinking I knew their music and I would learn the songs really quickly. I came in very confident, but my confidence was shaken, shaken to the core. I was really stripped down to my core. I almost walked away. I thought: "Maybe this isn't for me."

But then I thought: "Here you are. This is what you've always wanted. This is probably your all-time favourite band in the whole wide world. And this is a tremendous opportunity. And, if you go home now, you might never ever get over it."

Jaz at the Townhouse during the recording of Extremities, Dirt and Various Repressed Emotions
© John Bechdel

What am I going to say to people? "I had the opportunity of a lifetime and I walked away from it"?

After I prepared for a good two months at home, practising every day, we were beginning the official *Extremities...* tour. We were rehearsing in Chicago. The one song that had been plaguing me all along was 'Extremities'.

It had to be just right. It wasn't just random. Jaz would always play it when we rehearsed so I never really got much of a chance to practise it. Dave [Kovacevic, keyboardist] showed it to me. The way Dave did it made it look much easier, so I started to get it. I knew that was one of my biggest challenges.

We did a summer tour of Europe opening for the Pixies [June 1991]. The big arena crowds. It was intense, really intense. We were playing [at] supersonic speeds. I got to start 'Requiem'. I thought: "This is it." I practised these songs in the bedroom in smalltown rural Pennsylvania as a teenager and here I am in an arena and on stage and playing 'Requiem' with Killing Joke.

There was a lot of difficult times but there was a lot of great reward. Everybody had to have an initiation.

It was in the end a monumental experience. I was now the guy from Killing Joke.

I never had to audition for a gig again.

Birthday card for John Bechdel, 23 August 1990. Note that Taskmaster Coleman apologetically signs himself as "Jaz (The Bastard)" © John Bechdel

YOUTH

That [*Extremities...*] actually is a good album. They really started honing the industrial edge. Weirdly enough, I was upstairs recording Bananarama's album *Pop Life* while they were recording *Extremities...* in the basement. We overlapped for a couple of weeks. I saw Raven once.

✦ ✦ ✦

DREAM DIARY EXCERPTS
21 November 1990,
Chicago, USA

MICHE MARCISZ

I met Jaz at a party. He was so willing to talk to me. We talked about his book and his classical music. Sandy was there (my friend). She took some photos. Me and Jaz were sitting at a bar counter. When they left, I asked for one more photo with Jaz.

✦ ✦ ✦

EDGE OF THE LOOKING GLASS
19 December 1990,
Chicago, USA

MICHE MARCISZ

The real meeting happened thus: *Extremities, Dirt and Various Repressed Emotions* album-release party at Edge of the Looking Glass bar, Chicago. The first person I met was Raven! "Hello, I'm Paul." What a kind voice he had. Geordie was elsewhere. Martin was in a far corner, in pain. He had just scratched his cornea. Yikes! Then I saw Jaz across the room.

I moved closer by the bar. He must've sensed I was in the room because Al Jourgensen suddenly stopped talking to him and moved away. At that moment, something PUSHED me, and I walked up to him. When he looked at me, I felt the same assurance I experienced in the dreams. The feeling of a connection. He gestured for us to sit down at the table. "Hi, Jaz. I've had these dreams that we'd meet..." We talked of astrology, his book, the upcoming radio interview my DJ friend, Joe, was going to do with the band on [radio station] WZRD, his classical music, the upcoming New Year's Eve show at the Vic [Theatre], my 3D photos and how I wished for a photo pass for the show, and magick.

So, when did I consider myself a Gatherer? When I started meeting people at their shows that were like me: fanatical. But not as in talking only about the music, but the bond: the energy levels experienced, the dreams, the synchronicities we all had in common, the urgency when we heard they'd be playing in another part of the world and we HAD to be there despite all odds. We'd visualise it, then be there! Noticeable things would fall into place (often, when I'm looking at flights, a Killing Joke song will come on. This is no coincidence). And especially when I attended the 1992 Holland Park Lectures in London and in 1994 when I followed the band on the *Pandemonium* tour through the UK. This is when the family aspect became real.

MATTHIAS RICH

I'd just picked up my cassette of *Extremities*.... My GOD! Talk about a creative U-turn! It blew my mind. To me, this was a new Killing Joke: bold and brazen, full of savage honesty, a reflection of society with nothing held back. I listened hard. It was like a psychic weather forecast for the times to come, equally terrifying and exhilarating. From here on in, I made sure that any and all future Killing Joke releases were a day-one purchase.

✦ ✦ ✦

HOLLYWOOD PALLADIUM
30 December 1990,
Hollywood, USA

ROMEO PESTANAS, JR.

X concert with Killing Joke opening. There's not really much anyone can say about this show. The line-up speaks for itself! I'm just glad I was a witness to two great bands in one night!

TOM PAYNE

At the release of *Extremities...* in 1990, there was a number to call to get more info. Anyhow, I rang the number and Jaz himself answered the call! They had an office above a recording studio in Putney where they were rehearsing for the *Extremities...* tour with Martin Atkins in the drum seat and the short-lived Andy Rourke on bass, subsequently fired. Personally, I couldn't see how a member of The Smiths could be in a band like Killing Joke!

Anyhow, Jaz invited me down and, of course, I bunked off work and spent three days with them! What a time.

Jaz and I became mates and I went to his house in Notting Hill for dinner and met up a few times at a restaurant near the British Museum (he was always late).

I ended up in New York at the same time they were touring there and spent time with them there, too. They were a lot of fun to spend time with.

Access all areas for all gigs! Brixton Academy; NYC (can't recall venue but could have been The Ritz); somewhere up north for Geordie's 30th birthday, etc, etc.

I knew this guy at the time whose very wealthy father owned a stretch of the River Test and I took Geordie and his partner fly-fishing there. Other than music, fishing was his passion and probably still is.

We had to move to another part of the river as it was clear we had no idea what we were doing, and Geordie did. Very funny at the time. He thought we were idiots, although we got on well.

GEORDIE

That was a lovely day. My son was conceived on Kensington Church Street the night before. [We] all pile up there: me, the wife, Tom Payne, his girlfriend and another mate. Brandy hangover, Remy hangover. This beautiful ancient manor house. The water crystal-clear. Tom just slams the line down. About 16 trout just scatter. Fucking fish-scarer.

I hop this fence up to this beautiful hill up to a stately home, sheep grazing. Get into some brambles, got the brandy-sweat hangover coming. I suddenly come out – a tree-canopied stretch, dappled sunlight. You could see the trout feeding. I pulled five out of there. I'd just fished Prince Charles' stretch. Fantastic.

ANDY SEWELL

My first exposure to Killing Joke completely opened my musical horizons. It was sometime in 1990 or 1991, my first year away from home at college. At this time, I was a young metalhead and something of a purist. If it wasn't heavy and fast, I wasn't interested. I also listened to punk rock and Public Enemy, so I wasn't a total metal snob. One night, I was hanging out in a friend's dorm and he pulled out the *Night Time* album on cassette. "You ever listen to these guys?" My world changed. How was it possible to make such atmospheric music while retaining a darkness and intensity? I quickly acquired my own copy and that cassette became my de facto night music for driving around the Detroit suburbs. I felt an instant connection, a sense that it was a secret and cool to be in the world of this music.

I scoured CD shops for more music and managed to find *Fire Dances*, *What's THIS for...!*, *Extremities, Dirt and Various Repressed Emotions*, and the *BBC in Concert* live album.

✦ ✦ ✦

LE GLOB
11 January 1991,
Lyon, France

STEPHANE BONGINI
(aka Frenchy Frenzy)

In 1991, I had the opportunity to see the band for the first time and I didn't know what to expect because the internet didn't exist. That reinforced the mysterious side, but I will always remember for a long time the slap I received during this concert in my own city, Lyon, at the club Le Glob just after the Gulf War started. I didn't expect so much energy and brutality: I was blown away by the live power of the band.

1994 – the album *Pandemonium*: a magnificent concert in Paris Elysée Montmartre and then [22 May] 1996 – one of the rare concerts of the *Democracy* tour, in Lyon.

INTERNATIONAL 2
26 January 1991,
Manchester, UK

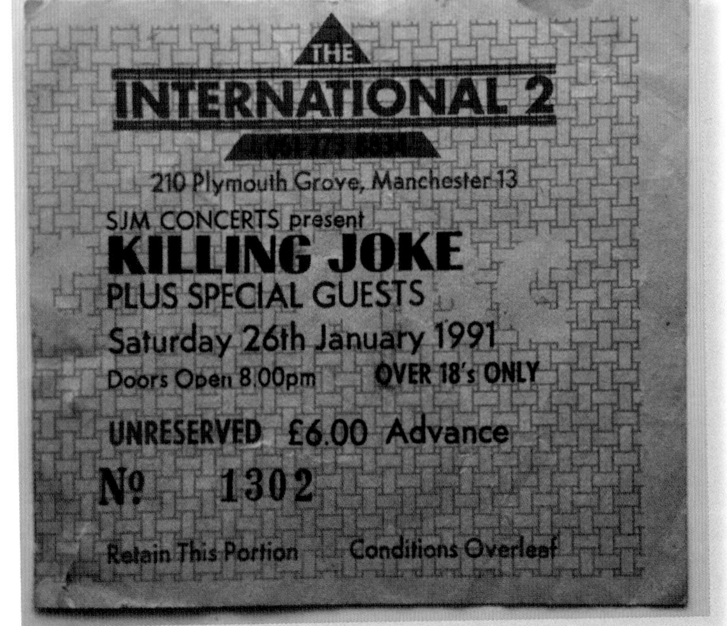

ALIM HAIDER

Being obsessed by Ultravox from the age 13, I would watch *Top of the Pops* and video the show. I videoed everything that they were on. Killing Joke came on one show with 'Love Like Blood'. It stuck in my mind. Humming it for weeks.

However, I never bought it for a few months – until I was on the No.50 bus coming back from town and Paul Gallagher was on. He was a massive Smiths and PiL fan. He later became known as the big brother of Liam and Noel. We got off and went to Mr Sifters Records in Burnage, a second-hand record shop. It was the centre of Burnage for us. We attacked the racks until we found something, then showed each other. I found *Street Sounds Electro 6* – £2.99. I showed Bod, as he was known.

"Look at this, Bod."

He dismissed it out of hand with an eye-roll. Bod had in his right hand a PiL album and in his left *Night Time*.

"That's not music – fucking clickity-click pop-pop. This is the real music."

Mr Sifter sold me *Night Time* when I was just 16. From that day on, I bought all my KJ vinyl from Pete, the legend of Burnage. Only because HMV was too expensive. But it's cooler to say you shopped in Sifters.

It took a few years before I went to see them – in Manchester, Plymouth Grove – International 2.

We went in – me, my girlfriend (soon to be wife) and a mate into Happy Mondays and the Manchester vibe. The smell of patchouli oil was heavy in the air. It was full of leftover punks.

[There was] no one I knew in the place. We walked in like we had just come from a rave – flares, baggy tops. We stood out like flies on a newly decorated wedding cake.

Feeling a bit out of place, I stood near the merchandising stand. Who should walk through the crowd? None other than Jaz. He walks straight past me. I shout over the sound of speakers blasting out the Roses: "Hey man, can I have your autograph?"

A stare that could melt fucking steel focused on me and said: "I don't carry a pen."

I don't know why I asked. I had no pen and nothing to sign.

He then turned completely different, a warmer person, when he saw he'd pretty much crushed me. He said: "Don't worry. I'll get one and return."

Of course, he didn't. But what a show.

I dumped the Madchester look that night. And went back to Mr Sifters and sold all my Ultravox.

LEE HOLFORD

KJ are back with a bang, 'Money', *Extremities...* – and a tour. I see them three times on this tour [Manchester; Birmingham Institute, 30 January; Birmingham Institute, 24 June). It was INCREDIBLE. So much darker and intense. Seeing them in this revitalised period was almost akin to a religious experience. I proper lost my shit dancing to these sets – exhausting, exhilarating, spellbinding.

SIMON ELLIS

I first got to see them on the *Extremities...* tour. I remember myself and my colleagues went to the now-demolished International 2 at Manchester, a 40-minute trip north from Stoke-on-Trent. I remember it looked like an old bingo hall, slightly in disrepair and in quite a rough neighbourhood.

We paid a pound to park on the car park to have the cars guarded by two burly security guards and a Rottweiler.

This all added to the tension, which inside you could cut with a knife as a full house eagerly anticipated the return of their heroes on the back of a mighty comeback album. I remember purchasing a Mike Coles-designed tour shirt and then taking a quick detour to the gents as my friends went to the bar.

As I traversed down the steep steps to the dank corridor below, Jaz emerged on the stairway. Slightly surprised, I could only utter the words "Good evening!" as he passed on the stairs. "Evening," he replied in a nonchalant manner. I couldn't quite believe I'd just passed my hero only to be somewhat stupidly star-struck.

Back down the front, the lights went down and the intro music played low. However, we must have waited about half an hour, the tension rising and the atmosphere thick with anticipation before the strains of 'Inside the Termite Mound' rang out. The lights hit the stage and Jaz emerged in full war-paint.

The set was immense, topped off with an encore where Martin Atkins threw his drumstick and it literally landed in my outstretched hand. The gig was over, but the audience that night had surely witnessed one of the greatest Killing Joke performances ever.

✦ ✦ ✦

DAKAR
1991
Senegal, West Africa

SIMON SLEATH

On my first visit to West Africa in 1991, I brought recent release *Extremities...* along for company. At first, no album could have seemed more incongruous in the relaxed tropical country of Senegal on the Atlantic Ocean, with its rolling 6/8 rhythms and lilting Islamic-inspired melodies.

Then Saddam Hussein shocked the world by invading Kuwait. TV screens carried images of desert warfare from places suddenly looking a lot like where I found myself, in the capital, Dakar. Oil prices had tumbled, international travel was suspended, and I didn't know if I was now stranded in a majority Muslim country that would turn hostile if the West intervened (I was much more ignorant about Islam then).

The unease and paranoia of *Extremities...* took on a new relevance I had not expected. The oppressive heat and teeming streets of Dakar seemed to accelerate the molecules of songs like 'Intravenous' and 'Slipstream' into a state of greater frenzy and relentlessness. Now feeling isolated and vulnerable, I found comfort in 'Solitude' and "surrendered to the will of God". With my new Muslim friends, we prayed for peace together.

The *Extremities...* album provided the soundtrack for another trip I made – to neighbouring country Guinea-Bissau. I had never seen such huge termite mounds, some about two metres high. One was taking over the Portuguese chapel – colonial splendour abandoned to ruins after communist rebels expelled the Europeans in the Seventies.

In the 2000s, I produced a record of my own in Senegal. Having long considered Geordie to possess the most intriguing guitar technique I've ever heard, I experimented with adapting something of his style to the acoustic guitar and transplanting it to an African setting. I wrote a song loosely inspired by some phrases from 'Adorations' and it led to a record deal with BBC Radio 3.

✦ ✦ ✦

ASTORIA
31 January 1991,
London, UK

MATT TIBBITS

The Gulf War was raging. The *Extremities...* album had grabbed me by the throat from the opening strains of 'Money Is Not Our God'. "They're back!" I took a friend who had heard a few Killing Joke songs but had never seen them live. He was amazed at the intensity of the atmosphere, the sheer visceral power of the music and the churning, turbulent throng all around us. When Jaz said "Israel. Palestine. 'Complications'!" he just looked at me, grinned and shook his head. I don't think he'd ever believed live music could be that relevant and vital. We left the venue utterly energised. As one reviewer put it, it was a relief to see the adjacent buildings still standing. Seeing this normally mild-mannered mate of mine vault the ticket barriers at Leicester Square tube, pumped full of adrenaline, summed it all up for me. Joyous, exhilarating catharsis at a time of extreme tension. No one else comes close.

ADRIAN WASON

Probably the loudest band I'd seen before this was The Stranglers, who were excellent and very tight. There was a lot of hype in the music press at the time about the fallout from *Outside the Gate* and Jaz's *Songs from the Victorious City* project with Anne Dudley, which was released around the summer of 1990. Incredibly, the first track from the album, 'The Awakening', was played on The Steve Wright Show on Radio 1 on a sunny afternoon. Also out at the same time was Youth's remix of Art of Noise tracks – *The Ambient Collection*.

So, I was living in Bath at the time and the main focus of my musical life was waiting for the *Extremities...* album, which I was guessing would sound like *Brighter...* or *Night Time*. I picked up the single 'Money Is Not Our God' and thought it was heavy and a slight change of direction. Many disappointed trips down the hill to Our Price and the local independent. Still no news on the album.

On what was effectively Black Friday back then in December, I did my usual search through 'K' in the CD collection more or less out of a hopeless routine – and there it finally was. I thought, "Brilliant cover", the band photos on the back even better.

On first listen, I remember thinking this was unlike anything I'd heard before. Every track offered something different, being very heavy with an agile sound, and still the melodies shone through.

The first thing I remember [about the gig] was the incredible atmosphere of punks with mohicans, people on the pavement asking for change and such a wonderful buzz of anticipation.

Finished our drinks and headed to the venue. The bouncer on the door said not to bother with the support Loud, which probably was a bit harsh, but the wait for Killing Joke was almost unbearable.

The place was packed to the rafters. I was at the front. I work out and I remember Raven saying you had to be physically fit to attend a Joke gig, and he was so right. Tracks from *Songs from the Victorious City* were played before 'Age Of Greed', about meat.

Then Martin Atkins came on in his stripy top, then Raven, who seemed to be immediately interacting with the mosh (as I would learn he always would). I didn't notice Geordie come on, but I'd never seen a band come on stage like this and it seemed an eternity before Jaz came on, but it honestly looked like he was walking on air or gliding as the lights were picking out his silhouette every few seconds, the place erupting, everyone trying to touch Jaz.

There was no pit then and we were practically hanging on to the monitors. I remember thinking Jaz's Velcro-strapped trainers were very non-Killing Joke, but otherwise he looked completely in a trance. 'Termite Mound' was incredible, especially the extended end, with Jaz gnashing his teeth.

The gig was off the scale and completely unlike anything I'd ever attended before.

The next day, I had friction burns on both arms and on my face. That was one rough gig. I have never been to a gig quite like that since and consider myself extremely lucky. Another outstanding memory was the smell of kerosene from the firebreathers.

PAUL RANGECROFT

My favourite gig would have to be London Astoria, '91. It was the height of (the first) Gulf War tension, the new album was an awesome return to form. London gigs were always a bit special. What a perfect opener 'Inside the Termite Mound' was. That really set the tone. Jaz was on fire, Raven obviously loved the new material and Geordie was as cool as ever. Unforgettable. As one music journalist put it: we were relieved to find the street outside still in one piece afterwards.

I had the pleasure of running a popular unofficial website for the band for a while. Raven was always very supportive. I remember getting a bit star-struck once when I spoke to him on the phone! I guess he was probably used to that kind of thing. He recognised me at a gig once and got one of the roadies to pass on a plectrum with the snake logo on, which really meant a lot.

MARK GEMINI THWAITE

I had moved from my home town of Birmingham and settled in west London in the late Eighties, which is when I was invited to audition for Kirk Brandon, who was reforming Spear of Destiny. The drummer working with Kirk at that time was Bobby Rae Mayhem, a tall, dreadlocked African-American from Philadelphia, who used to play in MDMA, and he was also jamming with Paul Raven around that time.

I recall meeting up with Bobby and Raven in a dark rehearsal room in London sometime in 1990, jamming together on a few new song ideas – with a view to forming or reforming another line-up of The Hellfire Club, if I recall correctly. But, shortly after, Paul was summoned back to the mighty KJ and I saw them on the *Extremities...* tour at London Astoria, this time with PiL's Martin Atkins on drums. I missed BPF, of course, but the *Extremities...* album and live show was a tremendous and ferocious return to form for the band after the disappointing *Outside the Gate*.

The next decade is a bit of a blur after I joined The Mission, then Tricky's live band, but I do recall catching KJ at the London Underworld in the early 2000s [14 August 2003] with the drummer from Prong [Ted Parsons]...

JASON MILLS

The Astoria gig, 31 January 1991, on the *Extremities...* tour, was another absolute standout – a truly brutal and barbaric evening.

TROY GREGORY

Extremities... came out. On that tour, I went and visited my Mom and Dad in Detroit and they [Joke] happened to be in Ann Arbor [4 February 1991]. Then they were playing in Chicago [2 March 1991]. I went to see them and found out something I didn't know about them – they don't really care who gets backstage, which I think is awesome.

JAZ

I guess we must be the only band that has an open-dressing-room policy. If you're brave enough to step inside [cackles], you're quite welcome. We've always done this. In 41 years, we've probably only had a couple of incidents. Generally, people are good, and we love meeting people. We see the whole thing of touring as a complete celebration. So, after a gig, I've gotta be honest, I feel completely cleansed on a spiritual level. This is why I do it. It's just such a fantastic experience for me.

It's also common knowledge that, wherever possible, we open the doors for soundchecks. That's getting harder and harder, but we manage it still.

✦ ✦ ✦

THE PALACE
21 February 1991,
Hollywood, USA

ROMEO PESTANAS, JR

Extremities... tour. There were at least three opening bands I remember. Everyone in attendance was there to see Killing Joke. Almost two hours passed before they actually performed. It was probably past midnight. The crowd was getting angry and yelling. Some were sitting on the floor waiting for them to play. Some even left the show. Killing Joke finally took the stage. They were brilliant! An onslaught of noise, beautiful noise! Jaz Coleman commanding the audience! Martin Atkins hitting the skins with force! Paul Raven and his choppy bass playing that I love! I stood in front of Geordie and was in awe of the sounds he got with the hollow-body guitar! One of my favourite shows ever!

✦ ✦ ✦

SIR GEORGE ROBEY
Early 1990s,
London, UK

PHIL TOLFIELD

Just thought of another one, although it's not directly related to Killing Joke. Back in the early Nineties, I was in a fairly shit band doing the London pay-to-play circuit and we had a gig at the George Robey (I think it was). Another band were on before us and the first song they played was 'Wardance'! Somewhat surprised, I legged it out of the dressing room to go watch them. They followed that with 'Intravenous'. Every song they played was either a KJ cover or sounded like they were trying to sound like KJ.

The guitarist, a hippy kind of guy with dreadlocks, was doing a not-half-bad impression of Geordie, but the singer was trying too hard to be Jaz, pulling the faces and staring enigmatically into the distance.

Unfortunately, he just came across as a bit of a twat.

When they finished playing, I went over to speak to them. The singer was far too important to speak to the likes of me and flounced off. The guitarist told me "That's Dave Kovacevic – he was in Killing Joke for seven years." Think he thought he still was.

AKI NAWAZ
(Southern Death Cult, Fun-Da-Mental, Nation Records)

My life at Nation Records also included Youth and his skills as a producer and a music lover. As a small-time skint label, I would offer Youth a brand-new TV or hi-grade speakers, stolen from some hi-fi shop in Bradford, as a fee. From stealing their records to giving them stolen goods for services rendered appeared to be a 'special relationship'. Youth remixed some great records for us, including the classic 'Temple Head' by Transglobal Underground.

Even more interesting, Jaz (sometimes with Raven) would come down to the Nation offices in Ladbroke Grove as he loved some of the music we were outputting. He saw it as important and advised me to contact Colonel Gaddafi for funds to help the label grow. I could not say "Jaz, you're mad" 'cos he knew he was anyway. But, as he was an inspiration, I kindly nodded and said: "Give me his number."

We discussed our ethnic origins and was excited that we shared some form of heritage and that he was very knowledgeable with the cultural history.

In Fun-Da-Mental, I did steal a bit of Jaz keyboard style, especially the intensity.

✦ ✦ ✦

FINSBURY PARK,
1 June 1991,
London, UK

TOBY GRIST

My first memory of Killing Joke was a poster. The 'Pope' [Catholic Nazi-sympathiser Alban Schachleiter] and Nazis poster. On my friend's wall. Oddly, I never thought for a moment they were associating themselves with the far right, but could see it was something ludicrous made to get attention. Something that immediately looked wrong but, even at quite a young age, I thought there was something interesting that needed to be investigated. I didn't have conspiracy theories back then but an inherent distrust of people in power.

Raven's hand-drawn set-list for the show at Cleveland's Empire Concert Club on 3 March 1991
© Kevin Colbert

In 1991, on a cold Saturday in June, I saw and heard them live for the first time. I cannot remember any of it. Too much alcohol and a massive regret. However, it must have got through because 'Money Is Not Our God', which was the first song played that day, has remained until this very day the best song I have ever heard. The album *Extremities, Dirt and Various Repressed Emotions* can never be bettered. It is as relevant today as the day it was released. As I've grown older, this band has been the only band to keep releasing albums that I not only love the sound of but feel like they are talking for me because I am unable to make as much noise.

ADRIAN WASON

Finsbury Park was special. Henry Rollins was amazing. I think the Joke started with 'Money Is Not Our God'. It was another cracking performance and I remember thinking how abrasive the band looked. We left after that and told the New Model Army and Mission fans that the best band of the day had already been on.

✦ ✦ ✦

LES BOURDAINES
8 June 1991,
Seignosse, France

FLORENCE CHARO

The other memory is a concert in 1991 [8 June] in Seignosse in the south-west of France, near the ocean. I absolutely wanted my boyfriend of that time – a musician himself, guitarist with Noir Désir and then Strychnine – to discover KJ.

From the first riff of guitars, the power of Paul's bass and Ferguson's drums, he was glued! But the most impressive was Jaz's charisma. In the middle of the concert, suddenly the music stopped. For a few seconds, there was a total, heavy silence. Jaz got close to the public and pointed his finger to a guy and said to him: "Don't you spit on me, dude! Do you hear me? Don't you dare spit on me!"

© Florence Charo

And from only one movement of Jaz's arm, the inferno machine restarted, even more powerful and vindictive, uncompromising.

When I was younger, I didn't realise the power of the lyrics, the politics and environmental commitments of the band. It was difficult to get access to the lyrics at that time; it is so much easier nowadays with the internet. I was more focused on the power of their music – it hit us in our guts straight away.

PARADISO
23 June 1991,
Amsterdam, Netherlands

STEVEN BORG

Finally, in 1991, I was able to see them live. I remember we ran into Jaz in the hall of the venue and I was flabbergasted.

When the gig started, we were standing in front and I had to hold tight to the stage not to get squashed by the insane crowd. I was obsessed by Jaz's performance. And I became obsessed by Killing Joke.

I've seen them live 12 times. I have briefly met Geordie, Raven, Youth and Big Paul. I'm wearing a Killing Joke ring made by Paul Ferguson and my friends call me a Killing Joke groupie. I practically buy everything. Books, DVDs and clothing. My picture is included in the booklet of the DVD *The Death and Resurrection Show* and it also passes by at the end of the DVD itself. My final wish is to speak to Jaz (even only for a minute) and to have a photo of the two of us.

I would be interested in his normal life. What does his regular life looks like? His hobbies? What is he doing when he's not into music?

The Paradiso gig was certainly the most memorable gig because it was the first time for me. I was blown away by his performance and was, of course, very eager to see them for a first time. After that gig, I knew what to expect and the element of surprise was gone. Of course, later on, when the original line-up was back, I was also excited to see them, although I've always had a preference for Raven above Youth.

UNIVERSITY
26 June 1991,
Sheffield, UK

COLIN BAMFORD

I went on my own to the Octagon, Sheffield [29 November 1986]. That was truly amazing. One of my favourite gigs of all time was KJ and the *Extremities...* tour. The gig was originally planned for the Octagon, but when I arrived it was switched to the Students' Union across the road. The place was full and you just could not move, then KJ came on and started with 'Inside the Termite Mound' – the whole place just moved as one. That's how it was the whole night, moving in unison, Raven pissed out of his head and Martin Atkins on drums looking like he had escaped from prison.

STANTONBURY LEISURE CENTRE (the gig that never was)
27 June 1991
Milton Keynes, UK

MICK HEAD

There were a couple of side-stories. Geordie's Mum and Dad had never seen Geordie play in all the years he'd been in the band; they'd never been witnesses to one of his live performances. The background was them turning up and having a nice meal all together before the gig.

As you can imagine, the leisure centre was a pretty vacuous hall. The promoter had hired a load of army camouflage and draped that all over the stage and on the speakers. He'd done quite a good job. It looked pretty good.

[Keyboardist] John Bechdel slept at mine [in Shipley, West Yorkshire] the night before. The next day, we're battling against the M1 to get to the venue in time for the soundcheck. We managed to get there.

The tour manager at the time said: "Come with me." With the promoter guy, we went through what seemed like a labyrinth of pathways. Eventually, we got to this office. The promoter handed over a wad of cash and some cheques to the tour manager and he handed them to me. What the tour manager didn't realise was that I used to work in a bank, my first job. So I put these notes down on the table and worked through them quite professionally. I counted the dosh and looked at the cheques and told him: "These are okay. Those are rubbish – no signature, postdated, the numerals to text don't match."

The tour manager pushes the notes in his pocket and gave the promoter the bad cheques back and then he says: "We're off."

Foolishly, the promoter had paid everybody – DJ, security, the hire of the hall, the support band – and had left himself well short of actually paying Killing Joke's fee. So the tour manager pulled the plug. "You haven't got the requisite readies. We're not playing."

Word of this gets through to the audience. We're trying to get the gear off the stage and the punters have got wind that there's not gonna be any Killing Joke gig and they're not too pleased. So they were legging stuff at the drum kit. So, inbetween dodging missiles, Raven comes along and says: "Mick, get us that camo, will ya." So me and Dave [Simpson], who was a punter at the time and is now Geordie's tech, we set about picking all this camouflage and stuck it in the back of Dave's van. We managed to get all the gear off with relatively little damage.

Apparently, Raven wanted the camo for his bass rig the next night at Brixton. In the end, we had to return the camo to the venue anyway.

The upshot was that Geordie's parents – after waiting all these years – still never got to see their son play. The gig that never was. And we all made our merry way down to Brixton Academy for the climax of the tour.

BRIXTON ACADEMY
28 June 1991,
London, UK

SIMON BARRINGTON

Brixton Academy – still in my top-five gigs ever. Atkins wrecked the kit/stage at the end of 'Pssyche'!

ADRIAN WASON

The Brixton Academy gig was strangely subdued, only the bottom [of the venue] was open and it seemed like the band had run out of energy by then, which was understandable with the performances they had put in.

ERIC SOLIS

Time passed and military obligations found me stationed in southern California. On a Saturday afternoon, I wandered into a record shop in Los Angeles' famous Venice Beach. Hanging on the wall was a Killing Joke t-shirt. The no-frills block lettering that composed the band's logo, coupled with the image of TV-watching kids standing next to a fallen adult, seemed positively Orwellian. Remembering how much I liked Metallica's version, I immediately bought the shirt, along with Killing Joke's first album.

I recall playing and replaying the tracks until 'The Wait''s two-note intro came through the speakers. The sound was reminiscent of a warning siren: something older generations might associate with an air raid or an incoming tornado. It was an ominous tone that impressed on the listener that something big was about to happen and, if you paid attention, you might just survive.

✦ ✦ ✦

HOLLAND PARK LECTURE
February 1992,
London, UK

ADRIAN WASON

This was a good day. It was a very unusual atmosphere. I think it was in an acupuncture centre. We had to take our shoes off and it was a bit awkward at first. Jaz came in and suggested we all introduce ourselves to each other as the atmosphere was not right. I was sitting next to a guy from the army who very generously later sent me a few 1989 bootlegs. About five minutes later, Jaz came back in, resplendent in green polo-neck jumper, sports jacket, smart slacks and shoes. I've lost my photo, unfortunately. The guy who did the rap on *Outside the Gate* was in the audience and Jaz played a lot on the piano, talked for a few hours and appeared to have drunk a whole bottle of brandy during the proceedings!

When he had finished, he tried to make a dramatic exit, but the door jammed! The food was very late (from an Iranian chef) but that was ideal as we all got to mingle with Jaz. I asked if I could take a few photos and he said that was fine as long as he had a cut! I then asked about his relationship with Raven and I think he said: "Bung him £5k and he'd be there!" The food was good. After, Jaz played the stuff he had recorded with Patricia Morrison and Mick from The Mission. I think the band was called G7, but it sounded like nothing I've ever heard then or since. I would love to hear that again, but Jaz claimed it was stolen.

PAUL RANGECROFT

One final amusing memory: Jaz gave a talk in Holland Park in the early Nineties and demand was such that the talk had to be given twice over two consecutive days. I attended on the second day. It was a very enjoyable occasion – good food, fascinating stories, a beautiful piano recital and so on. But my favourite bit was when Jaz was explaining that time was just an illusion. To demonstrate this, he declared: "We can of course smash the clock up!" He produced a broken and battered wristwatch... "Actually, I smashed it up yesterday!"

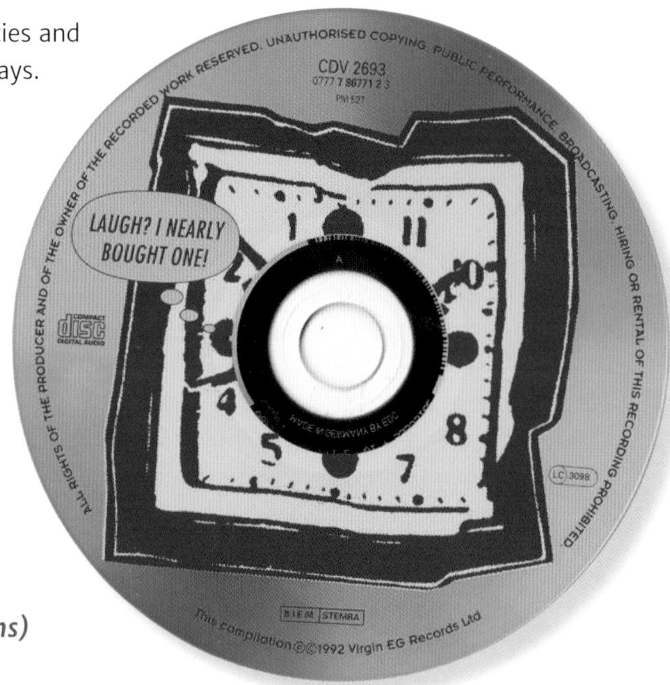

JOHN BECHDEL

(keyboards, Murder Inc.)

Murder Inc. was supposed to be a Killing Joke record. We were gonna make a follow-up to *Extremities*.... The plan was that I would come back over and we would do it all again.

CHRIS CONNELLY

(vocals, Murder Inc., featuring Geordie, Raven, Big Paul and Martin Atkins)

Murder Inc. came about because of a fight or disagreement in the band, where time was booked/dates were booked or something and Jaz refused to come.

I offered my services, or was asked, and Martin asked Big Paul to join us for a recording session. Martin and I were friends already and Paul was out of the [Killing Joke] picture. Martin introduced me.

JAZ

I was fired from the band. I was fired. I'm the only fucker who's been fired from Killing Joke.

CHRIS CONNELLY

I did not know any of them [Killing Joke], but I certainly liked them a lot. They started putting out records at the time I became an avid punk/post-punk fan. I was already an obsessive fan of Throbbing Gristle. The 'punk' of '77 had taken second place to a newer, deeper, often more aggressive sound: The Pop Group, Wire, early industrial and Killing Joke, to name but a few.

Killing joke had the appeal of extreme violence while being catchy as fuck. Their music reflected the times: if you want to put ME in that context, the zeitgeist was depression, dull, hopeless in the UK at the time, a long grey ennui that soaked you to the marrow. The music of Killing Joke, in a sense like Throbbing Gristle, kind of EMBODIED the feeling of the time without necessarily protesting against it, but they also had a very appealing mystique, and their sound was peerless: no one sounded like them.

They all had their own very strong personalities, which proved so true when I started collaborating.

We convened in Chicago and worked up a couple of ideas before going to a live-in studio in Minnesota with Steve Albini. Now THAT was a lot of fun. I would let the band work during the day and would go in myself at night and record with Steve most of the time, but we all got along well. There were shenanigans, of course, but it was a very pleasant experience. I liked all these guys individually very much. Still do. They were always really great to me.

There was John Bechdel as well, on keyboards, and two drummers. We did not have any expectations, which is a bit scary in retrospect. There was not a big plan, short of the same as always – "Let's make a fucking great record that will be HUGE."

Jaz is a brilliant singer and he is different from me. I am certain our spirits have much in common, but the way it comes out is different. There is no comparison. It's apples and oranges. I didn't feel like I was treading on his toes.

[On Murder Inc.'s self-titled 1992 album] I very rarely listen to old records, only if I have to relearn a song. That said, I am very proud of it. I don't think there is another record that sounds like it – and it's a fond memory.

GEORDIE

That was fun. We got to work with Steve Albini. In that studio [Pachyderm] in Cannon Falls, Minnesota, just before Nirvana were up there [for *In Utero*]. This fucking piece of land, 50 acres of a limestone gorge, reminded me of Derbyshire. Did that album in a few days. And then a few gigs. The Limelight was very, very good, with the two drummers.

JOHN BECHDEL

Raven was the one that came up with the [band] name.

As the music developed, it really wasn't Killing Joke.

Geordie would always throw me these beautiful chords, magnificent chords to play for the song 'Mania'.

Murder Inc. was the first time I met Paul [Ferguson] properly. I got to tell him what a big inspiration he was. Part of what I felt made Killing Joke such a great band was the tribal nature of his drums. I hadn't really heard that before. It was primitive. It really fit so well.

He and Martin both playing drums was really exciting. That was a good experience.

CHRIS CONNELLY

Jaz was doing other stuff at the time. As it goes, I think Murder Inc. happened parallel to the Killing Joke trajectory, not necessarily intertwined with it.

JAZ

I went through five years of litigation and it was a very unpleasant journey. I was hospitalised and had a complete nervous breakdown. All sorts of things happened. But the most important thing is we kept going.

1992–2000

"All my life I've been waiting for this moment"

YOUTH
I kind of always felt that there was unfinished business. We're a very dysfunctional family.

JAZ
I moved to New Zealand because I was inspired by David Lang, who made New Zealand a nuclear-free zone. We started my studio [York Street Studios in Auckland] on *Pandemonium*.

YOUTH
I met up with Geordie. The band was pretty dormant, even though we never officially split up. They were doing a compilation and Geordie asked if I would get involved.

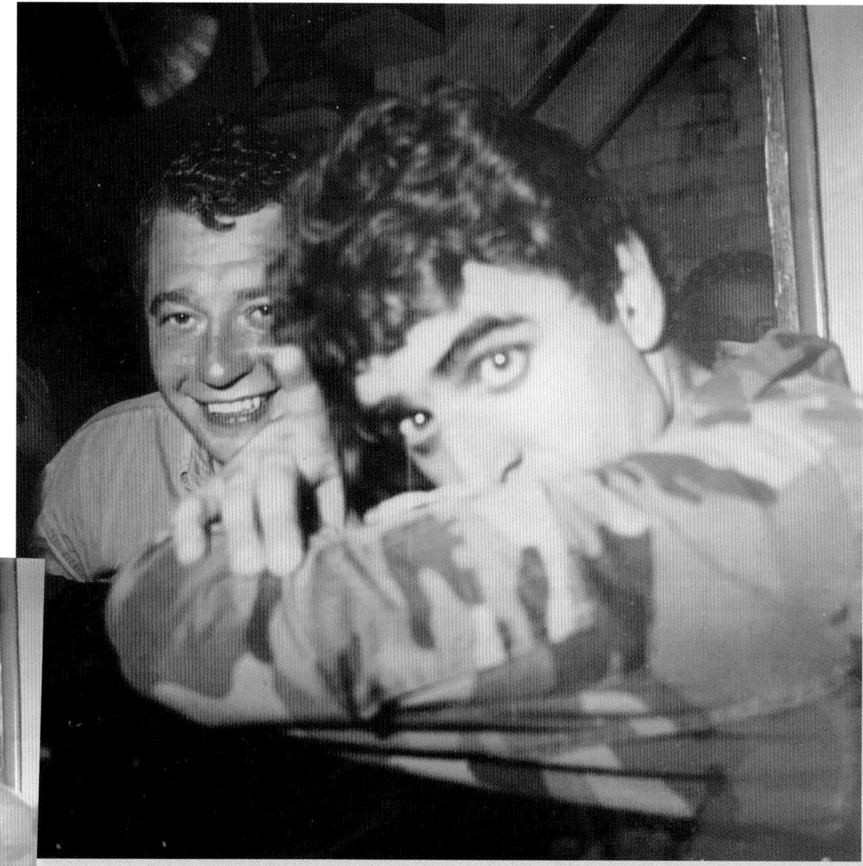

Vaughan Smith with Jaz at York Street Studios, c.'93/'94. "We look young there."

GEORDIE

Before *Pandemonium*, I compiled the master of *Laugh? I Nearly Bought One!* I wanted that picture of the Pope's emissary. That was in a book of Youth's. Youth got hooked in for the artwork. Then he said: "We should reform, man. It would be great."

YOUTH

We got involved with the running order and the sleeve. During that, I said it would be good to do something else. And then we agreed to go do *Pandemonium*.

Signed to my label, Butterfly. I had a budget. We could go do it in New Zealand.

JAZ

I always have to applaud Youth. It's great having Youth in the band. "C'mon, let's do this. Doesn't matter about the money. Let's go do this." I just love that.

I can remember being on the plane to Egypt. I said: "We got some great studios to choose from." He says: "I wanna record in the Great Pyramid" and, of course, we did end up recording in the Great Pyramid. When we collectively visualise something, it normally happens. Youth is great like that. We can visualise him saying things, and they happen. Life follows art, certainly. That's why we have to get our vision right at this stage.

YOUTH

I suggested we do strings in Egypt. Then I said, "Why don't we record it in the pyramids?" And Jaz said: "Don't be ridiculous." Totally dismissed it. But I had an inside connection. Mary [Lomando], who was a white witch, used to run the record plant in New York. She had a big coven, was living in Egypt and doing a lot of meditation work. Her ex-boyfriend, Bob Clearmountain, the legendary mixer, had put me on to her. She said: "I think I can set it up for you to go to the pyramids."

We met up with Mary and her group of people doing this occult meditation in one of the rooms in the pyramids and they had a connection with the Department of Antiquities.

We had to do this interview to get in. At one point, this guy from the antiquities goes, "You're not a Satanist, are you?" And Jaz goes, "I don't believe in Satan, so how can I be a Satanist?" The guy didn't seem particularly spooked, but the fact that he asked Jaz if he was a Satanist was telling. He didn't ask me. What I sensed was they [officials] were quite used to Americans and westerners coming over doing weird meditations in the pyramid rooms. There's a big American university there. A lot of esoteric Americans. Jaz's answer made all the women [in the room] laugh. It kind of lightened the vibe of it.

That seemed to roll us through. Cash was procured and offered, and we got in. I knew how it worked. I thought of Egypt as halfway to India and I'd been living in India for 10 years. The east is a baksheesh culture, which means that people kinda tip a lot. Oiling the wheels of industry, let's put it that way. You do it with everybody; everybody asks for it. It's a pilgrimage culture, everybody's on a pilgrimage. At some point, people ask for alms and everybody gives them. It's nice. I liked it. And it did cut through a lot of red tape.

For me, the main thing was its [the Great Pyramid's] location. It's so amazing. On the nodal point of earth energies and ley lines. The shape of it and numbers involved all give it this cosmic thing and this all comes to focus in the King's Chamber, and the Queen's Chamber, to a degree. I wanted to do a kind of Druid ceremony where we tapped into that universal energy and got some blessing and guidance. Certainly, we didn't want to harness it or sort of control it.

We had two nights. First night, it was really weird. I had to pick up the engineer [Greg Hunter] in the flats. The lift broke down. We had to jump out of the lift as it was going up and down, [or] it could have decapitated us. Jaz was already freaking out. He just collapsed on the floor and refused to get out. Eventually, me and the engineer just hauled him through this gap before it shut and decapitated him.

When we got to the pyramids, we found out that the women on their way there had gone through a similar experience in another block of flats.

We all crowded into the King's Chamber. Engineer Sameh [Almazny] freaked out. He fell asleep and woke up and infamously saw these Eyes of Horus coming out. He ran out screaming, never to go back again.

Jaz broke down in tears after two or three takes. He just couldn't do it. It was a bit messy that day.

I was in a very clear space and Jaz wasn't really. So I took charge of it and we gave up [on that first day]. The next day, I said, "Let's do everything in threes. I put the three women in the Queen's Chamber doing their ceremony and just three of us in the King's Chamber: me, Jaz and the engineer. Everyone else outside.

I did a Druid ceremony, cleared the space and got my intentions properly articulated in the ceremony. And then just let Jaz have two or three takes on each vocal. In the end, we got it really quick and it was really good.

Because I handled the ceremonial aspect, it was really clear, really fluid and we just soared on it, really epic, cosmic, like a thousand years condensed into half an hour. Really visionary. Like taking very, very strong acid.

As we came out, it was night-time and all these Bedouins were making fires. It was really beautiful, kind of almost Biblical. Jaz got a big buzz out of it.

I felt we'd unleashed an acupuncture point on the planet and unleashed some very dormant, well-stored beautiful light. It did feel like an opening.

✦ ✦ ✦

TOWNHOUSE STUDIOS
1993,
London, UK

GEOFF DUGMORE
(drummer, Pandemonium, Democracy)

My first experience of playing with the band was when I got a call to come and play on what was the *Pandemonium* album. I did not know the album title at the time. It was a Sunday morning at Townhouse Studio 2. I arrived at 10am and set everything up. The engineer, Greg, passed me something to smoke and, what felt like five hours later, Youth arrived and we started to work.

YOUTH
When we started mixing, we brought in Geoff Dugmore, and he kinda overdubbed nearly everything.

GEOFF DUGMORE
It was the first time working with Youth. I knew his name and all that he had done. I'd known Big Paul because he used to go out with a girl called Lesley, a friend of a girl I shared a flat with in Neasden called Toni Childs, so he used to come round. Big Paul was a great guy, so jumping into his seat was something I was aware of.

Youth told me I couldn't hear the songs [beforehand] and I was just to go in and play whatever I felt as the music came at me. We did three songs in the first sessions. I remember doing 'Whiteout'. It was so intense, and all that I played was gut feeling and first take. In fact, all the tracks were pretty much first or second takes. The music was so intense. It was playing by gut feeling and what was coming at me musically.

Youth was so great in giving me the vibe. I loved doing the sessions. We did the whole album over three days. I first met Jaz in the second session. He was really cool, a totally different character than when we toured the album. Geordie I wouldn't meet until we started rehearsing for the tour.

YOUTH
I knew that album was gonna be killer straight off. Apart from anything, I was on fire. I had started taking LSD again, living in India, confident and fully focused on what I was doing. I knew it was gonna work.

CHRIS BRYANS
Did you still feel like there was unfinished, unresolved business? Did you avoid listening to Joke or hearing of new releases or tours calling near to you?

BIG PAUL
Yes, indeed. Pissed me off afresh every time.

YOUTH
I thought we had the amount of talent and kudos between us on *Pandemonium* to do what Zeppelin had done on their first album. Actually, it's more like what Zeppelin did on Led Zep II. I think it's in that league of classic rock albums. It also pioneered the electronic element of rock that became so common after that. But we were definitely one of the first off the blocks. We'd already been working with that in the Eighties. I thought it came together really well on that album. 'Exorcism' and 'Whiteout' were definitely following on from 'Money Is Not Our God'. But we were also reaching into new areas with 'Pandemonium' and other tracks. I was really indulging our Zeppelin and AC/DC roots.

LUC TIRONNEAU

I reconnected with KJ with *Extremities...*, one of their best albums, unquestionably, and believed that the group was finished when the following years I saw no release. It was therefore with a huge surprise that in the car with a friend I came across the intro to 'Pandemonium' and this slightly metal bent, not unpleasant at the bottom, even if I will always prefer the sound invented by Geordie between '82 and '85.

ANDY SEWELL

Killing Joke came out with *Pandemonium* and changed my perception of what one could do with music again – this time showing a new way to play heavy music without it being metal or punk.

MIK RAVEN

The albums were a bit sporadic but the first place I always went to at HMV was the 'K' section. I remember, having thought KJ was no more, going into a record shop in Blackpool and finding 'Exorcism'. It blew my mind! Especially the dance mixes by Youth. You have to remember there was no internet for the masses back then, and I did not subscribe to the music press. My children had to suffer it on repeat in the car all the way home!

✦ ✦ ✦

METROPOLITAN UNIVERSITY
18 April 1994,
Leeds, UK

DARREN DAVY

I'm 47, born and raised in West Yorkshire, and lived in Northern Ireland for eight years. I was first introduced to KJ by chance. As a big Metallica fan, in 1987 I splashed out on the US import of *Garage Days Re-Revisited EP*. My standout track was 'The Wait'. But... who the fuck are Killing Joke?

Journey started there.

Now, I won't pretend to be a super-fan and I'm definitely not sycophantic about it! Some parts of KJ's back-catalogue I honestly don't like much.

But...

Some of their work is fucking amazing. Personal favourite: 'Euphoria'.

Been lucky to have witnessed them several times in Leeds, mainly at the polytechnic. I didn't get to see KJ until *Pandemonium*. I just admitted that, didn't I?

Shameful.

I'll get my coat.

But I had a stance then that makes no sense now. Bradford was my scene (about 15 miles from home). Leeds was around 25-plus miles but a taxi-home affair. Cost of taxi from Leeds could pay for two, three, maybe four gigs in Bradford.

My head said, "If you're not coming to Bradford... sod ya." There were so many gigs in Bradford (used to be... scene long dead).

Again, speaking honestly – KJ ain't always fantastic live. But, when they're in the zone, fuck me. Stonking.

The jester hood... The stomp... That glare. Honestly, thought I'd turn to stone after eyes locked.

Jaz is on my list of people I'd like to share a meal with, even if he does, in equal measure, both interest and intimidate me.

ROCK CITY
19 April 1994,
Nottingham, UK

TOBY O'REILLY
(aka Apple)

Manchester University
Students Union
Tel (061) 275 293
SJM CONCERTS presents
Killing Joke
+ Special Guests
FRIDAY 15th APRIL 1994
Doors 7:30 p.m.
£9 (Advance)
UNRESERVED
OVER 18's ONLY
00076
Retain This Portion
Conditions Overleaf
Students Union

I first got to meet the band in Nottingham. After the gig, I was asked if I would like to go backstage by one of the road crew – too right I would.

I was ushered through this side into the back room. Sat in chairs were Jaz, Geordie. Cross-legged on the floor was Youth. The room stunk of weed. I remember standing in the corner of the room while Jaz talked with some people. After 10 minutes, I asked Youth if it was okay to skin up. Sure it was. "Sit down and share it around." I pulled out of my fag packet a tiny lump of rocky and started to make a spliff. As I started to burn it, Youth looked over at me and passed me this leather pouch. "Use mine if you want." Inside was some of the nicest skunk I had ever had the pleasure to skin up with.

MICK HEAD

Dave [Simpson, now Geordie's guitar tech] would put me up in Bristol areas, south-west. Anything up north – Yorkshire, Manchester – I'd put Dave up. I had a young family at the time. This was the *Pandemonium* era. Dave's come up. I haven't told the missus that Dave would be staying overnight. In them days, Dave had the most fabulous, massive mohican. Dave's crashed out on my sofa with this fabulous mohican. My wife's up early to see to Damon, my first son, who is now Big Paul's tech. Lynsey goes into the front room and sees this bloke crashed out with the massive mohawk and thinks, "What the chuff's going on here?"

Dave – as he was wont to do – went to the shop and fetched Lynsey a big bar of chocolate and also bought my son a Subbuteo set for when he's old enough to play it. He's a good bloke is Dave. He's never lost sight of the fact that he was once a punter.

✦ ✦ ✦

ASTORIA
20 April 1994,
London, UK

ALAN MUSTAFA

Cemented in flesh, my first true gathering, in 1994 at the Astoria. Masks on entry, the ghosts swirling in the crowd, the Haka, the fire-eaters and that magic from the stage. The noise, the wonderful noise. Next year, the candle is passed around the crowd to commemorate a lost friend. Don't let it go out, says Jaz. It never does.

So many more times. Some big, some like the [Camden] Underworld in 2003, a sweltering, melting, privilege, so close to the heart of the storm. But, wherever the venue, whatever the time, they always bring you back to that glorious space between the soaring hymn and tribal drum. There's nowhere better.

The mask handed out to fans – including Alan Mustafa – who attended the London Astoria gig in April 1994. "Grotesque" was designer Mike Coles' apt description of the face he used as the basis for the end result

ADRIAN WASON

A choir, Maori warriors and Jaz appearing in a jester's hat, which looked totally otherworldly when backlit as he glided slowly on. I remember at the end of 'Communion', he threw the hat down on the floor as if in disgust, which I thought was strange.

COLIN MURDY

I didn't get to see the band live until much later, on their *Pandemonium* tour, which was a true experience of majestic sonic terror with a purposeful intent.

TORSTEN BOUR

In 1994, I was 17. MTV was really big and I watched it a lot. I remember one evening I fell asleep and, in the night, awoke suddenly. The TV was still playing, but I had my eyes closed and heard the sound of a music video. It was a massive, hard sound and I was very impressed. It was the music video of Killing Joke's 'Millennium'. What a great song. What an impressive video! It was in the middle of the night and I was totally blown away. I didn't know Killing Joke before. This was the first time I heard from this band. In the next days, the song was always on my mind, so I went to a music store. I found the album *Pandemonium* there, with the track 'Millennium' on it. I was very, very happy! The artwork from the CD cover also impressed me. It has a touch of mystic, I think. I didn't know anything about Killing Joke at this time. I'd only seen the 'Millennium' video once. But I had to buy the CD and for me this was a totally new kind of music, an absolute new sound. The influence of Arabic music sounds very mysterious, very special. I listened to the CD over and over again and love it from the first to the last song. It's unique, it's a masterpiece – even today! From this time on, I am a fan of Killing Joke. I love their heavy music and enjoy seeing them playing live. The 'Millennium' music video was the beginning for me to become a Gatherer.

KEVIN THIBODEAUX

My first contact with Killing Joke was at a Camelot Music store at Collin Creek Mall in Plano, Texas. I was mesmerised by the CD cover of *Pandemonium* so decided to take a listen. Up until that time, I was mainly into pure metal, but Killing Joke bridged the gap between the hard stuff I was listening to and something more spiritual. To this day, I own the vinyl of *Pandemonium* and love every song.

✦ ✦ ✦

TOP OF THE POPS
14 July 1994,
London, UK

BRIAN RICHARDSON

I moved around between genres. It wasn't until I saw a charismatic performance from Jaz Coleman on *Top of The Pops* in 1994 [the 'Pandemonium' performance] that I fully appreciated the Killing Joke sound.

Simon Mayo doing his best to introduce a band outside his comfort zone, screaming girls who looked more like pop fans, Jaz muting down the clown paint – but holy fuck! This was it. That incredible riff from Geordie, the keys, Jaz growling about how fucked our society really is to an audience of middle-class kids in nice sweaters and tidy haircuts. And then the close camera angle of an enthused Jaz Coleman. His voice was incredible and, even now, he remains a standout vocalist. So distinctive.

The song didn't feel right for that audience but it did for me, stuck in front of my rubbish 14-inch TV – I bought the cassette singles, the albums, played every track. Even the B-side, 'Another Cult Goes Down', for me was phenomenal. I think Mayo called Jaz a "mad axe murderer from hell" on the 'Millennium' *TOTP* gig [5 May 1994] but that just showed how mainstream didn't get it. I'm glad they didn't!

SUBTERANIA
15 July 1994,
London, UK

ADRIAN WASON

Unbelievable. Boiling-hot day. We entered just as the intro from 'Communion' started and, although the place was absolutely packed, we miraculously found our way to the front almost immediately in all the chaos. Bingo [Robert Bingham] was a star with armour plates and an angle grinder. From the video footage, I think 'Whiteout' is the most mental. We were all covered in white, blue and red paint.

✦ ✦ ✦

PHOENIX FESTIVAL
17 July 1994,
Long Marston Airfield, UK

ALAN MUSTAFA

Me and my mate Dan were very excited to see Jaz was going to do a signing. We waited in line nervously and debated what we might say to this scary, magic man, being well aware of his reputation. How could we make this a moment to remember?

As it turns out, Jaz did all the work with charismatic flair, a brilliant smile and a healthy dose of skewed wisdom.

"Where are you from?" he asked. "Um, Aldershot" I stuttered. "Ahh, where they make the bombs!" Jaz shouted. "Uh, yeah, the army town," I muttered. "Does your Dad make the bombs?" Cackle.

Panicky and red by now, I stuttered, "No, he's an accountant, at a cooker hood firm." Louder cackle.

"Ah well, I'll draw you a bomb anyway." And he did, diligently, on the band photo he was signing.

Me and Dan staggered away, confused but very happy. What a character! They were storming that day too. And, if ever where we grew up comes up in conversation, the joke is, of course, "we're from where they make the bombs". Cheers, Jaz.

ERIC SOLIS

Pandemonium made me a fan for life. There were a lot of exciting bands coming up at that time, but I couldn't pull away from Killing Joke's martial rhythm section and the swirling, engine-like guitar. And those vocals. That intimate croon that shifts into a threatening bark or a primal howl. This band really is the sum of its parts.

BRETT NEELY

I was 17 in the summer of 1994. During my two-week vacation from my fast-food job, I took a Greyhound Bus trip to spend a week at my sister's apartment, which she shared with her husband. They both worked full-time, so I was by myself during the day and had to come up with ways to fill my time. My sister gave me a hand-drawn map of the surrounding area so I could explore. She also loaned me a bike, but it had a flat tyre and didn't have a lock. So I took the bike to a bike shop, bought a replacement tube for the tyre (which I changed myself) and bought a bike lock. From there, with about 20 dollars left in my pocket, I found my way to a record store called Newbury Comics.

I locked the bike up and walked in, feeling rather accomplished compared to someone who could've sat on the couch in front of the television all day. And I heard something rather incredible on the store's sound system. I quickly found a store employee and asked what they were playing. They pointed to a little cardboard box holding the CD case for the Now Playing album: Killing Joke's *Pandemonium*.

© Alan Mustafa

While growing up, my big sister listened to pop music on the radio and my brother listened to classic rock. My friends at school were getting into grunge, seemingly pivoting from Bon Jovi to Nirvana overnight. I was still searching for something to call my own. Something with depth and power. Something that I could play for others and proudly say, "I discovered this." And, on that day, I found it, thanks to that Newbury Comics store in southern New Hampshire many years ago.

✦ ✦ ✦

KENTISH TOWN FORUM
19 October 1994,
London, UK

ADRIAN WASON

I was taking my mate Nick, who I shared a house in Bath with at the time *Extremities...* came out. Unfortunately, we got on the Old Rosie cider too soon and, even though the gig was one tube stop down the line, we ended up in a Mexican restaurant. My moment of shame.

✦ ✦ ✦

GARAGE
21 October 1994,
Glasgow, UK

IAN ROBERTSON

Something to get genuinely excited about again. Martin 'Youth' Glover was back in the fold, and *Pandemonium* was a true return to form.

I was living in Glasgow at the time and, along with the rest of rave cultural Britain, recreational hallucinogenics had been a regular fixture those past three years. Or was it four? 21 October 1994 at the Garage is indelibly etched into my cerebral cortex. To witness Youth take to the stage, attired in a kilt and antlers, while I played understudy to the magic of mushrooms, made for a quintessential experience.

CARSTEN DOIG

1994 was the year I became a Gatherer. I couldn't believe that this band were back. I bought the 'Exorcism' 10-inch single – coloured vinyl with the new logo on an opaque sleeve – and marvelled at this band for recording a song inside the Great Pyramid.

I saw them for the first time at Glasgow Garage that year. I was about halfway back but could still see the intensity on Jaz's face and Youth dancing around. I was fortunate to see Raven when they supported Mötley Crüe [in 2005], and later welcomed back Big Paul for the *Absolute Dissent* tour.

✦ ✦ ✦

HARVARD UNIVERSITY
October 1994,
Cambridge, USA

GREG SLAWSON

During the *Pandemonium* tour in 1994, Jaz (and I think Geordie) did a signing at a popular independent record shop on the Harvard University campus. There was not a big crowd there, so I was able to go right up to Jaz's table. Knowing that they were political, I mentioned that I was a Marxist. Jaz quickly bellowed in a loud voice, "So you believe a living body and a dead body are the same!" Being a bit intimidated, that was the end of the conversation.

✦ ✦ ✦

TOWER RECORDS
15 November 1994,
Hollywood, USA

ROMEO PESTANAS, JR.

I remember lining up with a lot of my Killing Joke vinyl covers to be signed. I also brought a Murder Inc. vinyl cover that I only wanted Geordie to sign since he's the only one that played on it. Somehow it got lost in the shuffle and the whole band signed it. LOL! I ended up talking to Geordie about guitars and amps while we were looking at CDs. I don't remember if they played that same night or the next night [the same night, The Palace]. Either way, it was a fucking great show!

✦ ✦ ✦

FIRST AVENUE
26 November 1994,
Minneapolis, USA

GEOFF DUGMORE

When we toured the *Pandemonium* album in the US, I remember we had a 30-hour bus ride from somewhere like Portland to Minneapolis, right across the top of Montana. It was Thanksgiving Day, 24 November, I think, and we were being chased by a massive snowstorm. The bus broke down and we were all on the side of the road, freezing our butts off. Eventually, another bus arrived and we headed off again, but the snowstorm caught us and we ended up in a truck stop, eating till it ended. We got to Minneapolis just in time for the show! It was a real cracker.

SAINT ANDREW'S HALL
29 November 1994,
Detroit, USA

ANDY SEWELL

I finally got to see them play. I remember being blown away (and annoyed by the tiny punk rocker in front of me who refused to dance until 'Eighties', whereupon he kicked me in the shins).

Time passed and my Killing Joke album collection grew. I even joined a few bands and brought the Killing Joke influence with me to the songs we played (never got to cover them, unfortunately).

I mourned the passing of Paul Raven, lamenting that I never got to see him play with the band (I lived far away from any music venues between 1994 and 2001).

✦ ✦ ✦

UIC PAVILION/CABARET METRO
1 December 1994,
Chicago, USA

FRED JAGGI

Back in the day, I lived in suburban Chicago, where punk and new wave were impossible to hear. Desperate to hear something new, I bought the 'Change'/'Requiem' 12-inch from a local record store. Spinning it on my turntable, I thought, "Wow, this is something really different. It's so dark and moody." After a week or so of listening, I had a thought. "Maybe this isn't a 33. Maybe it's a 45!" Oops! Since then, I've been a huge fan, but sometimes I still miss that 33.

In the early Nineties, a friend and I went to Chicago to see KJ play as one of the opening acts for the Twisted Christmas line-up. They rocked, of course. When they finished, my friend and I left the stadium and drove over to the amazing Cabaret Metro club, where KJ were playing again that night. As we waited outside the club by ourselves, who should walk up but the man himself – Jaz!

We told him we'd loved the earlier set. He told us thanks but also his voice was totally gone. Later, during the show, Jaz was clearly self-medicating with some serious alcohol. They again rocked it, but the banter between the songs was completely unintelligible.

PEABODY'S DOWN UNDER
5 December 1994,
Cleveland, USA

KEVIN COLBERT

I have a pretty good story from seeing Killing Joke during the summer of '94. It was the *Pandemonium* tour. Stabbing Westward opened and they were terrible, but Killing Joke was phenomenal. This was my third time seeing them and it was just brutal (in a very good way). But my favourite memories of this are from the events that happened after the show. First, Geordie gave one of his guitars a Viking funeral on the Cuyahoga River right outside the venue. It was totally bizarre and unexpected, and there were only a few of us to witness it (including a photographer, so it has to be documented somewhere), but he lit his guitar on fire, set it onto the water and pushed it off. After witnessing that, my brother Mike, my friend Big Ed (RIP) and I sat down and had a long talk with Jaz Coleman about everything from his favourite books (some of which he wrote the titles of on the back of an

© Kevin Colbert

enormous tour poster I stole from the venue) to his take on Chaos Theory (deep, deep stuff for a 1am conversation while sitting on the floor of a bar). I currently have the poster hanging in my garage [the background image on the previous page]. Jaz's autograph is pretty obvious, but I can't remember who did the other two. Probably Geordie and Youth? I can't remember who was drumming on that tour [Geoff Dugmore], but, if I had to guess, I don't think they signed it. Anyhoo, the experience was a dream come true for a diehard Killing Joke fan – one I'll never forget. It's one of those events that was so bizarre that, 26 years later, I started questioning it myself. But, fortunately, my brother was with me at the time and he remembers it as vividly as I do.

GEORDIE

He's a delusional fantasist. Fuck me. It's just absolute bollocks. It just never fucking happened. My memory's really good. I have absolutely no recollection of it. Fucking spare me.

I am not recalling the guitar in a boat.

Later in the same call:

It's kind of ringing a bell. But it's absolutely not one of my guitars. Not one of mine.

Different call, later the same day:

A photographer [was there] and not one fucking smudge of it? There you go. Just drop it.

Another call, the same day:

Cliff, a Native American... it could have been his guitar. He wanted to be my roadie. "All right, come along. Okay, could you change this plug to American?" He just looked at it. Fucking hell, he hasn't got a clue. Thing is, he set it [the gear] up, then he would just stand there and fucking stare into space the whole gig. It was the only tour I've ever done when *nothing* went wrong. Unbelievable. Could have been his guitar. It was absolutely *not* my guitar.

LIMELIGHT
6 December 1994,
New York, USA

GEOFF DUGMORE

The last show on that tour was at the Limelight Club in New York. It was an epic show but, in the middle of I think it was 'Communion', there was this kind of sound vortex happening, where it seemed that everything went totally quiet, although we were still playing.

I remember at the end of the song, we all looked at each other thinking, "What the fuck just happened there?" Now, if you think about it, the song is called 'Communion' and we were playing in an old church... Mmmmm...

When we finished the show, our tour manager said to us, "Let's get the fuck out of here quick!" We did.

TJ HEANEY

I was first exposed to Killing Joke on 27 December 1994. I turned 13 a couple of weeks prior. I was watching MTV's *120 Minutes* and the host announced their live guest. They performed 'Millennium'. It was love at first sound. Never before had I heard a band create such a sinister and primal sound. Sure, I had been exposed to other bands in a similar vein, such as Ministry and Nine Inch Nails, but I never felt that strongly about them. I used my birthday and Christmas money to buy the CD of *Pandemonium*. When the title track began to play, I knew I had found something to connect with.

TOWER RECORDS
26 January 1995,
London, UK

PHIL TOLFIELD

I'll also briefly mention the short four-song set the band played in Tower Records in London, around the time of the *Pandemonium* tour. Not your average Killing Joke gig – four o'clock in the afternoon in a shop basement! It was quite funny watching the 'normal' people get halfway down the stairs, see this very loud rock band playing, Jaz ranting and raving away at the beginning of 'Exorcism', then turn around and go straight back upstairs again!

✦ ✦ ✦

ROCK CITY
31 January 1995,
Nottingham, UK

MICK HEAD

Youth is now back on board and as equally accommodating and friendly as the other permanent band members. In fact, it was quite amusing at Nottingham Rock City to see Youth, spliff in hand, settle himself down next to Lynsey in the dressing room to watch *Brookside* and the infamous episode where Trevor Jordache's body was found under the patio by Jimmy Corkhill. An episode neither of them wanted to miss.

✦ ✦ ✦

THE TROUBADOUR
24 February 1995,
Hollywood, USA

ROMEO PESTANAS, JR.

Chris Connelly *Shipwreck* concert. I've always loved Chris Connelly's voice and went to this concert, being a big Ministry/Revco fan. I heckled Martin Atkins on the *Phenobarb Bambalam* tour a few years earlier. I ran into Raven near the bar and asked, "What happened, man?" He'd left Killing Joke. He replied, "I'm in fookin' Prong now!" He said it with such affirmation I didn't want to push the subject any further. Bought a beer and enjoyed the rest of the show. Paul Raven, man! Paul... fuckin'... Raven!

JOE COSENZA

It's strange the amount of details I remember about it. It was about June/July 1995. I was 12. For a really long time, I used to skateboard and would always be watching skate videos or even Eighties skateboarding movies and sometimes surf movies, though I didn't start surfing until my teens. One afternoon, I was watching Channel 11 and saw a commercial for a surfing movie called *North Shore* airing later that day. It featured a lot of good Eighties music, but I remember two songs in particular. One was 'Body and the Beat' [by Dragon], because of that funky bass-line, and the other was 'Chessboards' by Killing Joke. It was playing during one of the surfing scenes at Waimea and it worked really well with that scene. I remember the drums, the singer's voice and the guitar sound in particular. I have that soundtrack now and, obviously, I have *Brighter Than a Thousand Suns*, but, back then, I had no idea who the band was.

A few years later, I was watching another Eighties movie, *Weird Science*, and remember hearing 'Eighties' during the party scene and thinking what the fuck is that? You could straight up dance to it, but it wasn't exactly a dance song. During all this time, I'd been hearing influences of Killing Joke on other bands like Ministry, but I still wasn't listening to Killing Joke. I even saw Ministry on their *Rio Grande Blood* tour – with Raven playing bass – back in 2006. The concert was on a Saturday and my hearing didn't return until Tuesday.

YOUTH
On *Democracy*, they [the rest of the band] weren't around on the mix and were really pissed off about that.

GEORDIE
Youth has retrieved the [*Democracy*] multi-tracks and we're gonna remix. It was recorded really well. It all died in the mix. Youth wanted a mix for American radio.

YOUTH
There are things on *Democracy* that are really heavy. 'Absent Friends' is one of my favourite Killing Joke tracks, I think it's glorious, so epic. I pop it in [the live set] if I can because it's just glorious. I love it. Great at a funeral.

GEORDIE
There were loads of absolutely filthy, dirty analogue synth loops going on. That's getting resurrected. I wrote all the guitar parts high to fit in with that.

YOUTH
Geordie has famously derided the mixes. We always said to Geordie that, when we reissue it, he could remix it. I'm sure Geordie would like to have a go at that.

I wanted it to sound like our *Sgt. Pepper's*. It's always a bit of a battle between me trying to be ambitious with the sound sculpturing and the band wanting a dirgy, heavy sound. On *Democracy*, I had the freedom to do it differently and maybe a little lighter, which had some of the metal Killing Joke fans a bit disappointed, but I thought we had covered a lot of that on *Pandemonium*.

I'm seeing more posts from fans saying this is a much-overlooked album, we love it. We all love that album a lot. It's Dave Grohl's favourite.

BRIAN RICHARDSON
When KJ released *Democracy*, I phoned the marketing phone number where you could hear the special sneak preview.

TROY GREGORY

My wife is a bartender. This is later on in my story. She comes home and says, "The Killing Joke guitar player was in today." I thought it might have been some guy trying to say he was in the band. But Geordie was living here [in Michigan].

One time I ran into him when I was hanging out at the bar. He invited me and Laura for dinner. My wife and his wife were talking and Geordie wanted to play me the new mixes of *Democracy*. I was really digging it and we just hung out.

About two weeks later, I'm playing a show in Detroit and I get a message to call my wife. [This is] pre-cell phones. I call her from a pay phone. "Geordie called and wants you to call him." I call him back. He says, "Raven isn't doing the tour. We wondered if you wanna do it?"

When things like that happen, it is such an anomaly. It happened in such a nonchalant way. Divine nonchalance. It's that band's whole way of doing things.

There was two weeks' rehearsals in London. When we flew out, I got really sick on the flight. I think I had pneumonia. When we landed, we didn't go to Youth's place; we went straight to Butterfly Studios.

I think Jaz saw me as a Yank that used to be in a heavy-metal band. That's how he was looking at me. It [the sickness] started getting worse and Jaz was saying: "Smoke this spliff, drink this wine. This is what Killing Joke's all about."

I would never, ever do this ever again for a session, but *Pandemonium* I didn't know at all. Geordie had said, "Ah, don't worry about things." I should have just used my initiative and listened to the songs. And the sickness was getting worse.

They say [play] this song, this song and this song and I'm like: "I don't know that song." I tell you, that was a frosty day. Jaz wouldn't even look at me.

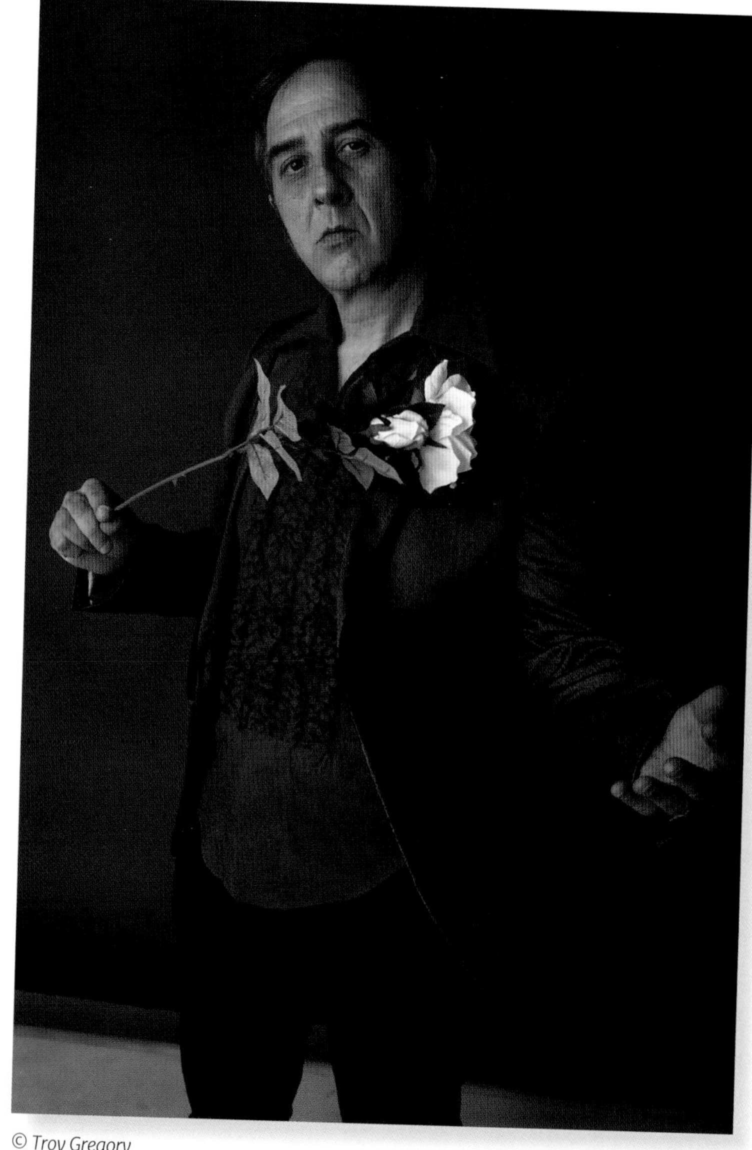

© Troy Gregory

I went back to Youth's and was up the whole night, going through every song and the *Democracy* stuff that was added. I was still really sick, but Nick [Walker, keyboardist] gives me this root, really hardcore herbicidal. I boiled it and it smelt horrible and I tasted it and it tasted horrible. But I woke up in the morning and I felt amazing. And I knew I had the set down.

The whole experience was surreal, especially because, at that time, I had only been there for, like, 48 hours.

EBULLITION
8 May 1996,
Bulle, Switzerland,

DIMITRI LORINGETT

Bulle, Switzerland – a small farmer's town in the middle of the Gruyère region. KJ were on the *Democracy* tour.

I got there early, around 7pm, and the doors were open. I stepped inside and made for the stage, where one of the two opening bands were rehearsing. As a venue manager was telling me to leave, none other than Jaz Coleman appeared and said it was okay and to join him backstage. He also asked if I had rolling papers, which I didn't, but he nevertheless led me upstairs to hang out with the band.

In the room, there was Geordie lying down on a sofa, resting. The other band members were just hanging around and Jaz went back to writing notes for a book on KJ (I think the project as such was never finished).

After getting Jaz and Geordie to sign the sleeve of an original 'Wardance' 7-inch single I brought with me (Geordie said something like, "Oh, that's a very old record!"), I started a conversation and, at some point, asked Jaz something about his interest in classical music.

At a certain point, Jaz asked me to leave as he and the lads had to get ready. I left him relaxed and 'normal', only to see him arrive later on stage with a war-painted face and wide-open and scary eyes, like in a trance. I reckoned he had found the rolling papers...

✦ ✦ ✦

LIVE MUSIC HALL
15 May 1996,
Cologne, Germany

MARCEL VAN DER WEIDEN

I used to be a metalhead and got into Killing Joke via Metallica's cover of 'The Wait'. I bought the first album and later on *Night Time* because someone played 'Love Like Blood' while I was depressed and lying stoned in a garden at the later stages of some party. What made me the fan I consider myself to be today was the *Pandemonium* album and especially 'Exorcism', 'Communion', the original 'Pandemonium' mix and 'Mathematics of Chaos'.

The first gig I ever attended was in Cologne during the *Democracy* tour, or the first real gig to be precise. I'm not a very esoteric person, but between *Pandemonium* and 2003, I attended three Killing Joke gigs in my dreams, which I find quite odd, since I have never dreamed of music, bands and such topics before or after except for these very three gigs.

My memory is a bit clouded, but the first one took place by the seaside on some kind of large jetty or pier. It was daytime and quite sunny as well. There weren't many people there, maybe 20, but the band didn't seem to mind that. They all had Jaz-ish war paint on and played a rather short and furious set, but I didn't recognise any songs. I think it was Raven on bass, which seems strange, since this must have taken place around the *Democracy* phase.

The second one took place in some unusual museum with several very different rooms stacked with huge artefacts of unknown origin and you could hardly see the band perform, since they didn't play on a stage or even in the same room, but seemed to wander through these different settings. Sometimes, they would appear out of nothing. Towards the end of the dream, some of the artefacts changed and looked more like stuff you would find in the warehouse of a theatre. Still huge, glamorous but with wooden planking on the back. Again, I don't remember recognising any songs or band members, but I remember enjoying the whole thing quite a lot.

© Mike Coles

The last dream-gig was probably the most realistic one, but too good to be true. There were ruins of what looked more romantic than a bunker, but without the splendour of a castle or some magnificent building in the middle of a glade in the forest. The band would play inside these ruins. It was a summer night and there was a whole bunch of people spread all over the forest and the glade as well as the ruins. There were lots of small fires burning and I remember drinking red wine, which seemed to be omnipresent. Jaz was in a very good mood and was chatting with everybody, myself included. All in all, it was a friendly, brotherly, if not loving atmosphere. When the band played, the sound was huge everywhere. I did not see them play but went to and fro from the glade into the forest and the ruins. There were shadows of the band dancing on the walls. In the dream, I knew they were playing some songs from *Pandemonium* – I'm sure 'Communion' was among them. It was an extremely enjoyable experience and I was seriously pissed off when I woke up and realised it was a dream. I wanted to stay.

Troy Gregory at the Paradiso, Amsterdam – 18 May 1996. Troy: "From a distance on stage, some people thought that I was Youth. They'd come closer and closer and then realise I'm not him. This horrible disappointment on their face" © Antoni Adamiak

TROY GREGORY

The shows [covering almost all of May] went well. My wife joined the tour about midway through. I smashed a bass at one show. I didn't mean to. I think my rocking got out of hand. I told my wife to bring my Rickenbacker from home. The other basses I was using were ones that Youth was okay for me to use, which was very kind of him.

I introduced her to Jaz and he said that it was nice when it's not just males, because they start to act like children. Having a woman there straightens our asses out.

By the time my wife came out, it made it seem like a vacation. The only difference was, I was playing with Killing Joke at night. It was great. Me and her had been married a year or so, so it was almost like a later honeymoon. It was just groovy. Everyone was cool.

They paid me well for that time. It paid the rent for at least three months, and that's helpful.

It was strange but cool to be on stage playing songs I have jammed in basements with friends, like 'Change'. And to be playing 'Change' and thinking: "God, this sounds so fucking right." Then you look up at the guys. Of course [it sounds right]!

It's weird. [It was] not one bit intimidating while I'm playing. It's one of the few things in life that I'm extremely comfortable with.

UMAIR CHAUDHRY

Killing Joke for me was like discovering a part of my own soul. I was first exposed to Killing Joke when a friend lent me a copy of *Democracy* at school. I was 15 at the time and exploring/consuming as much diverse music as I could find. Something about that album stood out from the pack, and I was immediately hooked by the emotional intensity. I purchased *Laugh? I Nearly Bought One!* and that gave me an overview of their career. I was spellbound from that point onwards. Tracks like 'Sun Goes Down', 'Wintergardens' and 'Darkness Before Dawn' revealed a yearning part of myself to me, a deep feeling that few other bands gave me.

I became a loyal fan, owning every release, knowing every lyric by heart. I would even go so far to say Killing Joke saved my life, instilling me with meaning, wonder and kinship in my darkest days when all hope was lost.

AL JOURGENSEN

(Ministry)

It was weird. We [Ministry and Killing Joke] would seem to do the same 'circuit' at the same time but always a day or two apart. It kind of became a running joke to the point where we, or they, would sabotage the dressing rooms knowing the other one was playing the next night. You know, the usual — faeces behind the couch, urine on the cushions, graffiti, etc... Juvenile stuff.

TROY GREGORY

We were sleeping on the tour bus and all of a sudden we were stopped. It was the French police. For days, everyone was swearing that there was some hash on the bus. It wasn't there anymore. Everyone was saying Geordie had nicked it. "I didn't nick it," he said.

The cops lined us all up in the countryside, the whole crew. They asked everyone to turn out their pockets. They go around everybody. Eventually, they get to Geordie and, sure enough, [he has] the hash.

And Jaz says: "Geordie, I *knew* it was you that had it." We were laughing, the cops were laughing.

There is a part of them that is very light-hearted and very silly, in a wonderfully absurdist way. But very joyful.

MICHAEL GAUGHAN

This one's actually a little funny. I'm 52 now so I was definitely 'living in the Eighties' at the right time. I liked all the 'mentioned in the same breath' bands like Ministry but, yes, seriously, my first-ever exposure to KJ was on buying the *Showgirls* soundtrack. I knew it had Bowie, it had Siouxsie, it had the Thrill Kill Kult, it had Toni Halliday's post-Curve gig.

When 'Hollywood Babylon' came forth from my speakers, it was a 'what the fuck did I miss?' moment. I honestly had no idea. Blame shitty American radio programmers for that one.

But, equally true, if 'Love Like Blood' had been on that soundtrack, it wouldn't have grabbed me by the fleshy bits and pulled as hard.

Immediately bought the CD of *Pandemonium*, which I will proudly note has cleared out three different house parties we were ready to end. Literally, halfway into 'Exorcism', the house was freakin' EMPTY.

FLETCHER STEWART

I suppose the way I first got into them is pretty crazy. I was in hardcore, surf and post-punk bands in my teens and started dating this really cool chick who made the scene when I was gigging early on around my home town of Knoxville, TN. She was my high-school girlfriend (even though I'd dropped out to gig more) and her Dad was a Brummie called Tony Smith, who happened to be tour-managing Metallica in the late Eighties and Nineties. He took a shine to me and used to pick me up in a Porsche 911 that he won in a bet with [Metallica guitarist] Kirk Hammett. He introduced me to all the amazing British bands that not only influenced Metallica, but that he had ran the board for back in the day. X-Ray Spex, The Slits, GBH, etc. I remember one day he played me a band that really affected me as a kid who grew up on Wax Trax! and more American 'industrial' stuff. It had sheering white-spark voltage blasts that infused with the hypno-tantric guitar over pounding, cyclical rhythms, up-front hook-laden bass-lines and malfunctioning fractured robo-cockney vocals. I was enthralled – my intro to the mighty Joke in Metallica's Porsche, which had of course a state-of-the-art sound system. It smelled like pipe smoke in a lambs-wool factory. The sounds had a lasting impact on me that would lead me to adventures in the UK many years later. Tony's favourite single of the day was The Verve's 'Bitter Sweet Symphony', which was on endless radio rotation at the time. Little did I know that one day I would end up smoking joints nervously and playing my demos in the living room of one of the UK's most important producers... That's another story...

thundergate.bandcamp.com/releases; @Thundergate; subgentsbandcamp.com; @Subgents

AARON COMBS

It was 1997 and my senior year of high school. My English teacher was a Scottish (ironic, I know) lad named Mr Page. He brought in a Killing Joke CD one day to play us a song which was relevant to what we were reading. I don't remember which song it was, but he then played 'Eighties', which I recognised from my favourite movie, *Weird Science*. A band that was deep enough to be played in English class and also cool enough to be in *Weird Science*? I was intrigued and then quickly hooked on their entire library.

MIK RAVEN

Late Nineties, when I thought KJ had disbanded, I found the internet and an email group called The Gathering. Only about 100 members at the time but I think we've all remained friends. Luckily, Paul Raven was also a member and kept us updated on what Killing Joke was not doing, but at least we had hope.

At this time, I realised there were no Killing Joke videos available for people to watch (pre-YouTube days – imagine that). I set out on a mission to get hold of as many as I could and make them available online (technology only allowed small videos back then) or on VCD [video CD] at low cost.

This seemed to keep people happy for a while, along with various bootlegs that were shared in the group. One highlight I had from that time (and I wish I still had the video) was Paul Raven wishing me a happy birthday then falling off his chair due to being drunk.

One day, I was at work and got a phone call. It was Paul Raven. You could have knocked me down with a feather. How had a member of Killing Joke got hold of my number? Turns out that another Gatherer gave it to him. But still… the bass player from your favourite band ringing you out of the blue at work? He had an idea about sharing all the videos publicly on a server farm. Sony put a stop to that idea pretty quickly, and also to my videos. Sony is a force that as an individual you do not want to stand up to!

One of Mik Raven's DVDs. Popular with Killing Joke fans; not so much with Sony © Mike Coles/Mik Raven

HOUSE OF BLUES
4 April 2000,
Los Angeles, USA

ROMEO PESTANAS, JR.

Being a huge Bauhaus fan, I went to this show and watched Peter Murphy and his interesting backing band of Eric Avery (Jane's Addiction) on bass, Peter DiStefano (Porno for Pyros) on guitar and Kevin Haskins on drums. I bumped into Raven first and said hello. I asked about the other members of Killing Joke and he pointed to Jaz. I spoke to him briefly. He was wearing a hat similar to the *Fire Dances*-era photo. He was very polite and nice. I asked about the friendship between Killing Joke and Bauhaus because I have a book where Daniel Ash says they're friends. Jaz said: "Daniel needs to play again. He's such a great guitarist. What a shame." Funny, I was thinking the same thing. I love his playing as well! I wish I could've chatted with Jaz and Raven more.

In the wake of Democracy, a second supergroup involving Joke members emerges, The Damage Manual, featuring Chris Connelly, Geordie, Martin Atkins, and Jah Wobble on bass...

CHRIS CONNELLY
(The Damage Manual)

When Martin [Atkins] called me up after [another of] many a falling out over Pigface over the subsequent years, I said yes immediately because it was him, Geordie and Jah Wobble AND I really wasn't up to much myself anyway. But, I mean, what a fucking powerhouse! That was an easy choice.

As with any collaboration (including Damage Manual), there was always a power struggle. I never took part in the power struggles. Maybe I should have. But those struggles are easily eclipsed by the creative force. I would do it again tomorrow, easily.

[Making the Damage Manual album was] sadly fraught. Martin was producing, and Wobble and Geordie hated his production. Their idea was a more stripped-down live sound; Martin's was a more modern (late Nineties) sample-ridden, bombastic approach. I could see the merits of both. The album is a compromise between Martin's work and Wobble enlisting Bill Laswell (which I was all fanboy about!). It's a hybrid all the way. I think it could have been so much better, but I still love it. But, Jesus, Wobble was querulous until the bitter death throes of the band, even calling me up to have his name removed. It was a hard band to be in because Geordie and Wobble were united against Martin. I just wanted to record and play. I think that band could have made some fucking great music.

In all fairness to Wobble, it was not the project he thought it was going to be, so of course he bickered and he didn't want to go to the States [on tour] with it because his heart just wasn't in it. If you listen to what he was doing at the time and just prior to the album, it's a very different animal. So that was that.

We carried on for a short US tour with another bassist and with Geordie. Then, after Geordie left, Martin and I even made another album, which was not bad at all.

I would absolutely collaborate again. I think we never tapped our full potential.

GEORDIE

I just thought of Martin Atkins and sighed.

2001–2007

"Burn, burn
Burn brightly
Burn, burn
Burn white heat"

GEORDIE
Jaz had kinda disappeared. I didn't hear from him for four or five years.

YOUTH
I think Jaz was actually sacked. When they did Damage Manual. He had to really fight to get it back, get the name back.

JAZ
All those times they say that Killing Joke had a hiatus... Well, all that time I was away, I was building something else. I was building another reality: an Earth Community, working towards permaculture.

JUSTIN BROADRICK
Godflesh had been covering 'Requiem' on the [2001] tour with Fear Factory, so at least I knew how to perform the song inside out. "Raven [who joined Godflesh following the departure of Ben Green] was like, "I'm getting Jaz down. He's in London. Let's do 'Requiem' with him." I'd never met Jaz at that point, so was very happy to have a childhood hero of mine on stage with me playing one of my favourite songs ever. It was ridiculous, but also, simultaneously, I was struggling with this new Godflesh. It didn't feel right. I was also very much battling alcohol dependency again. I knew I was doing it to get by, and generally wasn't happy and was very depressed. So I don't feel I ever really appreciated the moment, but it was, of course, amazing for me. Jaz seemed enamoured with the low-tuning aspect of Godflesh – he was performing the song dropped to B. He seemed to find that both challenging and exciting.

MARCEL VON DER WEIDEN
It was in late 2002 – if I remember correctly – when I had the chance to listen to a rough mix of *Killing Joke 2003*. [It was] before Dave Grohl laid down the drums and it only had programmed drums. I was playing keyboards for German alternative band Blackmail and we were recording a couple of songs at Andy Gill's – God rest his soul – studio in the Beauchamp Building in London. Jerry Kandiah was his engineer back then.

One day, I came back from some record store and Jerry asked me what I had bought. I showed him the 'Chop-Chop' 7-inch I had found and he said something like: "Oh, by the way, we just recorded their next album."

I didn't even know they still existed, given the long hiatus after *Democracy*.

They allowed me to listen that mix and I was over the moon, as you may imagine. Tears of joy. God, I love this band.

© Tony Woolliscroft

YOUTH

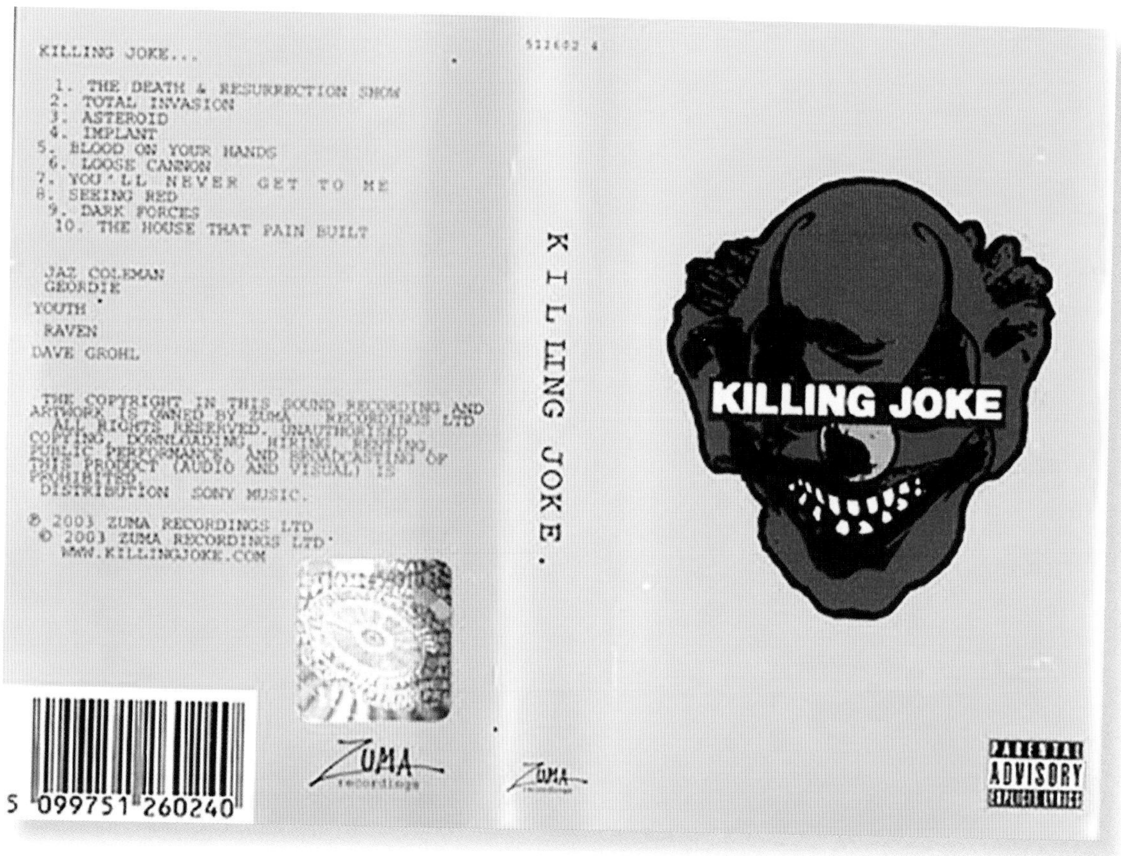

[*Killing Joke 2003*] was [done] a bit in a piecemeal way. Again, it was a tough time for the band. Geordie and Jaz were just sofa-surfing in London, and London had changed by then. It was no longer an easy place to live. It was getting expensive. The band hadn't been doing much, but we had this album deal.

I'd just had a couple of kids so wasn't that able to put in a lot of time, so we decided to get Andy Gill to produce it. That was good, because it [Beauchamp Building, Gill's London recording studio] was a neutral space and he was a neutral guy. Andy really kicked in on the vocals. Him and Jaz did them. I didn't get involved in that at all.

We were kinda writing it in the studio. There was a few things I'd written at home and brought in. Like 'Loose Cannon', which Geordie didn't really like. But, now we do it [live], he loves it. Time has erased his objections to it.

GEORDIE

Playing bass [on the album]? Not much at all. I think I just added a lower bass-line to 'Loose Cannon'. That was it.

YOUTH

Raven's on one track. The reason we brought Raven back in to do one track was because I didn't wanna tour it. He was prepared to tour it but wanted to be part of the album if he was gonna tour it.

We'd probably have about an hour of jamming around a riff or an idea. Maybe an hour and a half. Then they'd go down the pub. They'd crawl back about three or four. In that time, I'd edited all the jamming up into a structure. Sometimes it would be thrown away; sometimes they'd use it. When they came back, I'd go home and do the kids and they'd overdub to it and put keys on.

We'd been working with electronic drums and they sounded fucking amazing. When we were talking about Dave [Grohl] doing it, and Danny Carey had a go, I was like, "Are you sure? These drums sound so incredible." Be great if we could find some rough mixes with the electronic drums on. They were mind-blowing.

ANDREW ALEKEL

(assistant engineer, LA drum session, Killing Joke 2003)

Yeah, I did hear those. I remember thinking, "This is intense." Ha ha!

GEORDIE

I wouldn't do it [the album] by putting the drums on last, but it worked. Grohly did a load of people's albums that year.

YOUTH

Jaz told me that Dave did each drum [as a] solo [element]. So he'd do just the bass drum, then he'd do the hats, then he'd do the toms. He would do a whole take of just kick-drum, then a whole track of just snare, then toms, all overdubbed. Very hard to do that actually.

ANDREW ALEKEL

It is usually done to have total control of the ambience and bleed of the sound. It got 'known' because they talked about the process in interviews. It's a technique that's been done for decades, probably less now since so much can be done with electronic methods, programming and samples.

YOUTH

I've heard from other people that he likes to work like that. So it's almost like he's recording like he's a drum machine anyway. But he did do an amazing job. When I heard it, I was like: "Wow."

GEORDIE

I was able to mix this Killing Joke album with the engineer, just me and him in the studio. Clive Goddard, bless him, another one gone [Goddard died in 2018]. Really talented kid. I think he'd mixed 'Asteroid' and 'Implant'. Had three days. We mixed about four.

['The Death and Resurrection Show' riff] was not in the back pocket [before recording]. That was a jazz riff. And the fucking chorus just landed on me. Didn't even have to change key as well. Economical.

YOUTH

Jaz kept wanting all the arrangements to be really weird, not have any choruses. We had big arguments about that. But we did end up with choruses, I'm glad to say.

JOHN DORAN

I could make a really good argument for their comeback album of 2003, the eponymous one, being their best album. It's not super recent, but we're not talking 1979, 1980. The power of that album is absolutely phenomenal.

I love post-punk and heavy metal. Heavy metal is in some ways a more inclusive church than other forms of guitar music. Once they released that album in 2003, at that point, heavy metal really started celebrating Killing Joke. They've long since been regarded as pioneers in heavy metal.

FABIO FESTA

The Killing Joke album from 2003 was my company in the year my father died. A descent into hell and a very slow ascent to see the stars again.

Ted Parsons, drummer for live dates in 2003, at Faust Studios in Prague in what became known as the 'Basement of Hell'. The Czech capital city was soon to become a focal point for the band
© Faust Records Studio

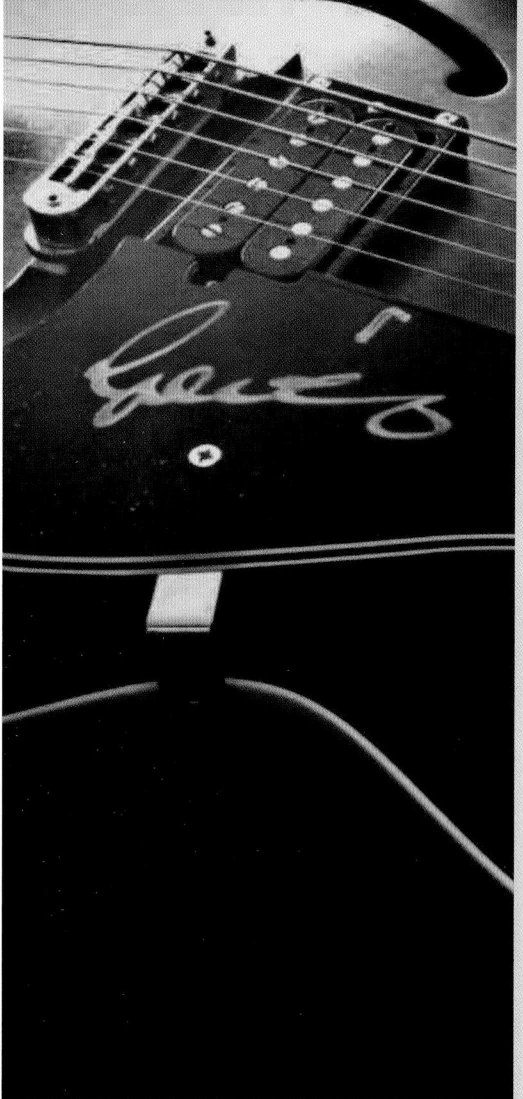
© Stefaan Kiekeman

LOKERSE FEESTEN
8 August 2003,
Lokeren, Belgium

STEFAAN KIEKEMAN

Time went by and, in the summer of 2003, I decided to go to a Killing Joke gig at the Lokerse Feesten. And there I was, front row, right in front of Paul Raven.

A few songs later, I realised this would be a gig to remember for ever.

Instead of observing, I absorbed all this energy blowing off the stage. Jaz looked scary, while Geordie looked super-cool.

His style reminds me of a James Bond quote while casting dice: "It's all in the wrist." Geordie creates these lovely tones with little movement of the right arm.

From this moment at Lokeren, it was the start of going to every KJ gathering in Belgium I could make.

A while ago, I picked up playing guitar again. I found a damaged archtop that I started to convert to a Geordie tribute.

A few years ago, at one of the Gatherings, I had the chance to talk to David [Simpson], Geordie's guitar tech. I gave him the pickguard of my guitar and a golden pen to ask to get it signed by Geordie. Half an hour later, David returned with the words, "You know Geordie can be a difficult person to deal with at times?" I listened carefully to what would follow – "but he's been so kind to sign your pickguard."

What a relief. The guitar is still under construction. It's getting a thicker neck and I am building a trapeze bridge to make it look and feel a bit more like the real deal. I look forward to playing some Killing Joke tunes on it.

ANDREW PENNINGTON

I thought I'd send you something different. In August 2003, I had my first child. We called her Jana. This is my girl wearing her Killing Joke-signed babygrow.

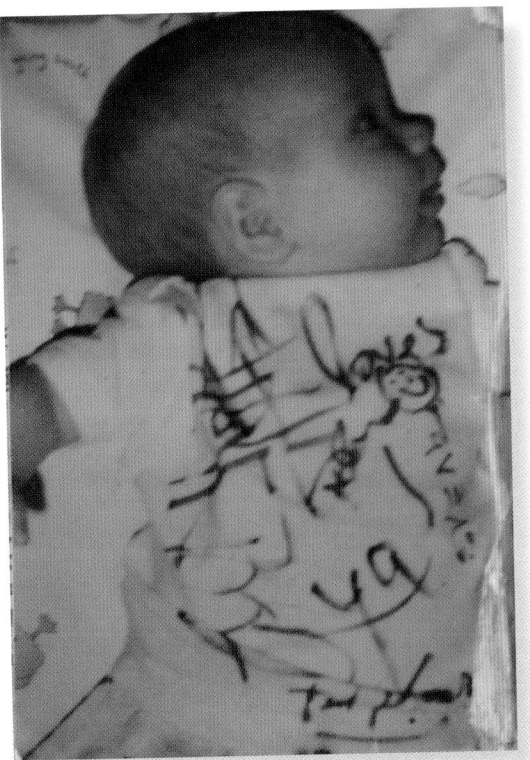
Jana wearing her Killing Joke-autographed babygrow

◆ ◆ ◆

M'ERA LUNA FESTIVAL
9 August 2003,
Hildesheim, Germany

MATTHIAS BOSENICK

Almost no moment was more thrilling than standing among thousands roaring 'Asteroid'. That was in 2003 when Killing Joke performed at the M'era Luna Festival. In broad daylight, Jaz Coleman summoned the masses with an oversized insect on his shirt. It was shortly after the release of the second self-titled album and I was amazed at how the people were around me. In the correct moment, everyone bawled the title of the new piece and Jaz gave us enough time before he got started with it, more intensely than a thousand-fold audience.

Unfortunately, I haven't had another live experience so far. A booked concert in Hamburg was cancelled. But I am confident.

✦ ✦ ✦

CAMDEN UNDERWORLD
14 August 2003,
London, UK

ALAN MUSTAFA

When I was a teen in the early Nineties, I saw a cuttings service advertised in one of the weeklies. You sent a list of the bands you were interested in and this bloke would send you a package every few weeks (or when you sent a cheque). It was 10p a cutting. I was obsessed with a few bands, so sent him a list (KJ, Bauhaus, Sisters, Christian Death). It was like getting a delivery of treasure every time it came, and well worth my paper-round money!

So I got a lot of KJ cuttings from the Eighties and then collected them myself in the Nineties. I worked with a bloke at HMV who was from NZ and knew Jaz. I lent him the folder to show Jaz, who apparently liked it, but was never sure if that was true. Mind you, the bloke did introduce me to Jaz's brother at the Underworld gig, so he was clearly connected. Had a slightly awkward small-talk chat with J's brother!

PETER LAMB

I've been a Killing Joke fan since I was 13 in 1980. However, the story I want to tell is much later on.

I've lived in China for the past 20 years. Like most Killing Joke obsessives, I've ranted on and on about how they are the best live experience. I could never find the words to truly describe Geordie's [guitar] tone. Anyway, in 2003, I was ecstatic to find out there was a new release and tour coming. It turned out that my best mate's sister's friend worked for KJ's management company at the time. My mate and I headed back to the UK for the summer to see KJ, and he came to the Camden Underworld gig with me. It was rammed and hotter than hell. When the roadie was getting Geordie's rig ready, he strummed that guitar and an almighty roar went up. I looked at my mate and he smiled and nodded. He knew I wasn't bullshitting. I was right down the front by Raven. My mate got caught in the mosh, then found me just after 'Change' finished. He was just brimming with happiness. I remember him telling me he couldn't believe how good Geordie was. My mate's been going to see them ever since.

After the gig, the friend of my mate's sister got us backstage and it was great. Got photos with them all. Jaz was very warm. Raven and Geordie were cool. Geordie made a joke about being an Englishman in China, which I can't repeat, and Ted Parsons was an absolute gent, lovely fella.

Happy days.

STEPHANE BONGINI
(aka Frenchy Frenzy)

The real turning point in my Killing Joke story. I go to see them for the first time in London.

I see the soundcheck and I meet Raven, who's really nice and I take a picture with him. I see Jaz for the first time up close. He's already drunk and screaming so I'm not going to disturb him. In a burst of enthusiasm, I tell myself that it's time to get them to sign the new album, *Killing Joke 2003*. I don't have a pen and I don't have any markers so I ask the only guy next to me if he can lend me one. Unfortunately, I run into the tour manager. who kindly escorts me out of the room...

Not bad but can do better; a frustrating feeling of having failed so close to the goal.

The concert is wonderful and there is an incredible energy with the incomparable feeling of attending it with 399 other lucky people. The walls of the hall literally ooze from the condensation released by the band and the boiling audience. At the end of the concert, thanks to Rob Moss – who lends me his photo pass – I get to see backstage for the first time. There I am, like a kid in a toy store. I remember a feeling of levitation between the venue and my hotel room. I was glad I came that night.

ADRIAN WASON
This was special. It was the first time KJ had played in the UK for a while and we were very lucky to get tickets. The place was absolutely jam-packed and possibly one of the sweatiest gigs ever. We heard there were people left outside who had tickets. The standout track for me was 'The Death and Resurrection Show'. The first time I heard this track, I was out running in the heat and I was choked with emotion. It did not disappoint live and it was the first time I'd seen Ted Parsons. He was like an animal drumming.

✦✦✦

L'USINE
21 September 2003
Geneva, Switzerland

STEPHANE BONGINI
I decided to bring my camera. It was the fabulous Raven who noticed me during the soundcheck. He said two or three words in French and got me into the backstage dressing room. Raven said: "You can film whatever you want for as long as you want: there's no problem". The beginning of an incredible odyssey. I owe it all to Raven.

The concert is great and I'm filming in excellent conditions, enjoying every minute. The after-concert is also very relaxed, with the singer of The Young Gods, and I feel strangely like a fish in water. In fact, I'm not at all in my usual environment but feel very comfortable.

Later, in Paris, I'll reap lifelong tinnitus thanks to Raven's bass on 'Asteroid'. I'm at the Astoria in London and then the anniversary concerts of 25 years of magic at Shepherd's Bush Empire in 2005.

There's a concert in Milan that will stay in my memory, as I spent the whole afternoon with Jaz and Raven relaxed and laughing, while Geordie is missing and arrives from Prague minutes before the start of the concert because he couldn't get on a plane in the morning.

ELYSEE MONTMARTRE
29 September 2003,
Paris, France

MIK RAVEN

So, now 2003. KJ came back! What a surprise and what a brilliant LP. This is the first time I did the tour – 13 dates and my first one in Europe. Loved the whole thing and met so many new friends.

One great experience was Paris. I was in a café near the gig with a couple of French Killing Joke friends I met on The Gathering. We were happily having a few beers and getting into the mood for the gig that night. Suddenly, there was banging on the window. It was [Paul] Raven saying, "Mik Raven! Mik Raven!" He came into the café, bought us all drinks and spent time chatting to us. He was like that. He loved to get to know the fans and had the ability to remember us. Anyway, after the drink, he had to go, but gave me a few CDs he had been given in Germany (a leather-bound Cradle of Filth CD included) and shook my hand. That handshake included a transfer of some cannabis!

After getting home, I smoked what I had been given. It would have been rude not to. It was good shit! What I later found out on The Gathering was that another Gatherer (a German teacher) had confiscated it from one of his pupils, then given it to Raven. He then brought it to Paris and gave it to me. I took it home to Wakefield in England. What a great story that pot had.

✦ ✦ ✦

THE GARAGE
4 October 2003,
Glasgow, UK

ANDY MAXWELL

2003 was my first experience of the Killing Joke live assault on my hearing. Why it took so long, I'll never know. I'm not proud to admit this, believe me. The second self-titled album was released. Mind-blowing is an understatement, to say the least. I still remember leaving to a chorus of 'Loose Cannon', my ears ringing from the sheer volume I had just experienced. Truly amazing.

Mick Head: *"I was support band (Lowrider) for my heroes [at Leeds Metropolitan University on 5 October 2003]. Raven prepared a bag of sweets for my son Damon [pictured between Raven and Geordie] and waited for him to arrive with me. His friendship was long-lasting and we subsequently followed him in Prong, Godflesh, Ministry and, of course, KJ"*

✦ ✦ ✦

ROADMENDER
9 October 2003,
Northampton, UK

SUZANNAH YOUNG

I must have been about 18. I hadn't heard of Killing Joke before, but a friend who was already a fan invited me to the gig and I decided to go with her. She was more of a heavy-metal fan than me (and a goth, whereas I wasn't) so I didn't know what to expect but went because we were into some of the same music already. There was a big goth and heavy-metal scene in Northampton at the time, so Killing Joke fitted right in.

As the band started to play, I experienced something I had never felt before and have not felt since. It was like this massive sound was washing over me. I was standing at the front, so the sound didn't have to travel a long way to get to me – it was really powerful. I closed my eyes and was enveloped in the music.

I haven't been to see Killing Joke again, but I've listened to their albums because of the experience I had at that gig.

RUTH HUMPHREYS

Killing Joke were a band I had long listened to, but never seen before. I'd enjoyed their extensive back-catalogue for some time and was, therefore, extremely excited to finally be able to see them. Even better, they were playing a small venue in my home town.

The Roadmender is a narrow, deep venue and was equipped with a powerful speaker set-up to push the sound from the stage to the back of the room. This meant that, if you stood near the front, you could expect things to get pretty loud! However, nothing really prepared me for the intensity of the wall of sound which hit me when KJ took the stage...

Pre-gig Suzannah Young and Ruth Humphreys © Ruth Humphreys

As Jaz Coleman appeared on stage to the intense tribal, pulsing beats of 'Communion', dressed in a brown hooded robe with white face paint, I was bowled over by the wall of sound which seemed to hit you right between the eyes. Jaz is quite the showman and KJ kept this intensity up throughout their set. They had recently released an eponymously titled album and weaved these newer songs seamlessly into their set alongside Eighties classics and more experimental Nineties offerings. My favourite album by Killing Joke is 1994's *Pandemonium*, and I was delighted they chose to open and close their show with songs from this record.

My overriding memories of the night are the hot, sweaty room, coupled with the wall of sound KJ produced, making for a trance-like experience at points. The ringing in my ears continued for well over 12 hours after the show finished!

Ironically, the experience left such an impression that I've spent the last 17 years actively trying to avoid seeing Killing Joke again, lest it not live up to expectations. I've not been entirely successful. They supported Guns N' Roses in Gdańsk in 2017 and, in that huge stadium environment, all the intensity the band had generated previously could never be replicated. It felt like I was watching an entirely different band.

ASTORIA
12 October 2003,
London, UK

SHUNICHI 'ISSHEE' ISHIDA

I was planning a trip to see some live shows in England and France in 2003. I can't remember which airlines I used [but] the flight from Tokyo takes nearly 12 hours.

At that time, I couldn't easily book tickets online, so the first thing I did when I arrived in London was buy *Time Out*. There was a live announcement of Killing Joke at the Astoria. Having just bought the 2003 album, I decided to go. This was the first Killing Joke experience. However, I planned to go to another live show that day so I went to Astoria to buy a ticket for the additional performance.

When I went to the Astoria at opening time, the message 'There will be a video shoot today' was displayed, so I rushed to secure the centre of the front row. The opening act was Queen Adreena. They were great, but I couldn't wait for Killing Joke. A solemn synth sound and the members come out. Jaz, Geordie and Paul Raven! There was also a violin player besides keyboard player and drummer [Ted Parsons].

'Communion' begins with Jaz's signal. Oh, how cool! An overwhelming performance focusing on the recent songs and the early songs. Jaz has a charismatic presence, with make-up that looks like a Kabuki actor. Geordie's guitars dominate the space, and Paul and Ted's rhythm corps are the driving force behind the tunes. A spicy keyboard and violin are added. A little less than two hours later, there I was, stunned. Of course, I wanted to listen to more songs, but I was satisfied with this first live experience.

✦ ✦ ✦

MOUNT STUART
13 October 2003,
Cardiff, UK

ADRIAN WASON

We were talking to Taif Ball, who was playing pool before one of the Forum shows in 2008. He lived in Barry at the time [of the Cardiff gig in 2003], about a 20-minute drive from the venue. He said he was invited to the soundcheck but said the stuff they were smoking was so strong he had to go home!

Anyway, there was a late venue change and the MS1 was much smaller than the original. Jaz came on and scowled, "Some of us are here through choice!" The crowd barrier was a waist-high scaffold bar which failed in the surge as the band came on and dropped to shin level. I still have the scars. Another hot and sweaty one. We drank the place dry – there was no more cider!

THE MILL
17 October 2003,
Preston, UK

PAUL STABLES

Never was a venue more fitting for this band – old, sweaty, low ceilings, struggling commercially (like the band themselves at this time). Best of all – a bar which wasn't so far away from the stage, therefore still affording a tolerable view of the band within a few short steps of purchasing your beverage of choice.

© Andrew Pennington

I hadn't seen Joke since the *Pandemonium* tour in the Nineties. On that occasion, I took my close friend Kev to the legendary Bierkeller nightclub in Bristol [30 January 1995]. Kev had never seen Joke before but trusted my musical influences most of the time. As we left the venue to catch the bus home, I asked what he thought. He replied enthusiastically, "They would have been the perfect backdrop to the end of the world." I still don't know if he liked the band, but I thought it was a fair summing up.

Back to the Mill at Preston. This time, I was with another good friend, Phil, but we met by coincidence other friends, Gary and his close friend Stewart, at the venue. Older than us, Stewart was your classic old-school punk in that he was there in '76 and therefore felt entitled to be very critical of a lot of the bands that emerged from that explosive musical period that continued into the Eighties and Nineties. Killing Joke were, of course, one of these bands and, sure enough, when 'Pssyche' boomed from the stage, in his opinion Raven was no match for the sublime bass-playing skills of Youth. Ignoring the old punk bore, I ventured forward, my interest piqued (another great thing about the Mill was it always seemed fairly easy to get to the front, probably because they rarely sold out any of the gigs I attended there). Jaz was in his now well-established boiler-suit attire and make-up, Raven with bob hat and face paint and Geordie ever so cool, no matter what nerve-jangling electric mischief emanated from his classic golden Gibson.

I'd never been this close to the band before and it was incredible, like a secret gig, very intimate, only a few hundred people present. A possible low point for the band? You would never have guessed that when balanced against the chaotic menace they seemed to be producing with ease that night. Jaz was still drinking at this time and demanded a large whisky from any member of the audience willing to acquiesce. I cannot recall as to how many whiskies were purchased for Jaz, but he seemed to be very happy, with a manic perma-grin on his face. They pumped out 'Follow the Leaders'. Jaz gave the audience every opportunity to sing along in a chant-esque mantra whilst staring on, microphone in the air pointed at the crowd, laughing hysterically. I was mesmerised and felt myself laughing hysterically at the whole experience. It was insane – Jaz laughing at us, Geordie oblivious to our existence with trademark ciggy dangling from his mouth, Raven simply staring at everybody with menace in spades. I had never previously seen these larger-than-life characters frighteningly close like this.

Whether or not this was a low point for the band, it was most assuredly a high point for me and one of the best gigs I've had the good fortune to witness. I could have stopped time and watched that crazy band for hours and hours but, equally, Kev was right. I really wouldn't have minded it all ending right there and then.

WEBSTER HALL
22 October 2003,
New York, USA

CLIFF MONK LIVINGSTON

2003 – [I was] in between albums. I had a feeling to look online to see if there was anything going on with Killing Joke. They were doing an album with Dave Grohl on drums. There was a Killing Joke fan website. I bumped into Paul Raven on there.

I offered to be a roadie for the Killing Joke North America 2003 tour. I did this for a month on the bus, travelling from New York to San Diego, two Canadian shows – one in Toronto, one in Vancouver – and then one week in Australia.

I got to play all the guitars every day. I was the stage manager and had to make sure the stage was set for them – duct-tape the cables down, set up the gear, make sure they had strings. Geordie didn't break a string the whole tour. Lucky me. I made sure the band had drinks. Geordie liked to have a straw duct-taped to his cup. Raven wanted incense lit and taped to his bass cabinet. I'd hand him his guitar when he walked on stage into a cloud of incense. It was a lot of hard work and great fun. I lost 30lbs in five weeks. All the guys were amazingly talented. When they hit the stage, it was 'show on'.

At the final show of that tour in Melbourne, Australia [23 November], everyone – including the crew – took a bow on stage and Jaz thanked me in front of the crowd for helping on the tour. There was lots of good downtime and I hung out with the band, having dinner with Jaz Coleman, getting to know the guys one on one. Geordie and I went guitar shopping and had lunch in Portland. I hung out with Paul Raven and Nick Walker, and we had a great Italian dinner in Sydney, with the tour manager. Good times.

✦ ✦ ✦

AXIS
25 October 2003,
Boston, USA

GREG SLAWSON

I remember their show in Boston during the 2003 reunion tour. Jaz, wearing his spider outfit, drooled on himself while his eyeballs were popping, with the spit falling right on his spider!

✦ ✦ ✦

EL REY THEATRE
14 November 2003,
Los Angeles, USA

JOEL GAUSTEN

The first time I saw Killing Joke – my all-time favourite band since childhood. I'd recently moved to LA from the East Coast and this was my first major night out. As '[The] Faith Healer' by The Sensational Alex Harvey Band played over the PA, I made my way to the front of the stage. The lights dimmed and my eyes soon met the menacing vision of Paul Raven – covered in war paint and looking like he wanted to singlehandedly break every audience member in half. It was on.

Geordie swayed in that inimitable Geordie way as Ted Parsons fuelled the band through 'Communion'. Parsons' live interpretation of the song – solid groove with a flowing hi-hat – remains my favourite. By the time The Black Jester made his way to centre-stage, the crowd was well in a trance, and stayed in one throughout the set. The White Heat was everywhere.

Outside the venue following the gig, I met a lovely young lady who had also attended. She soon took me on a few adventures around town and taught me some new things about the world. As for exact details, let's just say Killing Joke always attract a very colourful lot, and leave it at that.

✦ ✦ ✦

UTOPIA RECORDS
20 November 2003,
Sydney, Australia

GARY HOWES

Moved to Australia, met an Irish girl and brought her back to Middlesex. She liked the softer 'Love Like Blood' era, and Jaz actually sang on *Brighter Than a Thousand Suns*. Emigrated back to Sydney. Like Jaz was feeling, the UK felt like it was going nowhere and the sky was large in the southern hemisphere. The possibilities seemed brighter.

I named my Australian son Jaz. And the attached note from Jaz Coleman was to my five-year-old boy after finally meeting my heroes at a record-shop signing. Chatted with Geordie sitting on a wall outside – the most lovely bloke and, in my opinion, best guitarist in the world.

© Gary Howes

Was in Auckland, New Zealand, just as the virus spread. I saw the ferry leave for Great Barrier Island and Little Barrier Island every day from the wharf. Kept thinking – just get a ticket and wander around till I find myself in Cythera.

THE ARENA
21 November 2003,
Brisbane, Australia

VAUGHAN SMITH

I got backstage before the gig. As I walked into the back room, there's Jaz laid out on the floor. I had to step over him to get in.

There's Geordie and Raven.

So, naturally, drank the free booze, had a few smokes. Jaz woke up, then we had a good session, more of the same. Talked about some mutual friends. Tony Haggar was one of them – RIP. Had a good laugh, then I went down in the pit.

Words don't describe the concert – the awesomeness.

Then backstage again. Then on to the hotel room.

Had a bit of a deep 'n' meaningful conversation with Jaz. We were all in a bit of a state, as you can imagine.

Another never-forget night.

Didn't get any photos but rang a couple of mates in New Zealand. Geordie said: "What shall I say?" I said: "Tell 'em to fuck off. They will love it." And they did.

HI-FI BAR
23 November 2003,
Melbourne, Australia

STAN MANIATIS

I had to wait 18 years for the next visit [after seeing the band in 1985]. That was frustrating. We're just too remote and small a population here in Australia.

I purchased that [2003] comeback record from JB HI-FI. Much wider release and I purchased this record five or six times, plus the Japanese version. I turned Melbourne into a sales hotspot and they finally toured in late 2003! 'Total Invasion' created a lot of new fans with those vocals and that chugging metallic guitar.

Adoring fans [at the gig] and with Raven on bass guitar. The sound was great and it was a memorable Sunday night.

When you hear 'Unspeakable', 'The Pandys Are Coming' and 'Wardance' for the first time, you're either repulsed or hooked. I was the latter. Even *Outside the Gate* is a refreshing blast of air! 'Tiahuanaco' is one of their best. *Extremities…* and *Pandemonium* were great, too, after they went a bit mellow in the late Eighties. New generation of fans came through. The Joke just come up with great releases – unbelievable quality control.

By comparison, The Clash were cooked by 1982 after five years and released an appalling final album, *Cut the Crap*, while the Joke records *Pylon* 35 years after the first album.

Absolute Dissent was very diverse, too, 'The Great Cull' and 'The Raven King'. It was like a compilation of all their sounds: industrial, metal, new wave and melodic tunes.

Great memories and a very creative band. Not a nostalgia act. Their recent material is just as good as the old.

SCOTT MCCALLUM

I'm from Adelaide, South Australia, born 1964. It was 1978/79 – we were listening to Buzzcocks and The Clash when one of the group found Killing Joke. Wow! What a sound! What a voice! What energy!

From that day onwards, I became a follower. Being so isolated, it would be some time before I'd experience the band live – first in 2003. I've since seen them two more times – truly the greatest music experiences I've ever had.

I went on to play in multiple bands, always influenced by that driving sound. Favourite album: *Hosannas from the Basements of Hell*.

BRIAN DRISCOLL

As a 19-year-old on a stinking-hot 42-degree Melbourne day on the way to Kooyong to watch the tennis (I had a free ticket) in January '82, I heard 'Follow the Leaders' on 3RRR FM, an independent community radio station – the greatest in the world. I HAD to stop at Gaslight Records in Glenferrie Road, Malvern, to get my copy of *What's THIS for…!* From then on, I was a lifetime KJ disciple.

I had to wait many years before the band made it to Melbourne. In 2003, on the back of their eponymous LP, I had to have my mind blown all over again.

✦ ✦ ✦

KZND 87.7 RADIO STATION
2004
Anchorage, Alaska

CLIFF MONK LIVINGSTON

I DJ'd on Alaska's only alternative rock station, KZND 87.7, the first station in USA to use a low-power TV signal for radio. My DJ name was Monka. I tagged it on to my name to make CliffMonka. Paul Raven was a fan of the show, listening online, and said I should be CliffMonk instead. I've kept it that way since 2004...

DIMITRI LORINGETT

I visited Mike Coles in London in 2004. He showed me his studio and some of the original material used for KJ album artwork.

RON SYNOVITZ

(partner, Golden HIVE Studios, Prague, Czech Republic)

I met Jaz Coleman around mid-2004 in Prague's Old Town. I sat next to him by chance at a pub called Marquis de Sade. I'd been listening to Killing Joke since 1982 in the States and still have my ticket from my first Killing Joke show – Hammersmith Palais, London, [23] November 1986.

I knew Jaz was living in Prague. I'd read an interview he'd given in 2002 to an underground newspaper called *The Prague Pill*. And I'd seen Killing Joke play Prague's Palac Akropolis in August 2003 with Ted Parsons on drums. But it was still a surprise to see Jaz sitting next to me in a black hat. He had a dark aura. He told me about his work with the Prague Symphony Orchestra, and the group Čechomor in Petr Zelenka's 2002 film *Rok d'ábla - Year of the Devil*. He also spoke about a Killing Joke documentary in the works by Shaun Pettigrew – *The Death and Resurrection Show*. Jaz called it by its working title at the time, *Let Success Be Your Proof*. He said: "I've got Dave Grohl in my film."

He was passionate about Prague's mysterious "geomagnetic energy" – taking me outside to point out an obscure 'Black Madonna' statue, near Prague's Gothic Týn Church, hidden in a niche up on the façade of a centuries-old building.

We took a taxi across town to another pub – Alice Through the Looking Glass – to meet Paul Raven. He'd just arrived from the UK with a bottle of 12-year-old Balvenie Single Malt Scotch Whisky in hand. Geordie Walker was living in Detroit at the time. I first spoke [on the phone] with Geordie that night as well. We finished the bottle, and I told Raven my friends wouldn't believe I'd drunk a bottle of scotch with Killing Joke. Raven gave me the empty bottle and canister, signing it: "MT – Now. It's true – we were here with him! PR 04." Jaz scrawled his autograph sideways on the canister. After that, Jaz convinced Geordie to relocate to Prague. I remember overhearing Jaz at Alice one night talking to Geordie back in Detroit on the phone – saying, "Not to survive but to thrive!"

MAX FARR

Until high school, my musical tastes were pretty much dictated by radio play. I liked pop and some rock, all very commercial. Then, in 1982, my family moved from Texas to Oklahoma, and I found an opportunity to try to reinvent myself. I took cues from my older brother, who embraced a punk aesthetic. I put on various albums of his while he was out drinking to try to 'discover' new bands, so I could discuss them at school with the few friends I had. One I tried – but was too unadventurous enough to appreciate at the time – was Killing Joke's *Fire Dances*. I just didn't 'get' it.

Flash-forward to about 2004. I'd moved to Prague some years before and was a regular at a bar/café Jaz also frequented, as well as sometimes Paul Raven, Ben Calvert and, less frequently, Geordie. I didn't know his name, hadn't met him or even noticed him before, but a friend of a friend introduced me to Jaz one day.

She told me he was in a band. When I found out the band was Killing Joke, I wasn't particularly impressed. But he and I and our friends sat and drank and smoked and listened to him tell various road stories and jokes (a year or so before Jaz stopped drinking) and it was generally a pretty good time. Jaz, I soon discovered, was full of great stories and had a wicked sense of humour.

Because we were both regulars and so were our mutual friends, we ended up making a routine of it. That café – Za Zrcadlem, Czech for 'Through the Looking Glass' aka Alice – was close to where I worked and usually my first stop after work. So Jaz and I became pretty good friends fairly quickly. I always bit my tongue, never gave my opinion about what I thought of his band and music. Occasionally, when Raven or Geordie sat with us, I followed the same policy.

It turned out to be the right move...

RON SYNOVITZ

When Geordie moved into a flat in my neighbourhood in Prague, Jaz took me over there to meet him in person. His gold 1952 Gibson ES-295 guitar was hanging on the wall. He let me play it. The strings felt super-light. It was perfectly set up with the strings so close to the fretboard, all the way up the neck. He had two huge Framus amp heads on top of four cabinets, each with four speakers – 16 speakers. Together, they were as tall as Geordie.

His apartment was right next door to a mutual friend, actually in the same building – *Marie Claire* fashion photographer Ian Bull. So I'd bump into Geordie there, or at neighbourhood haunts that Geordie said he liked because they were "within stumbling distance from home". We'd talk about music and heartbreak, recording gear and fishing.

Geordie and Ben Calvert in the 'Basement of Hell' at Faust. Behind Geordie is the same amp/speaker set-up he had in his flat © Faust Records Studio

IAN BULL

(Geordie's next-door neighbor, Prague)

I became Geordie's drinking buddy. More like his 'drink everything in the house' buddy, getting rock-star smashed at three in the afternoon on wine and slivovice [plum brandy]. I heard a lot of stories from him. We were neighbours. An entirely different relationship than anyone else, probably. A neighbour, not a rock star.

We lived across the street from a place we called 'Murder Park' on account of body parts turning up there. And junkies. It was the exterior courtyard of a 16th-century church built on top of an eighth-century church that was built over a third-century pagan site. His apartment had a straight line-of-sight view of Prague Castle. I think we both lived on a ley line. He said the place was haunted. A bit of an understatement, if you ask me.

Our bedrooms were back to back. They shared the same wall and it was the thinnest wall in the flat. Geordie had these huge guitar amps against the far wall on the opposite end of his apartment near the door to the patio, and he'd play the guitar all the time. Loudly. Noise. He was working songs out. But I never told him to turn it down. I'd go over and bang on his door until he'd open it up, and I'd say: "Dude, just close your bedroom door." The acoustics were amazing in there. That's why he got the place. Except for the bedroom, the old stone walls were a metre thick, so he could crank it up. But his patio was like a speaker cone that amplified the music and blasted it up to Letná Park. You could sit in the park and hear him playing.

Loved that guy. After living next door to Geordie for years, I finally got to see Killing Joke play. It blew me away when I saw him in concert and went backstage. Then I understood the shenanigans. All his stories finally matched up. They were gods. When he moved to another flat in the neighbourhood, I moved over into his apartment. That place was totally haunted.

RON SYNOVITZ

Killing Joke gathered to celebrate Raven's 44th birthday at a medieval-themed restaurant in Prague called U Sádlů. It was 16 January 2005. The party included Raven, Jaz, Geordie and their new young drummer, Ben Calvert. I was invited along. There wasn't a car in sight on Revoluční Street on the way there. We all jay-walked against a traffic light. Raven led everyone in a Judas Priest chant: "Breaking the law. Breaking the law." There was a lot of laughter.

Jaz had discovered U Sádlů and the basement was booked. We had it to ourselves. We sat at a heavy wooden table – a medieval table set with goblets – surrounded by old suits of armour, animal heads and coats of arms. Jaz was in a lot of physical pain because he'd just lost a filling, leaving the raw nerve in his tooth exposed. He was tilting his head sideways and pouring whisky on it to numb the pain, wondering out loud how soon he could get a dentist.

Raven's 44th birthday marked the start of the *Hosannas from the Basements of Hell* era with Ben Calvert on drums. Raven had joined Jaz and Geordie in Prague about a week earlier. Ben came over that day to start rehearsals for two upcoming shows in London.

After the feast, Jaz tapped on his glass and toasted Raven's birthday. Then he announced the plans for the band. There would be Prague practices through mid-February at Faust, the studio where they'd rehearsed with Ted Parsons on drums for their 2003/2004 tours. Then a warm-up tour of the Czech Republic, starting in a small village called Vroutek [16 February] and ending at Prague's Palac Akropolis [21 February], then a flight to London for shows on 24/25 February at Shepherd's Bush Empire. Jaz said the London shows would be recorded and filmed for a live album and DVD. He already had the name: *XXV Gathering! The Band That Preys Together Stays Together*. After that, they'd return to Faust in Prague to work on material for a new studio album and prepare for a summer tour with Mötley Crüe.

I told Ben he must be stoked about recording with Killing Joke. He said he was just focusing on getting up to speed on all the songs he needed to learn for the tour. Jaz told Ben: "You'll be playing drums in Hell" and laughed. 'Hell' was the nickname of the basement at Faust. Geordie told me a few weeks later, before the tour started, that Ben had 'an accident' one night after playing in Hell. Blood everywhere. Stitches around his kick-pedal leg.

BERT NEVEN

(partner, Golden HIVE Studios; sound engineer, Killing Joke)

I met the whole band at the same time. It was in Vroutek in the Czech Republic, about a week before their 25th-anniversary gigs in London. They'd been rehearsing at Faust and were doing warm-up gigs in the Czech Republic, a four-gig tour basically preparing for those two London shows.

I was on the road on another tour, just ending, in the south of the country. I got a phone call from a friend, a driver for rock bands. He said: "An English band needs a sound engineer. What the fuck are you doing tomorrow?"
"What's the name of the band?" "Killing Joke." "Are you fucking kidding me?" Disbelief, basically. And it turns out it was them. I knew their albums. And I always loved 'Love Like Blood'. So for me, the next day, I had to get back to Prague where they had a car waiting for me to drive me to their gig in Vroutek.

I arrived at the gig three hours late for soundcheck. So they'd started with the local guy and were waiting for me. I guess they were happy that I arrived. I went backstage. They were all there. First, I introduced myself. Excused myself for being so late, and the first question was from Raven. "Do you have weed?" I gave him the weed out of my pocket with papers, with filters, and a cigarette, and I said I'm going to start soundchecking. I did the drums. It all went quite fast. Raven went on stage. Geordie went on stage. Jaz was standing in the hall listening to it, until his face lit up and he gave me a nod of approval – the moment he obviously thought things were ready for him to go on stage and sing. So he went on stage. And the whole thing started for me.

I don't know when Benny stuck his fucking foot through the glass in the front door at Faust. It was locked. He'd lost the key. He cut his leg. Real bad. His right calf. And he needed stitches from one side of his leg to the other side. It was one of those nights in Prague before the London shows.

Benny played all the Czech warm-up gigs like that with his right leg reddish and swollen up. I did sound for all four gigs. Then they went and played the two London shows. I didn't do those shows, but, when they came back, I started doing their live sound for years. I did the Mötley Crüe tour with them that summer.

✦ ✦ ✦

PALAC AKROPOLIS
21 February 2005,
Prague, Czech Republic

MAX FARR

Eventually, Jaz invited me to see a Killing Joke concert. I thought it would be rude to turn him down, but I wasn't expecting to enjoy it at all and agonised a bit over what I would say afterwards. So, strategically, I asked him for a plus-one for the guest-list, so I could take a date and tell him I spent most of the show focused on my date – I really didn't want to tell him that I thought he was cool and brilliant and funny but his band sucked.

The girl I took was apparently semi-obsessed with Jaz, but I didn't really know that when I asked her. But I did know that Jaz told me that they would hit the stage at 7.30 sharp, not late, so a few minutes before that I told her at the bar area that we should go into the concert hall (the show was at Akropolis, a nice small/medium venue in Prague). She took me by the hand and, like magic, led us straight up front. The crowd seemed to literally part for her like the sea parting for Moses. We were about third/fourth row in no time, with her in front of me.

The band hit the stage right on time and the girl grabbed my hands and put them on her breasts and started grinding against me – and the music wasn't anything like what I thought I remembered. It was powerful but heavily rhythmic too, and I knew from the first few notes that I was going to like it a lot more than I had expected. Early in the first song, Jaz made eye contact and I could tell he was trying not to smile but he seemed pretty happy that the girl was making sure I was enjoying myself – I had a fairly well deserved reputation for being hopelessly romantic and a general failure with relationships. To be fair, it lasted just a few weeks with this girl, but she helped make my first Killing Joke show quite memorable.

We didn't go backstage – Jaz was clear that he didn't want any girl he didn't know backstage. But he joined us later for a smoke and a drink. I've been backstage at every other show I've been lucky enough to see since then.

SHEPHERD'S BUSH EMPIRE
24 February 2005,
London, UK

MARK GEMINI THWAITE

Fast-forward a few years and I bumped into Raven in the after-show bar at the Shepherd's Bush

MGT and Raven get their heads together © Mark Gemini Thwaite

Empire show, right before I moved to Los Angeles for a change of scenery. I was no longer in The Mission, whom I'd fallen out with in late 2001 due to touring schedule conflicts with Tricky, who I also played guitar for.

I did end up being invited by Wayne Hussey to rejoin The Mission later that year for a tour in South Africa and Europe. Talking of Wayne, funnily enough, he was also friends with Jaz Coleman and Raven. I recall Jaz coming backstage after a Mission show at the Powerhaus in London back in 1993…

✦ ✦ ✦

SHEPHERD'S BUSH EMPIRE
25 February 2005,
London, UK

BRIAN RICHARDSON

I've seen them play more times than any other band, but the one for me was the XXV Gathering in London 2005. When I got the tickets through the post and saw the event was going to be filmed – that was insane. I'd introduced the band to a mate who wanted to see them too and we pushed our way to the front. I later realised I was actually under the camera and cannot be seen in the DVD, but it didn't matter. Seeing the band pummelling out tracks, Jaz on fine, passionate form in sweaty red war paint and jump-suit, waving his cross on a stick over the heads of fans, is still a benchmark in gigs for me.

ADRIAN WASON

Fabulous gig, very well attended. I love this line-up. It really worked for me. Probably my second favourite after the *Extremities…* line-up. The gig was filmed and Geordie looked a bit silly, like a character from one of Gerry Anderson's series. For me, the outstanding aspect of this gig was 'Sun Goes Down' and 'Darkness Before Dawn', which I'd never heard before live. Unfortunately, the chanting didn't kick in, so the track wasn't included on the DVD, but you heard the backing track, which is a thing of wonder, absolutely amazing.

JANE STEPHENSON

Like any sensible woman, I wasn't necessarily keen to embrace my 40th birthday (on Friday 25 February 2005) but my husband reassured me that many treats were in store to mark the occasion. We met friends after work for cocktails in a hotel bar in Holland Park, but, after an hour or so, with champagne fizzing nicely through my veins, I was ushered in the direction of Shepherd's Bush Empire for some musical entertainment: the second of Killing Joke's two 25th-anniversary gigs.

You wouldn't think a wide-eyed Jaz Coleman in his boiler suit, teeth bared, channelling the subliminal flash of the demon's face in *The Exorcist* and chanting "part of us is animal, part of us is alien" would be the perfect way to say "many happy returns", but Jaz was just hours away from his own 45th birthday and he knew what he was doing.

After 90 blistering, deafening minutes of relentless tribal music, a cake was brought on stage and the band blew out the candles and downed shots to celebrate Killing Joke's quarter-century. By way of farewell, Jaz cheerfully announced, "It's my birthday in 40 minutes, so fuck you all" as he departed. After 24 hours for rest and recuperation, my own birthday bonanza continued with a romantic trip to Rome, which proved to be a wonderful holiday. Yet somehow, 15 years later, it's not the gifts or the cocktails or the week in Rome that stand out when I recall the start of my fifth decade but Killing Joke's intense performance. As the band embark on their own naughty 40s, long may they continue.

MARK WHITE

My most personal memory is that of meeting Jaz in Prague, some 10/15 years ago. Myself, my wife and a couple of friends were sat in an alternative bar just having a quiet drink when this very dark and foreboding figure loomed on the horizon. Sure enough, it was Jaz. I entered into full-on fanboy mode. Determined to get an autograph, I plucked up the courage and spoke with the great man. After we went to great lengths to reassure him we were not from the press, he relaxed and joined us for a drink. Suffice to say, I never got the autograph. I never asked for it. It seemed wrong after he'd given his time to speak with us. He's one of the most engaging, intelligent and funny guys I've ever met. I will never, ever forget that hour or so he spent with us. He gave us a phone number and told us, whenever we were in Prague, to call it and, if he was around, he would come out for a drink. To date we have not been back, but thank you, Jaz.

DEREK SAXENMEYER

(vocal session engineer, Absolute Dissent; pre-production, MMXII)

Ben [Calvert] would practise drums in the 'Basement of Hell'. He'd play two or three hours straight, non-stop, so hard that the ladies working in an insurance company two floors up called to complain that he was making all their coffee cups rattle. It was probably Jaz that came up with the name for it. I'm not sure, but, after Killing Joke, everybody in the studio started calling it 'Hell'.

It's an untreated basement. Tile floors, concrete walls, big heavy pipes for gas lines, water, sewage. There's one ventilation shaft in the middle. When you don't take care to close it, that's when the people living four floors up above get pissed off about the noise. Altogether, it's 300 square metres, with three recording rooms and a long twisty hallway. It's musty as hell, and the metro runs directly below it. So you get a bit of rumble every couple of minutes. It doesn't usually affect recordings. It's obviously got a certain vibe. It's a really loud sounding room, which is awesome for tracking drums for rock 'n' roll. It's big enough to put a full band in and have them play together while still allowing for some isolation. It used to have an old VHS camera, like a hand-held camcorder, duct-taped to a stand and hardwired to a TV upstairs in the control room. The drummer could be downstairs and the rest of the band could play along upstairs.

BERT NEVEN

They'd been rehearsing at Faust and were just starting work on the *Hosannas...* album. Jaz was upstairs in the control room and the rest of the band was downstairs in Hell. There was a small room. Raven was in there. And Geordie was in the room in the back. Ben was in the big room downstairs. We were still working out how to get the best sound. We found some hot spots all over the place. Geordie did it together with Jerry Kandiah – the engineer for *Hosannas...* and the *2003* album. They'd walk around listening to the sound in different places, find the sweet spots in the room and put up a mic.

RON SYNOVITZ

During the *Basements of Hell* sessions, Geordie told me he'd discovered a 'secret' about recording drums in Hell. He was really pleased. Along with direct mics on Ben's drums, he'd found a spot near a wall away from the kit where ambient mics captured a huge sound. He also put a large condenser mic right in the threshold as you enter the drum chamber. It caught drum sounds rushing through the door. "You've got to move air and you've got to capture the air moving," Geordie said.

DEREK SAXENMEYER

Geordie liked to put two mics against the wall in Hell for ambient mics. It was a weird place to put them, but it worked. He knew of those spots.

✦ ✦ ✦

INTERNATIONAL ARENA
18 June 2005,
Cardiff, UK

ADRIAN WASON

Lovely sunny day and we got in early. The Mötley Crüe fans have got to be the dullest ever. I asked a guy in front of me who he was here to see, and he just said "Crüe". I asked if we could go in front of him as we were only here to see Killing Joke. He said no. Joke were spot on – they whizzed through a 45-minute set, Jaz shouted at Benny – "Keep up, Benny!" My mate Darren pleaded with me to come and see another gig – the legendary Cardiff band Shockhead – but I went home instead. I'd never heard of them at the time but apparently their gigs were mental and the sound was like a heavy floating sound, rather like 'Wardance' with Martin Atkins drumming.

BERT NEVEN

The Mötley Crüe tour in the summer of 2005 is where Diamond Dave [Simpson] got in as guitar tech. He was doing the backstage decorations and atmosphere. Geordie had a problem with his guitar tech. I said, "Why don't you get Dave in? He's brilliant." And, since then, he's been Geordie's guitar tech.

ROLLING STONE
30 June 2005,
Milan, Italy

PAOLO BINASCHI

I'm Italian, living near Milan, 51 years old, great fan of KJ since the Eighties ("And we sang, you do it this way…").

Many memories about them in connection with my life. I can tell you an anecdote related to the KJ concert in Milan. I was around the location long before the start of the concert having my drink. Suddenly, I recognised his silhouette running in front of me, heading for the club.

Obviously, I chased and called him. He turned to me. Stammering, I told him he had to sign me an autograph, but I didn't have any paper. So I pulled a 10 Euro note out of my wallet and he wrote me a dedication, showing off his mephistophelic smile.

Needless to say, the concert had a completely different flavour after that.

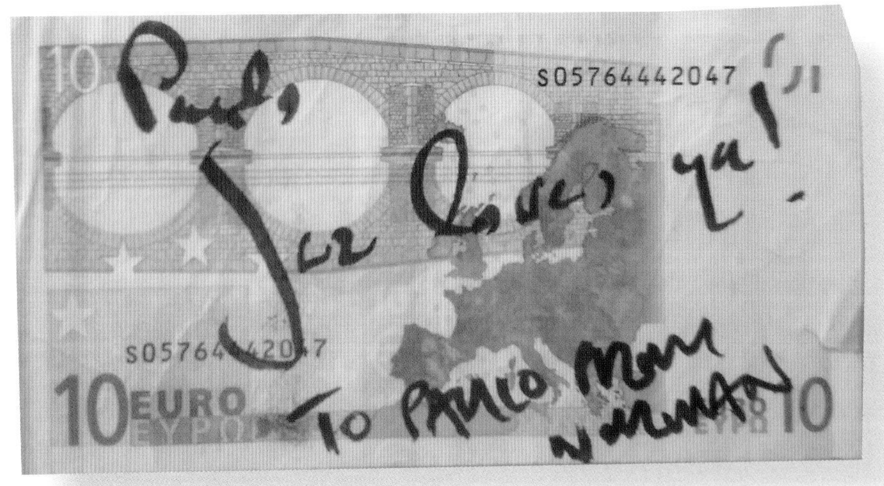

© Paolo Binaschi

SHERWOOD FESTIVAL
2 July 2005,
Stadio Euganeo, Italy

MICKEY E.VIL
(The Mugshots)

I'd like to share a memory of my meeting with Mr Jaz Coleman, hours before a gig in Italy. It was summer. That day, I was at the Radio Sherwood Festival early in the afternoon and I was wandering – still a few people around – among the stands when I spotted Jaz and asked if he would be available for an interview for Radio Onda d'Urto FM. He was so kind, down to earth and immediately accepted. So we sat behind a stand, smoked a pipe filled with hash and started to record the interview. I do not know if the hash was the motivation behind Jaz's openness: he actually seemed so friendly to me aside from the smoking. So I don't think that the hash influenced the interview that much, apart from the great amount of laughter!

I'm used to interviewing rock musicians (Alice Cooper, The Stranglers, Jethro Tull, Andy Fletcher from Depeche Mode, Midge Ure from Ultravox, Ace from Skunk Anansie and many others) and I found Jaz very easy to interview: no rock star attitude at all, great availability and lot of fun! Just like talking to an old friend, you know what I mean? I remember letting him hear The Mugshots' live version of 'The Wait' and asking, "Is it better than Metallica's one?" and Jaz went, "Well, it's not that difficult, ha ha ha!"

Later that night, I was at the gig: so powerful, entertaining and captivating. After the show, I just said to Jaz, "Great show. I will see you again someday."

✦ ✦ ✦

CAMDEN BARFLY
21 August 2005,
London, UK

PAUL BRANNIGAN
(former editor, Kerrang! and Planet Rock)

My introduction… or perhaps indoctrination… to Killing Joke came via my friend Matt Tibbits. Obviously, as a punk/metal/alt. rock-loving teenager, I knew of the band's existence prior to meeting Matt at Georgetown University in the summer of 1991, but, truthfully, my knowledge of the KJ canon didn't extend far beyond the 'Love Like Blood' and 'Eighties' singles. Thanks to Matt's tireless advocacy for the band, and some diligently compiled D90 cassettes, this would change over the course of nine months in Washington, DC. The notion of Killing Joke as An Important Band would become firmly imprinted in my mind.

Fast-forward to 2005 and I'm now, somehow, editor of *Kerrang!* with the authority to hand out 'gongs' – or more accurately chunky metallic trophies – at the magazine's annual awards ceremony.

So, when asked to decide who should be the recipient of 2005's Lifetime Achievement Award, Killing Joke were my first choice. In the week leading up to the awards, *Kerrang!* also planned to stage a series of gigs at the 200-capacity Barfly venue in Camden, north London, and, having already secured the services of Therapy?, Trivium and more, I approached Killing Joke's people about the possibility of the band playing one of the nights, and was hugely surprised when they actually agreed. For reasons which escape me, this led to me directly dealing with Raven, discussing the logistics. At some point, it was decided that the gig, scheduled for 21 August, would be held as a benefit concert for a respected member of the extended KJ family, Jester, which added an extra sense of occasion to what was already promising to be a special night.

Those lucky enough to have been in attendance will doubtless share my memories of the gig being a) very fucking loud b) very fucking packed and c) very fucking hot. Oh, and very, very good. Personally, I was just delighted it had taken place at all, given that approximately 72 hours earlier I'd had a conversation with Raven in which he mentioned the distinct possibility that the band might elect to remain in Prague rather than flying to London. Nothing like the prospect of a no-show to ease the nerves on the busiest week in the *Kerrang!* calendar.

In the end, the awards themselves were a stress-free blast. Long-time Killing Joke fan Dave Grohl made a warm-hearted, highly entertaining speech about his love of the band and their seismic impact upon 'our' world before presenting Jaz with the award, and the KJ guys seemed genuinely touched by the standing ovation they received from the room full of musician peers and music industry players.

As the ceremony blurred into a typically messy after-party, I found myself in conversation with Jaz at the bar and congratulated him on the accolade. In my pleasantly inebriated state, I'd convinced myself that we were getting on famously... right up until the moment that a manically cackling Jaz put me in a headlock and attempted – almost very successfully – to knee me squarely in the balls. It was, perhaps, intended to serve as a little reminder that Killing Joke might now be respected elder statesmen in the rock scene, but one should never, ever imagine they've lost their cutting edge. Or maybe Jaz simply thought I was a bit of a cunt. Whatever, a happy memory of a band who remain fabulously unpredictable, entirely untamed and utterly unique.

JAMES STOKES

I was always intrigued by the descriptions of Killing Joke in *Kerrang!* magazine back in 2005/2006: "apocalyptic industrial tribal dance disco hellish metal punk", and so on. Jaz's adventures at the 2005 *Kerrang!* Awards also made for hilarious reading and furthered my curiosity as I wondered who the hell this bloke was – and why was just about everyone falling over themselves to go speak to him?

Fourteen years, 10 incredible gigs and millions of listening-hours later, I'm a little closer to knowing.

PHIL TOLFIELD

I've seen Killing Joke many times over the years, but one that sticks in my mind the most is the London Barfly gig. I remember arriving at the venue with a couple of other Gatherers I'd met in the pub before, and bumping into Jaz and Raven stood outside. We stood in a small circle chatting. I'd met Raven before and he seemed to remember me, which was cool.

Suddenly, from an open window upstairs in the venue came the most enormous guitar noise piercing the London evening air as Geordie began his soundcheck. Everyone turned to look up at the window. People stopped in the street to look up. I mean – it was *loud*. Then Jaz looked back down, looked directly at me, threw his head back and let out a huge raucous cackle like only he can do! This was a great moment for me and something I'll never forget. The gig itself I remember as being very hot and sweaty as it's a really small venue, and it's significant for me as it was the last time I saw Raven playing with the band.

✦ ✦ ✦

ACADEMY
7 October 2005,
Liverpool, UK

CHRISTOPHER OWENS

It was May 2005. I was 19, had just been sacked from a job, discovered my girlfriend at the time was cheating on me and an uncle had been diagnosed with cancer. I went to HMV in Belfast with the last bit of money from my wage packet to buy a CD and, while browsing, came across the first album. I knew the name because of the Nirvana connection, nothing else.

After buying the album for £6.99, I walked out into the rain and found shelter at a bus stop. I stuck on the album and it's no exaggeration to say this was a moment that changed my life irrevocably. Aside from it being the greatest music I'd ever heard, it also exposed me to another way of thinking. This band taught me to never take anything for granted, to question everything and push yourself mentally.

As well as this, they gave me a new-found appreciation for music. Although I was already a bit of a music buff, Killing Joke led me to discover and explore other musical forms, like industrial, metal, punk, disco, post-punk and dub.

By the start of June, having played the first album to death, I noticed they were doing a UK tour in October for the 25th anniversary of the first record. I booked a ticket for the Liverpool show. I'd never been on a plane by myself, but, for this new discovery, I was prepared to take the chance.

By this time, my uncle had died and my relationship had disintegrated. I was at a fairly low ebb in my life, but 7 October was a revelation. It was like I'd been living in darkness all my life, then Killing Joke opened a door and invited me to step inside. Everything I do today (my radio show, reviewing, promoting gigs, writing fiction) can be traced back to that gig.

I often call it the first day of the rest of my life.

Since then, I've seen the band a further 22 times (2006–2019). It's never a chore. It's an exorcism of the senses.

So I'd like to take this moment to salute Jaz, Geordie, Youth, Big Paul, Raven and Martin Atkins. You warped my mind at a young age and I've never been the same since. Thank you.

IAN MATTHIAS

I got into Killing Joke proper around this time after getting a copy of the self-titled 2003 album. That record blew me away and changed my perspective on what music can mean.

I went to see them live with my good mate Ste Sadler, who was also a big fan. Watching them was like a religious experience, neither of us being that way inclined. The music washed over us and we just danced and sang through the entire set. I hadn't felt anything like that before. It was unparalleled! Killing Joke are a special band. The music means something mentally, emotionally and spiritually to me.

✦ ✦ ✦

UNIVERSITY
10 October 2005,
Newcastle, UK

ALEC MAJOR

My story concerns the birth of my son Jake in 2005. KJ were playing a gig next to the hospital in Newcastle-upon-Tyne, where my wife was giving birth. The labour was problematic to say the least and resulted in an emergency C-section after a marathon stint. As a result, I was unable to attend the gig. I still have the unused ticket stored in the back of his birth photo album. He is now 15 and likes KJ, too.

I pull his leg and blame him for missing the gig all those years ago! So KJ have a lasting meaning for both me and my son.

ASTORIA
14 October 2005,
London, UK

ADRIAN WASON

I really loved this gig and Bristol two days before it. I felt the sound was spot on and the set-list sensational. The Astoria gig was filmed. Highlights were 'Sun Goes Down', 'Darkness Before Dawn', 'Butcher'. For the encore, first up was 'Termite Mound'. I felt like I'd been transported back in time to the January gig 14 years earlier.

LUCERNA MUSIC BAR
4 November 2005,
Prague, Czech Republic

RON SYNOVITZ

The last time Raven played in Prague with Killing Joke. I saw Geordie before the show and asked how the new album was coming along. He wasn't very happy.

Geordie said: "For the first time in 25 years, I really don't care. There's only one good song on it." During the concert, Raven seemed to be struggling with the bass part on one of the songs. Geordie stood in front of him, playing face to face, so Raven could see where his hand was on the guitar neck. At one point, Geordie sat down cross-legged in the middle of a song. I'd never seen that at a Killing Joke show before. I grabbed the set-list off Geordie's monitor afterwards: 'Communion', 'Wardance', 'Sun Goes Down', 'Primitive', 'Darkness', 'Total Invasion', 'Requiem', 'Butcher', 'Money Is Not Our God', 'Frenzy', 'Asteroid', 'Whiteout', 'Wait', 'Complications', 'Ps[s]yche'. It lists the encores as 'Termite', 'Bloodsport', 'Pandemonium'.

MARK LUSARDI

(mixing engineer, Hosannas...)

You've heard the vocal and the song [on the title track]. It's fantastic. That was brilliant. He [Jaz] left a box of cigars in the studio. I've kept it ever since. Got no cigars in it now. I keep plectrums and things in it.

✦ ✦ ✦

HILTONGROVE MASTERING
Late 2005
Dunmow, UK

DAVE BLACKMAN

(mastering, Hosannas...)

Several of the members, including Jaz, attended the sessions, drank a lot of spiced rum and coke, and smoked some big cigars.

I remember that they were pretty buzzing about the record – everyone around it seemed pretty excited about it, including the guys at the label I was also dealing with. The mixes were solid, and they were pretty happy to sit and chat and pop out for the occasional drink and smoke.

The bulk of the stuff was done in a day, and they came back another evening (or two?) to re-do a few things, get everything where they wanted it. I remember Jaz chatting to me in the car park during a break about how he was going to launch an advertising campaign for me, which obviously never happened! I'd taken on the studio the year before, and this was my most high-profile job since then.

There was a sense of relief when they were happy, as there is with every job. I didn't really know a lot about their reputation going in, but they were pretty intense, in a good way, but very vibey. They knew when something sounded right. I always try to do my best work, no matter who the client, but obviously there's an added pressure when you're dealing with a name – I just didn't want to fuck it up!

They signed off on it, it got pressed. Still a great record, I think.

YOUTH

If you listen to *Hosannas...*, that reminds me of the third album. Sounds awful, I think. But, again, a lot of fans love it. I love the sleeve of *Hosannas...* though.

VICTOR SAFONKIN

(Russian artist, whose 1999 painting Inhuman Rearing was used for the cover of Hosannas...)

Today, the world has gone crazy from this virus and everything else, but, for me personally, nothing has changed. I do not leave the studio, working almost non-stop.

As for Jaz Coleman and the great Killing Joke, we met a couple of times in my gallery. As far as I remember, he was working in Prague then. Once, during a walk, he accidentally saw my gallery, where he drew attention to the painting *Inhuman Rearing*. Perhaps, thematically, this picture corresponded to the concept of the album *Hosannas from the Basements of Hell*.

In the modern world, you're shown destruction, pain and death, not in order to stop suffering, but in order to manipulate and receive preferences and profits. Perhaps Jaz was thinking about this.

When I saw Jaz, he gave me the impression of a solid, strong man. Then there was an association with a bird, a bird-man, I thought. Later, I realised this is the Gamayun bird – a mythical bird of paradise in Russian culture. In literary works of the 17th–19th centuries, it's a legless, wingless bird flying from paradise.

The band asked about using other paintings, but it did not work out. My manager did not agree to use another painting.

Those were good times.

FABIO FESTA

2006 was a magical year. I got a job in a company I'd loved for years (Bang & Olufsen). *Hosannas from the Basements of Hell* was what I detonated during the lunch breaks from the powerful BeoLab 5 speakers!

BERT NEVEN

I think Raven was living in the States when he was offered a tour with Ministry, and he just took it. So Raven couldn't make it to Prague when Killing Joke did a video clip for 'Hosannas...'. In half of the video, I pretended I was Raven on bass guitar, with pantyhose over my head. The other half was done by Michal Lajosh Trajer, the bass player of Kashmir 941. We were both wearing my jacket and the same pantyhose over our faces.

✦ ✦ ✦

DEN ATELIER
15 April 2006,
Luxembourg City, Luxembourg

NICO PLEIMLING

It took me quite some time before I could finally see the band live and, I must admit, I've got to see Killing Joke only once so far.

I made a first attempt during the Nineties when I was studying in Ohio and the band was promoting the album *Pandemonium*. Well, I guess you're familiar with the US alcohol regulations, that you need to be 21 before you can have a drink in bars, clubs or other public venues.

I thought I was smart enough to go to that place called Bogart's in Cincinnati where Killing Joke were playing that night [2 December 1994] and bring my passport in order to have a couple of beers at the show.

So, first of all, I ended up having a discussion at the door, because they'd only accept a valid Ohio State ID or driver's licence and, of course, the bouncers ended up marking both my hands with large Xs in order to point out that I wasn't allowed to have a drink at the location. "Fecking nazis," I thought.

After enjoying the opening act, Stabbing Westward, I asked a friend attending the show with me to get me a pint of beer after all. I barely managed to raise the cup to my lips before I had two gorillas on me who made me leave the premises. So much for seeing Killing Joke that night...

I had to wait until 2006 before I could finally experience Killing Joke. It was during their *Hosannas from the Basements from Hell* tour at Den Atelier back in Luxembourg City. Even though they did end up not throwing in their most popular song (some of the audience were obviously not very pleased about that), it was a great gig with many highlights – 'Asteroid' being my personal cherry on the cake.

Jaz signing a poster for Stéphane Bongini on the afternoon of 24 April 2006 before a gig that night at Le Transbordeur in Lyon © Stéphane Bongini

PRIME CLUB
27 April 2006,
Cologne, Germany

MANFRED ROLEF

I followed them with every record and nearly every tour and was lucky enough to meet Jaz three times. The first time I only saw him in the Columbia Hotel, London, not knowing that this hotel, where I spent my honeymoon, is frequented by rock stars. At the time, I was working at EMI Records, Cologne. A few years later, a friend of mine was the German print-promoter during their *Hosannas...* album and asked if I would like to meet Jaz. Of course. He was very nice and answered all my fan-questions while drinking wine together. Jaz told me of his experience of his *Freispiel* session in Cologne [*Freispiel* was a CD – released in 1994 – featuring music created at a four-day gathering in late 1993 that included Jaz and Geordie] and that he lost the album. I already had a copy at home and the next day returned to their gig in the Prime Club in Cologne and brought him two copies.

The gig was by far the loudest in my whole life and the result was acute hearing loss – which results still in a constant noise in my ears. Maybe it wasn't the best idea to stand in front of one of the speaker towers.

KOKO
4 May 2006,
London, UK

ADRIAN WASON

Was really looking forward to this gig but, unfortunately, Raven's commitments with Ministry were clashing. We saw Jaz at the bar and I asked him a few questions.

Were they going to play 'The Fanatic'? "We never play that!"
Were they going to play 'Darkness Before Dawn'? "We played that too much last year!"
Were they going to play 'Judas Goat'? "We may play it/not play it. Wait and see!" He knew full well they were not going to play it, but was keen not to let a punter go away empty-handed!
The gig wasn't bad but the sound was a bit fuzzy and it was hard to make out the track 'Majestic'.

TRUTNOV FESTIVAL
17 August 2006,
Na Bojišti, Czech Republic

LENNONKA

The first time I heard about KJ was in the Czech movie [2002 film *Year of the Devil*]. Maybe Jaz likes to think he played the Devil, but the greater devil in the movie was alcoholism. The movie is also about 'searching for God'. The very first song [of theirs] I heard was 'Exorcism'. I was completely astonished by the sound. It was unlike anything I heard before.

I'd noticed them playing in my home town, but it wasn't until a year later that I started listening to them. I used to listen to Queen and was thinking, if only I could find a band with invention, oriental influence, intensity, charisma, but also smarter lyrics and spiritual depth. Only to realise they've already found me! I've dived into their extensive catalogue and was finding gem after gem, micro-symphony after micro-symphony. I longed to see them live.

That summer, I was at a music festival with friends. My sister was trying to convince me to go to another festival to see her favourite band. I was fed up with crowds, so responded that I would go only if KJ played there. Several hours later, a flyer landed in my hand claiming KJ was going to play at a Czech festival next month.

So I went to see them. It must have been the worst of their gigs I've ever seen. They were barely half the original band – it was Jaz, who was drinking 24/7, Geordie, Benny, there was a stand-in for Raven, and maybe Reza on keyboards already. But at least I got lucky to meet them backstage! I was dying to try on Jaz's hat, which he let me, and my friend took photos of us posing with the hat. I caught myself entertaining the idea of stealing it. I've heard that someone else got to do it later. Damn!

My friend and I were invited to take a trip in their tour bus to Prague, which we accepted. Jaz tried to kiss me, but I wouldn't let him. He was sleeping in my lap and I was playing with his hair. Can you believe that?

A few days later, I was on my way to a university in the Netherlands on a scholarship. What happened next was curious. In the Netherlands, I was in a deep personal crisis, being far from home for the first time, smoking strong weed (obviously) and it resulted in my first spiritual awakening. I found myself in the centre of bright white light, where there was no concept of time and space, so I didn't even know how much time passed in the physical world. I was also receiving knowledge from high consciousness over the next few weeks, which doesn't come in the form of thoughts, and its translation into human thoughts can be erroneous.

About that time, I also started researching band history, got deeper into the lyrics, and, of course, into other related topics, such as Crowley. I could only grow more amazed. I decided to create the website known as killingjoke.cz and some of you might have been visitors to its forum. Our community even managed to transcribe lyrics of some of the unreleased songs. The best people, the Gatherers.

Luckily for KJ, they fixed their musical reputation when I got the chance to see the reunited line-up live in Berlin two years later. They were extraordinary! I even got to listen to my favourite, 'Mathematics of Chaos', rarely played live anymore, on their soundcheck. I was hoping to talk to Jaz and we were left alone to talk privately. He was a changed person in the best possible sense. He looked great and was completely sober. I am incredibly proud of you, Jaz.

I also got to smoke a joint with Youth, who was communicating with me without uttering a word. I adored him for that. I got to meet Big Paul, of which I'm not proud how it went, because I was like: "Hi Paul, just sign this poster for me." And, of course, sweet Geordie again and kind Reza. I didn't try to make an impression, because I thought it was over for me. Hilarious! The story hasn't ended there.

Thanks to their inspiration, I started composing music again and playing in bands as a keyboardist. When they can, why couldn't I? They are my muses in many aspects. Thanks to them, I advanced my English and my poetry. My sense of humour, too. And plenty more...

Brothers, I salute you. You've achieved the impossible. The new renaissance.

To me, KJ is The Beatles of the next generation. This is to be taken as a great compliment.

Let me close with a fragment of my recent poem:

'Our games for all the world to see
And will they ever?
Or is this just for you and me?
Is this only our
Ecstasy
And agony untellable?'

RON SYNOVITZ

I've jammed with Jaz. He played a simple riff on piano and had me repeat it on electric guitar. We played it over and over again, Jaz conducting with one hand like it was on fire, raising it up and pushing me to an intensity I didn't know was in me. It was empowering. I've seen Jaz do that a lot with people he knows in Prague – empower their creativity and bring the most out of them. I think it's a hobby of his.

BERT NEVEN

In 2006, Jaz told me he was going to turn me into a studio engineer. He was producing a Czech girl band called Gaia Mesiah. He fucking threw me in there, in the deep. So I learned how to work in the studio and engineered Gaia Mesiah's *Alpha Female* album together with Jaz. That's when I started working closely in the studio with him. Great experience. I learned about the studio and how to work with Jaz, which is not easy most of the time.

After that, I worked with Jaz on a project by a group called Les Tambours Du Bronx. It's a French percussion group. We did two songs, starting with a long percussion track already recorded by the group in France. We started cutting it up and turning it into a song. Jaz was there playing keyboards and doing vocals. Katka Morella, the guitarist of Gaia Mesiah, played the guitars, and Ondřej Smeykal played didgeridoo. Derek Saxenmeyer had just started working freelance at Faust Studio, so I took him in to help engineer. That's when he started working with Jaz in the studio, too. I think it's fucking brilliant that all these people started coming together at those sessions.

DEREK SAXENMEYER

I first met Jaz at Faust when he was producing a project by a group of French drummers. It was in the summer of 2007. Definitely summer. We walked in and out of the control room at the same time, met at the door. He was walking out, I was walking in. He looked at me and said: "Are you Australian?" I said: "No." He said: "All right then." Not long after that, possibly because of that session, Jaz started on *Black & Red* with Ondřej Smeykal on didgeridoo. There were two batches of *Black & Red* sessions. The first were recorded at a place Ondřej set up, the first five or six tunes. They recorded what they could there. Then we did some overdubs at Faust and got some basic mixes going.

BERT NEVEN

The earliest *Black & Red* sessions were in an underground venue in Prague called Final Club. Ondřej Smeykal was connected. I went over with Jaz and Ondřej for two days of demo recordings at Final Club. Ondřej played didgeridoo and Jaz played harmonium.

DEREK SAXENMEYER

We did overdubs on [the Final Club recordings for] *Black & Red*. It was just me, Ondřej and Jaz there for that. We recorded additional didge and Jaz's vocals. Ondřej found these giant Indonesian angklungs, shaken percussion instruments, in the trash outside of a school. He got a bunch of them. Each angklung has three notes and when you rattle them, they make sounds. He and Jaz used them to play chords. Those first sessions essentially functioned as demos. One track did make it through and ended up on a song that made the final cut.

MAX FARR

Jaz and I REALLY became close when I lost my job and he let me move in. I was there for several months, including the very sad time when Raven died.

That was an intensely emotional experience. Raven had been scheduled to tour with the band for *Hosannas from the Basements of Hell*, but instead chose to tour with Ministry. I remember the day after Jaz got the news [about Raven's death] I woke up and could hear Jaz sobbing in the kitchen. I stayed in bed for a while, so he could be alone in his grief. It made me realise how deeply Jaz had really cared about Raven.

It was a bit of a traumatic time to be staying with Jaz no doubt, but also a bit of an honour to have been one of his close friends during that period. He's been better to me than my own brother and my own father. I will always appreciate that, and I respect him not just as a musician and composer but as a friend and a person, and I am honoured that I am able to call him friend.

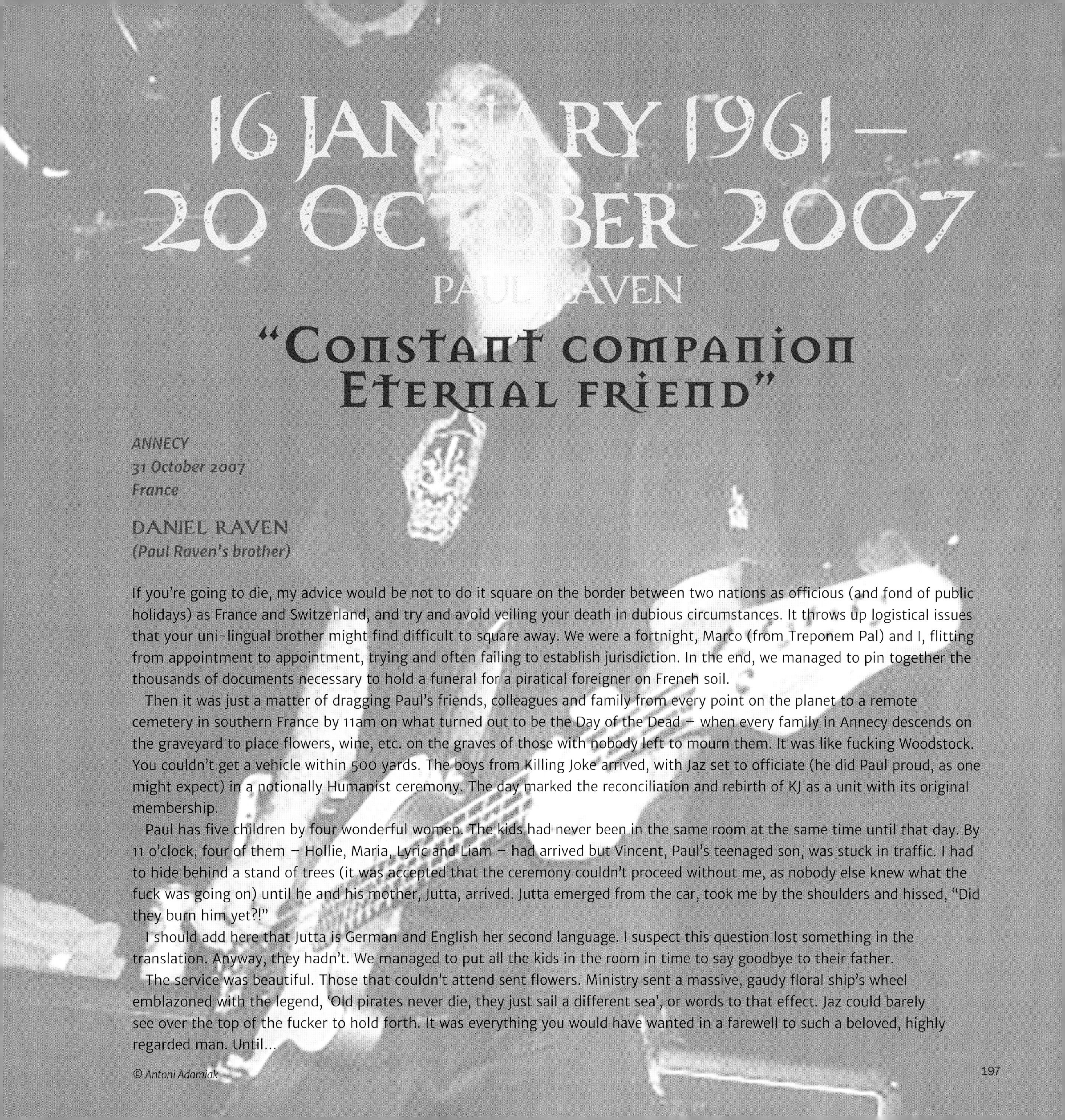

16 January 1961 – 20 October 2007

Paul Raven

"Constant companion Eternal friend"

ANNECY
31 October 2007
France

DANIEL RAVEN
(Paul Raven's brother)

If you're going to die, my advice would be not to do it square on the border between two nations as officious (and fond of public holidays) as France and Switzerland, and try and avoid veiling your death in dubious circumstances. It throws up logistical issues that your uni-lingual brother might find difficult to square away. We were a fortnight, Marco (from Treponem Pal) and I, flitting from appointment to appointment, trying and often failing to establish jurisdiction. In the end, we managed to pin together the thousands of documents necessary to hold a funeral for a piratical foreigner on French soil.

Then it was just a matter of dragging Paul's friends, colleagues and family from every point on the planet to a remote cemetery in southern France by 11am on what turned out to be the Day of the Dead – when every family in Annecy descends on the graveyard to place flowers, wine, etc. on the graves of those with nobody left to mourn them. It was like fucking Woodstock. You couldn't get a vehicle within 500 yards. The boys from Killing Joke arrived, with Jaz set to officiate (he did Paul proud, as one might expect) in a notionally Humanist ceremony. The day marked the reconciliation and rebirth of KJ as a unit with its original membership.

Paul has five children by four wonderful women. The kids had never been in the same room at the same time until that day. By 11 o'clock, four of them – Hollie, Maria, Lyric and Liam – had arrived but Vincent, Paul's teenaged son, was stuck in traffic. I had to hide behind a stand of trees (it was accepted that the ceremony couldn't proceed without me, as nobody else knew what the fuck was going on) until he and his mother, Jutta, arrived. Jutta emerged from the car, took me by the shoulders and hissed, "Did they burn him yet?!"

I should add here that Jutta is German and English her second language. I suspect this question lost something in the translation. Anyway, they hadn't. We managed to put all the kids in the room in time to say goodbye to their father.

The service was beautiful. Those that couldn't attend sent flowers. Ministry sent a massive, gaudy floral ship's wheel emblazoned with the legend, 'Old pirates never die, they just sail a different sea', or words to that effect. Jaz could barely see over the top of the fucker to hold forth. It was everything you would have wanted in a farewell to such a beloved, highly regarded man. Until...

© Antoni Adamiak

At the end of the ceremony, to the strains of 'If I Can Dream', it fell to the French official, who had missed his chance to officiate at an 'entertainment' funeral, to close the doors around Paul's casket. Did he ever make the most of it. He took up a stance redolent of a Vegas-era Elvis and proceeded to hide Paul from our view across seven excruciating minutes. 'If I Can Dream' played three times in its entirety before the dude was close to finished.

Paul's wake was held at an anarchist punk club in Geneva later that day. My most potent memory is of watching a KJ concert on the big screen there. At the opening synth blasts of 'Requiem', I began finally to lose my composure. Big Paul caught my eye, embraced me and whispered fine consolations in my ear. Scary fuckers with spongy hearts, those KJ boys.

AL JOURGENSEN
(Ministry)

We had run into each other from time to time. Raven knew Martin Atkins well when Martin played with us, then hooked me up with John Bechdel when we needed a keyboard player. At that point, with both of them in the band, we laughingly discussed renaming our band Minijoke. By the end, we had become quite close. One of a kind, yet he fit with our lot hand in glove.

Kindred spirit indeed! He thrived where others just survive. He left us too early but, damn, did he Gonzo this living thing! I'm sure we will meet again.

GEORDIE

We really got on, just like a house on fire. Massive Alex Harvey fan. Funny as fuck. If he got a hold of your funny bone, you were fucked. He would not let go. I remember rolling around a marble hotel lobby in Rome, hitting him to make him stop. Just one-liners, one-liners, one-liners. He'd have you in tears.

I created a little fantasy for myself to soften the blow. That he'd actually faked his own death and he's still alive down in Patagonia. If any cunt would do that kind of thing, it would be him.

MATT TIBBITS

Geordie and Jaz invited me over to Prague just before my birthday in the summer of 2005. The band were rehearsing and performing small, informal warm-up gigs for their tour with Mötley Crüe. Following a high-spirited afternoon at Faust Studios, the day ended with a glorious bar crawl and, afterwards, Raven very kindly put me up in his flat. He played me demos from *Hosannas...* on his laptop, buzzing with enthusiasm. The following day, he showed me his favourite haunts around the city, including a great cigar shop and bar where everyone knew him, and generously bought me a beautiful Cohiba Double Corona.

After Raven left us, I could never bring myself to smoke that cigar but always took it with me to Killing Joke gigs on the continent. Years later, in 2018, I had it with me at L'Usine in Geneva on the day Jaz performed a memorial ceremony for him there before the gig that evening. The next morning, the Cohiba was nowhere to be seen. After all those years and travels, it ended up disappearing at Raven's favourite hangout in one of his favourite cities, where the wake following his funeral had also taken place. It was as if Raven was saying, "If you're not gonna fucking smoke it, I'm having it back."

© Stéphane Bongini

© Mark Gemini Thwaite

MARK GEMINI THWAITE

I'd mentioned to Raven I was moving to USA and we met up in Hollywood a year or so later, after Paul heard some of my demos and suggested we form a new band – Mob Research – later to feature Kory Clarke of Warrior Soul on vocals. Paul was very excited by the recordings and Kory had laid down killer vocals on four songs on the album. Then we got the call that Paul had suddenly died of a heart attack at the age of 46, whilst recording bass with Treponem Pal.

I'd spoken to Paul just a few days before as he boarded the plane. He was booking Mob Research shows for October that same year (2007) and I was nervous that it was too soon to gig without a record out and expressed my concerns. His last words to me were "Stay positive". A great sentiment I keep with me to this day.

STEPHANE BONGINI

(aka Frenchy Frenzy)

Raven's funeral. I thought it was impossible not to go there to pay my last respects to such a sweet boy with such a great sense of humour and the one that made everything happen for me with Killing Joke. It was a very moving moment, with all of Raven's family with his various partners and children.

I really had the feeling of entering the intimacy of the group while remaining in my place, but it was a very, very powerful moment. Around 3am, when we left L'Usine in Geneva, where we finished the evening, I felt a new moment of fullness and near levitation.

I had the chance to witness the reformation with Big Paul after years of quarrels – it was during this evening that the idea of a reunion was born. It was a memorable evening where the guests wanted to enjoy life – I think Raven would have appreciated it.

© Stéphane Bongini

BIG PAUL

I couldn't *not* say goodbye. It was such a shock. But, yes, it was a challenge to see Jaz after all the terrible things I had wanted to inflict upon him. But, you know, the mind is a terrible thing to taste. (Thanks Al!)

We just hugged and shared our grief. But Raven's kids were there, you know. They lost their Dad. We were the sideshow. Why carry on with the bullshit and hurt?

JUSTIN BROADRICK

I remember Raven once proudly telling me Rat Scabies from The Damned had referred to him as a "dog with two dicks". He was possibly proud of the pirate label too. I wouldn't wish in any way to disrespect the memory of Raven, but it's somewhat understandable that he could be accused of being essentially a pirate, ha ha!

I guess he was an opportunist and would stop at nothing to get what he wanted, but he was also a gentleman – charming and wildly entertaining! And an amazing musician, of course.

IAN ORGAN

Members of KJ, including Raven and Reza, would frequently visit the chat site.

I saw them at Cambridge Junction, [8 May] 2006. By then, Raven had left and Kneill [Brown] had replaced him. The last time I saw Raven in KJ was in 2005, when we had a beer or two after the gig in Birmingham [11 October]. I kept in touch with him right up till the Sunday before he passed away.

Raven's funeral. I was all set to go to it uninvited. I wanted to be there but the logistics of getting there was too much. Just after, KJ reformed with the original line-up: Jaz, Youth, Geordie, BPF. Everyone descended on two nights in London – this for me was magical to see the original line-up that had not played properly since 1982.

ROB MOSS

Raven – such a delightfully shady character!

He was the one that always had a scheme or a plan. If anyone were to have their collar felt by the Old Bill, it's Raven. He travelled the world on a less-than-legit passport. I think it took 10 years off his age!

Raven once told me that the members of Killing Joke were all really nice guys. Until they all got together – and then there was a collective mindset that seemed to turn them into "a bunch of cunts!".

Raven produced Headcount's 2004 album *Die Monkey Die*. We recorded in a shed on a farm and also at the home studio of Martin Ratcliffe (ex-Neon Hearts).

Dope deals in pubs, driving round Oxford, where he would shout "Where's your muzzle?" to passers-by. Dirty jokes and his famous 'belt buckle' trick (use your imagination)! Great evenings with food and wine and talking late into the night. His production method was simple. We would run through a track and then he would say that we were about to do a take. Just before, the door to the studio would open, and he would growl "Don't fuck up!" We didn't want to let the man down at all.

His ears were sharp. If there was an overdub that wasn't right, he was on it and really enjoyed pushing us. Many of the vocal tracks were done in one take because he got the best out of me.

Münster, Germany, 18 February 1984 © Larry Bate

I remember he called me from Prague once in the hope I would do some tour-managing for them. I have no idea why he picked on me. No way was I going to get involved with that lot! I asked "What's in it for me, other than a divorce?", which was met with that mocking laugh. He was with Geordie and they were both rip-roaringly pissed, having a great time.

And, not long after, he was gone! Like that! Boom. No warning. His funeral was an amazing event, so many ex-wives and girlfriends all united in grief. But it was a joyous event. The evening in L'Usine was magical. He would have loved to have been there. Well, he was in spirit without a doubt.

After that, I had some interesting experiences. He left some personal effects at my place and I swear he was there sometimes. He was cremated on Halloween – how fitting. Later, I found a watch of mine that could show the date in French or English. It stopped, in French mode, on the day of his funeral at the exact time. 2.30 if I recall correctly...

DEREK SAXENMEYER

You mostly get a daily ritual going of how you work on the songs, so it's hard to recall specific memories in regard to each song. But 'The Raven King', for sure, was one of the more memorable ones because of the emotional weight that was tied to it. The atmosphere was heavy. It wasn't dark. I sat at the console and it was Jaz standing there behind my back for five or 10 minutes in silence. Then he said: "Okay, run the track." Jaz was obviously reflecting on Paul Raven. Then, afterwards, Geordie stopped in to have a listen. You could see them both in that same state of mind. That moment where you feel happy you've completed something that you feel is beautiful and, at the same time, the memories that go along with it, the thoughts that go along with it...

2007–2020

"I AM THE FURY THE SPIRIT OF OUTRAGE"

CHRIS BRYANS
When you got into a room with instruments – were you nervous? Did you have reservations?

BIG PAUL
The years still drop away, and we still play the same games. Arrested development. Reservations? Huge... and every time.

CHRIS BRYANS
How quickly did you decide to record again?

BIG PAUL
Must have been about five minutes in.

CHRIS BRYANS
The first release was The Duende Sessions, recorded at Youth's studio in Spain? Did you feel that you slotted straight back in again (and also swiftly absorbed the tracks you hadn't originally played on)?

BIG PAUL
It felt great to play on tracks I should have played on! But credit to all who sat in my seat. Great drummers all.

James Stokes: "The history of the band affirms them as the most interesting thing in music, bar none"
© JM Stokes

HERON MUSIC
2008
Bristol, UK

TOM DALGETY
(co-producer Pylon)

Killing Joke came into my life via Dave Simpson.

I was working in a studio in Bristol, on a project with Mushroom from Massive Attack. One day, I needed to pop into the local guitar shop (Heron Music). When I walked in the door, I was confronted by a wall of flight cases, all with the words 'Killing Joke' written on them.

At that point, KJ were my absolute favourite band in the world – so this sight nearly made me hyperventilate! When I asked the friendly shop owner what all the cases were, he replied, "Oh yeah, I'm Geordie's tech. They store all their gear here!"

Mind blown! That meant all the secrets of the mythical Geordie Walker stereo guitar sound were in these boxes right in front of me!

Once I'd calmed down, I got chatting to Dave and we bonded over a love of the Banshees (I'd recently worked on Siouxsie's *Mantaray* album).

Just before leaving, I half-jokingly said, "Well, if KJ ever need an engineer!"

This triggered a chain reaction that I still can barely believe – I recommended a studio for them, which led to me showing them around said studio, which led to me engineering a session for them, which led to flying out to Youth's studio in Spain to record Jaz's vocals, which led to me mixing part of the *MMXII* record. Which ultimately led to me [co-]producing the *Pylon* record a few years later!

YOUTH

We [the band] agreed to come out here... where I am now... in Spain, rehearse for a tour and make an album. Jaz was like, "I don't wanna make an album." I was like, "If we don't make an album or record, I don't wanna do the tour." There's always that sort of to and fro with me and Jaz. Between us, we tend to get it done.

We rehearsed here [at Space Mountain Studios], recorded a bit here and then did that tour. It was good fun, challenging but good fun.

Two dates in Tokyo marked the first gigs with the original Killing Joke line-up since 24 February 1982. And the first shows with Big Paul in place since late 1986

DUO MUSIC EXCHANGE
11 September 2008,
Tokyo, Japan

TIM MERRILL

I'd never been to Japan before, had no idea how to read Japanese or order tickets through a website. I ordered two tickets through a French promoter in Paris for $150 that were promised to be delivered. Booked a $600 flight for a 90-minute jaunt from Korea and secured a bunk in a coffin hotel. Talked my job into letting me book time off to 'attend a wedding in Canada', and it was set.

I sat on the plane and wondered if this was really going to come off without a hitch. Would I get my tickets? Would it even happen, as we all know about the 'cancellations'. The gods of good journey were with me, as I happened to meet a friendly Japanese gent on the plane, who not only bought me a vending-machine beer for the shuttle bus into Tokyo but took me right to my subway stop for Akebonobashi.

Showed up at the hotel, and my tickets in envelope were waiting for me at the desk. The stars were aligning.

Next day, show up in Shibuya at noon to suss out the club and spotted a familiar dreadlocked geezer in visor ducking into an art-supply store. It was *on*! Found the club in a back alley amidst a sea of love motels, singing rooms and other 'music venues'. I found my tribe.

A small group had started camping out in front of the variety store across from duo [Music Exchange], beers in hand, and despite the language barriers made me feel right at home.

Around three o'clock, a cube van pulled up and out stepped Jaz and the boys, ready for soundcheck. I nervously stepped up, gave him a Korean tea-set I brought with me as a gift. He thanked me and the band were shuttled inside. Instead of getting totally soused before the main event, I pissed off to Tokyo Tower and found an incredible Wax Museum dedicated to 'Fathers of Progressive Rock'. Many of them recorded with Conny Plank, who also produced *Revelations*. Another sign this trip would be legend.

Got back to the club and had to not only pay to stash my camera and gear, but, with any Japanese show, you are expected to buy a mandatory drink, and mine was an $11 beer. Could care less. I was ready for pandemonium.

After the standard Gary Glitter and Alex Harvey pre-game, I stared around the room of 600-plus and it hit me that I honestly felt like I was in a scene from *Blade Runner*, as the kids all wore PVC and wraparound shades, and I was immersed in it. While I'm having my thought, I suddenly hear the clacking of a keyboard over the PA and immediately recognised the voice of Harrison Ford. Holy shit! And the boys came out to the strains of Vangelis. The first night was to be the first two albums. Like a switch, the crowd turned on and sang 'Requiem' note for note. Jaz just stood back with a manic grin, amazed. Once it ended, the grand court jester reminded us that it was "9/11, and 9/11 was done by the US! 'Wardance'!"

Boom, the bomb went off and the crowd was lit.

A solid tribal mass of music fuelled by Big Paul's pounding on the tubs, beating them like they owed him fucking money. Youth was in his zone, holding down the groove, but it was Geordie that got my eye. Stood like a goddamn mannequin, almost motionless, like he focused every ion of his being into the Gibson and fucking roared the whole set, making it sound like an effortless symphony.

It's hard to explain, but those who know the Joke know that, once they find their pocket, it's like we're all not even there. It becomes a flowing rhythmic alchemy between band and The Gathering. The impossible becomes possible, the insane becomes sane and strangers become family.

The whole night turned into one cacophonous, glorious blur, but the highlights to me were 'The Fall of Because' and 'Who Told You How?', which they had never played before live.

They ended with 'Change' and 'Love Like Blood', then the crowd was hustled out. We walked out electric, wanting nothing but 'more'!

I managed to grab my gear and snake back into the club to the back. Big Paul was along the barrier signing flyers and I asked him to sign my EG Vinyl Box set. He was going to take it back to get the fellas to sign it, but then he gave us the wave and we were backstage.

For four guys who'd never played together in over 26 years, it was like the distance never happened at all. They were ecstatic. Geordie handed me a bottle of wine and I toasted the lads. I handed Jaz a copy of a Viktor Frankl book I thought he'd like. We got everyone together for some snaps. It was a victory for all of us.

I was grateful the boys gave me their gracious time. I never thought the first night would end like this. Felt like I didn't want to overstay my welcome, but, as we were about to leave, the club manager came in and told everyone we had

© *Tim Merrill*

to leave as the club was re-opening for its 11 o'clock disco. Totally fucking ridiculous to Killing Joke to force them to cut their reunion celebration short, but the boys loaded up and headed out the back door to power down and re-energise for the next night that was to come...

BIG PAUL

[I was] jet-lagged to hell mostly. Great buzz, though. For the others in the band, this was a continuation: same songs, same habits, different drummer. No big deal. For me, it was a different life! One I had put away. I had left my arrogance and self-confidence behind. I had to face my demons and do this.

JAZ

I always knew Paul would be back. There was never any doubt. Even through the worst times, I always knew he was part of it. And we did some fucking dark shit. It took an amount of time for everybody to get over it.

✦ ✦ ✦

ABART
22 September 2008,
Zurich, Switzerland

DIMITRI LORINGETT

Probably the most amazing live gig I've been to in my life. Big Paul was really cool and just mingled with the crowd while the others headed for the tour bus parked outside.

Dimitri, right, with the powerhouse that is Big Paul © Dimitri Loringett

✦ ✦ ✦

KENTISH TOWN FORUM
October 2008,
London, UK

TOBY O'REILLY
(Apple)

The phone rang around 11.30 at night. The band had been playing in London that night. I couldn't go as I had my young son and daughter for the weekend.

The [phone] conversation starts.

"Hi, how was the Joke gig? Good gig?"

The voice replies: "We were good, very good."

"Is that you, Jaz?"

"Yes, Apple, it's me. I have one question to ask you – why were you not at my gig tonight?"

I explained about the kids being with me.

"But Apple, that's why we have boarding schools so you can come to my gigs."

He starts his laughing and the phone goes dead.

KENTISH TOWN FORUM
3/4 October 2008,
London, UK

ADRIAN WASON

Of course, this was after Raven's death. That was a shock. I can remember where I was like it was yesterday. He was an enthusiastic member of The Gathering and always replied to our questions. Some of his putdowns were hilarious: U2 – "Balding Welsh midgets".

The Forum gigs were like a party atmosphere. The main things I remember were:

Talking to Taif Ball, who was playing pool in the pub next door. He was so funny he should have his own show.

'Who Told You How?' on the first night not sounding as scary as on record.

Second night opening with 'The Hum'.

Treponem Pal being absolutely amazing. I only bought the CD as it was Raven's last record, but there are some tunes on that.

TICKET NUMBER : 95 6
DOWNSTAIRS
AGE RESTRICTIONS APPLY
ticketmaster
ticketmaster.co.uk
MEAN FIDDLER PRESENTS
KILLING JOKE
PERFORMING PANDEMONIUM
AND SINGLES
THE FORUM LONDON NW5
SAT 04-OCT-08 DOORS 19:00
PRICE 20.00 S/C TOTAL 20.00
PARKING RESTRICTIONS
USE PUBLIC TRANSPORT

✦ ✦ ✦

LANCASTER GATE
5 October 2008,
London, UK

MATT TIBBITS

The morning after the second Forum reunion gig in 2008, I saw Jaz at breakfast in the hotel and he invited me up to his room for a cigar – a passion we share – and a chat. Whilst regaling me with his plans for the next year or so, he cajoled me into also sharing his hash from a smoke-filled, upturned wine glass. Big mistake! Not being used to it, I clearly overdid it and ended up having to make my apologies and leave, in a terrible state of mental time-slip and hallucination. Half an hour later, having manically packed my things a dozen times, I found myself stumbling along a short street in Lancaster Gate which suddenly appeared 10 miles long, in a desperate, vain attempt to get to the tube and eventually home. Forlorn and beside myself, I had to go back to the hotel, at which moment Jaz, Paul and some of the crew were checking out and witnessed my paranoid plight with great amusement!

Matt with Jaz in Brussels about a week before his 'experience' In London © Matt Tibbits

To my huge relief, I was able to check back into my room to try and sleep it off. Thankfully, things improved after a couple of hours. At the height of my horrors, I had called my wife, who was on important business with the Foreign Office and Russian government officials. Eventually, she was able to excuse herself and come and help me get home. Not my proudest moment.

FILLMORE NEW YORK AT IRVING PLAZA
11 October 2008,
New York, USA

JORDAN DINIZ

I stood in the middle of the front row and I remember the synth intro to 'Requiem' like a heartbeat bringing the ceremony to life. The shaman appeared out of the dark with measured step and a piercing gaze, holding the mic a certain distance from his body as if even he were wary of its power. Bathed in red light, he begins to sing while the crowd chants along. As the set continues, the effect of the merging of tribal, pulsating rhythms (the body), the fire-wash of Lydian scales (the spirit) and the forceful declaration of the vocals (the ego-consciousness) meets its culmination for me during 'The Fall of Because', and I feel the closest I had come that night to a ritualistic trance brought on by the relentless repetition, as the shaman, stone-faced and throbbing to the beat, stood straight with an outstretched hand to invoke timelessness from within the room. The music has particularly accompanied me alone on long drives day or night through the still lush and desolate parts of New England, bringing great synergy and catharsis to those moments, which always remain part of me as coordinates to those thin-veiled places. It's helped develop meaning and identity out of both inner and outer chaos respectively, and for that I will always be grateful to the band. It's done good in the world, not just by itself but through its influence on all the other artists that have had similar effects on me and so many other people, instilling the primal connection that sees us to our true humanity. As I write this, I'm not a five-minute walk from the grave of HP Lovecraft, so it seems appropriate to appeal to other Gatherers during this dark time and for the dark times to come to consider the joke that kills all fear – that "even death may die".

FILLMORE NEW YORK AT IRVING PLAZA
12 October 2008,
New York, USA

MATTHEW GAMMA

We were getting prepped at McSorley's Old Ale House. My girlfriend Kerry and my friends Ben and Keith came along. It was the first show I have ever been to that made me feel like I took two hits of ecstasy. I was in a groove of dance and rhythm and all I did was drink dark ale. When they played 'Wardance', it was like a steady locomotive train driving through the plaza. I'll never forget it – along with Jaz in the Heath Ledger-style joker make-up along with his grey jumpsuit. I've only seen them three times, but this was my first and best experience. Long live Killing Joke.

CLIFF MONK LIVINGSTON

Finally getting to meet Big Paul Ferguson and having tea backstage with Youth in NYC 2008 was too cool.

Killing Joke are my favourite band and it was a dream come true to work together on tour, get to know them better as people. Killing Joke continue to inspire my creativity.

Cliff's wife Ivy with Big Paul © Cliff Monk Livingston

HOUSE OF BLUES
14 October 2008,
Chicago, USA

DAVID LADWIG

There was a show here in Chicago at the House of Blues. There seemed to be some sort of psychic event as the stage started to move in a wave motion, undulating for five seconds. I remember blinking and looking down to refocus my vision. I chalked it up to having had a few beers, but I was truly gobsmacked when I later read that Youth mentions the same event in an interview. Wow.

HELLFEST
20 June 2009,
Clison, France

STEPHANE BONGINI
(aka Frenchy Frenzy)

The biggest music festival in France. I go there with all my equipment, plus the cheeses and bottles of wine. It's unbelievably hot and I have to walk around the site to finally get stuck by the security guards – and there the miracle happens. In the distance, I see Jaz and Youth walking and I think I've never shouted so loud in my life to wave to them and above all for them to hear me because it was my only chance to get to the festival, at least backstage. It's incredible – Jaz hears me shouting and he comes to see me with Youth – but the security guards won't let me through.

Jaz is forced to go back inside the festival to get me a pass. From then on, the trouble turns into total happiness. I don't know many other people who would have bothered to do what Jaz did for me. That's why I always take the trouble to do things right at the cheese dinners with attention to detail.

A civilising force that demands respect © Stéphane Bongini

Unlike some people (especially in big cities like London or Paris) who solicit the band without really knowing their music, I always try not to solicit them too much, even if I've made them sign most of the collector's vinyl records (that's my collector side). They are very careful to avoid stalkers or any kind of profiteers.

I think I passed the exam, but they want to protect themselves from psychopathic fans.

I was lucky enough to be able to film them in excellent conditions. Then we continued with the cheese meal. On average, there are at least five to six different cheeses, but that could go up to 14, all fresh and vacuum-packed with fresh morning baguettes and glasses that are never plastic.

All this on wicker trays – because presentation is paramount.

You can't imagine all the logistics behind it.

Lots of musicians come to see them backstage because they have a real cult following. There were the musicians from Amebix at this cheese meal and they were almost intimidated and especially surprised by the friendly side of the band members. I remember someone said in Berlin one day it was a change to find so many cheeses instead of the usual alcohol and cocaine in the backstage of the concerts...

VENICE AIRPORT FESTIVAL
31 July 2009,
Venice, Italy

STEPHANE BONGINI

Summer 2009 is also the year of an exceptional outdoor concert in Venice, Italy, with my buddies Jon Chapman and Cormac. A relaxed atmosphere – like all concerts in Italy – especially outdoors. We made an extraordinary cheese meal in a small house that bordered the festival grounds: imagine that, our hotel was 200m from the festival. To get back to the hotel, we were hovering without our feet touching the ground. We felt so much like we had spent an extraordinary day in the middle of nature listening to our favourite music played by musicians who don't play the stars – and Geordie played bass on a cover of Lou Reed's 'Walk on the Wild Side' at 2am.

WINTER GARDENS
9 August 2009,
Blackpool, UK

KALEM CLARKE

They're one of the few bands I can go see with both my parents as they're just that good and it's impossible not to enjoy them live. My Dad got me into punk and brought me to see them for the first time when I was 12. To this day, it's one of the greatest sets I've ever seen. I'd never witnessed anything like it before. It felt more like a religious ceremony than a gig. The image of Jaz coming out in his war paint still sticks in my mind 11 years later. They really set the benchmark for live music for me. Since then, I've been lucky to see them every time they've come to Dublin. My mother wouldn't be too fond of punk and bands like that, but she never misses a Killing Joke gig! It's a real family affair when they play here and I'm sure others feel the same way.

GEORDIE

It had been building for a while [the impetus to make a new album].

It was a nice venue, Youth's studio, all very spread out. You could get your own space. We had a lot on the table. I'd gone in with Jaz over here and got a good few ideas up and Youth had a load of ideas, too. Landed in that Pink Floyd studio [Britannia] down Putney way, so we all had quite a lot on the table for that.

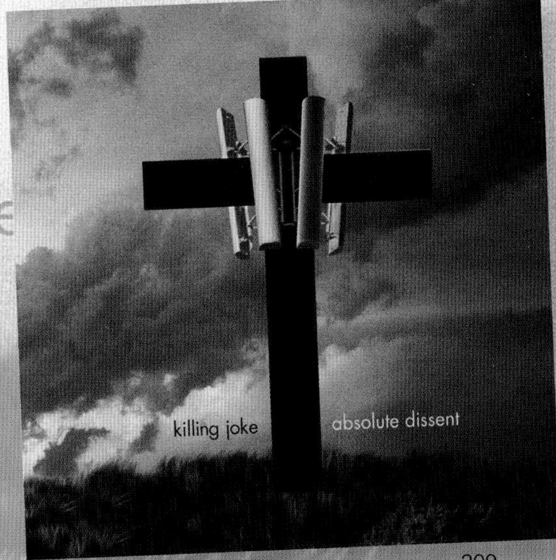

"'Cheeseboard'? Was that on *Brighter Than a Thousand Suns*?"
© Stéphane Bongini

STÉPHANE BONGINI

An incredible moment for me – attending three days of the recording of the album *Absolute Dissent* in London [in late 2009]. I discover a world that I do not know: the recording of an album is the very meticulous work of adjustment of all the songs. It is there where one realises the titanic work to conceive an album of music.

The atmosphere is relaxed and I film unique moments and I realise I am extremely privileged to be present at these moments of creation to which no one is usually invited.

I had info about the place and the date, but I never know in advance how it will happen. I always bring my secret weapons – cheeses and wines – which are the best ambassadors of brotherhood.

DEREK SAXENMEYER

I came on to do *Absolute Dissent*, starting in December 2009. Just recording vocals. Jaz added keys to one or two tracks. But I don't know if they re-did that in the end. It might just have been an idea. We were in the studio for about a month-and-a-half or two months. They'd been working on the album with Thomas Stiehler, a German producer and engineer [*Night Time*/*Brighter Than a Thousand Suns*] they knew from Hansa Studio in Berlin. Thomas and Jaz had already started vocal sessions. But Thomas had some family matters and had to leave. So I stepped in. I'd already recorded Jaz once. But that's when I started actually putting Jaz in the control room with me. Thomas had set him up that way. There wasn't a lot of space in the vocal booth at Faust [Studios]. So Thomas put Jaz behind him in the control room. I kept Jaz that way because it was comfortable for him to sing like that. Also because, being in close contact, that feeling of intimacy sometimes helps everyone to be in the zone together. Most singers usually sing in a recording room that doesn't have anyone else in it. It's kind of impersonal. Being in the same room together offers a proximity where you can lead off each other's energy. It affects the performance. You get an actual performance when there's people there. Well, having Jaz belt at the back of your head for hours is heavy. That's the only way to describe it. It's intense. When a singer is pushing that much energy out, it's almost like an extreme sport. It's actually tough on their body, their throat. And emotionally tough if they're *in* the song. Each take, you're waiting on the edge, in suspense, to see if that is going to be THE take. There's a limit to how long a singer can belt, so you try to capture as much intensity as possible without them frying their voice out. To do that, the engineer has to be on their toes. I did the vocals on all the songs on the *In Excelsis* EP – 'In Excelsis', 'Endgame', 'Kali Yuga' and 'Ghosts of Ladbroke Grove'. They were songs that were released ahead of the album, but they were all recorded in the same batch. And I recorded all Jaz's vocals for the *Absolute Dissent* album with the exception of two or three they'd already done. Jaz was writing his book at the same time – *Letters from Cythera*. Clive Goddard mixed *Absolute Dissent*, so I'd been in contact mostly with him while we recorded the vocals. He would send me instrumentals for Jaz to record vocals on. Big Paul sent a couple as well, and I was sending my files back to Clive in England.

INMUSIC FESTIVAL
31 July 2010,
Zhangbei County, China

SPIKE T SMITH
(drummer)

For one night only? Spike T Smith (centre) © Spike T Smith

As I sit here at home in this pandemic lockdown [in July 2020], I cast my mind back to 10 years ago, when I would have been travelling to China, the country where the virus was born, to immerse myself, play drums and be cocooned in the wonderful world of the mighty Killing Joke! Original drummer Big Paul Ferguson was unable to commit, so, at very short notice, I was drafted in, given the set-list to learn and the necessary paperwork to fill out to get me into the country.

The second Zhangbei Grassland Music Festival, aka InMusic Festival, was the event the band were booked to play. It was held in Zhangbei Grassland in Zhangjiakou, Hebei Province – basically, a getaway spot for people living in Beijing. It was a very remote area and, as I remember it, close to the Mongolian border.

Brief brothers in arms: Spike T Smith with Jaz in China © Spike T Smith

Rehearsals were to take place in Beijing, which is where we all collectively flew into from our various home destinations around the globe. These rehearsals would be a mixture of super high-intensity and rolling about with laughter. For me, the opportunity to be playing with the three original members and in a country that was a first for all of us to perform in was both mind-blowing and inspirational in equal measure.

We rehearsed hard for two days and got the set in good shape, then made the arduous 12-or-so-hour trip (we were told it would take about four!) by a very 'basic in comfort' bus to close by the festival site.

On arrival, we were told the show may not go ahead due to the extremely bad weather forecast for the following day. Fortunately, it did and I live to tell the tale. As quickly as the whole adventure started, it was over and I found myself back in the UK focusing on my next musical adventure – a much richer man for the experience!

BERT NEVEN
(partner, Golden HIVE Studios, Prague; Killing Joke live sound engineer)

China with Killing Joke. One show. July 2010. Fucking hilarious. It was really fucking weird. Because first of all, we heard that in China there's an absolute ban on whatever kind of drugs. So everybody had the idea not to take anything with us. We went to a rehearsing centre in Beijing for four days of practice before the show because we had a new drummer from the UK. His name was Spike T Smith. I think he played only that show with them. Youth was back already. But I think Big Paul had a problem somehow and wasn't there. That's why Spike was there. We were going to the show and it was only a 300km drive from Beijing. We drove past the Great Wall of China. There was no time to stop, but we saw it. I thought we'd be at the show in about three hours. But there was an absurd traffic jam. It took us eight or 10 hours, ridiculously long, with Jaz sitting, nagging, in the back, saying, "Are we there yet?" and "How long?" Youth, during the drive, wrote a beautiful song on his computer, wearing his headphones. Geordie was in need of lime juice to mix with his tequila. Reza was Reza. Their guitar tech, Diamond Dave, was a diamond like always. And Spike T was sitting there, probably thinking, "What the fuck am I doing here?" I heard the traffic jam lasted all summer and got so bad in August that it took two weeks to make that same drive.

Diamond Dave – 2010 in Prague © Ian Bull

RON SYNOVITZ

When Geordie got the final mixes of *Absolute Dissent* back from England in the summer of 2010, he came over to my apartment to listen through studio monitors. I had an analogue audio mastering chain there, Manley gear – a Massive Passive EQ, a Variable Mu compressor and an ELOP (electrical optical limiter). After that, Geordie started giving me tapes of demos he'd been working on in Detroit, then came to Prague, where he lived next door to Ian Bull. He said: "Run it through the meat grinder." There were guitar-synth instrumentals using a Roland R-8 drum machine. One tape was labeled 'Elevenses' and another 'Primobile'. They included an early version of 'Primobile', which would turn up on Killing Joke's *MMXII* album, and a song based around a guitar riff that became 'Big Buzz' on the *Pylon* album. When I told Geordie there was a whole album worth of songs, he said: "Call it *Animal Pharm*." Some had already been put out for fans as unmastered MP3s on Geordie's official Myspace page. His track titles were 'Legs Eleven', 'Anno Zero', 'Love Kills', 'Genotron', 'Angel with Dirty Secrets', 'Dang Skippy', 'Replay', 'Hidden Plein', 'Young Retriever' and 'Choral Exe'. I mastered another unreleased recording that Geordie made with Youth. Geordie gave it to Mont Sherar – a photographer who'd been a friend of Killing Joke since the 1980s. Mont used it for the soundtrack of a short hockey film he made called *Sini vs. Smidt*. Geordie also asked me to master tapes with early working recordings of Damage Manual. He called it *W.A.W.* for Walker-Atkins-Wobble. It had Martin Atkins on drums and Jah Wobble – the bass player from *Metal Box*-era Public Image Ltd. They were instrumental mixes done before Chris Connelly joined as vocalist, and before Martin Atkins chopped it up and moved bits around on the grid. Geordie said it sounded "human" to him. The tapes were labeled *Berwick Street*. There was one song with a vocal – 'The Streets Belong to You' – with the late Alex Harvey. Geordie said, with great admiration for Alex, they'd taken his voice from a flexi-disc interview for a 1974 British rock magazine.

THE FLEECE
25 September 2010,
Bristol, UK

LEE COTTERELL

I first got into Killing Joke in 1982. I got into punk around this time just as many of my school friends were getting bored with it and managed to buy a lot of their unwanted records cheap. Among these bargains were the 'Follow the Leaders' 10-inch and *What's THIS for...!* album. They both blew me away. From there, it was seeing 'Empire Song' on *Top of the Pops* (although I was a bit baffled by Jaz Coleman's absence at the time).

I continued buying their records but didn't get to see them live until the *Night Time* tour and was completely blown away by their live performance. Apart from one dip in interest around the time of *Outside the Gate* (I couldn't get into that album), I remain a firm fan, continue to buy their records and get to as many live gigs as possible. The highlight was seeing them play a cosy warm-up gig at the Fleece in Bristol in 2010. And to think the guy who sold me those records all those years ago warned me I'd get bored with them after a little while!

ADRIAN WASON

Great venue, although, apparently, Jaz doesn't like it. Notable highlights: opener 'Tomorrow's World', 'Fresh Fever...' and 'Depthcharge'.

✦ ✦ ✦

AÉRONEF
30 September 2010,
Lille, France

JEAN-CHRISTOPHE VAN THIENEN

After that gig, I was standing right next to Youth at the merch stand and simply said "11 Portland Road". He stood back, rather bemused, and asked how come I knew that address, so I told him the story and he invited me backstage and told the story in turn to Jaz, who offered me a drink with a big grin on his face.

JUSTIN BROADRICK

[On his remix of *Absolute Dissent*'s 'European Super State'] I'm still not as happy with it as I could've been, but I was very happy that, according to Youth, he and the rest of the band

Killing Joke at Lucerna Music Club, Prague – 4 October 2010 © Ron Synovitz

were happy with it. But this was after a few other attempts from me, which they weren't into so much. They [the versions] were more extreme. Ultimately, I wanted to go further, but – unfortunately here – I was being asked to remix one of my favourite bands of all time just as I'd switched over to a whole bunch of new studio equipment, which was quite literally about to fundamentally change the way I'd been working for some time. So, I was in the teething stage with this equipment, had barely got anywhere near accustomed to it and was having to remix Killing Joke! I was nowhere near comfortable with working with this equipment by the time of the deadline, so I've never been truly satisfied with the remix, but I think it does 'something'.

I'd love to remix KJ again, especially with my current studio set-up and working methods. Who knows if that could happen again? But I do know that, collectively, Killing Joke like my work and feel that I am an ally – that's enough for me.

✦ ✦ ✦

NOSTURI
11 October 2010,
Helsinki, Finland

ANTTI LAUTALA

Killing Joke toured in Finland around 1984. Then there was a long pause until they returned to conquer this land with the reformed original line-up in 2009. They played an open-air festival called Ilosaarirock in Joensuu. To my disappointment, I had to skip that one. Gladly, they returned to play Helsinki next year. I was there in the packed venue. They were absolutely awesome. Right after that, I was at every show they played in Finland. So far, it's five in total. Let's say three of them were brilliant, but there was a fill-in drummer at two shows and you could say it was different. You can play like Big Paul, but replacing him is impossible. He has a special drive that can't be replaced. I think that is also a problem with Killing Joke records that don't include Big Paul. Martin Atkins was the only one who could come even close. Amen.

✦ ✦ ✦

HAMMERSMITH APOLLO
16 October 2010,
London, UK

ADRIAN WASON

I saw Gregg Wallace from *MasterChef* at the bar.

✦ ✦ ✦

IRVING PLAZA
3 December 2010,
New York, USA

FRED MASTROMARINO

I finally got to see them in concert while touring for *Absolute Dissent*, and it was truly pulverising. They knew exactly how to use the space to give a track like 'The Great Cull' immense power on stage as well as making songs from the first album continue to seem timeless. I was delighted to see them again with Tool as recently as [19 November] 2019 and was riveted with every song they played.

'Eighties' is still my favourite song of all time.

PARADISE ROCK CLUB
4 December 2010,
Boston, USA

JOEL GAUSTEN

The original Killing Joke back in action, three decades after the release of the first full-length album. And those eyes – piercing, focused and beyond intense behind the drums. Big Paul Ferguson, finally back in his rightful place. Killing Joke have had a slew of brilliant drummers – hell, I've played alongside two of 'em – but none of them played 'Change' with his balance of fury and precision. That's HIS song.

DEREK SAXENMEYER

Late in 2010 or at the beginning of 2011, I did pre-production sessions just with Geordie for the *MMXII* album. We recorded two songs, Geordie hashing out demos for 'Rapture' and 'Pole Shift'. I don't think there were previous demos and I don't recall there were any vocals on it. He did guitars, keyboards and bass. We recorded on to a drum track prepared ahead of time. For guitars, Geordie brought over his gold Gibson ES-295, going through a splitter into his Bell Electronics ADTs. Those went to two Egnater Rebel 20 amps with matching 1 x 12" cabs. We mic'd it up with two Royer R-121 ribbon mics. For the keyboards, we used a Dave Smith Instruments Prophet '08. They [the band] went to Doghouse Studio, Oxfordshire in 2011 to record most of the album.

Geordie and Derek Saxenmeyer recording demos of the tracks 'Rapture' and 'Pole Shift' during pre-production at Faust for MMXII © Faust Records Studio

ROCK CITY
30 March 2011,
Nottingham, UK

ADRIAN WASON

First time I'd seen 'Unspeakable' as an opener, which was brilliant.

RON SYNOVITZ

In August 2011, Geordie called and asked if we could run a concert recording through the Manley chain. So we mastered Killing Joke's *Down by the River* album together. It was Geordie's pet project. He'd recorded the concert at the Royal Festival Hall, London in April 2011 without telling the rest of the band. He said performances on previous live Killing Joke albums were affected because everybody knew they were being recorded. He wanted to avoid that, so had the Royal Festival Hall gig recorded secretly. He mixed it with Clive Goddard and Marcus Butler in Henley-on-Thames – The Doghouse Studio. He said it was fitting it was recorded and mixed at two locations on the River Thames. Plus, he could go fishing during downtime at Doghouse. To finish up the master, I took Geordie down to the Vltava River in Prague – a studio called Golden Digital near the Vltavská metro station. It was built by Michael Šťastný, aka Amak Golden, the future chief engineer of the Prague *Pylon* sessions.

AMAK GOLDEN

(partner, Golden HIVE Studios; Prague Pylon sessions)

The first one I met from Killing Joke was Geordie. He came over to the Vltavská studio for the masters of *Down by the River*. Jaz came over after that to do vocals for his *Black & Red* album [with Ondřej Smeykal]. Then all of Killing Joke came together to jam and write songs.

RON SYNOVITZ

It was a windowless basement space in a building that had been a communist-era 'youth culture palace'. The lower realms of the building were rumoured to have been used by the Gestapo during the Second World War. It definitely had a creepy vibe. Amak called it Golden Digital. Then we pooled together a lot of analogue gear, teamed up with Bert Neven and moved to Prague's Vinohrady neighbourhood. That's where Jaz rechristened our studio the 'HIVE'.

Jaz and Geordie returned to Prague around the time they were finishing *MMXII*. They invited me over to Faust to watch them record a bonus song for the CD release. Jaz said the working title was 'Great Uprising'. It was released as 'New Uprising'. Reza Udhin was engineering. Geordie sat next to him in the control room, his guitar amps mic'd up in an isolation chamber. You could almost sense spirits hovering around him while he played – like the ghosts that follow the musicians in the film *Rok d'ábla* or the angels in Wim Wenders' *Wings of Desire*. Geordie was no-nonsense in the studio. So focused, nailing all his parts in one take. Then he left while Jaz worked on his keyboard parts and got a mix with Reza. They spent 14 hours arranging the song. "Slow is FAST," Jaz told me the next day when it was all finished. Killing Joke threw a pre-release listening party for the *MMXII* album at Final Club on 21 February 2012. Jaz thought that date relevant for a world premiere because it was a palindromic number. Friends were invited. Jaz handed out autographed folders with memorabilia from the sessions – handwritten lyric sheets he'd used when recording vocals, plane tickets from their travels, cigar rings from celebrations. At exactly two minutes after nine o'clock, Jaz looked at his watch and told me: "It looks like the perfect time to start." Then he turned to Bert at the Final Club mixboard and said "Crank it at welding volume" – 21:02 on 21.02.2012.

BERT NEVEN

There was a lot of Killing Joke activity concentrated in Final Club, an underground venue in Prague. They threw their parties there. They screened an early cut of documentary film *The Death and Resurrection Show* downstairs. Youth came to Prague for that. Geordie and Jaz were both there too. And Jaz and Geordie threw a world-premiere listening party down there for Killing Joke's *MMXII* album before it was released.

✦ ✦ ✦

O2 ACADEMY
5 March 2012,
Bristol, UK

ADRIAN WASON

Loved the set-list. 'In Cythera', 'Fema Camp', 'Unspeakable', 'Sun Goes Down', 'Bloodsport', 'Pole Shift', 'Chop-Chop'. I thought that, of the last three albums, *MMXII* was possibly the best. I'm sure 'Colony Collapse' was played, although it's not on setlist.fm. This was one of my favourite gigs recently, mainly because of the set.

✦ ✦ ✦

ROUNDHOUSE
8 March 2012,
London, UK

FLETCHER STEWART

There I was, in the circular structure at the dawn of what was to be the apocalypse in 2012. Steam crawled from the stage and wafted throughout the old engine shed now known as the Roundhouse, where so many legendary performances had commenced before. Killing Joke took the stage as Geordie raked a chord that shattered the tension in a harmonic firestorm of sound. After years of hearing the records and yearning as a Tennessee boy to see this enigmatic band live, there I was, gazing at the iconic silhouettes of these four alchemists of joyous terror as they decimated the audience with a sonic leviathan that seemed to unleash upon their summation. Seeing them revealed nothing – the mystery of where this power came from only deepened.

✦ ✦ ✦

ACADEMY 1
10 March 2012,
Manchester, UK

MIK RAVEN

Let me tell another story. I had a pretty shitty time in the late Noughties. My wife of over 20 years decided to have an affair with the guy over the road. Fair enough. This stuff happens. Broke my marriage, though. At the time, I was going through a bad time mentally. Eventually, I came through it and met my current wife (who at the time was not a fan of KJ). We decided to marry and,

on the night of her hen do, I was at a conference in Manchester. Killing Joke were playing that same night in that same city! What the fuck! I was there and one of my wife's memories is my text to her as Jaz came on stage to the intro to 'European Super State' – "It's fucking Killing Joke!" It had been quite a while since I'd seen them.

✦ ✦ ✦

O2 ABC
12 March 2012,
Glasgow, UK

REZA UDHIN

Keyboardist Reza in Prague in 2010 © Ian Bull

For many years after I joined Killing Joke in 2006, the original members used to tell me of these almost magical, unexplained episodes which happened to them on stage during their sets. They were not regular; they happened a handful of times in their career. But, when it happened, they all knew it. From what I gathered, it would occur at a point of ultimate ecstasy, when the music and crowd were tuned into a certain frenzy frequency.

I believe they said the first time it happened was early in the band's history at the Hexagon in Reading, UK [1 February 1985]. The band could feel the energy of the audience rising and then, out of nowhere, sudden silence fell on stage. The band looked at each other. They were all still playing and the audience still dancing but they could hear nothing. They knew this was something very special in that moment and they all acknowledged it. Then the sound reappeared and they continued the gig, the audience none the wiser as to what had just happened.

They told me they were sure this was going to happen again, since the original line-up got back together. I believe this happened in Glasgow – 12 March 2012 at the O2 ABC. The show was going great, energy was rising. We started our 13th song (read into that whatever you will!). The song was 'Corporate Elect'. The audience were absolutely buzzing, the energy so high. Then, halfway into the song, I experienced that silence for a few seconds. I believe the rest of the band did, too... complete silence – but we were still playing and audience still moshing, but it was all too short-lived. The lights went out, power down and the venue was dropped into complete darkness!

We were ushered through the dark corridors and stairs with torches into our pitch-black dressing rooms. Candles were lit. We were informed that the audience had been ushered out of the building, as the power was completely out. Some of the band's friends came into our darkened dressing room, Ally McCoist, at the time manager of Scottish football club Rangers, and Derek Forbes, formerly of the band Simple Minds. By this time, the fans outside were stirring into a mini-riot outside the venue, as they wanted us to finish the gig! We were speaking in darkness about how we'd apparently knocked out the electricity in the building, then someone in the room, I can't remember who exactly, said, "Not just the room, guys. You knocked out the power in the entire block – all the clubs, venues, bars. Everything!"

CHRIS BRYANS

Have you had many of those white-heat moments since you've been back in the chair?

BIG PAUL

Few and far between, but they've happened. A gig in Philadelphia on a recent tour comes to mind. A transcendence, everything locked in, no more effort, almost blissful.

TROY GREGORY

I didn't know that [the white-heat moment] was a thing. But there was a show and it was 'Pssyche'. There was a part of the song in a keyboard drone where Geordie and Nick [Walker] are both playing. It felt like it went on for about 12 minutes. It was like it was in slow motion. I fucking love that moment. I didn't know that was a white-heat moment, not until I saw the trailer for Shaun's film [*The Death and Resurrection Show*]. Shaun came out on that tour for a bit. I definitely experienced it before I knew what it was. All the frequencies all at the same time, rattling around the cage.

O2 ABC
12 March 2012,
Glasgow, UK

DEREK FORBES

Last time I saw Killing Joke was in Glasgow at the now defunct, destroyed ABC. It was the night the power went down, around halfway through the show. Jaz was on top form that night. He commanded the stage with some incredible tribal moves, and was vocally superb. Geordie was every bit as cool, swaggering around the stage with the same majesty only the greats can produce – Page/Ronson/Cleminson, to name but three!

Paul Ferguson is an incredible drummer in my eyes, and gelled with the wonderful Youth to create a sonic river of sound that was the beating, pulsing heart of the band. The Glasgow audience were loving it, and then the electricity took an early bath, and the band left the stage.

Rivers of sound, power cuts, Japanese sipping saké and a half-eaten kebab – a typical night with Killing Joke for Derek Forbes © Derek Forbes

I was there with my wife, Wendy, and sons Kai and Dylan. My great friend was there, too, as he had been many times before – the polecat Ally McCoist. We went backstage to meet up with the band. Nicest guys you could ever meet. Geordie passed round a 30-year-old bottle of Japanese sipping saké.

Jaz was incredibly generous with his time, regaling stories to Wendy and my boys, who loved the band. I ended up lying back on the dressing-room couch, with Youth unable by this time to bite my fingers. I woke up the next day with a half-eaten kebab in my pocket. Ally must have left just after the demise of the refreshments, and so we wait until The Joke come back again. I, for one, will definitely be there.

ANDY MAXWELL

When my son Finlay was 13, I decided it was time for him to have the Killing Joke experience. Although most venues don't allow under-14s in, even accompanied by an adult, I decided to take the chance – and it paid off big time. It was 2012, on the *MMXII* tour.

Finlay's account will tell you the rest.

Jaz signed this photo for 13-year-old Finlay Maxwell © Andy Maxwell

FINLAY MAXWELL

It was a brilliant night until Sauchiehall Street had a power cut, which meant the set got cut short. We waited outside for a while and eventually managed to get backstage to meet the band, who were all so lovely and welcoming. We got pictures with everyone. Jaz gave me his t-shirt, which he'd been wearing on stage that night. It was drenched in sweat! Jaz also gave us his manager's number and told us to give him a call whenever we wanted to go to a show, and we would have free tickets for life.

ANDY MAXWELL

I remember having a lengthy conversation with Jaz about punk in general and he was telling me Killing Joke used to rehearse next door to The Clash, and that he still misses Joe Strummer terribly. It was a member of the road crew that invited us backstage that night after the power had been restored. The band couldn't have been more welcoming to us, telling us to help ourselves to food and drinks and get as many photos as we wanted.

Unfortunately, I had to drive 70 miles back home after the gig and Finlay had school in the morning, so no alcohol for me!! Finlay was buzzing all the way home. I nearly had to peel him off the roof of the car when we got there!

✦ ✦ ✦

WULFRUN HALL
14 March 2012,
Wolverhampton, UK

PETER LAMB

Jaz came on for an encore of 'Wardance' in his dressing gown. That was very funny. He didn't want to come back on and was cursing the others, who were laughing hard. The crew snapped plenty of photos.

PYRAMIDS CENTRE
16 March 2012,
Portsmouth, UK

NICOLA FROUDE

Eventually, I moved to Hampshire with my partner. We saw a few gigs: Beady Eye, The Stranglers, Paul Weller. And I remember my partner said to me, "You talked about this band, Killing Joke." They were playing the Pyramids Centre in a couple of days.

I worked in Southsea, about 10 minutes from the Pyramids. I said, "Let me wander down, maybe I can gatecrash the soundcheck."

I had the most surreal experience. I walked up there, not expecting to see them, anybody, anything at all. Who did I see sitting on a bench? Big Paul, looking out to sea. I thought, "My God, he's going to get the shock of his life."

I said to him, "This is weird. I'm getting goosebumps here."

He asked if I was coming to the gig. I said we didn't have tickets and he said he'd put us on the guest-list.

It was great to see all these people, looking a bit older. I went back[stage] beforehand. I hadn't seen them for years.

Heavy-duty atmosphere going on [at the gig]. It was loud, it was raucous, it was dangerous. It was everything you wanted it to be. Everything you remembered.

We'd got tickets to see them in Coventry [17 June 2020] but the gig was cancelled because of all this horribleness going on.

I have to say what stays with me and will always stay with me so much was how wonderful the music business is. I've been so bloody lucky. Finding your way through on your journey through the music business in the Eighties, which was the best ever – it was hard work, but we did have a good time. I just loved going into work. It was a joy. I miss it so much, even now.

They [Killing Joke] meant the world to me. I was there for them if they needed things. A little bit dark, a little bit intimidating, but they weren't really.

✦ ✦ ✦

LE TRANSBORDEUR
19 April 2012,
Lyon, France

STEPHANE BONGINI

My first big European tour by car (7,776kms, if memory serves) and it's great, because you disconnect from your habits for total immersion in the music. You drive from one concert to another and you realise that the rhythm of a tour is gruelling.

When you go to see a unique concert in your city, you can't imagine the waiting.

It's an enormous amount of waiting for giving an hour-and-a-half concert. I also realised in a band it's extremely timed all day long, with a very tight schedule. I was amazed that they are always very punctual.

They were coming to play in my city, Lyon, so I organised a cheese dinner party in the cheese factory where I go all the time. A magical evening, people happy to share these unique moments where time is suspended. Jaz isn't there, but joins us the next morning and we visit a museum where I manage to organise a private visit. It's called the Abode of Chaos. The owner is a madman but got on very, very well with Jaz.

FLETCHER STEWART

Shortly after seeing the band at the Roundhouse [8 March 2012], I found myself free of the rat race that I was in while working in London's once-legendary Tin Pan Alley on Denmark Street amongst slimeball guitar dealers and their hipster cronies. I kept my head down while I was working in a shop there and ended up discovering that my passion for musical equipment had revealed a hidden talent, which took me places I never thought I would go. After blogging about my favourite unsung guitarists and their gear for a year or so, I was hired by the world's premier pedal publication, *Tone Report Weekly*, as part of the original team. I'd finally found my footing among like-minded music freaks not satisfied with the never-ending guitar-magazine revolving door of Clapton, Page, Gilmour, repeat.

I amassed an incredible collection of boutique effects units that were as unique and inspiring as the wonderful folks who made them. I decided I should see if I could get some of these machines in the hands of some of my favourite musicians to see what musical magic would happen.

✦ ✦ ✦

POSTBAHNHOF
2 May 2012,
Berlin, Germany

TORSTEN BOUR

Over the years, I became more and more a fan, but unfortunately missed the two concerts in Berlin in 2008 [24/25 September]. The next tour was for the album *Absolute Dissent*, but they only played Hamburg and Cologne in 2010, not in my home town of Berlin.

In 2012, the time had finally come and they came back to play a concert in Berlin for the *MMXII* tour. I can clearly remember I was very excited to see them play live. The played in a small venue. I remember someone from the crew came on stage right before the beginning and lit a kind of incense candle or something like that. It burned throughout the whole concert and somehow it made up a mystical vibe for me.

Mike Coles: "One of the many [cover design] variations leading up to Killing Joke's MMXII album. This album didn't actually have a title. I put MMXII in just for balance and it stuck"

When the band came on stage and started playing, I was totally blown away. The massive sound of the drums and Geordie's guitar sounded unmistakable: this was Killing Joke! Much harder and more intense than on CD. Jaz was in his element right from the beginning. You could literally feel his energy.

I liked it very much that they played six songs from the new album. Unfortunately, the track 'Millennium' from 1994, which made me become a Gatherer, was not in the set-list. But it was still a great concert! Since then, I've been going to every concert from Killing Joke in Berlin and was able to see them live in 2016 and 2018.

For me, Killing Joke concerts have something magical, mysterious and their sound is amazing. It really is the sound of hell!

SANT'ELIA ARENA
13 July 2012,
Cagliari, Italy

STEPHANE BONGINI

A memorable concert, where I was welcomed in a magnificent way by the organisers.

The right set of circumstances, as I call them.

I arrive by plane and get to the hotel. By chance, it's the same hotel as the group. I find myself propelled with them into an evening where we go to eat in a good restaurant where tourists never go and discover the city with people of extraordinary kindness. Geordie asks how I arrive at the right time with people I didn't know before? It's simple – I'm a damn Frenchman and I'm resourceful.

JAMES FRYER

My ultimate ambition as a fan was to find like-minded Gatherers and musicians to play the music. Tribute bands are a bit naff to many people, but I just wanted to play the music to other KJ fans who want to hear it – just an extension of being a KJ fan and a different way to express it.

In 2010, I found some kindred spirits and we got together and practised many of the songs. Various personnel changes later, we properly gigged in 2012 and have been ever since (though not as often as we'd like to).

Originally known as Absolute Dissent, we changed the name of the band to Pssyche – The Killing Joke Tribute in 2018.

We have many great friends among the Gatherers who come to see us wherever we play. For that we are immensely grateful. It would be easy to be negative about what we are doing, but they are tremendously supportive. At the end of the day, we are all just enjoying KJ's music in our own way.

Thanks to bandmates and friends Mick and Damon Head (Damon having served as Big Paul's drum tech on recent tours), I've been lucky enough to go backstage and meet the band on a number of occasions – they are aware of our humble tribute and have only ever shown interest and an appreciation that we are just fans finding another way to celebrate the music – but probably have a chuckle about it at the same time, God bless 'em!

© Adrian Wason

DEREK SAXENMEYER

The second batch of *Black & Red* recordings was about five years after the first batch. They re-recorded everything completely. We recorded all the instruments at Faust.

ONDREJ SMEYKAL

Jaz has worked with Ondřej Smeykal (above) for the album Black & Red. "No one's done anything like this," he says © Ron Synovitz

I play didgeridoo and I play on the album *Black & Red* with Jaz Coleman. *Black & Red* is a combination of human voice, Indian harmonium and didgeridoo. But it's not actually didgeridoo. It's something which comes out of the didgeridoo, something I call Electro Tube. It's a sort of synthesiser inspired by this ancient instrument. One way I work with it is rescaling the instrument by the sliding of two tubes – like a trombone. But there's also a technique of changing the position of the lips and air pressure and the amplifying of these things through my system to get out a kind of chromatic scale. It's not completely chromatic. But you can get a lot of notes in combination with the sliding instrument. You can cover whatever notes you want to compose with. So it becomes a kind of synthesiser.

DEREK SAXENMEYER

Ondřej was set up in the recording room at Faust. He has his own effects mixer so he could tailor the sound to taste. We also had an SM7B microphone set up in case Jaz felt inspired and felt like going at it with a vocal. He could just jump on it and go. He jumped up there a couple of times. He'd record a section and then say: "Just leave it for later so I can remember what I did." For the harmonium, we used three Shure SM57 mics. That's a weird combination for an acoustic instrument. It's a colourful mic to use. We ended up putting phasers on and distorting the harmonium quite a bit, so that was a better fit for what Jaz was after. The mood was cool. They were both in a tribal and animalistic frame of mind.

Jaz laying down vocals in 2012 for the Black & Red album © Ron Synovitz

RON SYNOVITZ

Jaz came to the Vltavská studio to record vocals for the second set of *Black & Red* recordings. Jaz said he wanted to force the Australian government to recognise that didgeridoo is the 'classical instrument' of Australia. Those vocal sessions were the first time Jaz worked with Amak Golden as an engineer.

AMAK GOLDEN

I recorded only the vocals with Jaz for *Black & Red*. He asked me if he could stay in the control room with me. So I decided to use a voiceover microphone, a Shure SM7B, with double compression through the Manley Variable Mu and a Universal Audio 1176LN. The double compression boosted the presence of his soft singing but kept the signal in check when he threw his head back and roared. I used this on all Jaz's vocals for the *Black & Red* sessions I did. I've used that same set-up with him ever since. I used it on all the Killing Joke sessions for *Pylon*. I used it again at Golden HIVE when Jaz came in to add vocals on Killing Joke's unfinished BBC Maida Vale recordings from 2015. That was in April 2016. The songs were 'Dawn of the Hive', 'Autonomous Zone', 'Euphoria', 'I Am the Virus' and 'Wardance'.

JAZ COLEMAN

The album is called *Black & Red*, which is the anarchist's flag, which is dear to the sentiment of the recording. We've made a proper listing of the best didge players in Australia, all of them, and no one's done anything like this. It's basically just two instruments. I gave myself limitations of a small harmonium... an Indian harmonium that you pump with one hand and play with the other. Then, with the developed didgeridoo, which Ondřej calls the Electro Tube, you can send multiple signals of the instrument in different directions. You may think it's a drum you're listening to. It's not a drum. It's actually the wonderful instrument Ondřej has developed. And, sometimes, you might think it's an electric guitar playing. It's not. It's the instrument Ondřej developed, again. There's multiple sine waves, there's multiple layers of the one instrument.

ZOMBIE HUT
14 March 2013,
Corby, UK

PETER LAMB

I once again uncannily synched a business trip back to the UK with some Killing Joke shows. Corby? Never heard of it! The Zombie Hut, I believe, was a converted rugby hut. It was a very square box, like a two-storey building. Very small too; very low stage. No barriers; no security. I saw Reza before they went on and asked if there were any surprises in the set-list. He smiled but said

When Killing Joke came to town, there was a different kind of contact activity in the former rugby hall known as the Zombie Hut © Peter Lamb

nothing. This was like Killing Joke in your living room at full blast, a couple of feet away. Jaz without make-up but still intense as ever. Geordie was piercing and crystal-clear. I made the mistake of being in front of Youth's speakers. Pleasure and pain. Seeing BPF operate up that close is a joy. Him and Geordie are very alike in their playing. No histrionics; just understated power and grace. 'The Beautiful Dead' made a welcome return from many years of disregard. They have far too many like that which need an airing. 'Follow the Leaders', 'Chop-Chop' and 'Sun Goes Down' were other notable additions. The gig had a nice vibe; lots of people dancing and struggling with balance issues, but all in good spirits. We're already too old. At the beginning of the encore, I recall Youth asking, "Any requests?"

"Requests? Nah, you got the wrong band..." © Peter Lamb

He followed that up with: "We don't do requests." Just how Killing Joke is that? I believe the Zombie has gone. What a shame. Brilliant venue.

✦ ✦ ✦

KENTISH TOWN FORUM
16 March 2013,
London, UK

MIK RAVEN

So, I had a new wife with no great love for the mighty Joke. What could I do? Obviously, take her to see them. The opportunity arose at the Forum. We went down and it was packed as usual. I will say at this point she is a massive Siouxsie fan, but the Joke gig blew her away. Not the performance of the band, but the audience. I was near the front, but her description was that the whole audience was dancing. Front to back! Not something she'd experienced before at Siouxsie gigs. That's the Gatherers for you.

Since then, we've been to many KJ gigs around the world. Thankfully, nowadays I can afford it (unlike in my youth). What I love is being able to introduce fans to the band where I can. I don't know the band very well myself but have some sort of influence being a known face and every now and then I can help a fan to meet a band member or get an autograph. Gives me a warm feeling inside. I've got a lot from Killing Joke through my life, but that is one thing that gives me a warm feeling inside!

ADRIAN WASON

This day was more memorable for sporting reasons than anything else. We piled into the pub at the bottom of the hill in Camden and watched Wales hammer England 30–3 [in the rugby union], which was unexpected and great if you were Welsh. We were half-tempted to go and see Claudia Brücken at The Borderline, but thought the [Killing Joke] set-list would be better than it turned out. Only 'Corporate Elect' being played from *MMXII*. I was despondent and really thought why bother churning out the same set-list time and time again. I put on The Gathering [message board] that it was time for Killing Joke to stop, for which I had a lot of abuse. We went back to the same pub in Camden and watched qualifying for the Australian GP.

✦ ✦ ✦

PARADISE ROCK CLUB
20 April 2013,
Boston, USA

JOEL GAUSTEN

It was less than a week after the Marathon bombing. "We want to be part of your healing!" announced Jaz from the stage during the most blistering KJ set I've ever seen. Killing Joke: forever a beacon of light amidst the madness.

✦ ✦ ✦

UNION TRANSFER
21 April 2013,
Philadelphia, USA

BOB CAMPBELL

It wasn't until 2013, over 30 years of being a fan, that I finally got to see KJ live. My nephew and myself were maybe 15ft back from the stage on Geordie's side. Quite a few times Youth and Jaz came over to that side, which was great being able to see everyone better, except for Big Paul, who obviously couldn't move. I joked that they did this to give a long-time fan (me) a better show but, in reality, there were some knuckleheads on the other side of the stage slinging their drinks all over, so I'm guessing they moved more to get out of the way of flying beer.

© Bob Campbell

EMPTY BOTTLE
27 April 2013,
Chicago, USA

ANDY SEWELL

I donated to the *Down by the River* project and got to see my name in the liner notes. Fast-forward and I was bringing my wife and brother-in-law to the show at Chicago's Empty Bottle. They were Killing Joke newbies and blown away by the performance. I danced like crazy. We went again in Columbus in 2018 [9 September]. In 2019, I may have been the only one in the arena at the Tool concert there to see Killing Joke. Tool were great too.

BILLBOARD THE VENUE
7 June 2013,
Melbourne, Australia

STAN MANIATIS

Only had to wait 10 years this time rather than 18 for the next Killing Joke gig. This was for the 1979–2012 compilation.

Billboards in the city on a clear but freezing winter's night – in front of hardcore fans, many middle-aged but some youngsters as well! Youth was in a Hawaiian shirt, which impressed me. Big Paul was missing – hand injury. They had a stand-in drummer.

Got a great t-shirt from 2013. Much better quality than the orange skull from 2003.

I have two sons. The younger one, Elias, does not appreciate my music but needs to attend the next Killing Joke show to understand its beauty. He sometimes secretly hums some of the tunes I play, especially The Smiths. I reckon a live performance would make a huge difference.

The range in Jaz Coleman's voice is amazing as he's got older. He can sing melodic new-wave pop songs one minute, then do industrial and death-metal-type vocals the next.

My wife was shocked at my taste in music. I seemed like a mild-mannered accountant. I've been an accountant since 1989.

Vaughan Smith and his wife with Jaz at the Melbourne show in 2013 © Vaughan Smith

STUDIO THE VENUE
13 June 2013,
Auckland, New Zealand

JASON MILLS

After emigrating to New Zealand in 2002, I feared and frustratingly accepted that I'd probably never see KJ live again.

Eleven years later, in June 2013, my wish was answered. KJ was coming to little ol' Aotearoa! A few days before the gigs, I was walking down Symonds Street in Auckland CBD, coffee in hand, head down, minding my own business, when, as I lifted my head, I caught a brief glimpse of a chap in a denim jacket, with thick, black, long hair, walking past me.

I thought, "Blimey, that looks so much like Jaz." I turned around, inquisitively said, "Jaz? Is that you?" If I'd looked up one second later, I'd have missed him. Even though I was a bit tongue-tied, we chatted for around half an hour. He was the most accepting, humble and humorous guy, a world away from what seemed an aggressive, angry creature on stage back in the day.

Apart from KJ playing their first two gigs in NZ (Auckland and Wellington [14 June], attended both), Jaz was there for another reason – the premiere of *The Death and Resurrection Show* (which I attended, met Jaz again, and [director] Shaun Pettigrew).

In all the years of following KJ, the NZ gigs were meant to be my first time seeing the original line-up, but it wasn't to be – Big Paul had to pull out. Gutted. But what an unforgettable few days it was!

In February 2016, Jaz was back in Auckland for a spoken-word evening. Again, Jaz spared me his time and we sat and spoke again at length after the show, a very humble chap.

✦ ✦ ✦

THE DEATH AND RESURRECTION SHOW

2013

SHAUN PETTIGREW

For me, even today, filming and listening to Coleman for all those years, ha ha! What a fucking lucky break for a filmmaker.

Just a bit of background. *The Death and Resurrection Show* was really two films if you like – an earlier version of the film called ***Let Success Be Your Proof***, directed by Jaz, about the original elemental occult experiment, and the final one you see now. Jaz and I started ILC [Productions] as a small film production business to capture Killing Joke's music and Jaz's classical personas. It was an absolute fucking blast! For the next 10 years, it developed into *The Death and Resurrection Show*.

NFT1
THE DEATH AND RESURRECTION SHOW + Q&A WI
THU FEB 19 2015 - 7:50 PM
£14.50
B21
Order No. 1560331
DOOR 4

I'm just chuffed that the film has been received well over the years – Jaz's outlandish anecdotes, arcane philosophy and the band's blistering music. Perhaps a bit dated now, but it was made under KJ's innate beliefs. I quote:

"The only way to deal with the horrors of this unfolding world and its relentless march towards oblivion is to laugh the laughter that overcomes all fear, laughing at mankind's tragic stupidity. The only thing that makes sense to me is a double-barrelled expression describing the shocking process of realisation in which the penny drops and the horrendous truth suddenly dawns. 'Killing Joke' as a general term was quite perfect. It portrayed this experience perfectly whilst simply being a front, always masking, concealing another agenda. From the genesis of Killing Joke, there were essentially three objectives. When asking ourselves 'what do we want out of Killing Joke?', our answers were as follows. To inspire others, to quite literally create a renaissance. To have a real understanding of the true power complex and its aims in the modern world. To create change in accordance with the will, to prove the existence of magick through a number of experiments." Jaz Coleman – *An Irrational Domain*.

God knows what we were on, but it was never to be a long-term love affair. Having said that, I believe I still have a seat at the table on the island of Cythera. The memories are etched into my KJ experience and still today make me smile.

STEPHANE BONGINI

2013 – I'm lucky enough to attend rehearsals in a studio in London. Really incredible moments. It's a bit like being in your living room sitting on your sofa comfortably, a glass of wine – well, several – in your hand, the cameras rolling and there it is – happiness. You attend a live concert just for you. There are only seven people – including you – in the front row and Jaz sings as he does in concert.

Of course, we interrupt the rehearsals with a small cheese meal each time because it's become a ritual over the years and I admit there's a soothing side to this moment of sharing and discovery of unknown tastes.

Tensions fade with this gastronomic break.

Aside from these extraordinary moments, I can add my modest collaboration to the shooting of the video clip that takes place in the rehearsal studios for the song 'Corporate Elect'. What's great is that I filmed Geordie up close. He hates that – so I'm lying on the floor under his guitar filming, and he can't say anything.

RON SYNOVITZ

Golden HIVE Studio records show the earliest pre-production sessions for the *Pylon* album were from 25 September to 8 October 2013 at Amak Golden's Vltavská basement. They were songwriting jam sessions. It was Geordie's idea. He said he wanted to write songs together the old way, like they'd done for Killing Joke's first three albums in the early Eighties. Youth and Big Paul said it was important for them all to try songwriting sessions Geordie's way. For two weeks, the four original members of Killing Joke reunited in Amak's basement studio – telling stories and catching up. Big Paul shared recordings of percussion and spoken-word pieces he'd done in New York. They'd jam, throwing spontaneous musical ideas back and forth between them, inspiring responses with riffs and rhythms that could be used for new songs. Geordie told me later it was the first time since 1982 that he, Jaz, Big Paul and Youth were all in one room just to jam and write songs together. Something definitely happens with the chemistry between those four when they get together in a small room to jam like that. Jaz says not many people have seen it. It's different from the Killing Joke chemistry with Raven and Ben – a collective connection between all four of them that goes back further and deeper. Geordie told me it was "all about the groove". To document the occasion, they invited their trusted photographer friend Mont Sherar. Mont's work methods were unobtrusive, despite the difficulties caused by the band's insistence that they play in a dimly lit room. A chapter in his book, *Twilight of the Mortals*, intimately captured the spirit of the sessions.

MONT SHERAR

I authored the photograph-based book *Twilight of the Mortals*, attempting to show a side of Killing Joke rarely seen both on stage and off. One chapter portrays a time in 2013 where I had the honour of being embedded in a tiny studio with the band when they were writing the songs for *Pylon*, many of them from scratch.

Being able to witness the process of how their music was created and be allowed to document it photographically was something I still pinch myself over.

Youth, Geordie, Jaz and Paul are as compatible as you could imagine on many fronts, but that doesn't mean there isn't any friction between them, because there is – loads of it. Tension is always in the air – until broken by sudden bursts of laughter. No wonder their music is wholly unique and totally incomparable to anything else.

So, while photographs are one way to tell a story, here we are today, with an opportunity to express it in a textual way. The birth of a Killing Joke song, if you will...

It's early in the afternoon (early morning by Killing Joke standards). Geordie, relaxed in his chair, begins strumming something he's been working on. Jaz, having just entered the room, stops in his tracks, clearly showing great pleasure in what he's hearing. Next, Jaz and Geordie are discussing various things like alternative chord changes and other musical lingo far outside my scope of knowledge.

Jaz suggests something, pointing to an area on Geordie's guitar. "Concert C?" Geordie asks while performing the tweak.

Suddenly, Jaz is jumping around like popcorn, swinging his arms like the conductor that he is in his 'other' career. "I've got the perfect sound for that!" Jaz shouts, then places himself behind his Prophet [keyboard], hitting a one-finger, single note with the tone of the apocalypse.

Over in the shadows sits Big Paul, softly playing around with different approaches as to what kind of rhythm feels right for the evolving track. Geordie and Paul begin shouting tempo rates back and forth, ultimately landing on the perfect sweet spot. Once that is settled, Paul unleashes an avalanche of complex, thunderous grooves, meshing all the bits and pieces together. A monster of a tune is on the way.

Suddenly, the door opens and Youth walks in, spliff in hand, of course. [He] sits down and begins to pluck away at a bass-line on his Rickenbacker.

"No! No! No!" Jaz shouts, staring directly at Mr Glover. "Too dubby, too reggae!"

Everything comes to a stop. Complete and total silence.

Within seconds, Geordie and Paul turn to each other – then burst out laughing, followed by Jaz's trademark cackle that overpowers everyone.

"Actually, it's brilliant!" Jaz admits. "Now, who wants a cup of tea?"

Killing Joke in 2013 © Tom Barnes

RON SYNOVITZ

Killing Joke wrote more than a dozen songs in those two weeks. One that didn't make it to the *Pylon* album started off with the title 'Pneumatic Drill'. It got relatively far along in the songwriting process, but not far enough to receive a vocal. It was based around a guitar-and-bass riff reminiscent of Gary Numan's 'Cars'. But it was darker and less sterile – a diminished variation that rocked harder and was more dynamic. "It's different," Jaz says. Youth brought in an idea for a song Geordie dubbed 'Barry White'. Industrial Killing Joke Motown. They worked on it quite a while before eventually dropping it because it sounded too close to a Barry White song. 'Lizard' got a full live workout at 7:45, with Jaz adding guide-vocal screams at the end of the choruses to signal the band back to the main riff. 'Reality Tunnel' was also fleshed out as a complete arrangement. 'Mutant Rockabilly' was fast and aggressive, eventually mutating into 'Apotheosis'. 'End Of M' became part of 'Into the Unknown', and 'Stacker' was an excerpt from a jam that would get used in 'Star Spangled'. 'Silver' and '3 A.M. F' had loose arrangements with Jaz shouting out cues for changes between verses and choruses. Working titles for other ideas they sketched out together included 'Bad Vibes', 'Karma Neurosis', 'Great Wall', 'Baza Black', 'Youth Jam', 'Troll', 'Triple Red', 'Fella' and 'Chorus'.

AMAK GOLDEN

When the songwriting sessions were over, I made reference mixes of the things they wanted to work on more. Jaz left for Australia to focus on his Nirvana Symphonic project. Big Paul returned to New York and Youth went back to his residential recording studio in Spain. Geordie stayed in Prague and kept working from the ideas in the reference mixes.

Amak in the control room at Golden HIVE Studios © Adam Janosik

RON SYNOVITZ

Over the next year, Geordie worked up and recorded arrangements in his new apartment. He used midi-triggered drums – playing his gold Gibson guitar and the Prophet '08. He also played a 1972 Yamaha bass through a small Burman GX3 pre-amp from the early Seventies. I lent him a two-channel TRP ribbon mic pre-amp so he could record his guitar through two small Egnater amplifiers. Overdriven, he could get a decent sound at a low volume without pissing off his neighbours too much. He had two Chinese ribbon mics and put one on each speaker cabinet to get a stereo spread on his guitar. He recorded on to a DAW [Digital Audio Workstation] machine with a CD drive that lets you print mixes straight to CD-R. Every so often, he'd bring a CD-R with a song or two to my flat and I'd help him transfer it to the music publisher in London. He let me keep all the CDs he brought over. I have nine discs with his handwriting – songs and titles evolving from early January into September 2014. 6 January – 'Reality Tunnel', 'Pneumatic' and 'B.V.', aka 'Bad Vibes'; 13 January – 'End of M', 'Baza', 'Silver Troll'; 21 January – 'Lizard'; 4 February – 'Stacker'; 10 February – more work on 'Bad Vibes', cutting it down to 4:38 and changing the title to 'G.V.'; 11 February – 'G.G.V.', a remix of

'G.V.'; 6 March – 'Shaftsport' demo arrangement in progress; 'Faction Strasse'; and 'Stacker (Strasse-Faction Version)'. 16 May – nine instrumental Geordie demos with arrangements in progress – 'Shaftsport', 'End of M', 'Faction Strasse' 5:40, 'Lizard', 'Real T', 'BZA', 'Silver T', 'Stacker', 'Pneumatic'; 30 August – 'Infadelicia' and 'Pneumatic', with the bass re-amped through Geordie's Burman and "new drums by Big Paul – midi mapped". 1 September – 'Stacker' with a new bass-line; 7 September – 'Silver Troll' mix with Burman bass pre-amp.

BERT NEVEN

Working with Killing Joke as an engineer inspired me in a very big way. Then Derek took over some things in the studio, recording vocals with Jaz. Then Amak Golden came in and took over some more things. They managed to put things together. And Golden HIVE Studios came together out of it.

RON SYNOVITZ

Geordie introduced me to Dutch sound engineer Bert Neven when he threw Bert a birthday dinner party. Bert had stopped working at Faust and moved to a new studio space in Prague's Vinohrady neighbourhood – the future location of Golden HIVE. By the spring of 2014, Amak and I moved all our recording gear there, pooling together with Bert and Czech engineer Filip Jelínek. In the beginning, it was being called No 1s Studio.

✦ ✦ ✦

TRADES CLUB
8 August 2014,
Hebden Bridge, UK

STEPHANE BONGINI

The Trades Club at Hebden Bridge in 2014 – the lights go out after a few songs and you can see the power of the band continuing to play as if nothing had happened.

✦ ✦ ✦

PICTUREDROME
14 August 2014,
Holmfirth, UK

SIMON ELLIS

I never thought I'd see the original line-up but, when they announced a gig at Holmfirth Picturedrome, it looked too good to miss. My friend and I travelled to the venue, never having been there before. What we found was one of the north's best-kept secrets, a picturesque setting on the river, very old and antiquated, with a lot of history.

It was particularly hot that summer night. We took a drink outside the venue and sat exchanging stories with other Gatherers. Nothing, though, could prepare me for witnessing the original line-up in the flesh. When they came out, the place erupted. It was a sweatbox and I was blown away.

I'd seen many incarnations of the band since my first time [Manchester, 26 January 1991], but this was like that – a ferocious assault on the senses that would leave us with a drive back home debating which of these two gigs had been the best. It's a split decision to this day.

These shows really left an indelible ink on my life.

FLEECE
15 August 2014,
Bristol, UK

ADRIAN WASON

Another cracking gig at the Fleece. I was working in Plymouth at the time so just about made it. Jaz looked in good shape, dressed in a t-shirt, looking like he'd been working out.

A Fleece of many colours © Adrian Wason

SHEFFIELD 2014

NIGEL CLARKE

I managed to sneak 'Colony Collapse' into a popular science talk I gave entitled Physics on my iPod, where I selected a few songs that had reference to physics, in this case self-assembling nanobots and a grey goo of nano sea, to expand upon the physics ideas behind the lyrics. I'm still working on how to include KJ in my Physics of Music course. I've managed to insert references to Einstürzende Neubauten, with their unusual home-made instruments illustrating some nice physics, and Sonic Youth, whose use of non-traditional tunings is fun mathematically. I'll figure something out for KJ eventually!

Nigel Clarke occasionally swaps the lecture theatre for the stage as drummer with Spontaneous Emissions

REMIXING, REMASTERING AND RARITIES

SCOTT THOMPSON

I've always been a musician, since the age of 15. I've always been in and around music.

I was going through a bit of a bad time in about 2015, 2014. Feeling pretty low. I did one or two [Killing Joke] remixes – and then ended up doing about 40. They're all on YouTube. I just decided to pile into it, keep myself as busy as possible. Originally, it was just to get my mental health back, but then it changed into something completely different.

I started to really take pride in it, get better at it. It became a very massive project. [It] took me the best part of probably about two years to do the 40 remixes.

The way I do my work is by finding strange sources. Rather than taking the samples from the songs direct, I lift them from things like tuning up or the spaces between songs and the outros of songs. I try to make it an original remix rather than just lifting direct samples of Killing Joke songs. I thought, I'll use my imagination to find different Killing Joke sources. The remixes I've worked on, all the audio has pretty much been created from very non-obvious parts of Killing Joke recordings.

© *Scott Thompson*

Then I started to make the videos as well. I just love making videos, being creative. I'm always trying to keep myself busy with music – and Joke especially.

It's been a fascination of mine to pick up rarities, from wherever I can really [for Scott's KJ Rarities channel]. And then clean them up, make them shine.

Last night, I did a bit of tracking. I read a message somewhere. The person couldn't find [Killing Joke track] 'Drug (Black Sun Mix)' for love nor money. I went deep into the internet and found it on a Russian blog site. I spent six or seven hours making a video, which is now online. [I] put it up last night.

I'm always looking for stuff. I'm forever searching blog and chat sites and Killing Joke forums, Facebook sites, the lot. As soon as I see a Gatherer saying, "Oh, I've never heard that", I go looking for it. It's just [a case of] being patient. They're all there. A few years back, I was on a fantastic blog site, Killing Joke Forum CZ. A lot of rarities were shared, and that's where I got a ton of bootlegs from.

The best I ever got were the 2009 Geordie demos, which were exclusive from me. From Geordie – to me!

I did a load of remastering as well, [on] the old kind of rubbishy bootlegs, full of hiss – [I wanted to] maximise them, optimise them. I made sure Youth got a copy of everything I did, all the remixes and remasters.

From that point, we got talking on Facebook, also with BPF and Mike Coles. [They] all gave me a huge amount of encouragement. I had a lot of encouragement from the band.

We found a really kind of crappy, hissy, noisy old audio cassette of 'Killer Dub'. I spent the best part of three months - doing eight-hour shifts - on that track, trying to sort it, which I did. Cleaned it all up, polished it up, sent it to Youth. Next thing I know, he'd included it ['Requiem Third Party Dub (The Ultra Rare Last Laugh Mix)'] on the *In Dub* album [on the bonus disk]. That was a real honour. I'm very proud of that. They're like my long-lost brothers, the band.

The Mat Stagger stuff that he [Big Paul] did in 1977. That's would be the Holy Grail of rarities, the golden ticket. Desperate to have that on the rarities channel. You can but try.

I am currently doing collabs with Anthony Angströms, the guy that does all the KJ guitar tabs on YouTube. A brilliant musician. I'm doing vocals for his KJ-inspired original songs. It [all] became something I thoroughly enjoyed. It became an obsession, if you like. I never stop really. Back to normal these days [in terms of mental health]. We all go there, mate.

AMAK GOLDEN

Before the *Pylon* album sessions started, we did a couple more pre-production sessions with Geordie. We worked on demos on a hard-disc recorder Geordie had at home. It had songs from the pre-production sessions at Vltavská and the work Geordie had done since then. They're great!

RON SYNOVITZ

By the time Jaz got back from Australia, things [at the studio] were running pretty smoothly. So Killing Joke gathered there in October 2014 for the start of the *Pylon* sessions.

BERT NEVEN

Reza Udhin came in with Geordie to Golden HIVE for a last bit of pre-production in the autumn of 2014. Reza was helping set things up before Youth arrived. Jaz was already there. Once Youth arrived, we started to record the *Pylon* album.

AMAK GOLDEN

The album sessions started around the end of October 2014. At first, they said it was going to be two weeks. When we finished two weeks, they asked me for more time. I remember we were working through Christmas. They asked me to book a couple of weeks more. We ended up working for four months.

RON SYNOVITZ

It stretched into 106 session dates. A total of 16 songs were recorded, all released as the *Pylon* deluxe edition. Killing Joke self-produced the Prague *Pylon* sessions with Amak Golden as chief engineer. Bert Neven was the HIVE studio manager for the sessions and is credited on the album for 'convivial vibes'. The band picked up with Geordie's instrumental demos and other ideas from pre-production. But they also worked up fresh song ideas at the new Golden HIVE location.

BERT NEVEN

Convivial vibes? It was about the atmosphere at Golden HIVE and keeping things together. Come in early in the morning, have the tea ready, just to be there like an assistant to Amak. When Amak wanted to take a break, I could take over. It was a really nice atmosphere. I think so, yeah, it was. The *Pylon* sessions were very intensive. There was pre-material and it was amazing to see how Jaz worked with ideas and turned ideas into songs. That was, I think for Amak and me, a very mind-opening experience. Although I knew that already with Jaz, but this was much more intensified.

AMAK GOLDEN

The first day, Geordie and Jaz and Youth were all there. So we started with all of them in the studio. We started with Youth putting down some more ideas onto the pre-production demos. Then we started working on song arrangements. Some of the *Pylon* songs were new ideas that began in the studio with Jaz's keyboards. Jaz would put down some drones, then started gradually building up the songs in layers. Usually, the drones were like 10 or 15 minutes long – really long drone songs. He slowly built up vocal melodies, all the keyboards, then we'd tighten up the length. He was working on lyrics in the studio at the same time. He recorded vocals with lyrics in the early stages, but they didn't all end up on the final versions recorded. He would change it all the time. Almost every day, Jaz would rename a song and change the arrangement, moving the chorus and changing the structure of the songs. Most of the final lyrics came later.

RON SYNOVITZ

Jaz told me he wasn't going to finish off the final lyrics for *Pylon* until the backing tracks for all the songs were completely finished. He said he wanted the lyrics to be inspired by the album in its entirety and kept saying: "Slow is FAST!"

AMAK GOLDEN

Jaz was definitely working on the lyrics as we were going along. He had the studio filled up with books and magazines about conspiracy theories. Almost every day, he'd start working on a song by giving it a new conspiracy-theory title or putting some conspiracy theory in the theme of the song – you know, chemtrails, microwave transmission towers, the government already has the extraterrestrials and is mixing alien genes with human genes. The way they would work together to get into the right frame of mind for recording is worth mentioning. They would be sitting in the recording room together and smiling. Everything would be great. Then they'd decide they were ready to record something. So they'd come into the control room and start screaming at me, being really pushy and agitated. They actually started the creative process with this confrontation to get themselves worked up into this nervous, aggressive frame of mind. One thing about it was really crazy. The air would seem to disappear from the room. You know what I mean? They'd start screaming. Then no air. They literally transformed the atmosphere in the control room.

BERT NEVEN

For me, as I'd worked with them for so long, I'm used to that kind of stress. If you're not used to it, it can be difficult. They are demanding. It's their goal to be confrontational. They've been like that ever since I've known them. But it's all for the best result. To get the most out of it. I think a lot of times, Youth would take over in the control room himself. When he had an idea, he'd just do it. He did some engineering things as well, setting up mics and amps. The album's co-producer, Tom Dalgety, recorded drums in England. I think they re-did the guitars in England too. But we did the keyboards, bass, vocals and initial guitars. Then Killing Joke took the multi-tracks to Tom Dalgety.

RON SYNOVITZ

Geordie told me how Tom recorded fresh drum tracks in England with Big Paul. Geordie also ran through his guitar parts again for the whole album in its entirety, as if he were performing the songs live in concert. Tom aced the final mixes. I'm not clear exactly how much of the England recordings made it to the record. But it's fair to say most of the *Pylon* album was written and recorded at Golden HIVE in Prague before Tom finished it all up.

✦ ✦ ✦

SIDEWAYS
12 June 2015,
Helsinki, Finland

SUVI JYRINKI

How I got to know Killing Joke or consider myself a Gatherer is some kind of luck. Or blessing. Or something that just had to happen.

I was born one day before their first album was released, which means I could have had a chance to hear their music for all my life. But, when I finally got to hear 'The Wait' for the first time, in 2012 (as far as I know for sure), it was a point of no return. Then collecting almost every album in just a few years (still searching for the missing ones) got me even deeper into that rabbit hole. No other songs have spoken to me so deeply. Killing Joke are the only band I really need. Hearing them was like a religious awakening. If you didn't know better, it's something that could have even been mistaken for Stendhal Syndrome [in which the beauty of art can be so overwhelming as to cause distress]. It has affected everything in my life and the artwork I make myself.

I've seen them live three times, twice in my home country [Sideways, Helsinki, 12 June 2015 and Tavastia, Helsinki, 28 November 2016] and once in London [Roundhouse, 17 November 2018].

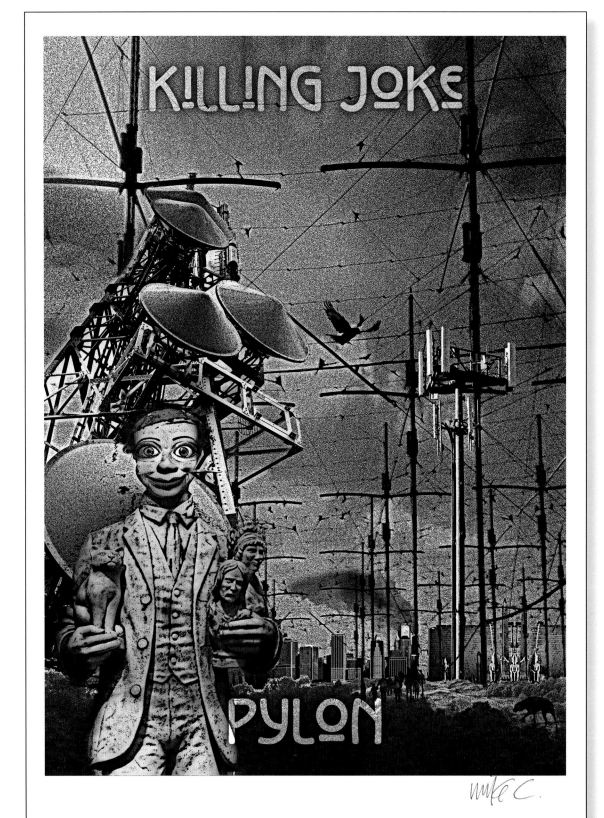

One of 250 limited-edition, signed prints from the Pylon project © Mike Coles

Alone every time, but at those shows I attended I never felt lonely. I've never got to meet them, obviously a shameful unfairness, and that's why they have remained somehow mysterious.

RON SYNOVITZ

One of the *Pylon* songs was called 'Dawn of the Hive'. When *Pylon* was released, Jaz credited our studio for the Prague sessions as the 'HIVE'. That's how Jaz Coleman named the studio. When I asked him about it, he said there was always "a buzz of activity". In fact, we were ready for a name change. We'd pulled together so much analogue gear that the studio had long outgrown the name Golden Digital.

DEREK SAXENMEYER

The HIVE. It's a cool name. It's funny. There's not only the song 'Dawn of the Hive' from *Pylon*. It's also partially one of the names of a *Black & Red* tune, 'Hive Mind'.

STEN SAWICZ

Now, we know personal tastes are subjective and a band's career can wane and wander over 40 years, but, up until 2015 and the release of *Pylon*, I'd always considered their first album to be the best, but this last album just rewrote my KJ history for me. Mind-blowing, astonishing, speechless. They were just a few adjectives to describe it. Bewildered at the sound and ferocious power I was being bombarded with, it instantly, in a nano-second, became my favourite album of theirs and the best album I'd heard in 20-plus years, such was its magnificence. Five years down the line, it's still mesmeric.

RON SYNOVITZ

When the *Pylon* album was released, the week of Halloween 2015, it shot straight up to No.1 on BBC Radio 1's Top 40 rock album chart. Jaz was right when he said: "Slow is FAST!"

✦ ✦ ✦

Y PLAS
25 October 2015,
Cardiff, UK

ADRIAN WASON

A nice change – a gig on my doorstop. I got rather excited pre-gig, hearing 'Absent Friends' was on the set-list. Jaz came on in now-personalised boiler suit to 'Autonomous Zone', then 'Absent Friends', which was absolutely amazing. I never thought I'd hear that live, but that was the last thing I can remember from that gig.

Joke hadn't played the Welsh capital for over a decade before the date at Y Plas © Adrian Wason

CONCORDE 2
26 October 2015,
Brighton, UK

SCOTT FORD

I met Youth for the first time in 2015 at the front of the Brighton gig – he was selling these little oil paintings and his son Jake was on the merch stall. It was like being 18 again with your hero. I wasn't too sure what to say. I always thought he was cool as fuck – he was the bass player in my favourite band and was this huge music producer. So, when I got the chance to get a photo with him, I was pleased as punch and he was such a chap too!

In 2017, I interviewed him on Soho Radio with my sister Kelly and found out more about his choice in music and interesting stories about The Verve's 'Bitter Sweet Symphony'. It was nerve-wracking but, again, he was very generous with his answers. I've since done music videos for him and artists on his Liquid Sound Design label.

Scott Ford and his special Soho Radio guest © Scott Ford

O2 RITZ
1 November 2015,
Manchester, UK

CONSTANCE GORDON

My story begins many years ago when I didn't know Killing Joke as a band.
But I met a charismatic man with incredibly strong magical radiance, Jaz Coleman, when he worked with Czech music band Čechomor on [2002 film] *Year of the Devil*. It was that moment when I found out Jeremy had his own band, Killing Joke. I sensed that Killing Joke was a part of his soul. Over time, I became a big fan of them and still love this band, because I appreciate what Killing Joke has been and is doing. My biggest memory doesn't consist of just one memory but from fragments of many small memories. First time I saw Killing Joke was in England 2015. I still remember the whole gig. I remember the energy around everyone. After this experience, I tried to go their concerts every year. Each concert contributed to my unified best memory that I have now. In 2018, during the Laugh at Your Peril tour, I was able to visit backstage a few times, and saw one fascinating thing which doesn't happen very often. The members of the band are functioning as one person, are complementary and have a very strong bond with each other. For me, it has been the most beautiful experience to think about how Killing Joke works. I felt the bond and chemistry between them.

From my point of view, each band member had great spiritual and energetic vibes, which affect everyone that listens to their music. Their music touches everyone who wants to listen and understand. It was beautiful for me to see and experience the moments when this music was affecting the fans and Gatherers. During a gig, I saw and felt the communication between the band and listeners, an amazing moment. It doesn't happen often that fans give such a big response. I'm impressed that Killing Joke can still do it today. It still fascinates me that Killing Joke have deep spiritual meaning within their songs. Every concert I attended was amazing, totally unreal. It didn't matter where it was – America or Europe – the magic could be felt all around. It was brilliant. My experiences and life were enriched by unforgettable meetings backstage and I felt it as a special privilege. And

Killing Joke have a big repertoire of songs. It is hard to choose a song which has most influenced me. For me, each is unique. Every song they've recorded has deep hidden meanings. I like every song equally. Killing Joke affects me in several ways. Thanks to Killing Joke, I've met and interacted with people who changed my life for the better. As well, I started to educate myself, because Killing Joke is all about self-education. I think that music where the artist puts their own heart and soul in is therapeutic for the hearts and souls of everyone open to it. Music from Killing Joke goes deep into your inner self. The meaning and energy of the words from lyrics inscribe themselves into your psyche, while your physical body is in deep trance from the incredible melody created by the other band members, Youth, Big Paul and Geordie. The members performing together create an incredible energetic explosion which shakes the emotional depths of everyone's inner selves. Killing Joke, with Jaz at the top, gives me hope and encouragement of a better future for our world. I really feel glad and grateful that someone is helping humanity survive in this dark and hard age with how our planet exists currently. Thank you, Jaz Coleman. Thank you, Martin 'Youth' Glover. Thank you, Big Paul Ferguson. Thank you, Geordie Walker.

SIMON SMITH

When I was young, I liked nothing more than getting into the mosh-pit, bouncing up and down and getting generally knocked about by a usually genial group of fellow fans up for the same experience. As time passed, the amount of time spent in there grew less and less. My musical tastes broadened to encompass styles of music that did not lend itself to such antics, while my waist broadened and made such physical exertion something that was difficult and challenging.

I put both of these things down to the passage of time, that I was maturing like a fine wine, whisky or cheese. Being unfit and overweight had become a way of life: a love of beer, wine, whisky and cheese being, amongst others, contributing factors to that increasingly sedentary state.

Around three years ago, I decided to do something about it, realising if I wanted to maximise the likelihood of seeing my young family grow up, I needed to become someone who did not accept that being nearly 23st (320lbs/145kg) was normal, and needed to do something about it.

I managed to lose seven stone (44kg), but something happened that made me realise just how far I'd come in that time and why I must never go back to how I was.

I went to see one of my favourite bands, Killing Joke, on two separate occasions in Manchester and Leeds [4 November 2015]. At both gigs I found myself, once again, in the mosh-pit. The previous time I'd seen them was in March 2013 at a festival [Hammerfest] where they played a relatively short set. I also found myself in the melee at the front.

The difference was stark. In 2013, still very overweight and unfit, I remember feeling horribly out of breath and massively sweaty after only one song. Fast-forward to 2015 and I made it through a 90-minute set of constant dancing and buffeting twice in a week. Yes, I was tired and sweaty at the end, but at no point did I feel out of breath. I felt hugely vindicated for the changes I've made to my lifestyle over the last couple of years, and seeing Killing Joke again provided me with the benchmark I needed to cement my sense of achievement at a time when I was just starting to backslide on those changes.

There are, of course, questions about whether a 51-year-old man should still be getting himself in the mosh-pit. But I had so much fun and connected so much with my younger self in a way that was genuinely surprising. This was not out of a nostalgic longing for the person I used to be, but a celebration of the person I am now.

Thank you, Killing Joke!

✦ ✦ ✦

LEEDS BECKETT UNIVERSITY
4 November 2015,
Leeds, UK

FLETCHER STEWART

Right around the time my band The Sub-Gents started, I made a series of experimental demos on the side. My older-brother figure in life had recently passed away under cruel circumstances in prison in the Philippines and I was exploring my grief through electronic soundscapes. I brazenly sent these demos to Youth online with some kind of fever-dream manifesto that must've intrigued him, because, much to my simultaneous elation and horror, he invited me to his house to chat about the project. When I arrived, it was a radiant autumn day. Youth had a beautiful canopy of red ivy twisting and filtering sunlight above as I approached the hippy side-door. As we sat talking in his living room, it obviously came as a surprise that I wasn't on a label and had no budget. These were understandable lines of enquiry, Youth being one of the world's most prolific and inspiring producers, but, through me showing up in all my naivety and his kind words of advice, we became friends. He played me some records that were in the direction he thought I could go and opened my eyes to what was needed to make my vision work. I told him about the amazing pedals I had come to curate and he very kindly invited me to meet the band in Leeds.

KILLING JOKE
Leeds Beckett Students Union, Leeds
WEDNESDAY 04 NOVEMBER 2015
Doors open 19.00
STANDING
22.50 (Subject to booking fee)
14+ only. 14's - 16's must be accompanied by an adult
50282553 LITTLE
633
888535
$48967732
www.seetickets.com TICKETS ARE SOLD SUBJECT TO THE TERMS AND CONDITIONS OVERLEAF
See

© Neil Little

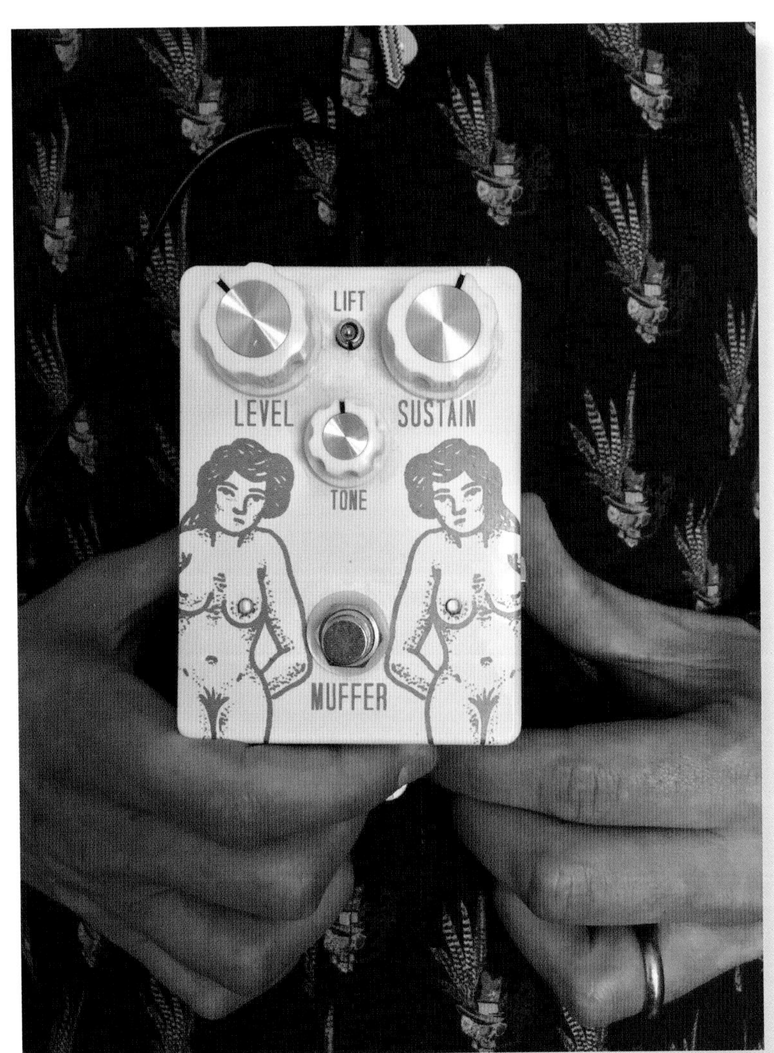

A "rather naughty pedal" used by both Youth and The Jesus and Mary Chain © Fletcher Stewart

Serendipitously, Robert Keeley had just released the 30ms Automatic Double Tracker, which was sent to me for review, so I packed it up with a few other stomp boxes to let Youth and Geordie have a go. Geordie famously utilises a similar effect in the form of his big Seventies bucket-brigade analogue Electrolabs ADT effects, so I thought Keeley's new stomp box might interest him. I was excited and nervous about meeting this incredibly enigmatic genius hydra of a band I had listened to for so long. When I arrived backstage and introduced myself, my wife Kyra and drummer Shaun, we were greeted and welcomed warmly by the band and crew. The show was, of course, a tornado blinder.

After, I had a chance to chat with Geordie for the first time about the joys of hollow-body guitars and show him how the new pedal worked. I found him to be very down-to-earth, a fellow gearhead of course. His knowledge of electronics and how gear worked under the hood was evident. The pedal never made it to become part of Geordie's permanent rig, but, having owned a rare variant of his old Seventies units, I can say nothing quite does what they do in the analogue realm and they are definitely not chorus units. To be clear to the gearheads that chase the dragon, Killing Joke's guitar sound *is* Geordie – his inimitable style comes from his melodic, textural and dissonant senses, not to mention his wild circular picking style and transcendent channelling of overtones.

After this first meeting with the band, I would loan them pedals at soundchecks from time to time and even did a session with Youth at his atrium treetop home studio, tweaking the Source Audio Nemesis Delay while he dubbed out on a beautiful Ovation bass. I'm pretty sure that pedal is part of Youth's rig now and a few Gatherers have heard its more experimental voice during the siren section of 'Turn to Red'. On the *Pylon* tour, Youth was touring with my Tomkat Violet Muffer Fuzz with magnificent light-up nipples. This rather naughty pedal was also used extensively by The Jesus and Mary Chain when they recorded their most recent album, with Youth producing. I'll treasure that box for ever.

✦ ✦ ✦

ROUNDHOUSE
6 November 2015,
London, UK

Kilimanjaro Live presents
Killing Joke
& special guests
Friday 06 November 2015
Main Space
Doors:8:00 pm
Level 1
Standing
Unres
£25.00
Ticket ID: 416
2572623
3988900
Mr. Chris Bryans
456722
ROUNDHOUSE
www.roundhouse.org.uk | London NW1 8EH | 0300 6789 222

IAN ROBERTSON

The Roundhouse's enviable reputation had preceded it. I was ecstatic at the prospect of seeing Killing Joke perform where The Doors, Hendrix and The Pink Floyd once stood. On that night, for me, it seemed as if the band and venue almost cancelled each other out – too many restless souls in that hallowed machine hall, reverence for both, somehow nullifying expectation...

A long journey was rewarded for Adrian Wason by hearing 'Into the Unknown' from Pylon © Adrian Wason

ADRIAN WASON

I was really looking forward to this one, hoping to meet some of the Gatherers, like Matt Tibbits, but I was in work that morning and the traffic on the M4 was disastrous. Walked down Haverstock Hill and the pubs were absolutely jammed, like I'd only seen before at Joke gigs in the early Nineties. Plan B was to pop into Sainsbury's Local, couple of packs of sandwiches and two bottles of prosecco and I was ready for the gig. It was worth the rush as I got to see 'Into the Unknown' played live, possibly one of their best-ever tracks.

KILLING JOKE BEER
2016
Hopcraft Brewing, Pontyclun, South Wales

GAZZA PRESCOTT
(now with Team Toxic Beers, Merseyside)

Why do brewers name beers the way they do? What's behind the names? Often, simply a conversation and a quick scan through the MP3/Spotify stream!

The idea of a Killing Joke beer was a natural progression for me as I'd made a habit of naming beers after bands, songs or lyrics I particularly liked; I see them as a homage to some of my favourite artists who have influenced my taste in music over the years. Most are songs from my formative years, where my love of punk, goth, ska and alternative of many shades has crystallised into my current Spotify playlists and MP3 collection.

We'd been offered a quantity of a brand-new, vaguely secret British hop called Jester, which sounded great but, as usual in a busy brewery with me doing pretty much everything, the beer got brewed before we had a name for it!

This is much more common an occurrence than you'd imagine in the industry. Many brewers I speak to claim that naming beers is the hardest part of running a brewery. I'd disagree and point to being doused in corrosive chemicals on a regular basis and moving tonnes of wet grain about with a shovel, but it's all about opinions, I guess.

The hops arrived and the brew was quickly rushed into the schedule as, like most brewers, we weren't averse to a bit of cock-waving. We were one of the first to get these new hops and we weren't backwards about being forward with them.

© Gazza Prescott

Come brew-day, the hops were smelling pretty damn good; in all my years of being involved in brewing, I can't remember many times where I've been sat in the office doing 'important manager stuff' on the computer and been able to smell the hops when the bag was opened!

Now the beer was in process, we needed a name, and quickly. Step forward my musical influences!

We'd recently done beers named, with a tip of the hat, to Type O Negative, Fields of the Nephilim, The Smiths and Joy Division, so I had a casual flip through my MP3 folder on the PC – laughably, this now sounds anachronistic with streaming having taken over playing actual MP3 files. I guess I felt the same wrench of realisation when society shifted from vinyl to CDs and then, again, to MP3s – but nothing really jumped out at me. It's usual in this situation to play random playlists or have a chat about names with the other guys, but nothing was shouting "me! me!"

Then I had an email from a fellow brewer who somehow knew (the bush telegraph was obviously in full swing) about our acquisition of the Jester hops.

OB: All right, mate. What you doing with these Jester then?

Me: Pale ale, see what they give... smelling lush!

OB: Yeah, just opened ours... Bloody hell. They smell like blueberry-pie filling!

I nodded in agreement, and was about to type a superbly witty response when up this popped:

OB: And I remember you always saying UK hops are a joke... Well, these kill that theory!

flash of inspiration

Me: Oh... I think you've just solved my naming problem.

OB: Invoice in the post, mate.

That was that! Killing Joke had done the usual thing with our beer names and, by luck and circumstance, had become the name. To expand on this a little, old-school British hops are often derided by progressive brewers as 'old fashioned' and 'tasting like twigs', because they are great for making bitter and mild but not great for much else, whereas these brand-new hybrid hops, which oozed fruity juiciness, really did smell like blueberry-pie filling.

The 'Killing Joke' name had the double meaning in that using UK hops is often seen as a joke by metropolitan-elite hipster brewers, but these would pass as American or New Zealand hops on a blind sensory test by anyone who knew hops. There's no way I'd have guessed they were UK grown. Hence, using UK hops is often labelled a bit of a joke, but these would kill that joke dead once the finished beer was tasted.

Happy with the morning's work, I relaxed and poured myself a 'tank sample' to celebrate the hard graft naming the beer and wandered back to the brewhouse to check on progress. All went well. Within a few weeks, the beer was released into the wild; all 26 casks sold well and we received excellent feedback but couldn't brew it again for over a year as there simply weren't any Jester hops around to use.

So, there we have it - a beer named after one of my many early music influences. Most people would have no idea why the beer was named Killing Joke (although I had a few emails congratulating us on yet another choice of top music!) but the main thing was that I'd name-checked one of the favourite bands of my youth. That always felt good. More importantly, the beer tasted good.

Bearded Theory Festival, Catton Hall – 27 May 2016. Mick Head: "Myself, Fil Legonidec (long-time Eighties/ Nineties KJ roadie), Geordie and Jaz share a laugh backstage" © Mick Head

MATTHEW HUTCHISON

I got into Killing Joke very late, the *Pylon* era to be exact. I knew of them before, but never gave their music a shot before this experience.

In summer 2016, during a drive back from the Joshua Tree area on Route 62, my photographer played 'New Cold War' in the car. We were in a Tesla Roadster, so the handling of the car mixed with the grainy, picturesque canyon scenery one sees while leaving Yucca Valley. The palm-muted riffing of Geordie's guitar mixed with Big Paul's beat really enhanced the experience, as if the car was in cadence with the two. I remember the chorus kicking in when we left the canyon and Jaz's voice echoed in perfect timing when the car exited the canyon and we were met with sprawling desert landscape, pretty desolate actually, and the glorious San Jacinto mountain ranges in dead centre of our vision.

That experience – mixed with their music – really stuck with me. It's a moment in time I haven't forgotten and has got me hooked on Killing Joke ever since. I've been lucky enough to see them once in Los Angeles and [then] interviewed Jaz [on 20 October 2019] during their tour stop with Tool for a website I write for. It was the anniversary of Paul Raven's death, making the interview that much more special.

Since 2016, Killing Joke's music has been present in a handful of joyful and distraught moments of my life.

I'm grateful they're still here. They make me feel alive.

✦ ✦ ✦

THE ACADEMY
30 October 2016,
Dublin, Republic of Ireland

ED NEIL

We were sitting in the Adelphi Bar, pre-gig. I'd booked four nights in Ireland (two in Dublin, two in Belfast) to catch two Killing Joke gigs with my (many say long-suffering) better half, Dina.

"They never play anything from *Revelations* anymore," I despaired, between sips of Smithwick's. It was the first Killing Joke album I bought and an enduring favourite. I'd read the band, and Youth in particular, weren't too keen on said album. "Perhaps you should just send them your personal set-list and they'll play all the songs you want to hear," she countered, rolling her eyes, shaking her head.

Getting to Middle Abbey Street hadn't been a cinch. Earlier, a chancer of a taxi driver, assuming us to be thick Scottish tourists (two out of three ain't bad!) tried to rip us off. "Just stop the car here," Dina demanded as he motored towards the wrong area of the city. The car halted. We bailed out. We eventually found the venue, and were now in a nearby pub. I chatted with fellow Gatherers. I ventured downstairs, where the men's stainless-steel, trough-like urinal had a large image of then-presidential wannabee Donald Trump. Unable to resist, I took aim and fired (when in Rome... well, Dublin actually). I also photographed the installation for posterity.

We got to the venue in good time. The Academy was quite unlike its vast Glasgow namesake. An unassuming three-tiered venue, it seemed incredibly small, particularly the bottom tier, which I guessed would at most hold not much over 200. I was overjoyed. This would be Killing Joke-up-close-and-personal! We took our usual spot near the front between Jaz and Geordie. As the support act finished, Dina was hit smack in the face by a coin. There's always some arsehole at a gig. Nearby Dubliners apologised profusely for their countryman's shitty behaviour.

The venue darkened. Jocelyn Pook's otherworldly music droned through the speakers. Cheers, whistles and roars went up. Plastic beer tumblers were thrown; dregs of beer arced through the air. The band, minus Jaz, strolled on stage. Geordie Walker strapped on his Gibson ES-295. A ferocious yet hypnotically familiar sound emerged. "He's playing 'The Hum'!" I yelled wildly at Dina. She, of course, couldn't hear me. Then Jaz, ever the showman, resplendent in a black Nehru collared coat (a definite improvement on that boiler suit), emerged from the gloom and started to intone the lyrics.

In many ways, it was a classic Killing Joke gig. Familiar crowd-pleasers, several tracks from the latest album (*Pylon*) and some deep cuts ('Complications' a welcome return). The band were as tight and powerful as ever. Big Paul, the thunderous heartbeat; Youth helping anchor the sound with rubbery bass-lines, bounding across the stage with child-like glee; Geordie, producing uniquely monstrous riffs and searing psychedelic arpeggios, and making it all look so effortless.

Then, of course, there's the force of nature that is Jaz Coleman. Undiminished, unstoppable, unforgettable; manically gesticulating, convulsing, ranting and exhorting the Gatherers through the band's mighty back-catalogue.

More than that, his actual singing (something he gets scant praise for) seemed to have improved markedly from the hoarseness of the early Noughties. He was in magnificent voice.

As 'Pssyche' finished the main set, the band trooped off. Only to re-emerge a short time later, minus Jaz. "Do you like to dance, Dublin?" asked Youth. And the band launched into 'Bloodsport'. I pointed out to Dina, Jaz, by the stage door, dancing along, his raven-black mane shaking in time to the relentless beat.

He returned to the stage to join the band for an extended encore just as Geordie's guitar signalled another well-known riff. 'Empire Song'! Surely not? The song that, for me, started it all. I was 16 again. I was back home in my small town In Ayrshire. *Top of the Pops* was on in my parents' living room. Thirty-four years later, the same band were playing the same song a few feet away from me. I whooped with delight. Mind. Totally. Blown.

"Maybe they got my set-list after all," I said to Dina as we emerged from the light, sound and sticky heat of the Academy and into the chill darkness of an autumnal Dublin night.

✦ ✦ ✦

LIMELIGHT
31 October 2016,
Belfast, UK

IAN ROBERTSON

Last time I saw Killing Joke was at the Roundhouse in London. I didn't write a review of that gig – what could I possibly say that hadn't been said before? All those countless acres of print, over the course of their generation-spanning career.

Besides, I felt somehow afraid, unworthy...

Then it struck me, in the lyrics – "Till the fearless come and the act is done, a love like blood." What I could say was simply my love for these blood-brothers, my experience, my perspective. That was mine, nobody else's.

As with the Garage in Glasgow, the intimacy of the venue fanned the flames with furious intensity. Tonight saw the band return to the land that spawned their first album cover. Don McCullin's iconic image of protestors fleeing CS gas in Derry during The Troubles, reimagined as artwork by Mike Coles.

© *Ian Robertson*

The esoteric carpet ride saw all points of the Killing Joke rose compass alighted upon – the set-list surely leaving little for anyone to grumble about. Okay, so the encore segment may have been a little stunted, due to time constraints, but the rapture evoked was such that it made barely a dent on proceedings.

The night and the crowd belonged to Killing Joke – Geordie prowling the stage, his cascading choral crescendos a wailing wall of angelic anguish; a bouncing, ebullient Youth, his bass, strung-out ley lines, thrumming to Danu's earth goddess hum; Big Paul, the pounding, tribalistic drum major, vanquishing all in this demilitarised zone; and Jaz – the Shin personified, the defiance in his haka – a clarion call for Gatherers old and new, the rejuvenation in his Supersynthesis, continually nourishing his Tree of Life...

In these troubled times, the standout track capturing the zeitgeist is 'European Super State' – "The origins of the European Union are Jan Huss from Prague in the 1600s. His original idea is worth studying because it's based on the arts, it's based on spirituality. At that time, Prague was a bastion of hermeticism and Rosicrucianism and alchemy against the Roman Catholic church, so it's worth looking at our roots there" – Jaz Coleman.

There, I've written it – the fear has gone. Killing Joke – the laughter that overcomes the fear.

THE HUM
LOVE LIKE BLOOD
EIGHTIES
AUTOMONOUS ZONE
NEW COLD WAR
EXORCISM
REQIUEM
CHANGE
TURN TO RED
ESS
COMPLICATIONS
DAWN OF THE HIVE
UNSPEAKABLE
THE WAIT
PSYCHE
DEATH OF RESA
EMPIRE SONG
BEAUTIFUL DEAD
WARDANCE
PANDEMONIUM

ARTS CENTRE
3 November 2016,
Colchester, UK

TOM KANE

Wow, crikey and jeepers! The best and loudest post-punk combo, one of my all-time faves, playing my local venue, a beautiful thousand-year-old church, capacity just 400. Yes, I was very excited.

I booked the tickets for this Brixton warm-up within 10 minutes of them going on sale. They were all gone soon after. The old church has fantastic atmosphere and great acoustics, but rarely (i.e. never) hosts big names like Joke. In fact, this whole swathe of the east is a major gig-circuit dead zone, so a rare local treat was in store.

Me and my old mucker Mitch pitched up in good time, after a couple of liveners, and there was clearly something big going down at our beloved local. The massive tour buses could barely fit outside the venue. The crowd was buzzing. Inside, the two bars were rammed.

The boys were kind enough to invite local band So Called Humans to share the stage, their excellent set followed by tour support Death Valley High. Then it was time. The band emerged amidst the swirling lights and the opening portentous jangle of 'The Hum', Jaz's demonic countenance looking at home in the sacred interior of the former place of worship. The sound was loud and clear, and throbbing, the acoustics excellently suited to the Joke noise. 'Love Like Blood' and 'Eighties' followed. Mitch, not previously particularly acquainted with KJ, had a big grin on his face, as he immersed himself in the sound and vision.

Fibbers, York, 2 November 2016. Mick Head: "[My son] Damon working Big Paul's kit. Warm-up for his first European tour as crew" © Mick Head

We stayed near the bar at the back, one beauty of the venue being easy access to refreshment and still being close enough to see the black of the singer's eyes. Halfway through, we decided it was smoke time. On the way back in, poor Mitch stumbled and fell. Mr Bouncer thought (wrongly) this meant he was too far gone to be allowed re-entry. After much pleading, to no avail, we had to, sadly, give up. Well, Mitch did. Sorry, mate, but I wasn't going to miss the rest of the set. Let's meet up after?

Feeling somewhat guilty, I returned for the rest of the full set, highlights being 'Requiem' and 'Change'. Finishing to huge acclaim, and two encores ('The Death and Resurrection Show' and 'Empire Song'), this warm-up must surely have delivered a great show to the much bigger crowd at Brixton the next night.

© Tom Kane

Afterwards, Jaz and Youth hung out by the merch chatting to fans, signing and gladly posing. I managed to get a snap with Youth, which topped up a great night.

Mitch forgave me for abandoning him. After all, though he only caught half a set, I had introduced him to a great band.

TIM FOSTER

Yes, I drove from east London to Colchester just to hear the sound of KJ. I confess to retreating to the back of the church they played in and then outside the building due to the ear-bleeding volume. My ears are not what they were. I'm still hoping for an acoustic record, but it might be a long wait.

◆ ◆ ◆

BRIXTON ACADEMY
4 November 2016,
London, UK

IAN ORGAN

In 2016, KJ played in London. Before the gig, I proposed to my now wife, Julie, in front of a pub full of Gatherers (it was her third KJ gig!) and was met with rapturous applause! We are now Mr and Mrs EmpiremanKJ.

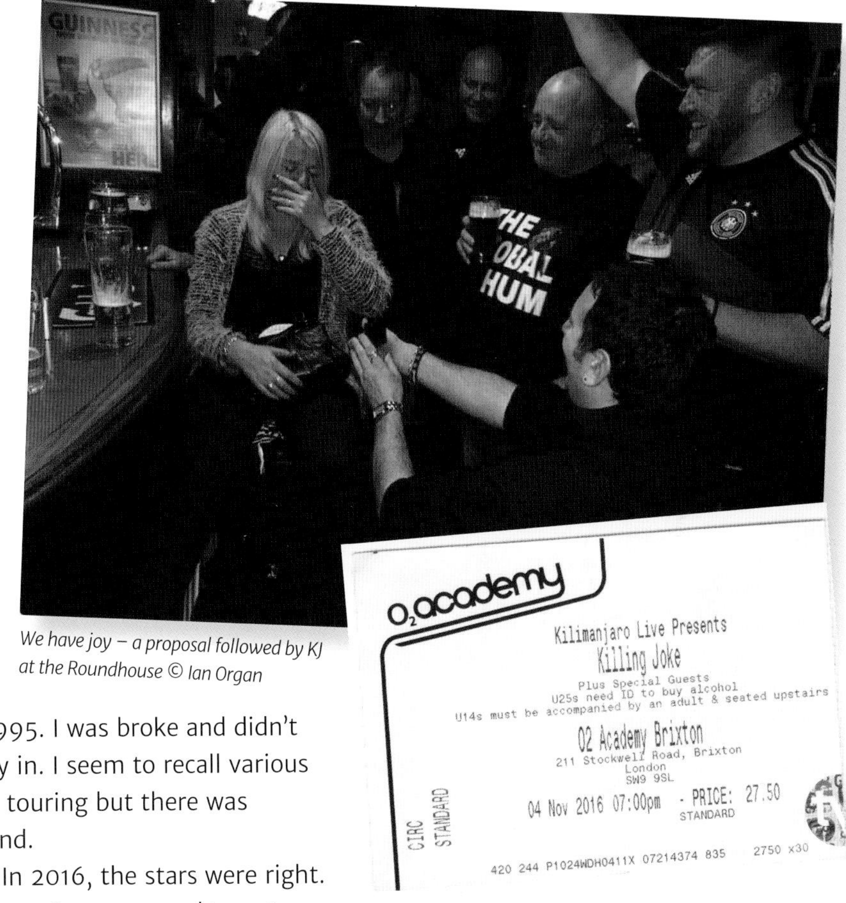

We have joy – a proposal followed by KJ at the Roundhouse © Ian Organ

MATTHIAS RICH

I've only seen Killing Joke live once. I sometimes have to ponder why. The CD of their live show in Le Pied [Toulouse] in June 1991 is one of my all-time-favourite live recordings of music that was arguably from one of their best albums – *Extremities...* I'd happily sell a kidney in exchange for a time machine that would send me back to that show.

I remember missing them play Bristol during January 1995. I was broke and didn't have the necessary chutzpah to attempt blagging my way in. I seem to recall various other dates after that point where I was aware they were touring but there was something always preventing me from being able to attend.

I've spent many years shrugging it off as just bad luck. In 2016, the stars were right. My wife, also a paranormal entity from a Lovecraftian dimension, managed to get some tickets to see the band play in Brixton.

It was a blazing show and a delight to see them at last, after a pitiful litany of missed-gig opportunities. My only gripe was that the mixing-desk team seemed to think Youth's bass was more important than Geordie's razor-sharp riffs. In this respect, it was a preliminary taster of *Killing Joke in Dub*, but I didn't think this was the effect they were after. No sane person should ever dampen down Geordie's guitar playing, FFS! As it turned out, this was Killing Joke's one entry into the world of drum 'n' bass. I'll

ILLUMINATION ILLUMINATION

MARK OUT THE POINTS BUILD THE PYRE

PUT ON YOUR MASKS & ANIMAL SKINS

KILLING JOKE

THE GREAT GATHERING

ILLUMINATION ILLUMINATION

conclude this ramble by rewinding back to the release of *Killing Joke in Dub*. I'd somehow missed the early albums. I don't know why, but I just hadn't ever got round to listening to them. There had been a melodic itch in my head I could never scratch – the tune my temporary stepbrother had played back in '81. I'd gone as far as trying to replicate it and played my rendition to a few friends who were old punks. Nobody seemed to know what It was, so I assumed I'd be ever stuck with the enigma. *In Dub* was released. I was loving every minute of it and then 'Tomorrow's World (Urban Primitive Dub)' began, I heard those spooky keyboard notes from the original bubble up from the depths and realised with utter irony that the mysterious track I'd heard in my childhood was actually by one of my all-time favourite bands. Needless to say, this was the Killing Joke and I managed to scratch the ancient itch by finally buying and listening to the first album.

JOE COSENZA

It was years before I would go see Killing Joke in concert, but I knew it had to be the 'right' one. "You always remember your first" the saying goes and that holds true for Killing Joke concerts too! Several years ago, my best friend died from a heroin overdose. He was someone I'd known since I was 13 and used to go skateboarding and surfing with. He started bodybuilding and consequently herniated three discs in his back so was on painkillers (opiates). Not long after, his addiction escalated to heroin and he lost the fight.

For months after, I was completely lost, feeling like I was left stranded on a deserted island with no sight of a passing ship to signal for help, no one I could talk to. I always heard people say, "This song helped me through..." and, it's such a cliché, but, after losing my friend, when it happened to me, 'Absent Friends' became that song for me. It's taken on a different meaning now he's gone. That was us completely! Now the years have gone by and I've forgotten the sound of his voice, I'll never forget the laughter. I remember that more than anything else. We were constantly making jokes, laughing at the absurdities of life.

A few months after he died, I saw Killing Joke would be playing a concert on my birthday in London. That was the show! I had to be there. I'm an introvert. My friend was always pushing me to do things, so I decided I would go, for him. I asked my cousin if he wanted to go with me, so we both flew to London. I remember that, as we were a block or so away from the O2 Academy in Brixton, we stopped at the light waiting to cross the street and Big Paul walked up and stopped next to me, also waiting to cross. I was too shy to say anything but whispered to my cousin, "That's the drummer."

Normally, whenever I go to a concert, I stand way back and just listen and watch. For whatever reason, I went right up to the stage, close as I could, one row between myself and the stage.

The next few hours were spent jumping, singing, definitely not being my usual quiet, shy self. It felt so good that night to be around so many people who love this band. My cousin, who stayed farther back, later told me he was talking to a few people, one of whom bought him a beer (thank you, whoever that was). Some may think The Gathering may be just a glorified name for the hardcore fans. I think it's much more. It's people who want to feel like they're part of something great. People frustrated with the way the world is and know it can be better. People who, despite differences in their personal beliefs, share a fundamental love for freedom and this band. The most recent time I saw Killing Joke, I brought my cousin again, his brother-in-law and my friend. I was right up front again. There's something about this band that pulls me out of my shell. Since I've started listening to them, I feel I have this 'strength', but I don't think they gave it to me. I think they just let me know I've always had it.

ROI ROBERTSON
(keyboards)

When I'm asked by people what I 'do' in life, I tell them about my band Mechanical Cabaret, my DJing, work as a musical composer and sound-effects creator and the fact that I write for a monthly magazine on the subject of dream analysis. Most of this is taken in their stride quite casually, accompanied by them saying such tantalising morsels as "Oh, that's cool", "Sounds interesting" and "Ooh, I had this dream, right..." They often then trail off into some long-winded description of a dream they remember having. "Well, why not type it out and send it to me to have a look at when I've got time to have a think about it?"

I usually say, followed by me tactfully changing the subject. Then, if I think I've gauged the person as appropriate to tell this to, I mention the other thing I 'do': "Oh, and I also play keyboards for the band Killing Joke."

"Killing Joke? What? Really? Fuck off! *The* Killing Joke?"

This tends to be the most common response I receive. Frequently followed by an atrociously apocryphal anecdote about them from the past, some questionable story or other regarding their reputation, or an item of 'trouble' they allegedly caused or were involved in. Some of which, however, might occasionally be based on actual facts. But that's none of my business, of course.

Well, how would you react when a fellow party guest tells you they play keyboards for Killing Joke?
© Tony Woolliscroft

Having met Geordie a few times many years ago through a mutual friend, I'd had an initiation into things Killing Joke from his perspective quite a while before I became friends with their 2006–2016 keyboard player Reza. Reza would often invite me along to their after-show parties and such like, when the band were in town, which meant I'd met Paul and the rest of them at various points. So, I guess I was at least a vaguely familiar face to some of them for a while before he asked me to cover for him on their 2016 EU and Scandinavian tour. He had booked a tour for his band, which it turned out clashed with the KJ tour planned for autumn that year. After talking to Killing Joke, he asked if I would consider covering for him, which, after thinking about it for a few days, I agreed to do – but what would I be letting myself in for?

Evidently, I relented, and embraced the prospect of performing with them, just for this 2016 tour, and then I would go about my business elsewhere. Or so I had thought.

Six weeks before it all kicked off, I learnt as many songs as I could, although I didn't know for sure exactly which songs would be chosen by the band to be played live. Just to make things even more tricky, the laptop I was due to use, with the software and sounds for their songs installed inside, wasn't given to me by Reza until two weeks before rehearsals. He had to get hold of one for me to use, on to which he was to install the MainStage music software, and copy the sounds and samples, as he wanted to use his own one, which he also used for KJ, for his own live tour, and I guess it just took as long as it took to get that sorted. So he bought an old, second-hand MacBook Pro for me to use, which, unfortunately for me, and the band, ended up malfunctioning so many times on stage. It kept crashing, frequently hindering and haunting my performances with them. Not ideal... at all.

Plus, I was to discover he usually performed with them without any kind of back-up equipment on stage in case things went wrong with the main set-up. Wot, no safety net? Yikes!

Anyway, I set about practising by playing along to live recordings, making some of my own sounds to rehearse with in the interim, to at least get a feel for things, before the proper sounds and relevant keyboard mapping were in my hands. There are several parts and samples per song, sometimes quite a few, all placed in specific places on the chromatic scale via MainStage for supposed convenience, so it's not just a simple matter of playing the parts on any old sound, where they would occur naturally on a keyboard.

As Reza wanted to play the UK leg of the tour before I took over the reins, which meant he had to rehearse with the band as a priority, I didn't actually get to properly rehearse or play with them until after the UK dates. I set up in the rehearsal room in Ladbroke Grove, me listening to what I was playing in my headphones, as they all rehearsed together – I also set up to the side of the stage at the last two UK gigs, doing the same thing, as they played the shows, hiding just out of sight of the audience behind the curtain at Brixton Academy, until my first actual gig with them in Germany at Substage, Karlsruhe, on 6 November 2016.

As it turned out, things went fairly well, shitty MacBook aside – we all got on all right, they liked my playing and told me they felt I fitted in. I played the rest of the 2016 shows around Europe and Scandinavia, and it was really enjoyable. Also, the crew were, and indeed still are, splendid people. Together with the band, the main sound emanating from our tour bus and dressing rooms was laughter, almost the entire time. Lots of taking the piss, every way imaginable, as is par for the course with a bus full of British people.

It was made clear to me that the band wanted me to come back and play with them again. I politely declined, several times, being that they had a regular keyboard player I still regarded as my friend, and thus I returned that cursed laptop to its rightful owner over a curry in Kentish Town. Later in 2017, however, I was contacted by the band and tour manager, inviting me to join them for their next tour, including two shows supporting Guns N' Roses [Gdańsk on 20 June; Hanover on 22 June]. I was informed they no longer required the services of Reza, and now had a vacancy in the keyboard department, which they would prefer me to fill – so I tentatively accepted. And, for whatever reasons best known to themselves, I've been invited to do so for every tour and live show they've played since. So, there you have it.

✦ ✦ ✦

TIVOLIVREDENBURG
8 November 2016,
Utrecht, Netherlands

MARJOLEIN KEIJSER

I was about 14 or 15 when I first heard Killing Joke – 'Love Like Blood' to be precise. I lived in a small village (Heino) and had only just started buying singles. I didn't go out yet, so got my musical inspiration from radio and TV. About once a month, we went to the city (Zwolle) to buy things that weren't available in our village, like music. I remember going to the record store and listening to *Night Time* with headphones on (a ritual you hardly see anymore, but then again there are hardly any record stores left). I loved the entire album. Not just 'Love Like Blood', but all of it. This time, I didn't just buy a single – I bought my first LP. Killing Joke was unlike anything I'd ever heard. I loved the guitars and Jaz Coleman's voice, especially what he did with it. To me, his rendition of 'Eighties' was almost sexual, especially combined with the lyrics ("push, push, struggle").

It took me more than 30 years to see Killing Joke live. It finally happened in 2016 in Utrecht, but was everything I hoped for, and more.

RIVER SEINE
9 November 2016,
Paris, France

ANTHONY ANGSTRÖMS

This puts a BIG SMILE on my face every time I think about it. On 9 November 2016, after a long night and no sleep in a bus to travel to the KJ gig in Paris, I had to find a long-time friend working at the Point Ephémère in Paris, Quais de Seine. I invited him to the gig and he invited me to stay in his flat after the gig.

I was tired, it was cold and it rained. Walking along the Seine, two girls told me I was going the right way, then a woman told me I was still going the right way, but with two miles to walk. "Holy shit!" Tired, very tired. "I'm a warrior, I'm a warrior, I'm a warrior, etc." Then I met a guy. I was doubtful about having two miles still to go. Here's the dialogue: "Please, can you tell me where is the Point Ephémère?" "Yes, but you have to go back. But don't worry. I pass in front [of it] so we will do the route together!" "Great, thank you. I'm going to see Killing Joke tonight at the Elysée Montmartre, so have to find my friend who is going with me..." "Oh, really? Killing Joke are playing tonight? I didn't know. I love them."

© Anthony Angströms

Then he sang me 'Pilgrimage'. Very well, to say the least.

"That's fantastic!" "I made some kind of karaoke from stuff I found on YouTube. I love their new single, 'Euphoria'. On YouTube, I found a guitar cover and then I was able to make karaoke from it." "Really? And did you write a French comment above the video, saying: "Merci, j'en ai fait un karaoké." "Yes, I did, but... what the fuck?" "Ahaha. I'm the guy who recorded the vid, played the guitar, etc." "Holy shit, this is what we call synchronicity." "Agreed, mate. Nice to meet you!" He showed me the place I was searching for. From the moment he told me about the 'Euphoria' vid, I knew the day and the gig and the after-gig would be perfect.

I ended up for the night in the tour bus with Geords and Youth's acoustic guitar. I played 'Pilgrimage' and Youth sang the chorus while I was playing. It was extra special in front of Geords. I was drunk so it felt kinda natural. Phil, a friend, was there saying, "Play this one, Anthony!" Geords was telling me if I was playing it the right or the wrong way. I think we stayed one and a half hours in the bus, drinking and playing this guitar. Geords showed me a few things, but I can't remember. So drunk! He showed me how he played 'Jana', but so quickly. I can't remember the chords. I remember bringing them a nice bottle of good wine. I think they appreciated this. [It was] part of the reason we ended up in the bus after going backstage.

Just needed to share this anecdote with you. Killing Joke followers are aware of synchronicities... Life is fantastic.

DYNAMO
11 November 2016,
Zurich, Switzerland

HELENA WEINBERG

I come from Prague. I'm a church organist and singer and grew up only with classical music, and have stayed that way. But when I heard and saw Jaz Coleman's orchestral works in Prague, I realised I had one of the most brilliant musicians of this century in front of me.

In 2016, I was at the live concerts in Zurich and Cologne [3 December], plus 2018 and 2019 in London. It was all unexpectedly amazing; wonderful and shattering experiences. The way they start, when the crowd of people has finally got through the often-unbearable noise from the support band and is finally ready for something else, to hear something special. Then The Special One begins. That deep, soulful voice that sings as if speaking to us from some ancient past to remind us who we are, what we are, why we are, wherever we go. This is revealed to people through the unique music and singing.

Humanity has made a covenant with the darkness of matter, but has not lost its connection to its true home – the cosmos – as long as it actively cares about it.

✦ ✦ ✦

HUXLEY'S NEUE WELT
4 December 2016,
Berlin, Germany

FRANK VOLLMANN

File under 'All class, all the time'. It's not every day you get to make a drunken fool of yourself in front of your musical heroes (although, fortunately, I've had more opportunities than most). But, when you do, just hope it's someone as patient, understanding and up for the mayhem as Jaz Coleman.

I've always been a big fan of Killing Joke and, as a musician myself, from a band running nearly 25 years, I'm still in awe of how valid and relevant all their work is year after year, when other bands have just become nostalgia acts.

A music/video producer, our videographer (who also took the photos, Sebastian Vogt) and some other industry cronies had gotten me backstage to meet Jaz after they played Huxley's in Berlin. Not realising how drunk I was nor that Jaz himself had quit drinking a few years before (nor that I could have easily got myself into a punch-up, according to rumours) I'd taken it upon myself to 'gracefully' place myself on the couch between Jaz and a couple of ladies talking with him. If that wasn't bad enough, as the camera was rolling, I continued to fall, drop my drink, spill it everywhere and somehow live to tell about it. Luckily, everyone was super-cool about it and, as seen in the photos, Jaz even had a laugh at the whole thing.

Luckily, my friends ushered me out of there before I could make this story more interesting.

frankvollmann.com/frankthebaptist

Every picture tells a story... © Frank Vollmann

NIGEL CLARKE

A few years ago, 2017 I think, I was invited to be a guest on BBC Radio Sheffield's lunchtime show. It's like a mini-version of *Desert Island Discs*, where the guest selects one song around which we'd chat about what it meant to me. I chose 'Eighties'. All was good until I arrived at the studio, at which point we entered into a fraught debate about whether I could think of something more listener-friendly. (I couldn't... Swans, Neubauten... Tool...?) The presenter, Rony Robinson, was really cool about it, and a great host who really made me feel at ease, but, understandably, he and his producer were concerned about how their bosses might respond, since they weren't sure it would appeal much to the average listener. When I explained my reasons for choosing 'Eighties', Rony decided to take the risk and go with it anyway and seemed to quite enjoy the chance to play something a little edgier than usual. I suspect Killing Joke haven't been played too often during a primetime lunch slot on local radio!

AMAK GOLDEN

After *Pylon*, Jaz asked if I could mix his Killing Joke symphonic orchestra album. His manager sent me a hard drive with all the files from the St Petersburg Philharmonic Orchestra sessions where it was recorded. They flew me to Granada and I drove a rental car to Youth's studio in Spain. Jaz was there when I arrived. Just Jaz, without Youth. We started uploading the songs and mixing. I decided I wanted to use all the analogue equipment Youth has up there. The console was his TL Audio VTC – the big blue one with 52 channels. I made a lot of stereo submixes from the St Petersburg sessions, because there were almost 100 tracks per song, sometimes even up to 120 tracks. Jaz gave me a stack of paper with notes for all the songs. A stack of notes for each song. I decided I was going to make stereo submixes, stems, from the St Petersburg multi-tracks – running through the analogue console for all of the songs. I would submix those 100-plus tracks down into 10 stems containing the different sections of strings, horns, percussion and vocals. I mixed all that down in real time, then collapsed those 10 stems into the final stereo mix for the album. The mood was so nice. Jaz was so nice and funny. We had a great time, jokes and everything. We would make trips to Granada. The rest of the time, we were listening to classical music all day long.

Jaz listens to Killing Joke Symphonic stereo submixes at Youth's studio in Spain in May 2018. The album was later released as Magna Invocatio © Amak Golden

EL CORAZÓN
1 September 2018,
Seattle, USA

SHIRLEY WONG

This was at a club called El Corazón and my friends were waiting for the band (another time I didn't really want to hang out and wait). Jaz finally comes out of his dressing room wearing a black bathrobe, black ankle socks with slippers and strolling a pink suitcase!

✦ ✦ ✦

REGENT THEATER
5 September 2018,
Los Angeles, USA

NICK LAUNAY

So... 35 years later. Here in LA. KJ are playing. I hadn't seen them in years. It was so good. It was at the Regent, downtown. And, of course, it's the original line-up. I went backstage. Either they'll be obnoxious and I'll leave... or they'll be nice. I thought at the very least it would be an amusing encounter.

Everybody's very happy. It had been a great gig. I talked to Youth. He's all loveliness. Paul's right there. He looks at me. Youth says, "It's Nick." Paul gives me a huge hug. We talked and talked. Jaz was talking to my friends. Jaz sees me. Immediately, he goes, "The Padre has returned!"

Geordie realised and was super-nice as well. The chocolate cake story came out. I ended up sitting down on this couch next to Geordie. There's this goth girl sat next to him. Geordie turns to me, then looks at her. He says, "Do you know Nick?"

She goes, "No."

So Geordie says, "This is Nick Launay. He produced our second record."

This is Nick Launay. He produced our second record. Gotcha!

Geordie gets up, starts banging his head with his hands. "Oh fuck. I can't believe I fucking did that."

Jaz looks at him: "You didn't?"

"I did."

Total revenge.

Maybe I'll get to make another record with them. And I'll be very wary of any chocolate cake. As a joke, I might even insist the album is called *Produced by Nick Launay*. I think *Padre's Pride* is also a good name for an album.

ROMEO PESTANAS, JR.

I was with my friend Alfredo, driving to the concert. We were listening to Big Paul Ferguson's *Remote Viewing*, with the great Mark Gemini Thwaite on guitar. Strange occurrences that night. We walked in and saw Geordie talking to some people in the lobby near the entrance. We walked towards him and told him we were both huge Killing Joke fans and asked if we could get a photo with him. He replied, "I'll be late!"

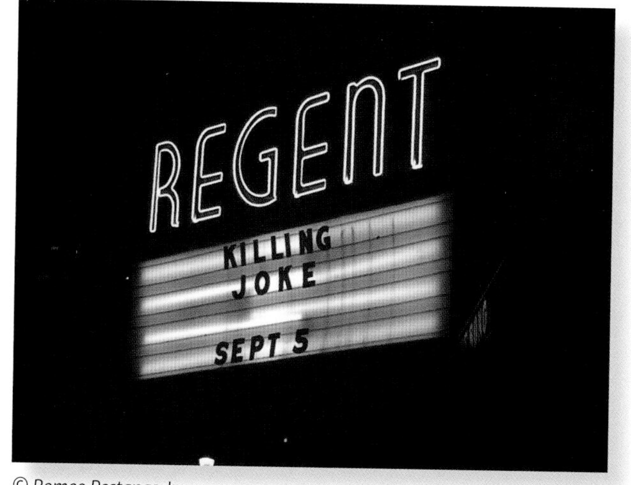

© *Romeo Pestanas, Jr.*

with a smile on his face. He put his arms around both of us for a photo and off he went.

While we were waiting for them to take the stage, Youth walked right by us heading backstage and Big Paul was eyeing the crowd from the left side below the stage. I saw him, raised my beer to him, and he nodded in acknowledgment. Killing Joke was great as always!

Romeo and friend Alfredo either side of Geordie
© Romeo Pestanas, Jr.

✦ ✦ ✦

REMOTE VIEWING EP
2018

MARK GEMINI THWAITE

It was the unlikely passing of Raven that brought original members of Killing Joke back together for his funeral in late 2007. It was great to see Big Paul and Youth back in the fold. Funnily enough, Big Paul drummed on a Warrior Soul record back in the Nineties after he left KJ. Small world.

I'd sent Big Paul copies of the Mob Research album to listen to and pass on to the guys in the band (the album later came out in 2009 on a European label). This started the beginnings of a friendship with Big Paul.

Mutual friend Mont Sherar suggested to Paul he collaborate with me to add guitars and bass to a solo track for the *Twilight of the Mortals* vinyl singles, featuring a solo track from each member of the band. We worked on 'The Great Motivator'. Before we knew it, we had seven songs demoed, culminating in the *BPF Remote Viewing* EP, released in 2018. It was incredible to think I had now collaborated with not just one but two seminal members of one of my favourite bands. Amazing.

✦ ✦ ✦

ORIENTAL THEATER
7 September 2018,
Denver, USA

TJ HEANEY

The first Killing Joke show I saw. I took my best friend. We arrived early to have a meal before the show. Little did we realise, we were extra early and had some time to kill before the doors opened. So we decided to walk around the neighbourhood and grab a couple of pints at a brewery.

As we wandered around, we encountered other Gatherers. Everyone was friendly and welcoming – total strangers that saw each other as family. Laughing and joking together, sharing stories and, on one occasion, cannabis. When it was finally time to go, a veritable army of Gatherers travelled over to the venue together.

Typically, I tend to be relaxed about concerts. Not this time. To me, it was the culmination of nearly 25 years of memories. As they took the stage and burst into the first song, I was in awe, smiling ear to ear, singing along for much of the show.

Initially, I was at a reserved table, thanks to some friends that also went. But, as the night progressed, I could not resist the siren's call to get closer to the stage. Seeing such untamed fury, feeling the energy of the band and crowd, I was euphoric, participating in a shared experience that left me feeling a sense of fellowship with the other fans that were there.

✦ ✦ ✦

SOUNDSTAGE
10 September 2018,
Baltimore, USA

MICHAEL JAMES STIPE

My life has been a different story since I got into Killing Joke. I was staying in Toronto for a few days with my wife. One afternoon, after going all over town, we decided to put on a post-punk YouTube channel and take a nap. As I fell asleep, 'Love Like Blood' came on. It was weird. I was asleep but could still hear the song. I woke up just as it was ending and scrambled for the remote to get back to that song so I could get the artist name.

I have been so taken with this band ever since. It's the first band I ever loved that was not about ego. They don't sing about romantic relationships *and* don't subscribe to super-left or right-wing politics. They taught me so much about being a concerned citizen and how to make art that is not about myself – more so about the greater good.

To go further on that last thought... I was a struggling musician for over a decade. After hearing Killing Joke, I started a new band called Northern Gloom, thanks to an interview with Jaz Coleman in which he references Killing Joke being called 'Southern Stomp' and Joy Division 'Northern Gloom' by the UK papers. I've toured nationally and internationally with this band now and owe everything to the music of Killing Joke. The mirror effect they have is *very real*.

My love of Killing Joke led me to see them on two occasions. First, on their 40th-anniversary tour and the second with Tool [Wells Fargo Center, Philadelphia, 18 November 2019]. Honestly, I enjoyed the show at Soundstage more because it was a room filled to capacity, with only Killing Joke fans. There was so much energy in the room and the band harnessed it. They put on such a great show. Jaz's voice was in top form, Geordie's guitar was huge as ever, Big Paul was flawless, Youth's bass was hypnotic. I brought two people with me who weren't necessarily Killing Joke fans. They were completely blown away. A show I will not forget!

There's no other band that has put out 15 albums that still has that kind of passion on stage and in studio. They're truly the best band to ever walk this planet. Well, they're at least the most important. If you Google all the bands that have been influenced by them, you will see how much they changed the world with their mirror effect.

KJ will never be forgotten and I hope to be another musician that carries on their legacy of inspiring other musicians to stop talking about themselves and start creating something revolutionary.

BOB CAMPBELL

The second gig, where I met Jaz, was in Baltimore. He came out and was getting pics with people. He was very nice, signed my shirt, posed for a couple of pictures and chatted briefly. Really, he listened to me spouting off about being a long-time fan and how my friend couldn't make it because he was bit by a possibly rabid raccoon (true story). Being a noisy setting, I'm not sure how much of it he understood but he smiled, put his arms around me and flashed a typical big, smiling Jaz face for a picture. I would have had so many questions if I wasn't so much of a fanboy meeting a legend! I really want to meet Geordie too, as he's been a big influence on me as a guitar player. Maybe next time.

PARADISE ROCK CLUB 11 September 2018, Boston, USA

STEPHANE BONGINI

Even by Jaz's standards, there are not many conversations that have included talk of a potentially rabid raccoon (see previous page) © Bob Campbell

For the first time, I'm going to see them in the United States. Without telling the band members, to give them a little surprise. The principle of these concerts is not just the concerts but before, during and after. You just have to have a Killing Joke t-shirt and – even if you don't know anybody – you go to a pub around the venue and immediately meet other Gatherers, who are very surprised and blown away that you come from so far away to see the band: people all want to buy you a beer.

The concerts are indeed moments of meeting other people with whom you create an immediate musical connection, as I knew it with Jon Chapman or Rob Moss, for example.

I noticed a guy on Facebook seeing all the shows on the US tour and thought: "I have to meet this intriguing guy."

We meet up at the Boston show and it really feels like we're on a different kind of dating site when we meet David Molyneux, who we've been chatting with a bit before.

The next day, we meet up in New York at the after-party, where Youth is going to mix, and the alcohol helps us have a great night.

JOEL GAUSTEN

Killing Joke have always been a cult act. Those who have embraced the band's power and magic – affectionately known as Gatherers – often travel great distances to experience the band live. Not surprisingly, an intense spirit of camaraderie was felt in the air when the band hit the stage at the Paradise Rock Club in Boston on 11 September 2018 and broke into 'Love Like Blood'. The right band, the right show opener, the right date. With Killing Joke, there is no separation between artist and audience; for 90-plus minutes, all souls in the Paradise were one.

RIOT FEST
15 September 2018,
Chicago, USA

DAN PARKER

Seeing the band perform live over the years did humanise them a bit: Geordie and that beautiful goddamn Gibson ES-295, wry grin on his face; Jaz not breaking character (is it a character?); on bass over the years, the not-to-be-trifled-with Paul Raven and fashion-indifferent Youth; I saw three different drummers playing for them live over the years, but getting to experience Killing Joke with Paul Ferguson at Chicago's Riot Fest in September 2018 as the sun set was an absolute high-water mark.

Geordie and his Gibson – a finely tuned relationship © DM Parker

I've been a hobbyist photographer for close to 30 years. Being able to shoot them twice, once at a sweaty Chicago club in 2013, as well as during the aforementioned Riot Fest in 2018 from the lip of the stage, was a thrill beyond description. On one hand, after seeing hundreds of bands, it's another show: the band walk on stage, pick up their instruments and play.

But seeing Killing Joke play those songs felt liberating and dangerous. These are underground anthems, after all.

✦ ✦ ✦

GRANADA THEATER
17 September 2018,
Dallas, USA

COLIN MARSH

Jaz and the band brought the crowd together. Beautiful gestures like: "Look at the person on your right, shake their hand, get to know them." That's what I've always appreciated about KJ. There is an underlying current of positivity mashed with angst and concern for people and the planet. Right up my alley. After the show, Jaz and Geordie joined several of us at the bar attached next door. And then, that's right, Jaz and Geordie spinning discs with the DJ! We danced after-hours.

As I'm in the middle of divorcing my wife of 25 years, I'm playing Killing Joke more than ever. Especially 'You'll Never Get to Me' and 'In Cythera'. Both are quite applicable.

Youth: "Yeah, this software package is like having a whole home studio on your laptop." Jaz: "Great. Which is the 'On' button again?" © Colin Marsh

AUGUSTINE RODRIGUEZ III

I cannot tell you how many missed opportunities I had trying to see them before. Took my son, 16 at the time, to his very first show. Who better? He grew up listening to KJ, aged 10 I believe, and has since been a fan. We were inches away from Jaz in the venue in Dallas. I was star-struck, in awe of his presence while my son held his composure (we seemed to switch ages). I desperately wanted to say hello and ask for a photo, but the memories are far greater. Jaz was extremely exhausted after that performance. I didn't want to bother him while he was making his way to the bus. We were parked inches from it. I simply said: "Thank you for coming to Texas. We've missed you!" He politely acknowledged, waved and said thank you!

Augustine Rodriguez III was at pains to point out that he and his son didn't attend "that awful [Journey] tribute show" five days after Killing Joke © Augustine Rodriguez IIII

JASON MILLS

I turned 50 and KJ were on their 40th-anniversary tour of the US, a double celebration, a no-brainer. Flights were quickly booked from New Zealand to Houston, along with Dallas and Austin gig tickets.

I met Big Paul outside the Dallas venue as he agreed beforehand to personally hand over a bronze statuette I'd purchased from his Boneyard store. The statuette was too expensive for me to pay to have it posted to NZ, so he very kindly agreed to put it in his tour kitbag. We chatted for a while, then he invited me to the soundcheck and meet-and-greet session.

Big Paul was a true gent to me that day, a very charming and unassuming individual, a top geezer.

Both gigs were amazing, especially Dallas. Jaz was on form and the whole band seemed to enjoy themselves. I must admit to being a bit overcome with emotion as they took the stage that night in Dallas. I met the band at length and attended both after-show parties, shared a beer with Big Paul in Austin, had plenty of photos. Jaz even kissed my wife. I let him off, just this once though! I also met some amazing US Gatherers, some of whom I am still in contact with today.

© *Erin Powell*

ERIN POWELL

This would be my first time to see Killing Joke live, and I had no idea what to expect.

The concert itself was phenomenal, the band putting out so much energy and volume, and Jaz being the consummate front man: pulling faces and gesturing, sweeping the crowd into a frenzy. They sounded in top form. Still processing the spectacle we had experienced, my group of friends staggered out of the venue at the end to go next door, where Youth was to do a post-show DJ set.

We were sat at one of the outdoor tables when Jaz Coleman walked up and was welcomed to sit with us. I offered to get him a drink of my own concoction, the Bullwhip, which our group liked to enjoy on outings together.

Roi Cabaret was there, too, and accepted a Bullwhip, but Jaz informed me he didn't drink. At that moment, he procured something from his pocket and said, "But this is special", or something along those lines. It looked like an innocuous little plastic tub of jelly or jam that you'd find on a restaurant dining table. He peeled the lid back and offered to share the contents with us. He said it was just some THC [Tetrahydrocannabinol] jelly. I normally do not partake, but when Jaz Coleman offers to share a substance with you, how can you say no?

I let him use my Swiss Army knife to cut up the jelly and it was divided between the five of us at the table. A photo was snapped in the moment and later altered by my wife to make it look like Jaz was working on a pocket watch! That made it safe to share on social media and confused many people wondering why Jaz Coleman was working on my pocket watch. I maintained that was exactly what he was doing... until now.

Jaz stated we'd "be flying!". I didn't think much of it at the time. We ended up having a fantastic conversation with Jaz about astrology and several other things. I was happy to see my friend Oliver Sheppard, who DJ'd the show, engaging with Jaz in person as he had previously done a phone interview with him. This was their first time meeting face to face.

The conversation was short-lived, however, as Jaz was whisked away by a few feminine fans. I went inside to get myself a Bullwhip and returned to our table. I was told by my wife that Geordie and Youth were in the women's rest room, having fun and posing for photos.

By the time I finished my drink, I felt... odd. When I stood up and went to the bar, it felt like my flesh was dropping off my frame with a promise of getting worse. I closed my tab and informed my wife we'd better leave.

It was a good thing, too, as by the time we got home I was thoroughly incapacitated by that jelly. I spoke with a couple of friends who had taken it. None of us felt 'normal' for a couple of days. 'Flying' was an understatement.

It was as if Jaz were some trickster shaman figure gifting us with a bit of chaos, and for that I am grateful. What a ritual, what a night!

THE MOHAWK
18 September 2018,
Austin, USA

ERIC SOLIS

The Holy Grail, of course, was seeing Killing Joke live. For a decade (then two) I waited for an announcement, but it seemed that the band was concentrating on limited European dates or working through personal and life events (RIP Paul Raven). Understandably, a US tour just wasn't on the cards. There were a couple of close calls in the mid-2000s, but those dates ultimately resulted in cancellations.

Finally, in September 2018, after almost 25 years of waiting, Killing Joke came to Austin. The show was amazing, more akin to a quasi-tribal, apocalyptic tent revival than a typical rock show. There's no point in going into details; I don't have the vocabulary. Like marriage or near-death, it's something that must be experienced in person to really appreciate.

Like all good things, the show wrapped up and a happy crowd began to hit the exits. I decided to wait out traffic and made my way to The Mohawk's rooftop bar, where I walked into Geordie and Martin having drinks and cigarettes at a picnic table. Hesitantly, I approached, introduced myself, shook hands and chatted for a bit. Turned out they were two of the nicest guys you'd ever want to meet. After blurting out how long I'd waited to see them play, Geordie gave me a surprised look and exclaimed: "25 years! Fucking hell." I couldn't help but laugh and told him it was worth it.

WAREHOUSE LIVE
19 September 2018,
Houston, USA

AARON COMBS

I was finally able to see Killing Joke live in 2018 after decades of wanting to. They don't make it Stateside too often. I was blown away by their energy and performance. I thought that maybe, since they were a bit older, they might play a short set and just the hits. They played the hits and so much more. A super-fun, crazy and lengthy show. It was a bit weird because it was like a set-list tailor-made just for me. They played a bunch of songs off *Pandemonium* and the 2003 self-titled album, which are my favourites. Hope to see them again soon!

Frenchy Frenzy's Tour of South America

CARIOCA CLUB
23 September 2018,
São Paolo, Brazil

STEPHANE BONGINI

I accompanied Jaz Coleman to the United Nations offices in New York and we discussed the band's upcoming first tour in South America. Jaz told me it would be good if I could attend and advised me to go to the last concert – in Lima, Peru.

I go back to France, start to think about it, then tell myself if I'm going there, I might as well do the concert in Santiago de Chile and make the most of the trip. Then I realise I've never been to Brazil or Argentina, so it's either Chile and Peru or Brazil and Argentina. My wife and children tell me not to hesitate, make myself happy. "Why don't you do the last four shows in one go?"

Plans for Stéphane's South American adventure began to come together during his time with Jaz in New York
© Stéphane Bongini

In the meantime, I contact David [Molyneux]. "Do you want to come with me to South America?" He answers in a single minute – "All of them: I am in!" Then the adventure begins – we find ourselves leaving together for a 24,920km journey between France, Brazil, Argentina, Chile and Peru, even though we hardly know each other!

A few days later, I'm in São Paulo and experience the principle of the Gathering: I really meet Brazilians thanks to Guto [Diaz], who I only know through Facebook and who takes me to restaurants to taste local specialities.

In fact, you're never alone when you travel to any place in the world to see Killing Joke. It's kind of like a big family.

I hid backstage to surprise them and start 10 unforgettable days.

We breathe Killing Joke, we think Killing Joke and we enjoy these rare moments.

I was stunned by the enthusiasm of the Brazilian fans, who were having a hard time realising their favourite band was coming to play. It was an ocean of smiles and immense respect. Everyone waited patiently for their turn to get up close and personal as they left the Carioca Club concert hall: no pushing and shoving, no security cordon, no excessive demands, just admiration.

I noticed how much pleasure it gave the band members to interact with their audience without a filter: they are simply very friendly.

I felt indirectly what I felt 15 years before, when I first met them: zenitude.

✦ ✦ ✦

ROXY LIVE BAR
24 September 2018,
Buenos Aires, Argentina

STEPHANE BONGINI

The distances are very long in South America. After a day's travel, we landed in Buenos Aires for another extraordinary day. The people are so welcoming and it's the same fervour of spectators.

I understand better now why a lot of bands come to film their concerts in South America then release them on DVD: I've rarely seen such a mixed and reactive audience. With Guto, our Brazilian accomplice, who followed us to Argentina, we formed a terrible trio: like three 20-year-old kids who think only of messing around...

The Argentinian leg of the South American odyssey, with David Molyneux, Guto Diaz and Stéphane Bongini © Stéphane Bongini

For the band, it's a little bit the same: I often have the impression I see four completely different guys but, when they're together, there is a kind of alchemy which is created and they really look like 20-year-old kids because they know how to stay very young in spirit, to have fun and let out thunderous laughter while drinking tea and smoking lots of stuff. All this creates a magnificent atmosphere.

The day off in Buenos Aires fell on the day of a national strike, never seen before, and we don't even know where to eat so take refuge in the restaurant of the band's hotel, where we can still eat and end up listening with Jaz in his room to the future symphonic album of Killing Joke, months before its release.

A privilege like that can't be refused and the listening is almost religious. A feeling of incomparable quietness.

✦ ✦ ✦

BLONDIE
27 September 2018,
Santiago, Chile

STEPHANE BONGINI

Already, Santiago is waiting for us – quite surreal to see that, on the other side of the world, there are people who love Killing Joke and who come to celebrate them for the first time in their country.

Jaz and Stéphane outside the Principado de Asturias hotel in Santiago © Stéphane Bongini

While I'm in the lobby of the band's hotel (because the promoter gave us the road book, requiring total discretion on our part) and while I'm watching Jaz being interviewed by Chilean radio station, Radio Futuro, Jaz sees me filming the interview and, while he's talking about these famous cheese-meal rituals after the concert, he calls me over. It's all completely improvised and quite surreal. I find myself answering in English to the questions of the Chilean journalist, all immortalised on video: a real hallucination. You can see Jaz is a really nice guy who impresses people a lot.

After my moment of glory, we were at the terrace of a café with Jaz and David. A Chilean woman comes up to us to offer a painting representing Jaz (painted by her).

She's very impressed by Jaz, if we can believe her halting speech and trembling when he started talking to her. She was completely turned upside down and upset and it was quite touching to see her approach her idol (even if I don't like the term).

Jaz is very approachable, very caring and friendly. I think people don't expect that, because Jaz is actually two people in one – the one backstage and in private and the one on stage. Jaz once told me he didn't know this person on stage with hallucinating eyes.

© Stéphane Bongini

FELIPE VIDAL ENCINAS

Here in Chile, KJ is not a popular band. Its different releases are not heard on radio stations, nor are they massively found in stores. But that's what draws attention and what personally caught me in a magical way, paraphrasing the mythical character of the band, as Jaz describes.

I remember it was about five years ago (I'm not a lifelong fan; I'm 27). The truth was that my discovery of the band was explosive: I heard 'Love Like Blood' then 'New Cold War'. I already knew 'The Wait' from the cover by Metallica. However, I was not attracted to anything about its interpretation. But all these songs unlocked something hidden in me, a natural force that taught me how to appreciate the darkest, most apocalyptic sounds I've ever heard.

The sense of what KJ personally means goes beyond that their compositions are good and cover a broad musical spectrum in terms of genre (discovering that *Hosannas from the Basements of Hell* or *Democracy* was related to the *Night Time* sound was one of the musical shocks of that year I discovered them).

They express in an energetic, rampant and convincing way how to stimulate the listener to question their own senses about how we should receive their music. It's not ordinary post-punk, nor is it danceable new wave, much less industrial or punk rock. KJ symbolise rage itself.

They symbolise a power to reject all I grew up with in Chile – a long dictatorship that suppressed all our individual liberties and made us less sensitive to corrupt governments that annihilate us day by day because of private interests or deepen that damn class/social inequality. They represent the background of what 'Complications' or 'Change' narrates. The band fill your senses in a sublime way, interpreting daily living, as a challenge to awaken that 'sixth sense hidden' in artistic appreciation, that we all have stored.

I saw them, I shared with them, in 2018 – the only time in my life. The humility and simplicity of these four people made me think that perhaps the path they have charted is the correct one. Loving what they've done, doing it for people, for us, their Gatherers, is the most beautiful thing one can discover being a music lover. Their live strength, the atmosphere they manage to create, is something indescribable, having seen more than 300 concerts in my short life, including those great glories like Metallica, Black Sabbath, Rush. None of those shows compare to how valuable it was to have seen them play; the trance – and explanation of its greatness – demonstrated before my senses.

Killing Joke has been a process to see how I can find myself, with everything that simply sounds like rock music, but that fills every cell of your body, taking that musical catharsis to a spiritual level, which makes you say as a follower: "It's not just that I like KJ – I like being part of this beautiful spiritual community."

HUXLEY'S NEUE WELT
19 October 2018,
Berlin, Germany

GILES SIBBALD

They've been a consistent influence in my life, the highlight a mini-Euro jaunt to Berlin, Warsaw and Prague on the 40th-anniversary tour, culminating in the massive [London] Roundhouse gig.

I met others in Berlin – maybe 20 or 30 Gatherers. Five of us made our way by train to Warsaw, met another few people, then moved on together to Prague the next day, where there was another large gathering, some of whom had come from Berlin and missed out Warsaw, others who came especially for Prague from the UK, Holland, Norway and the USA.

Prague was where Jaz announced he was leaving the city and going nomadic again – quite an emotional goodbye to the city. I had a chat and photos with all the band (except Geordie) in each city, which was awesome. Jaz, Youth, BPF and [keyboardist] Roi were out chatting and laughing with the crowd afterwards. The Roundhouse was one of the most intense and fervent celebrations of the Joke.

◆ ◆ ◆

STODOLA
20 October 2018,
Warsaw, Poland

DAWID LEWANDOWSKI

My journey with Killing Joke began not in the Eighties, Nineties or even Noughties. It began somewhere in 2017, when I was in high school and I was about 17. I met a girl in my class that I really liked, but at first she wasn't interested in any form of relationship. After some time, I got over it, but then out of nowhere she told me she'd noticed something in me and wanted to develop our relationship. The sad part was that I wasn't very interested anymore (at least in something serious), but we decided to become friends.

When we got to know each other, it turned out she was a pretty toxic person with mental problems. It wasn't easy to maintain contact and we hurt each other a lot during that time, but there's one thing I'm grateful for: she was (probably still is) a huge Nirvana fan (especially Kurt and his lyrics). One day, she sent me two songs that had a similar riff to Nirvana's 'Come As You Are'. Those songs were 'Life Goes On' by The Damned and 'Eighties' by our mighty Killing Joke.

I remember admiring Geordie's guitar in the music video and decided to try out more of their songs, next being 'Love Like Blood'. There was something magical in the main riff and Geordie's sound, in Raven's deep, rhythmic bass-line, in Big Paul's machine-like drums, in the creepy synth parts, and Jaz's mournful voice, singing these now-classic, touching lyrics.

After hearing those two songs, I decided to buy myself the *Night Time* CD and immediately fell in love with it. I then began realising my goal of acquiring their whole discography. I got into side-projects of band members, bought Jaz's book, the Malicious Damage clock by Michael Coles, and other KJ-related stuff.

I then had the pleasure of attending one of their concerts – in Warsaw in 2018 on 20 October (the anniversary of when our beloved brother, Paul Raven, died).

I'm not a veteran who has managed to attend the band's first concerts or anything, but, after discovering their music, I found something I've never experienced in any band before. It's hard to describe, but I'll try by using a trivial phrase to illustrate it – their music has soul. I love it, even if it's dark, greedy and apocalyptic.

I just love this band. I honestly don't know what I can add – it's such a personal experience.

CABARET SAUVAGE
27 October 2018,
Paris, France

DYLANE WOJIEK

Killing Joke are a big part of my father's life [see page 45], and mine. I'm 26. I grew up with this band. Their songs support me at many times of my life. I finally saw Killing Joke on stage for the first time in 2018 for their 40th-anniversary tour. By seeing them live, I definitely feel what my Dad felt before – this transcending sound, something so powerful.

Like father, like daughter, I am a Gatherer.

✦ ✦ ✦

BARROWLAND
6 November 2018,
Glasgow, UK

ANDY MAXWELL

Not long after *Pylon* was released, around January 2016, I was in a bit of a dark place for around three months. The one song that helped me get through this was 'Euphoria'. Whether I was at home or out in the car, that song was played at full blast and helped me through a very tough time.

When we went to the 40th-anniversary show at Glasgow Barrowland, I was asking Jaz how the symphonic album was coming along. He got up from his seat, went into his bag and brought out an iPod. He told me it was finished and asked which song I wanted to hear. It could only be one song, as I'd heard a clip of it on Pledge when it was being recorded. I told him 'Euphoria', so he gave me the earplugs and let me listen to it. Emotion doesn't even come into it. What a masterpiece he's created.

I could feel my eyes welling up. To hear part of the album a year before it was released was an honour. Jaz, you should be so proud of what you've accomplished with *Magna Invocatio*. Pure brilliance.

It was such a privilege to be standing at the side of the stage [in Glasgow] when Youth, Geordie and Big Paul walked on to rapturous applause. Jaz was standing right next to us at this point as the crowd awaited his appearance. As soon as he started to make his way up the ramp to the stage and the Scottish crowd caught a glimpse of him, they went mental before the band burst into 'Unspeakable'. Absolutely amazing! And the rest of the gig was tremendous. We were able to watch some of it from behind the stage to see the reaction of the crowd, and we watched the rest from the front.

FINLAY MAXWELL

The Laugh at your Peril tour. This time, we got given AAA passes. We got to see the band before and after they went on stage and could go up the stairs and watch from directly above the stage, which was really cool.

An unusual perspective – a band's eye view for Andy Maxwell and his son © Andy Maxwell

For the occasion, my Dad got a bottle of whisky with a personalised Happy 40th Anniversary label with the Laugh at your Peril picture on. He also got miniature bottles with each band member's name on. They seemed very touched by them.

When the show was finished, we were backstage talking to all the band and I was telling Jaz three of my friends and I had formed a band. We call ourselves The Lutras and play original indie rock. He told me to ask Youth if he would remix one of our songs, which he agreed to do, although we've not done it yet. I play drums and take some of my inspiration from Big Paul.

A measure of Andy Maxwell's appreciation for the band was this gift of a personalised bottle of whisky © Andy Maxwell

✦ ✦ ✦

O2 ACADEMY
10 November 2018,
Bristol, UK

ADRIAN WASON

Cracking gig with the opener again 'Unspeakable', which is a fabulous opener, but I wish they would open with 'Termite Mound' again or even a leftfield choice like 'Another Cult Goes Down', which I reckon would be well worth it.

✦ ✦ ✦

GUILDHALL
11 November 2018,
Southampton, UK

MANNY BALDWIN

I was into Sabbath, Hawkwind, Crass, Priest, UK Subs, Stranglers when I heard 'Eighties'. It was phenomenal. Such a great sound and energy. Killing Joke's strong connection with fans, tracks you can relate to and reflect what's going on. A hard riff and bass sound, experimental and different – that's what I like about this band.

I met Jaz at the Southampton Guildhall gig, had a quick chat and he autographed a print of my watercolour painting of punks and rockers at the Buttercross [monument in] Winchester where I grew up, with a great music scene. The signature joins The Vibrators, UK Subs, Steve Ignorant and The Members as I continue to watch live bands. 'Love Like Blood' live keeps me going.

Manny Baldwin with Jaz at the Southampton Guildhall gig © Manny Baldwin

CORN EXCHANGE
13 November 2018,
Cambridge, UK

SAM TESTER

I was with a friend. We were walking around the corner. Big Paul was there. I said, "Hi, thanks for your music." The first thing he said was: "What's your name? So nice to meet you." Then Youth and Jaz followed. They were so lovely: friendly, happy to talk. All three gave me a hug. I still talk to Youth and Paul. This band are humble and thoughtful. They have time for their fans and treat them as friends.

YOST THEATER
22 May 2019,
Santa Ana, USA

ROMEO PESTANAS, JR.

I was with Alfredo. We were listening to the Dream Syndicate album *These Times*. We'd never been to the venue before and were looking for a bar to drink at before the show. We found one and a few pints later decided to walk in. I loved the venue. I took a few pics of the stage before they went on. Killing Joke sounded awesome that night! After the show, I approached Youth at the merch table. I spoke to him a bit, asked what the requirements were for him to produce or mix my music. He said: "Send me the music. If I like it, I'll do it."

We took a few photos together and off he went, speaking to other fans. Really an honour to speak to such a great producer and bassist!

© Romeo Pestanas, Jr.

Music from Romeo's solo instrumental project, Hourglass Slide, is available on Apple Music and Spotify

A post-gig Youth with Romeo Pestanas, Jr
© Romeo Pestanas, Jr.

THE ROXY
23 May 2019,
Los Angeles, USA

NICK LAUNAY

We ended up hanging out really late. We got talking about acid and Youth was explaining how doing acid had helped his imagination and he was able to produce all these amazing records. I reminded him about him being delivered to the studio in a straitjacket [during the making of the second album], completely out of it. "You didn't know what day it was. And, a few years later, you were one of the top record producers in England, producing these big, big hit records like The Verve." I couldn't work out how this guy went from being so far off the planet to… I mean, you have to be pretty on it as a record producer. There's a lot of organising.

I said: "Do you think taking acid changed your brain and you suddenly became this organiser of musicians?"

He said: "Hang on a minute, I wasn't delivered to the studio in a straitjacket. No, no, that happened on the next album. That wasn't the album you did."

I said: "Let's just think about this for a minute. I was 21, I hadn't done any drugs and I wasn't drinking. This was a very important record for me, and I remember everything about it. You, on the other hand, had an acid trip.

"So who's a more reliable source to say what happened?"

So he says: "'Ere, Jaz, what album was it…"

And Jaz remembered it as the third album. They started arguing with me about it.

This went on for a while.

I said: "Ask Paul. He's the sane one."

Paul goes, "I think Nick's right."

I wasn't involved in the third record. I wasn't there. So how could I know all the details?

I mentioned the fire extinguisher thing. Youth said: "What do you mean? The fire extinguisher thing?"

"So, there you go. See? You're not a reliable source."

I told him the story. He says to Jaz and Geordie: "You cunts. Really? Why would you do that to me?"

STEPHANE BONGINI

I'm going back to see them again in the USA but this time in California, specifically the mythical Roxy in Los Angeles, where after the concert we devour a multitude of cheeses: Americans are always very surprised to taste these unusual things.

I'd been dreaming for a long time of going on an American tour and seeing them in San Francisco and Los Angeles.

NICK LAUNAY

Backstage at gigs, they have a French guy who travels with them who has wine and cheese. Amazing. It's such good cheese. He's dressed like a waiter. They're the most elegant band backstage. It's great. I love them for that.

NATHAN WELBOURNE

I finally got to see them for their 40th-anniversary tour at The Roxy in Los Angeles. It was incredible. Everything I thought it would be. It was truly a special night. Everyone in the audience knew it, too. Watching them perform was magical, and it was an awesome set of songs, hearing 'Tension', 'Requiem', 'The Hum' and 'Pandemonium' live was an experience unlike anything I'd ever seen or felt. There was so much power. I've never had the chance to interact with anyone in the band but, from what I've seen and heard, they're all solid guys and very cool to their fans. The only interaction I've had with anyone involved in the band is having former drummer Martin Atkins comment on things on my Instagram page, getting to chat with him. I'd love to meet or chat with the band. The one guy I heard was a super-kind guy was Paul Raven, who I wish I could've met. He's my favourite bass player ever. All his bass-lines on albums like *Fire Dances* and *Night Time* made a huge impact on me. So much so, I learn Killing Joke bass-lines. Anyway, I'm a lifelong Gatherer and always make it a point to show folks Killing Joke, because they are a special band to so many people and deserve all the love and admiration from fans, both famous or not.

✦ ✦ ✦

KK'S STEEL MILL
8 August 2019,
Wolverhampton, UK

JAMES STOKES

Of the many happy memories involving KJ, the biggest and brightest has to be shooting the gig in Wolverhampton, 2019, at KK's Steel Mill. I'd spent years wanting to try music photography, researching and saving for better equipment, and KJ had been my favourite band for many years – so there I was, finally doing a 'proper' gig, with an I'm-so-professional-doncha-know camera.

They unexpectedly played 'Seeing Red' – the first Killing Joke track I ever heard, a decade before. It was a beautiful moment where several dearly important things all collided: music photographers rarely get to shoot their favourite bands and I ticked off the No. 1 band at my first assignment.

A security staffer kindly let me perch near the sound-desk for the rest of the gig. On getting there, the sound promptly cut out! As the band restarted 'Complications', I prayed nobody saw me there and thought I'd pulled a cable out by mistake.

Looking back, there was Wolverhampton 2012, where Jaz did the encore in his dressing gown; attending *The Death and Resurrection Show* premiere at the Southbank; 'Absent Friends' unexpectedly being dusted off for part of the *Pylon* tour; seeing Jaz and Big Paul embrace at the end of the Camden Roundhouse 2018 gig. I may have arrived very bloody late to the story, but completely respected the emotional weight of that moment; realising the venue for 2019's London gig [Subterania] used to be Acklam Hall, site of the launch show of the *Killing Joke* LP.

Smugly, I met all four of them after the Wolverhampton 2012 gig. Telling Jaz it was my first ever Killing Joke gig, he jabbed me in the stomach and said: "Yeah? Make sure it's not your last one!"

I've stuck to that ever since.

ANDY BOTT

I was always too broke to see them in the Eighties, but of course I bought *Night Time* and *Brighter Than a Thousand Suns*. I never lost the taste for KJ, but, over the years, I was always unavailable when the rare tours happened. This carried on for years, due to their habit of touring around the time of my wife's birthday. The collection of CDs continued to grow. Then, in 2019, my chance came at last. A bit of a drive, but I couldn't hold on any longer. Front row. In front of Geordie. Mind totally blown, cherry popped.

SUBTERANIA
10 August 2019,
London, UK

LEE HOLFORD

I always love the smaller gigs, like the 2003 'comeback' (I got ticket No. 1!) at Camden Underworld. The Barfly in Camden 2005. Maybe my favourite – Holmfirth Picturedrome in 2014. Incredibly loud. My head pounding in the speaker and my innards reduced to swill. Perfection!

The last time – the hot as hell Subterania gig in August 2019. I'd seen them at the same venue in the Nineties [15 July 1994] so it was great to be back where they played early gigs when it was called Acklam Hall.

Roll on the end of the world. Killing Joke will be the soundtrack. Hahahahahhaha...

TOBY GRIST

Later in the [Subterania] gig, the smallest and hottest gig I've ever seen them at, Jaz collapsed due to the heat and I spoke to him – from my head to his head. "I've got you. It's okay. I've got your voice." Not only do I not know the lyrics properly but also I never, ever sing out loud. It felt like, if I had his voice, he could just stand there and be okay. Sounds odd writing it. Felt even odder at the time. It was like magic. A moment within a moment. No matter if it was real or imaginary. I've never felt that before at any gig by any band.

IAN ORGAN

Roll on to 2019 – last time I saw KJ was Subterania in London, a hot and sweaty club where 600 Gatherers saw once again how KJ are forever in our hearts.

LUCY AND LAYLA SWINHOE

We couldn't believe we'd never heard of this band before. They were one of the best live bands we'd ever seen! The first album we heard was *Pylon*, and we then went through their back-catalogue to find that every album was brilliant! Their music/lyrics are a manual for what is happening now, alongside being a healthy catharsis. This makes them a very important band. We had the pleasure of meeting Youth and Paul at the Subterania and then all of them at the Concorde [2] in Brighton [12 August 2019], where we were welcomed by a lovely group of people. We later met Jaz again for his *Magna Invocatio* album signing at Fopp, London [29 November]. Looking forward to the next album!

Lucy Swinhoe (left) and twin Layla (right) either side of Big Paul © Lucy and Layla Swinhoe

CONCORDE 2
12 August 2019,
Brighton, UK

ADRIAN WASON

Back in 2017, we went to Brighton's Gay Pride Festival, which was a cracking laugh. It was my daughter's birthday and she wanted to go to Brighton. We had a really long walk to the new marina and passed the Concorde 2, which I thought would be an ideal venue for Killing Joke. I see they've played there a few times. So...

Lightbringers – Brighton Concorde 2, 12 August 2019 © Adrian Wason

[12 August 2019] It was a lovely day and I met [fellow Gatherer] Zoltan Usher outside with a spare ticket. The spare was for my wife. We had a quid pro quo where I was to attend a gig of her choice and vice versa. I had to put up with two hours of Barry Manilow in 2016 and she has still not fulfilled her part of the bargain, but she is very, very busy.

Anyway, the venue was hot, intimate, the support was brilliant and the whole gig was full of so much energy, Jaz coming on perfectly choreographed, picking up the mic from Diamond Dave, who was kneeling down. Not my ideal set, but probably one of my favourite Killing Joke gigs - the band absolutely nailed every track.

SCOTT FORD

I got a chance to meet all the band after the Brighton gig and enjoy one of their famous cheese-and-wine post-gig sessions.

STEPHANE BONGINI

We ended the summer of 2019 with a UK tour, including Brighton [12 August], where Jaz doubled his energy after collapsing on stage two days before in the suffocating heat of Subterania, London [10 August].

MELKWEG
16 August 2019,
Amsterdam, Netherlands

DAZ BROWN

Ask Larry [Bate] about his meeting with all four of the band outside Melkweg in Amsterdam last year. Jaz passed around a spliff dipped in LSD. I missed out on it as I was still asleep in the hotel after an overnight bus ride from Cologne. Brilliant.

LARRY BATE

The famous Jaz 'grenade'! Very funny. He just left it and walked off. Came back to find us in a right mess. He picked the stub out of the ashtray and said: "You did, didn't you?" and started pissing himself laughing. My God, it was a good one! Daz certainly dodged a bullet that day.

Larry Bate's foreign excursion to see Killing Joke in Amsterdam included a surprise trip © Larry Bate

STAPLES CENTER
20 October 2019,
Los Angeles, USA

MARK GEMINI THWAITE

Fast-forward to last year. I had the pleasure of catching up with Big Paul and Killing Joke live in Los Angeles last summer [2019], supporting Tool at the Staples Center in downtown Los Angeles. As always, the band were in superb form and surprisingly loud for a support act. They played a killer set, mixing new and old material to a sold-out 10,000 capacity crowd, and went down really well.

Here's to another decade of the unperverted pantomime...

FISERV FORUM
31 October 2019,
Milwaukee, USA

FRED GRABARA

Back around 1991, I asked the cute girl at the record store to suggest some music. She gave me three tapes – one of them was *Pandemonium*. I loved it and played hell out of it.

I later read that it was a departure from their regular sound. I liked it so much I decided I wasn't interested in anything else.

Then, 28 years later, I stumble across 'Love Like Blood' on YouTube. I immediately realised what a horrible mistake I made omitting the rest of their work.

I seek to correct this error and make sure I own all their albums (but only if someone gives me *Outside the Gate*, sorry). I'm currently two short of that goal.

I also got to fill a bucket-list item when I saw them open for Tool in Milwaukee. As an added act of contrition, I made sure to buy two shirts and a hat.

In short, I love Killing Joke and all they've done – even the stuff I don't like.

Lemme know if you guys make it back to Wisconsin after this whole pandemic blows over. Miss you!

✦ ✦ ✦

SCOTIABANK ARENA
12 November 2019,
Toronto, Canada

MICHAEL CANNON

First time I heard of Killing Joke was after The Police new-wave picnic Oakville (Toronto) summer 1981. The bill was mostly new-wave and power-pop bands like The Go-Gos. Reading the review and some live footage of a new band Killing Joke, they were described as post-apocalyptic metal and, IIRC, alternative metal – a decade before the term came in vogue. A 'metal' band in 1981 that could play on a new-wave/ska/punk festival? Beyond awesome!

I was intrigued and followed their career from that point. Didn't see them live until the Fall of 2003 (Raven RIP) and love the Jaz Floyd classical CDs. Saw them in November 2019 open for Tool at the sold-out Toronto ScotiaBank Arena.

AKI NAWAZ

Some recent work with Youth has seen interesting bridges created between the power of 'Requiem' and spiritual nature of devotional Qawwali music.

I feel like I've spent a life timeline with the band, and that's just probably me thinking it. Everything about them is about me – that's about the best 'lie' I can steal!

Killing Joke – Zindabad!

Written from the northern mountains of Pakistan… stranded!

LUKE BRADBURY

I was brought up listening mainly to reggae/ska/northern soul (my parents' choice), but at high school I met a friend, Jack Wilkinson, who was a big KJ fan. His dad, John Wilkinson, and his friend (Sean Riley) were original band followers. They got me more and more into the band. I remember the first KJ song I ever listened to, 'Love Like Blood'. The haunting sound of Geordie's guitar was sublime – and then Jaz's voice. I fell in love with the sound. Authentic, passion-filled and gifted. Then I began to listen more and more. I've seen the band live many times and each time, to me, they sound better and better.

Now, I've always been religious. I'm a Catholic and I'm currently training to be a Catholic priest. I'm not sure how many priests are KJ fans. Well, I've always liked to be different. Nothing wrong with that. The music of Killing Joke speaks to me. Maybe not in a spiritual way, but, rather, in a more ritualistic way.

I heard the orchestra version of 'You'll Never Get to Me' and thought: "This needs to be played on the organ!" A great song that means a lot to me. My mother loves it.

Trainee Catholic priest Luke Bradbury has faith in the passion and authenticity of Killing Joke's music © Luke Bradbury

GEORDIE AND HIS GIBSON ES-295

"I'M NEVER AWAY FROM IT. HANGS ON MY FUCKING WALL"

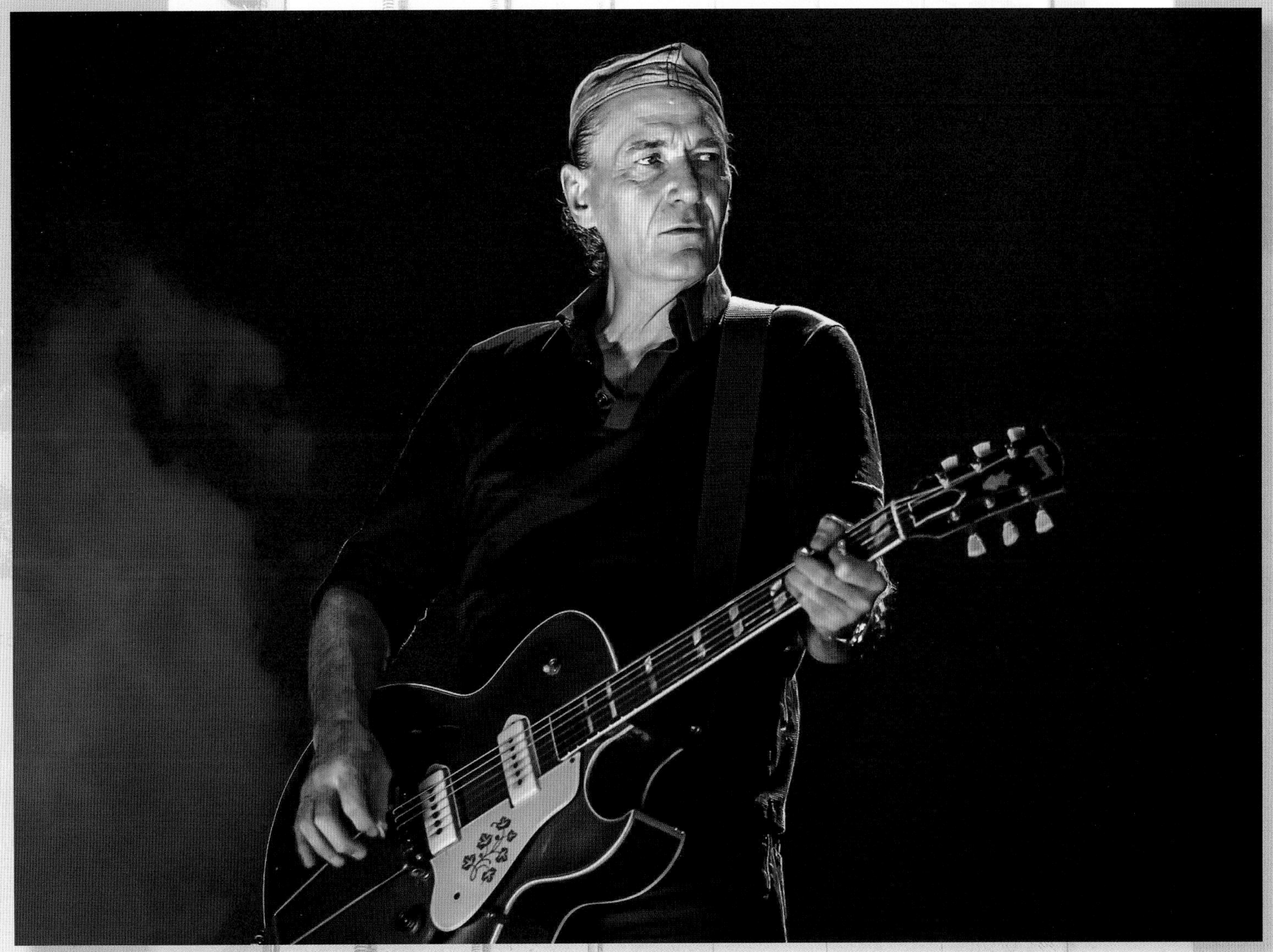

© Bobby Talamine

GEORDIE

I kinda realised early on that, if you've got a distorted guitar sound and play complex chords, the chords disappear in the harmonic distortion. So I thought: "I'll get a semi-acoustic and one of those transducer stick-on microphones and I'll blend the two."

So I got a reprint of a Gibson catalogue and there it was – "Oh, fuckin' hell, look at that. Look at *that*!" One turned up at Peter Cook's [Guitar World, in Hanwell, west London], £640. I plugged it in and the sound was there. Basically, it's a big wooden microphone with strings on it. So, when you're shifting a bit of air with amplifiers, it's talking back very cello-ey. You don't have to drive it as hard to get a raw sound.

By the time I could afford a second one, a couple of years later, maybe three, I go down to Vintage 'n' Rare Guitars in Earl's Court, as it was then. "You're the geezer out of Killing Joke. I've got one left – £1,300." I priced myself out of the fucking market.

ROB MOSS

I had the pleasure of seeing the band in rehearsal in west London with Mike Coles and my wife and son, Noah, in 2014.

There's a pub across the road, a bit on the rough side. I'd bought a round of drinks. Geordie had a cider. There was something black and evil in it, but he still wanted to drink it. I insisted on a replacement. Imagine if it was toxic and I killed the Golden Harpist. No way! The landlord drank it – I do not know his fate!

Anyway, as a guitarist of sorts, I got talking with Geordie about set-ups and what you use here and there. I asked how come he doesn't change guitars for sounds needed. He said he didn't need to. His did everything. How come, says I? A Strat is a Strat, a Les Paul is a Les Paul, etc.

Come with me, says he. And there I am. Both harps in front of me and he grabs one and says: "Try this". Fuck! I'm being asked if I wanna play the Harp!!! Does the Pope shit in the woods?

He slings the strap around me and says: "Bridge pick-up does this. Neck does this – here's the expresion pedal." The sounds are worlds apart. This, I learn, is because he likes to play with the electrics and polarity of the pickups. Yeah, me neither. Then he says: "Play something!"

Er, um. I'm playing the Golden Harp in front of Geordie. Trembling, I instantly forget how to play. Finally, I remember some riffs and play. My wife's looking at me, my son's looking at me and Geordie's sat in a chair, lounging and grinning because he knows and I know. The power and the feel is otherworldly. Honestly!

A few brief moments later, I'm done.

"Wow, Geordie. Thanks. I can't believe you trust anyone to do that," says I.

He looks at me. He laughs. He winks. "I don't!" says he!

NICK LAUNAY

He's got a huge guitar sound. It takes up the whole room, yet he plays very lightly. If you look at his strumming hand, he's playing so lightly. Guitars stay in tune better and you can hear the notes better. That, to me, is the sign of a really, really good musician. A great musician. It's fascinating to watch him play. He moves around the stage so graciously. He's a very elegant man. He's in command of his space.

GEORDIE

Every room is different. If I get a hardwood floor and a high ceiling, I'm in heaven. If I'm on a fuckin' ping-pong-table stage and a short ceiling, oh, it is fucking hard work. Moving round, trying to find the sweet spot – and then don't fucking move. As soon as you stop playing, turn it off. If you stop playing, you're in trouble.

MICK HEAD

I've played it. It's alive. I've got a replica now of an ES-295 and those big, fat hollow-bodied things are alive. You have to try and tame them like an animal. When it's gonna feed back, how it's gonna feed back. It's part of his [Geordie's] person. He's got two of them. He takes one home and Dave [Simpson] looks after the other.

GEORDIE

The beauty of it is the wrap-over bridge, which a lot of people took off because it slides around. Just fucking put double-sided sticky tape under it, you muppet. You've got your right hand resting on the bridge for damping and chugging. But you can actually press that bridge in, so you get an almost semitone drop. You can play arpeggios. The most playable instrument.

I know you get that instant gratification when you double [track] a guitar, you get that spread. But the price of that is losing the intimacy. You can make it sound as big with one guitar.

DAVID NICHOLAS

If there was ever any question about approximating Killing Joke's sound just by virtue of kit and hardware, it can be quickly settled from my experience. Like so many other guitarists, my whole concept of what a guitar can do has been shaped and changed by Geordie Walker. What he conjures with his Gibson ES-295 defies traditional rock guitar constructs. His sound is so singular and innovative. The only paltry gesture I could manage was to acquire a 295 when I had the chance, knowing that's where the connection would stop. To have the same model would be superficially satisfying enough... so I thought. Some years ago, I had the occasion to have him play mine. He offered to make the adjustments to put it into his tuning and playing action. We volleyed, playing it unplugged back and forth. Guess who sounded like who? That his sound comes from within was reinforced even more when I had occasion to play his (plugged in, at earth-shattering volume) and again learned the lesson that his sonic architecture comes from a much deeper, unfathomable place. His mystery remains intact and inscrutable as ever. As it should.

GEORDIE

Influences? It's amazing what one soaks in. I was over in the States, early Nineties, flipping through the 78 channels – Canadian Broadcasting [Corporation], 'cos I was in Detroit. What's the fuck's this secret agent man? It's *Danger Man* with Patrick McGoohan. I hear all the incidental music. Absolutely soaked into me. That's where I got it from. That's where the fucking shit came from. A lot of time [it goes] into the subconscious rather than the conscious. The conscious brain isn't always a good thing.

One of the records I bought that always stayed with me was an album by John McLaughlin, called *Devotion*, with Hendrix's drummer [Buddy Miles] on it. I dug that out again. That really sank in. I said to Danny [Carey, Tool drummer], "A word to the wise, check this out". "Yeah, man, I know. My big brother had that. I thought it was a bit 'hairy' then, but it's fucking magical," he said.

The chugs are deffo Zal Cleminson. The bell-like chords – I learnt *Live at Leeds* all the way through when I was 15, 16, so that was a big influence. Solos? As soon as you do a solo, all the drive and balls disappear. I learnt that very early on when I was rehearsing at school with a couple of mates.

Matt Tibbits with Geordie's ES-295s at Faust Studios in Prague

NICK HARPER
(guitarist, singer/songwriter)

Of Geordie Walker: High Priest of the Church of Doom Boogie and Riffmeister General.

At the end of the Seventies, shit got real. The winter of discontent and the dawn of the Thatcher era gave rise to the unmistakable voice of authentic, sustained dissent. Most of us mildly inquisitive adolescents of the late 20th century, searching for the answer to life, the universe and everything, looked to music for guidance. In 1979/80, for the national and political I found Gang of Four, and for the global and spiritual there was Killing Joke.

When I first heard Killing Joke, the reaction was visceral. I felt I was being spoken to on another level. This wasn't fashion. This band were serious and wanted to actually effect change with music. I'd done a school chemistry project on what was known then as the Greenhouse Effect, and here was a band saying, "Butcher the womb and expect her to bear." A+. I was in.

I'd been taken to loads of gigs as a kid, from Zappa to Zeppelin, but this was music I would travel to see on my own. That first gig was mind-blowing. Thundering, volcanic drums and bass that, let alone questioning the seating of your breastbone, left you wondering whether they were the result of, or had the potential to cause, fissures in the tectonic plates of the Earth. Seemingly led by a perfectly crazed Colonel Kurtz figure, every bit the escapee from Conrad's carnage on the River Congo or Coppola's Mekong (or our very own... Severn?), exploring the deepest depths of the human soul so we didn't have to. And, on his right, a destroying angel, all steel and blades, wielding his six-string scimitar like a Hell-bound Hashishin. My ears were still ringing two days later. Bliss.

I was learning guitar then (still am) and I've never heard anyone like Geordie. On the 'Wardance'/'Pssyche' single and on the first album, there were some chords I recognised. Cool. But there were odd things going on that I hadn't heard before. The augmented note at the start of the riff in 'Requiem', for instance. That note was a choice I don't think any other guitar player would have made. This wasn't just dissonant noise; it was melodic, yet unsettling and very exciting. I was swept up in the flow of the collection of anti-anthems that album is, but at the same time knew this was no ordinary guitar player. I was hooked.

When *What's THIS for...!* arrived, his playing wasn't just unusual, it was in its own sphere altogether. As was the whole album. From the hypnotic, unrelenting riffs of 'The Fall of Because' and 'Tension' to that scimitar, now reflecting the light of a dark-choked sun, in 'Unspeakable' and 'Madness'. That album signalled this man as a singular guitarist. An original. Then he somehow topped that on the next album by writing Wagnerian overtures on an electric guitar on songs like 'The Hum' and 'Empire Song'. *Revelations* was the definitive soundtrack for the dystopian backdrop of 1982, Britain at war in the Falklands and a government on a collision course with its people.

I've been listening for 40 years now and, for me, Geordie's playing has always evolved yet always been true: strident, discordant, oblique, full of irresistible riffs, medieval brutality and unnerving changes, all with a kind of terrible beauty and, of course, always totally original – there can be only one!

As the years have come and gone, Killing Joke have carried the burden of actually living Killing Joke (blimey) whilst I dip in to get healed every once in a while. Music has always been a major gateway to freedom for the mind, the soul. The black poor in early-20th-century Mississippi sang the blues on their tin-shack porches to rid themselves of poverty and oppression, however briefly. Though their tin shack is a global music marketplace, Killing Joke do the same. The need is the same. The result is the same: catharsis, transcendence and healing. And we all need a bit of that from time to time, right?

Oh, did I mention on top all that they're a fucking good rock band?

AMAK GOLDEN

There are a lot of things to say about Geordie's guitar playing. I don't know if I can describe them for you. Geordie was always sitting in the studio tuning up his guitar to Jaz's keyboard drones, listening to the lyrics and scratch vocals. He'd usually tune his guitar open to the root chord of the song. Then, when he'd start recording guitar after at least some guide vocals were down, he'd come to me in the control room. He'd take a drum throne and sit there playing guitar. He'd barely touch his left hand to the neck because the guitar was already tuned to the root chord, and his right hand was loose and free, just flowing. One take for the left channel, one take for the right. That's it. Always just two guitar takes. Then he was done. That was genius, and the groove was absolutely genius.

GEORDIE

There was a question I was asked years and years ago. "So when did you start listening to jazz?" I've never listened to it.

A lot of the time, you make yourself so relaxed and you're in kind of a trance, then something will just land on you. "Whoa, fucking hell, what's that?" Something that gets the hairs on the back on your neck standing up.

Funny thing is, years back, I got hold of the Hebrew Gematria. Stuck my name in. And Geordie Walker came up as 'fingers'. Then I put my christened name in, Kevin Walker, and that came up as 'a choir of angels'.

"Killing Joke is simply a mirror – you look at us, we look at you"

London Roundhouse, November 2018 © Tony Woolliscroft

JAZ

It's really like going out into your front room and all your friends are there. I'm talking about 41 years of going around the world in multiple countries. The people who put food into our stomachs are welcome in our home and our home is our dressing room. We have so much fun seeing old faces and new faces.

MARK WHITELEY

If you explore the depths of your soul, each and every time you come up for air, you're in danger of decompression and death. I let this realisation guide me... away from the rocks below. Hence, I can sit down on a Covid-19 lockdown day, reflect on our delightful, indolent nation and bathe in rage and adrenaline with no immediate threat of sanction. As we drift in 2020 towards a geopolitical climate that looks spookily like a dark New World Order, I'd like to share a memory or two...

One particular group of artists have informed my attitudes and insights into this insane but beautiful world - Killing Joke.

My love of their music was unconditional. The ideas they tussled with were fascinating. They spoke in a language I connected with almost immediately. I was already a passionate fan of punk and reggae. Killing Joke mirrored my emotional turmoil, my political views and spoke to my interests in the mystical and spiritual.

SEAN RILEY

Jaz has been telling us all for longer than I can remember how the world was on a path to self-destruction. He's been mocked, ridiculed and no one ever really believed him. But, when you look back and see where we are now in 2020 – with songs from 'Butcher' (from 1981), telling us how man was taking everything from nature and polluting the atmosphere and doing nothing to replenish the world, to 'I Am the Virus', when we now have Covid-19 – you have to admit he had a point. A very valid one! It looks like his premonition was correct...

As for Geordie, that guitar sound. One guitar that can throw out such melody, such anthemic riffs and sound like 10 guitars at the same time. How does he do it? Nobody knows, but we're glad he does. Youth has always been the life and soul of the band, and, of course, Big Paul – and we shouldn't forget Martin Atkins, of course. As for the spirit of Killing Joke, well, the Raven King identified with the fans so much. It was a two-way thing. The fact his untimely passing at just 46 years of age had such a profound effect on his friends on and off the stage, and that it should bring back together the original line-up, just shows the mark of the man. RIP, Paul. As for the rest of us, Laugh at Your Peril never seemed so relevant as it does now. There should be a Killing Joke museum, there really should...

BRIAN RICHARDSON

This is something I've always felt with KJ – they couldn't be crowbarred into a specific sub-genre and perhaps the media never liked it – but who wants to be like that?

Every album seems to produce a different sound, a new concept, but it's always Killing Joke and, while they may now be different to the likes of 'Wardance' or 'Bloodsport' or the more mainstream 'Eighties', it is still them. The same passionate, non-conformist views on society and unapologetic music. It's far easier for bands to sell out, but the real reason I've been listening to them for 31 years is because they have stuck to their values.

Bob Campbell: "Let's just say that seeing Killing Joke is the closest to a religious experience a person can have"

PAUL RANGECROFT

Thank you, Killing Joke, for all these memories and so many more. Not just a band – a philosophy, a way of life, a way to cope with the insanity of it all. Forever in my heart.

RUSTY EGAN

They are somehow, to this day, an all-consuming gift of a sound that, like a tornado, lifts up all and everything to a level, like an exorcism. Not [get] out, more, "Come in, be a part of us."

My last time was November 2018 at the Roundhouse. I had a support DJ set with Peter Hook a year before and made it a dark, Germanic sound. When I saw KJ, it was as if the Roundhouse was possessed. That is KJ to me. I've loved them since 'Turn to Red', but can't copy or even emulate. It's the four of them or nothing.

HONEY BANE

If we were to run into each other, it would be like they'd always been there. It wouldn't be strange. They were really good times.

TROY GREGORY

It was a good time, for sure, a time that's made me reflect. If someone had said this was gonna happen – the older me who lived in a different country...

That idea of ending up in a band that you listened to is fun. That's not lost on me. I'd never be like: "Fuck yeah, I deserve it. That's mine." I'm like: "That was a wild ride, wasn't it?"

MATTHEW LAMBETH

Still the same noise and intensity to the gigs – no compromise. Just a great band.

ALEX JEMETZ

Killing Joke is a band whose music has never been out of sync with global events and the sound is one I enjoy no matter what mood I am in. I like that they have a mystical and slightly occult component/presence in their music and live performances that come across as authentic and not as other bands may use to heighten their popularity as part of their act. I feel lucky that they are still producing amazing music – *Pylon* is incredible and on it you can hear bits of their creativity from all of their previous works. Being a fan of Killing Joke is like being part of a secret society. Only others who are in it understand your passion for their music.

JUSTIN BROADRICK

The first four albums were albums of my youth, records I literally grew up with. Like most people, the records of your youth are the most important records of your life. These records become myths almost, intangible.

There's always something in Killing Joke I directly communicate with. It's become spiritual by now. I would consider KJ's openness an inspiration, but they were always direct, but that heap of influences the band converged upon to make this magnificent whole was mind-boggling – post-punk, dub, reggae, rock, krautrock. I hear all these things in the first album alone, and more! I always strived to encapsulate many styles but be very direct with the delivery. I also realise that expression is complex. It's wide and all-consuming. The best art is. I want it all. Like Killing Joke and inspired by Killing Joke, I'm greedy with sound.

Kirk Brandon
(vocals/guitar, Theatre of Hate/Spear of Destiny)

I first met Killing Joke as my then girlfriend was Jennie Smith (Scotch Jennie). She it was who was managing KJ at the start of their career, alongside Brian [Taylor]. [*Editor's note:* Big Paul says Jennie's role was more linked to strategy – "if such a thing was or is ever possible with KJ".] They were very much a Notting Hill Gate/Portobello Road band and several of them lived there at the time. I always got on well with Paul Ferguson, the powerhouse drummer. His girlfriend also played in an all-girl band at the time. Paul said a few times that the band thrived on the tension that existed within the band. Having met Jaz, I understood why. But many bands, Theatre of Hate included, were 'on the brink' virtually daily themselves.

Jennie was enthusiastic about the band and their music and I went along with her to quite a few early shows. It's hard to exactly say why, but all the grungy/industrial rock bands that came in their wake owe KJ a big tip of the hat for taking onboard their ideas and using them.

Initially, especially in London, their gigs were electric. It was original music with stops and starts, mixtures of Youth's funk bass-line/phrases together under Geordie's full-on guitar.

Three-quarters of the band at Britannia Row Studios in London during the making of Absolute Dissent © Stéphane Bongini

Geordie and an amped-up Jaz at Chicago's Riot Fest – 15 September 2018 © DM Parker

However it came about, my band Theatre of Hate were offered the support slot on the first major UK KJ tour. It was a good opportunity to showcase Theatre of Hate.

I remember in a soundcheck, Jaz had written magical symbols on a pentangle on the floor of the stage in chalk, a fairly wacky thing to do, everyone thought. Why he did this I don't know. Maybe it was his idea of humour, someone said.

Both bands were at the top of our game at the time, and the positive press we received by being on that tour certainly helped with our career. After about four shows, Jennie said we were to be taken off the tour.

Relatively shortly after their first album, I believe they changed management and Jennie and Brian then parted ways with them. The band was getting bigger at a rate of knots.

Killing Joke were and are a unique and brilliant band, of that I have no doubt. Their many ideas – lifted by other bands – stand witness to that even today. Their music leaves a brilliant legacy.

ALAN MCGEE
(co-founder, Creation Records)

Killing Joke changed 1980 for me. I was 18, had moved to London and rocked up to what was the band's second show at the Lyceum, with Pink Military. I got down the front and went crazy. 'Requiem' blew my mind. In Glasgow, we didn't get that many punk bands going up there, so five bands in one night that were all great blew me away. I bought the records and always loved them. Through the Britpop thing, I became mates with Youth. I was a bit in awe of the man, but he's so great. We became firm friends since that day. Jaz is a genius, a one-off musician – and the rest of the boys are all brilliant. I love them still and still buy their records the day they're released. Seminal.

ANDY MAXWELL

I'd like to doff my hat to rock 'n' roll's true survivors.

A massive thank you to my brothers in Killing Joke for the last 40-plus years. They've always been a band way ahead of their time.

Jaz Coleman – one of the most truly amazing, intelligent, polite, knowledgeable, kind gentlemen we've had the pleasure of being in the company of. Ever! A true legend.

Geordie Walker – your guitar playing is an inspiration to thousands around the world. Thank you for keeping it real for over 40 years. One of the loudest and best guitarists I've ever heard, and also a true gent, kind and funny, always has time for a chat... and a drink!

Youth – down to earth and chilled is an understatement. An amazing bassist, and a wizard at the controls, either in the studio recording and producing, or DJing. A legend at mixing and dub. Always a pleasure to sit down and have a chat with.

Big Paul – what can I say? One of the nicest human beings we've had the pleasure of meeting. Genuine, kind and always has time to talk to fans. I'm surprised some of the stages he's played on have survived after he beats the living hell out of a drum-kit for nearly two hours. Absolute respect.

Not forgetting our dear brother, Paul Vincent Raven. An amazing bass player and massive part of Killing Joke – Rock In Peace.

TOM PAYNE

We lost touch as the band had a break and my life took a different path and we've not caught up since, although I still go to every gig I can and even have my son now as a massive fan.

Despite age, they're as awesome now as back in '83 when I first saw them. Fond memories of the greatest live band on the planet.

JAZ

I really care about the standards of KJ live. We all do, but I really care. This is just symptomatic of the passion we have for what we're doing.

MANFRED ROLEF

For me, it's still impressive how relevant and powerful their musical output is and that nearly each album has a unique sound. My favourite album is *Democracy* and the album I really cannot listen to is *Hosannas...* Nearly each album has standout songs and it was a pleasure to see them on their 40th-anniversary tour, together with my 20-year-old son in the mosh-pit. A new Gatherer generation...

MICK HEAD

I'm really lucky, having had the privilege to witness not only the acclaimed gigs but also the creative process, meeting the supporting cast, the band's highs, their lows and all the amazing stories in between.

I've even taken my family to see the band, and they've struck the same friendships up. My son [Damon] is now entrusted even more than myself, being part of the touring crew for several years now.

LUKE BRADBURY

The music has power, the lyrics have depth. KJ have and will always have a special place in my life!

LUC TIRONNEAU

I have never stopped and will never stop being a Gatherer.

FLORENCE CHARO

From the first album until *Pylon*, the aim to shake the capitalist system is there. This consistency is still there today, after the band's 40 years career, and it is undoubtedly needed even more than ever in today's world. Amazing!

I am always surprised and rather disappointed to see KJ is very often forgotten in books that talk about the rise of punk in the late Seventies. They are for me one of the most important bands many others feel accountable to.

I will say only one thing – I love you guys!

CARSTEN DOIG

Now, 35 years from when I first heard them, Killing Joke are the only band that have lasted with me throughout my life. I shall go on with them to the end.

ANDY SEWELL

I follow Killing Joke with great passion. They have become the soundtrack to life and are scarily prophetic. They provide an odd sense of comfort as we slide into the abyss. No better music for dancing to the culmination of mankind's folly, it appears. Thank you for everything, Jaz, Geordie, Youth and Paul!

COLIN MURDY

My admiration for the band is an ever-evolving process of love.

LEE HOLFORD

(Nuclear Boy)

Over the years, I've seen them 55 times. A lot of these I have Geordie Jim Ireland to thank for driving everywhere! Every one beyond great – Rock City, Leeds Uni, Brixton Academy, Astoria, Roadmender, various Academies and Apollos, Glasgow, Rebellion.

MARK COWLING

I just saw them on the Tool tour, and there wasn't a song or lyric I didn't know. I had to apologise to the people around me as I was making a complete dolt out of myself, dancing, singing, etc.

From the first time I saw Killing Joke, I was absolutely enthralled, enveloped, totally captivated by them. They became my absolute favourite band and I've been playing guitar for, oh jeez, since I was eight and I'm 63 this year. Ugh.

NICK LAUNAY

I've worked with a lot of very difficult, abrasive artists in my time, starting with Johnny [Lydon]. Nick Cave and The Birthday Party, pretty intense and full on. Also Lou Reed, quite a character.

They are just people that are very focused and determined and have an idea of what they want to be musically. They're hell-bent on getting it and need someone to help them in the studio to do this. I like experimenting and my taste in music is exactly their taste in music. I think that's why I've ended up doing so many records in that dark wave area, that anarchistic approach to rock music.

Killing Joke have all matured. They're nice people now. They're still intense but they're mostly really funny. Jaz is a scary-looking guy. But these days I find him to be very sweet. Super-intelligent. He's scored entire orchestras. It's not just rock music. The man's a genius.

FRANK JENKINSON

What brought me back into them was the book [*Killing Joke Picture Book*. Check out Frank's Facebook page of the same name]. I have a lot of photographs and that book was only the autumn of 1979. There's another year and a half of photographs to be sorted.

I've been backstage at most places at London gigs since they started touring again. I saw them in Hammersmith, Shepherd's Bush and the Royal Festival Hall. As a bunch of people (including their fans, with whom I've become better acquainted) they are all remarkable.

SEGS

(The Ruts)

Youth and I recently drove to Bristol together for a 'bass-off' with RDF [Radical Dance Faction]. By the time we got down that way, we were chatting away, listening to dub in the car, telling stories – quite stoned. Missed the turnoff for Bristol and were 30 minutes late. Great fun and great to see him.

We influenced each other a bit, I'd say. I loved 'Pssyche' and played the bass-line at the bass-off rehearsal when Youth arrived. Don't think he even noticed!

TROY GREGORY

Killing Joke-ish moments? The shrine of a dressing room. I go in the dressing room and it was posh, wonderful. Kick back on these big pillows. Beautiful tapestries. Just the whole place. You couldn't recognise it. You get so used to horrible dressing rooms. The people from the club could've walked in and wouldn't know the place. They'd look around, say: "We're in the wrong place."

Jaz says to me: "You see? You were laughing at us about this. Isn't it nice not to look on the wall and see a bunch of dicks?"

That whole environment was interesting. Before coming out on stage for the very first night. Lighting the torch. I appreciated the ritual aspect of it.

MIKE COLES

Now we're all grown men, we actually get on... sort of... They all have completely different ideas and opinions. It's a full-on battle of wits. I've had stuff almost ready for print, only to have the whole thing scrapped and started again.

I understand them because I know them so well. We have the same sense of humour and the ridiculous. As Big Paul said in a recent interview: "Mike Coles was and is a blessing to Killing Joke. Because Mike gets it, all of it: the pathos, the sinister in the ordinary, the fucked-upness of it all. The Joke."

NICK LAUNAY

What a great band Killing Joke are. What a combination. Just a great band on every level. They're a force unto their own.

DEREK SAXENMEYER

On Killing Joke sessions, it can be really intense. But it's great working with musicians of their calibre. You have the feeling that you're working on something that's really worthwhile.

IAN ORGAN

Into the Nineties, saw them at every opportunity I could – UK, Europe – including Prague, which KJ regarded as their second home. Then the 2000s – loads more gigs. By now, I'd been going to KJ gigs nearly 20 years and started to see the same fans, so we talked and made friends. The birth of the internet – KJ exploded all over the internet. There was a Gatherer in Alaska – Cliff

Monk Livingston – who set up a KJ chat room. We all joined. That's where I cemented my name EmpiremanKJ to all other Gatherers. We would find streams of live gigs that KJ were playing, so we wouldn't miss out.

Since then, I've graced as much as I can for every tour, meeting fellow Gatherers and enjoying each other's stories time and again.

UMAIR CHAUDHRY

I've seen them play around seven times over the years in Oxford and London. Every time, the sense of communion and sheer energy is immense. I sing along to each song as if they are my own. Few bands compare. I describe the gravitational pull towards this band like a moth towards a flame. They will always hold a special place for me, and have been a massive influence in terms of my own music.

STEPHANE BONGINI

(aka Frenchy Frenzy)

How could I have imagined that, 30 years after listening to a cassette in a car, I would find myself at a radio interview in South America and, more exactly, in Santiago de Chile with the singer of this band I didn't know back then: this surreal situation is a bit of my story with Killing Joke and its singer, Jaz Coleman.

The question I'm asking myself is why do we hang so much on one type of music and then on the music of a particular band when we listen to a lot of other bands and a lot of different music?

Following Killing Joke on tour, Stéphane Bongini has assisted Jaz during a radio interview...

... as well as helping to capture the band's live shows... © Stéphane Bongini

Maybe it's the certainty of hearing something unique and singular: a sound, a style, which you can't hear anywhere else.

MARCEL VON DER WEIDEN

Since the *Democracy* tour, I went to see every tour they played and have never been disappointed. I don't dance, but I've danced to 'Pssyche', laughed with joy over 'The Death and Resurrection Show' and cried over loss during 'Exorcism'.

DEREK S – FALKIRK

I have continued to congregate with all other Gatherers to stand and take in the brilliant, psychological din of Killing Joke. Onwards, Gatherers.

DAZ BROWN

They are sublime. Intense. Strange. One can never quite put one's finger on it. I honestly don't know what it is about this band I love...

One thing I do know is that, 32 years and over 40 gigs later, I am still intrigued and fascinated.

RICHARD FARRELL

I've been passionate about other bands and different types of music over the years, but just don't ask me where I heard any of them first. Many have made a long and lasting impression, just not quite like Killing Joke.

STEVEN BORG

The difference between Killing Joke and other favourite bands is that listening to Killing Joke gives me a certain power, confidence and feeling of being invincible. Most of all, they have a unique sound which never bores me. I'm still listening to their albums, which I've been listening to since the Eighties. Meanwhile, listening to other bands I like sometimes bores me. Then I need to stop listening to them, sometimes for years, before being able to enjoy it again. This never happens with Killing Joke. I'm proud to tell people I'm a huge KJ fan, even if they've never heard of them.

For me, Killing Joke is a way of life. If I die, Killing Joke will be played at my funeral, because that is who I was!

VAUGHAN SMITH

Killing Joke – even the name was overwhelming. It meant everything to me.

I had a son in August last year [2019] and named him Jaz. Yep, after Jaz Coleman.

Having grown up in Hull, I lived in New Zealand for 17 years, then came to Australia in 2002.

MARC JONES

I've seen this sublime band many times and I'm happy to say they are still immense and one of my favourite bands to this day.

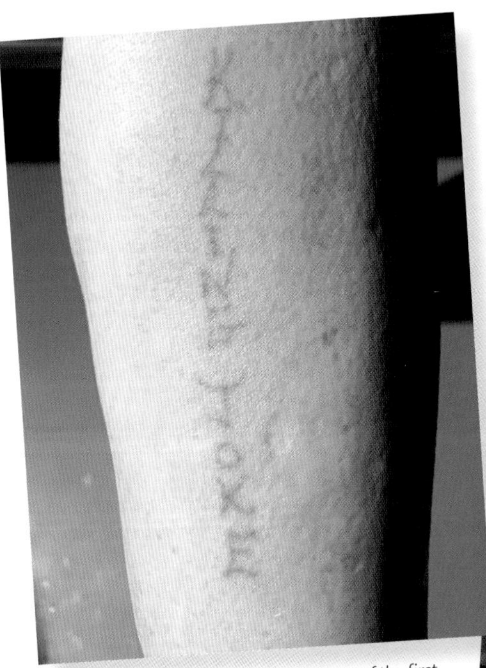

Vaughan Smith: "Oh yeah, I might be one of the first to get a Killing Joke tattoo – '83. Home-made."

Vaughan's son Jaz with his mother

JAMES FRYER

I won't bore you with my views on all the albums over 40 years – needless to say, I've stuck with them throughout and found something new in every change in style and in each new release (even forgiving them 'Me or You?' and *Outside the Gate*).

Geordie has always been my favourite guitar player. Over the years, I learned how to play many of the songs. After a fashion, you understand. No one could ever come close to the magic of 'Geords the Chords'!

GEORGE WASYLENKO

It took me many years to truly understand what Killing Joke represents. Their ideology is profound. Jaz Coleman is truly a musical genius. From Killing Joke to his classical compositions, Jaz is inspirational. Killing Joke - highly underrated and misunderstood.

IAN ORGAN

Even before Facebook, there was Myspace, where I had one of the best Killing Joke tribute sites. It was frequently visited by band members, mainly Paul Raven (RIP, KJ brother), who said it was awesome. After 38 years, I still wear the shirts, play the music every day, watch gig videos, collect KJ-related merch. This band influenced so many others. Not only will they have their place in history, they'll always have a place in my heart.

Gigs are not just gigs – they're a place to meet the KJ family and keep in contact with like-minded Gatherers all over the world.

© Sean Riley

SEAN RILEY

They had you under their spell. The 'Pope' t-shirt (God, I wish I still had it now). All the thought-provoking imagery from the wonderful Mike Coles – the drowning liberty, the jester and children in front of the Centre Point tower block, the street scene depicting youths confronting the British Army etc. and the huge tour poster – all were duly purchased. This wasn't just a post-punk band. It was some kind of movement, a crusade. Jaz was like the Pied Piper, and we were all following his tune.

I've grown up with the band, seen them on every visit to Manchester and a lot more places besides. People I've met in my life always remember me as 'the one who is into Killing Joke', although, to be fair, Theatre of Hate were also a huge band for me.

I've supported the band through the lean times - remember ODIC [the Order of the Distant Island Charter fan club, around the time of the *Extremities...* album]? And I was fortunate to make contact with the late, great Raven through email when that was the new thing. I cherish that, along with all the posters, cuttings, records and CDs amassed over the years. The Gatherers introduced me to so many people who share the same passion for Killing Joke. If I thought I had the addiction bad, I know plenty more who've got the obsessive-compulsive disorder the band drives us all to.

TJ HEANEY

I grew up in a very conservative small city/large town in the United States. There was a very heavy influence of Christianity, something I could never really accept. I had trouble fitting in. It didn't help that I was also the weird ginger kid with nerdy hobbies like Dungeons & Dragons. I genuinely felt I had no outlet for my youthful angst.

Then came Killing Joke, a gateway to seeing beauty in the bizarre. They taught me bravery to break the mould of normalcy, [to show] compassion and acceptance of what would be considered deviant or bizarre. To look beyond the 'what is' and aspire to the 'what could be'. They made the coming years of high school much easier to weather. They showed me there is magic in life.

Since then, I've continued to fall in love with them over and again. Sometimes, I drift away to explore new things, but always return, as if they were my closest friends. For that, I'm grateful to be a Gatherer.

DAN PARKER

In the late Seventies, I'd listen to Black Sabbath's 'Children of the Grave' in the dark to scare myself as a kid. In the early Nineties, 'Goat' by The Jesus Lizard brought on the heebie-jeebies. And in between, and to this day, *Night Time* and its monolithic aural depth-charges does it every time.

As I write this in America in June 2020, it appears Killing Joke already wrote the soundtrack for this nightmarish movie: a reality-television star-turned-president-turned-despot sowing seeds of chaos; a global pandemic killing hundreds of thousands; police with empty stares murdering people of colour with little fear of reprisal; furious citizens hitting the streets in protest.

Even just a sampling of Killing Joke song titles over their career – 'Bloodsport', 'This World Hell', 'Follow the Leaders', 'Age of Greed', 'I Am the Virus', to name but a few – paints an evocative picture of a planet barely holding on. Coupled with the music, one wonders whether this band is merely a mirror or have they actually helped create some of the madness that surrounds them?

FLETCHER STEWART

It's such a special thing to me that my passion for musical technology somehow guided me to meet my favourite band. And they are more relevant and stronger than ever. Though larger than life on stage, they have a true interest in their fans' lives, and every interaction with them has been lovely and enriching. The impact on the musical landscape Jaz, Geordie, Youth and Big Paul have imparted is immeasurable. May the furnace burn for years to come. Laugh at the peril and honour the fire.

JOE COSENZA

When I first started listening to Killing Joke, not hearing but *listening*, I knew what it felt like when humans first discovered fire. Things I'd noticed for years that were happening globally were in their songs. I no longer felt alone in my thoughts. It's become commonplace for bands to sing about war and the leaders who got us there, but I didn't know of any others singing about geoengineering, Monsanto pushing their GMO seeds and their cancer-causing pesticides, wiping out bee populations, or the central bankers running their operations to keep everyone in their financial system and under their control. The list can go on but, for the first time in a long time, I felt there were others genuinely concerned about all this stuff besides myself. Thank you, Big Paul, Youth, Geordie, Jaz and Raven, I am eternally grateful. Killing Joke is my Prometheus.

HELENA WEINBERG

I admire the genuineness and honesty of Killing Joke's musicians. They perform it so directly on stage and let people feel they are there for them. At these moments, none of the people there are lonely or desperate! They are carried by a common, real spirit.

I cannot thank you enough for these experiences.

ALEX SMITH

If you're looking for a tell-tale sign of musical greatness, search for a band that eludes concise classification. Killing Joke are just such a band. Prone to garnering a wide host of colourful descriptors, yet impossible to accurately pigeonhole, Killing Joke have remained a provocative, pugnacious, often polarising moving target for the span of their 42-year career. While certainly born of punk, the elements the original members brought to the table far exceeded the stagnating stylistic limitations that eventually hemmed in that genre. And despite Killing Joke's penchant for a stentorian heft to their sound, they've never quite been a heavy-metal band, their palette far too polychromatic for that similarly limiting tag. Their rhythms have embraced thundering primal tribalism, trippy dub, motorik pulses, unabashed four-on-the-floor disco beats and beyond. They may periodically share certain aesthetics with the so-called goth and industrial communities, but Killing Joke are neither a goth nor an industrial band, and never have been. As if.

If ever there was a catch-all label that practically applied to Killing Joke, it might be post-punk, given the specifics of their origins, their sensibility and their timeline. But peruse any purportedly authoritative text on same, and far too often their name is excluded from citation alongside more easily defined bands as Gang of Four, Public Image Ltd, Joy Division and other more celebrated outfits of the post-punk era. Killing Joke's dogged reluctance to adhere to any easily marketable signifier may have earned them a fervent army of bug-eyed, easily riled followers, but it did not especially endear them to record-company bean counters looking for seamlessly accessible product. It's not that Killing Joke didn't want to sell records — very much the opposite — but rather that, all too often, the sheer impact of their actual sound and particulars of the lyrical content made for a variant of sonic cocktail that didn't exactly go down easy. Considering the band's original intention was to replicate the sound of 'the earth vomiting', one imagines their often-chilly reception in the fluffier circles of the music industry shouldn't have been too much of a surprise. Oh well.

Phoenix Concert Theatre, Toronto, Canada – December 2010 © Michael Dent

JOHN DORAN

I've always loved music that hybridises, that recombines, that recontextualises. I think Killing Joke did that really well.

They were clearly into disco. If I had to do a DJ set, say, at the Berghain [nightclub in Berlin], and wanted people to dance – this is a crazy concept, but let's just go with it – literally the first thing I'd pack in my DJ bag would be the copy of 'Change' – 135bpm, absolute banger. It's classic disco drumming, classic driving bass. Killing Joke are almost more like A Certain Ratio in that respect. Killing Joke really, really work on the dancefloor. The drums on Killing Joke and Joy Division are some of the most exciting things ever. Everyone talks about the reggae, everyone talks about the punk – but, really, Killing Joke at their root were a disco band, I think. I remember saying this to Jaz and he was a bit defensive, saying: "We weren't really a disco band."

I wasn't saying it as a diss.

STEPHANE BONGINI

We often talk about the small joys of life. Killing Joke symbolises a lot of small joys, like being able to listen to a preview with Jaz in his hotel in London of tracks from the soon-to-be-released *Pylon* album. Like spending three days in Youth's Space Mountain Studios in Spain, with Jaz and Big Paul watching the production work on the *MMXII* album and enjoying the pool under the blazing sun. With Jaz making me tea...

It's the privileged feeling of hearing your favourite music before anyone else, especially in their working versions.

The observation of this creative phase is fascinating when you compare snippets of tracks and/or demos with the final version of the album.

Attending the Golden HIVE studio in Prague at such a moment of creative process for the song 'Panopticon'. Jaz encouraging Geordie to explore his riff genius is a magical moment of intimacy and aural enjoyment.

The little joys are also when I got a phone call from Geordie for my 50th birthday. It may sound simple, but, when you've been a fan of a band for so many years, when you've seen them live, on TV or in video clips, how can you imagine for one second that the guitarist who plays 'Love Like Blood' will give you a phone call for your birthday? And that you will also receive videos from the singer and the drummer and a note from the bass player for your 50th?

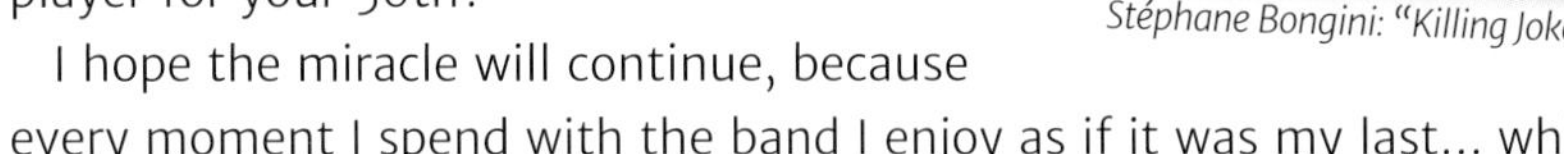

Stéphane Bongini: "Killing Joke symbolises a lot of small joys" © Stéphane Bongini

I hope the miracle will continue, because every moment I spend with the band I enjoy as if it was my last... which will inevitably happen.

In short, life's little pleasures.

SIMON ELLIS

I've seen loads of bands over the years, including the likes of Nirvana, Smashing Pumpkins, all as they were beginning and when they hit the top, but nothing ever really comes close to a Killing Joke gig. This band keep hooking you back in decade after decade. That makes them so different and so damn good!

IAN ROBERTSON

I struggle to think of any other band with this longevity or vitality – name another band, still going 30-odd years later, whose last three albums bristle with the same fire and originality as their first three. Killing Joke stand tall, their integrity still intact, burning brighter than a thousand suns.

JOHN DORAN

It's important to say they're one of the few bands who've done really good work late in their career.

MATTHIAS RICH

Above and beyond the music, Jaz Coleman's lyrical barbs worked on a level which mentally prepared me for the end of one millennium and the beginning of a new one. At the time of writing, in 2020, with a pandemic-stricken world teetering on the brink of the abyss, I take no comfort from the circumstances which have brought us here, but feel Killing Joke provided me with a suitable mental buffer zone which had enabled me to feel emotionally and mentally prepared for the world we now all live in.

Maybe someone's already said their music is the soundtrack for the apocalypse, but, as I find myself driving around in this world of insanity with KJ blasting from my stereo, the shoe just fits.

JAMES STOKES

I've never encountered a band that goes further, sounds louder or punches harder than Killing Joke. The collected works is a soundtrack to losing your existing worldview, then becoming a set of tools for putting together a new one. The history of the band affirms them as the most interesting thing in music, bar none: the weirdest Zeppelin legends and the most unbelievable tales of Mark E Smith's – (RIP) – treatment of journalists pale in comparison to Killing Joke.

IAN RABJOHN

For me, the second LP was the peak. I carried on going to see the band for the next couple of LPs but lost interest around the time of 'Love Like Blood', which didn't really appeal. Too smooth/polished. But I've seen them live in London a few times in recent years and they are back on fire. Maybe they never lost it, maybe I just stopped going as my music taste changed, but I'm glad I'm back in The Gathering again.

IAN LIDGETT

I've met the band a few times – Nottingham Rock City was the first time. All signed my CD and were up for pics. Went to see Jaz at St Pancras Church [17 June 2015] and had a chat with him after the lecture. A true gent and fascinating to hear his life stories.

Waiting with anticipation to see the band live is like no other experience I've had at a gig. The band never miss a beat and give 100% every time they play.

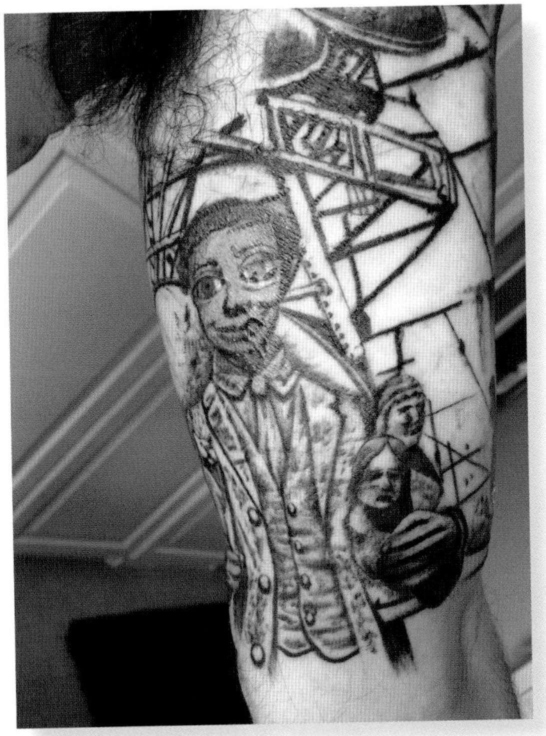

Ian Lidgett: "Jaz, Geordie, Big Paul, Youth, Raven (RIP) – thanks for life-changing memories"

JOHN DORAN

Like a lot of post-punks, to what extent are they really hippies? I don't think Geordie is, but I think Youth is.

MARK WHITELEY

Many years later, I can listen to 'In Cythera' and, on a human level, feel for the struggles Jaz laments. It felt similar when I first heard 'Prozac People'. Anyone who's tossed and turned in a cold sweat, checking the clock hour by hour, desperate to overcome an addiction or psychosis, will get it. For others, those songs are educational, informative and speak to the compassion that lies within even the darkest hearts.

NEIL BURKDOLL

At 43 years old, I still listen to the band regularly and, in fact, I think *Absolute Dissent* and *MMXII* are two of their best albums, along with *Night Time*. Killing Joke has always been in my life and I expect they will continue to be. Godflesh has been my favourite band since 1990. It was always obvious they were influenced by KJ and it really showed everyone how ahead of their time KJ were.

TOBY GRIST

I've never met any of them but I would love to. I think it would be a shame to miss that opportunity. I would be scared and maybe scarred, but it would be sacred. I almost got the nerve up to say hello to Jaz outside the Subterania [August 2019] but, as I was about to speak to him, a couple of selfie-huggers jumped him and visibly irritated him, so I left it.

Their music and ideas have permeated my adult life. Made me feel part of something. Made me understand I am not alone. They feel like brothers, like family, as do their fans.

LARRY BATE

I continue to travel and see this wonderful band and will forever be a KJ fanatic.

Liverpool Royal Court, 20 December 1983. "I will forever be a KJ fanatic" – Larry Bate © Larry Bate

STU BIRD

They didn't play to any rules and ploughed their own furrow. Something they still do now. Nearly 40 years later, I still look forward to Killing Joke gigs like a teenager, and they never disappoint. This is indeed music to march to...

AKI NAWAZ

Without doubt, Killing Joke as a band are unique and utterly original, occupying a special place for the rebellious punk years of the late Seventies onwards. That space, as a band of influence, cannot be played down and I can with an element of gloating and pride say every band I formed managed to support them at some concert somewhere.

The sound and landscape of their creativity stands alone, nothing to be compared with and nothing comparable with them.

DAVEID PHILLIPS

A 40-year love affair, punctuated by releases like the 'Follow the Leaders' 10-inch I just about wore out. I can still play it today and it feels as fresh as it did back then in my bedroom,

I've seen them countless times over the years, sometimes on my own, sometimes with others I think are just humouring me and don't really get them.

I never cared because, every time I see them, I'm transported back to the moment I discovered them as a kid and the first time I saw them, crushed at the front of a heaving punk rock crowd with my arms open wide, my eyes locked on Jaz as it felt like my internal DNA was being added to with the power that is Killing Joke live.

I recently bought Jaz's *Magna Invocatio* and it reduced me to tears, happy and sad tears.

He can still do it; he still has that extraordinarily seductive power I felt when I first heard his and Killing Joke's music. They will forever be 'my band'.

JAZ COLEMAN
St Petersburg
Philharmonic Orchestra
MAGNA
A Gnostic Mass for choir and orchestra
inspired by the sublime music of Killing Joke
INVOCATIO

JOHN DORAN

Don't you think Killing Joke have the perfect name? The name appertains to humour and, when you meet them, they're humorous people. How often does the figure of the clown crop up in their artwork? Maybe we're being asked to investigate what the actual nature of humour is.

ANGELA WARD

(astrologer, funeral celebrant and druid)

All of them have a special place in my heart. Raven for his volcanic passion and magnificent wit. Paul – like a pure flame of energy. I watch him work and I'm always floored by what he can do – huge capacity but sensitive and wise, artistic yet so humble. Youth, well, he's as generous a person as you could meet in his open-minded and inquiring attitude to the human animal. He's deep in the rhythm of life – laconic, dry, observant, endlessly creative, the soul of an artist, free spirit and traveller. Geordie is the person with whom I can tramp around in the hedgerows, pore over maps and find brooks and rivers for the best fishing spots – Geordie's real passion. Good long lunches, fine wine, old radios, precision engineering, fish and chips, patron, something to fix. Wily, clever, and acerbic one-liners to make you fall off your chair. And, of course, that sound, hewn in white heat and ice and sung by a thousand sonic angels.

And Jaz. The channel for it all that we connect with at the front of the stage. He stands at the edge of the veil and sees beyond the next horizon. Between this world and the next, he articulates something utterly profound and, for me, utterly personal. He is feral, wise, compassionate and a true visionary with the best and the worst of humanity in his understanding.

I have laughed, ranted, cried, danced, fought, sung, travelled, advised, loved and created with these men. I have been honoured to be their friend, companion and fellow traveller for all this time. There will not be another such as Killing Joke.

© Tony Woolliscroft

JAZ

We see the ceremony that we do before we go on stage as so powerful that it banishes all negative, all evil forces.

We do the opposite of a banishing ritual – we do an invoking ritual. We not only invoke the spirits of where we are, but we call on our ancestral spirits. That is, our forefathers who are in the other world. All our dads are dead. We call on our fathers to be here and everyone else who has loved us and loved Killing Joke who moved into the other world. We call them all to be with us. We put our foreheads together. We hug each other. Everybody says the prayer.

I can't tell you exactly what is said, but it start with the words, "Spirits of this time and place, be here now..."

We wouldn't dare start without it. It has a very, very powerful unifying effect on us. And we feel protected – completely.

ANDY BOTT

Coventry booked for 2020. Cancelled. This cannot be the end. I won't let it...

When will Killing Joke next grace the stage at London's Roundhouse, a semi-regular stamping ground in recent years? © Tony Woolliscroft

"Shoulder to shoulder until the end"

JAZ

At this stage before a Killing Joke album, you can feel it coming. I can feel my brothers out there. It's coming. Although I'm not in the same continent, I'm with all of them. I know exactly the hour that Geordie wakes up every day, 'cos I always wake up 10 minutes after him. When you've been together long as we have, oh my God...

Backstage at the Roundhouse, 17 November 2018 © Tony Woolliscroft

Jaz: "We know we can beat all of the albums that we've done. And that's the task that is ahead of us" © *Tony Woolliscroft*

BIG PAUL

It's been a long time. It's been difficult. Sometimes, commitments have clashed, which has made choices very hard. Each of us live on different continents, which makes rehearsing/writing a difficult and expensive proposition.

GEORDIE

It's always better if you play 'em [new tracks] in [before recording] but we're all over the fuckin' world. We made it a lot fucking harder work.

JAZ

Every Killing Joke album is utterly traumatic. I don't know why it has to be like that. Don't ask me why it has to be like that. It just is like that. And whatever you think it's gonna be like, it's not gonna be like that. It's gonna be like whatever it wants to be like. You have to have an open mind. It's a kind of open workshop.

BIG PAUL

[We are] not locked into a style and each of us has massively different tastes. Who knows where the clash of wills will lead us? Usually to a good place.

GEORDIE

My criteria of songs is what would I stand on stage in front of a load of people and play, then look them in the eye. That's how I judge all of it. That's what I'm thinking when I'm writing songs or coming up with music. Would I be in communion with this?

JAZ

We know we can beat all the albums that we've done. That's the task that is ahead of us. Everyone's taking a deep breath in. It starts like this: "Whatever you think is good is shit. Whatever you think is even coming from God is not good enough." And that's our starting point.

As the late, great Paul Raven said: "Don't peak too soon."

GEORDIE

We'll fucking get there. I did eight tracks with Tom Dalgety in two days back at the end of January. He's just so fucking quick – psychic producer.

BIG PAUL

They [the albums] all have a different flavour and I've loved every one. With the exceptions, naturally, of *Outside the Bollocks* and the others I wasn't on!

A sermon from Reverend Walker? No swearing, please © Tom Dalgety

YOUTH

A lot of kids today are super, super-fearful of putting anything out. But they do it as avoidance. Perfectionism as avoidance is a common theme I have dealt with as a producer with artists. We're guilty of that as well with Killing Joke. Absolutely we are, Jesus. We're super-adept at all the avoidance techniques between us. Which is one of the reasons it's very hard for us to ever get anything done.

But, once we're actually in the room together, we're really focused and we get on with it. And that's what you gotta do.

GEORDIE

I like capturing the stream of consciousness.

YOUTH

It's almost impossible to rationalise what that magic is, but I suspect and sense it's the chemistry. Like in a test tube when you put two opposing elements together and they fire up. Simply that. Plus some old karmic energy that hadn't been worked off that brought us together in this way.

GEORDIE

You gotta get back to the roots. Where's the gig? Where's the stage? What works there? That's the default position. Get back on stage. Keep it simple. Too much of a cerebral concept? It can disappear up its own arse. You have to keep a rein on it.

JAZ

If you are living the life the right way, when we get together it just comes out. It just oozes out. There's no analysis. Nearly all the albums have been written in the studio. Sometimes, Geords and me do a bit of prepping. Generally speaking, it just comes together because of the friction we create between each other. They don't change, these guys. Our dynamic is forever the same.

YOUTH

We've remained friends and colleagues for over 40 years and we're still making a lot of fire and sparks together.

JAZ

Once we lock into this energy, this current, it's so heavy. We're so good now. Killing Joke's so good now. I'm thrilled just thinking about it.

YOUTH

You've got to commit to it. And sacrifice possibly 80% of the rest of your life. And it's just got worse [over time]. Probably 90% now.

JAZ

Killing Joke tours are never long enough for me. I like the life. I'm a bit like Raven there. I'm a nomadic person. I'm on the move. When haven't I been on the move? It's very hard to keep still. I'm a bit like that, bit of a restless soul. I can't wait to get stuck into touring. I wish we could do a hundred gigs non-stop. I've got a big appetite for concerts. I wanna visit Baghdad. Definitely go to Lebanon to record the new album. Haiti. I wanna feel the mass of humanity. I wanna feel what's happening and let it profoundly affect me.

GEORDIE

The rehearsals can be a pain in the arse. Locked in the tube with a fucking nutter in the carriage. Can get a bit like that.

JAZ

You miss it after a while. It's a way of life. It's our university. It's our everything. It's very hard on the body and mind but it's addictive. And then there's how we are as a band on the social level. Our tradition of truly black humour. People don't understand how we talk to each other. They say, "You lot hate each other." Nah, it's just like that. Everybody in the band knows every muscle in everybody's face and there's nothing that can be hidden. I'll be honest, Youth and Geordie are never happier than when things are falling to bits.

GEORDIE

If anything gets pined for, it's being on stage.

JAZ

The Killing Joke tour bus. The back lounge is the bad boys' room and the front lounge is no smoking. There are so many books... It looks like a travelling library. There's so much vinyl there, it looks like we've been living there for 100 years.

On top of this, there's things like antlers and all sorts of rubbish Youth buys and puts everywhere. One time, we were finishing

© Tony Woolliscroft

a tour in New York City and I was banging on Youth's door at the Gramercy Park Hotel. I opened the door and I tell you what – he gathers so much stuff on tour. We had an extra trailer to bring all the rubbish Youth picks up.

It's all worthless stuff. It's stuff like illuminated statues of the Virgin Mary.

I walked into his room and it was piled to the ceiling. And Youth's trying to negotiate how he's gonna get all this stuff back to London. It looked like *Steptoe and Son*. It looked like he'd been there all his life in this room. He's a part-time rag and bone man.

YOUTH

I definitely believe that opposites attract.

JAZ

It's been amazing for me and for us to leave high school with no exams... Everybody's achieved so many things. All of this was made possible through punk and its philosophy of 'no fear of failure' and 'I'll have a go'.

I intend to return to New Zealand and make a real difference there in my remaining years. [PM] Jacinda [Ardern] knows I support her. She's steered our country through this crisis in a way that makes me proud to be a New Zealander. She puts so much money into the arts. All the musicians love her.

I wanna be more active, not less active. I feel energetic and super-aggressive about what I am doing.

YOUTH

[On his interactions with LSD] The whole life – this studio, the music I've made for the last 30 years since that experience – has all been informed by it. I needed that to shake off my pseudo street-punk persona I built up: a rudderless ship of a spiritless, Neanderthal, self-serving... You know... It wasn't pretty. Although I did have a lot of fun, I had to get rid of that. I had to be reduced to my element then be re-informed and re-invented in terms of purpose, meaning. Absolutely it's the most important experience I've ever had. Absolutely the most powerful positive experience, even though it came quite close to killing me.

From that experience, [I've learned] how to be fearless, how to take risks, how to trust, how to see the universe as essentially a benevolent thing, enough to throw yourself into it. It's a paradox. It killed other people. They never actually managed to come back through that Alice in Wonderland door. Most people can't come back the same person. If you do, how you rebuild your ego... I was very lucky. I had some very good mentors around me, and friends.

JAZ

Personalities in Killing Joke haven't changed. There was a point after 2008 when I thought Paul had gone pretty zen. Until I saw him grabbing someone, probably our road manager, around the throat. And I thought: "Nothing's changed."

Youth: "You don't wanna go through life with fear" © Tony Woolliscroft

BIG PAUL

We are who we are, no one trying to be something else, and there is an acceptance of that. We never change. It changes around us.

Vale Studios, 2015 © Tom Dalgety

JAZ

One of us in the band is going mad at any one time. But you can't do it all together. You have to do it in turns.

BIG PAUL

It's always a struggle, and there is deep affection.

JAZ

Myself and my colleagues, we were born in the shadow of the war. It's forgotten by subsequent generations. We're hard-wired against fascism. I lost family members in the last world war.

My father took us to Germany once. He made us go to all the concentration camps, drummed it into us that this was because good men didn't speak out. The more people speak out about the trend towards fascism, the better. So, when I see evil trends, of a technotronic age that is tantamount to slavery, I'm gonna keep speaking. I resist it with all my being. None of us in Killing Joke believe in suicide so, if anything happened to me, it wasn't an accident.

The years are passing, the anger is still increasing. I'm furious. I feel sad for humanity and, of course, my grandson. I feel compelled to speak out as a citizen. There is a moral obligation for me to fight for a better world. I know it puts me on the spot. And I've had quite a lot of weird experiences because of it. And I suppose it doesn't do me any good.

Look. Let me be very clear. We must evolve to planetary consciousness. When I say that, I do not endorse any fascistic New World Order, which is normally associated with a unipolar world. What I endorse is a polycentric world in which nation states all have a say in the future development of mankind. That's what we've learned the hard way through Brexit.

People have forgotten the fact that they have the major say in what kind of world we wanna live in. This is a wake-up call.

YOUTH

Face the sun and the shadows fall behind you. You don't wanna go through life with fear.

JAZ

I'm very proud to work with Youth because of his undying belief in counter-culture. [We had] a fantastic conversation on the last tour. We were talking about the origins of counter-culture. The truth of the matter is, the origins of counter-culture – and you can refer Dr John Coleman's work – is that the counter-culture was actually created in a laboratory. People like [Theodor] Adorno and the Frankfurt School of Psychiatry. The counter-culture of the Sixties was definitely manufactured – there's no question about it. It's pretty much declassified now, all that stuff. We know about that.

What was amazing about this reflection on the tour bus was that Geordie and Youth spoke up and said: "We don't draw our counter-culture from this line. [We take it from] the Nature Boys." Of course, there was that single 'Nature Boy' [popularised by Nat King Cole], which Geordie told me about.

These were conscientious objectors in the First World War who believed in permaculture and Earth Communities close to the land. We had this incredible conversation, concluding in the point that, when it comes to counter-culture, Killing Joke didn't draw its roots from the counter-culture of the Sixties but in the Nature Boys, the conscientious objectors of the First World War. You'd never have a conversation like this with any other band. This is kind of a normal day with Killing Joke.

There's never been any doubt since I started this band that it would be there in my life for the remainder of my life. There's never been any doubt.

YOUTH

I believe in reincarnation. I definitely feel we've worked together before in different ways.

Probably as pirates.

Jaz at Nottingham Rock City in 2018. "There's never been any doubt since I started this band that it would be there in my life for the remainder of my life" © Tony Woolliscroft

A PROPHECY FULFILLED

JAZ

You have to understand that Killing Joke started with Big Paul and myself taking that oath. That's how serious it was and is. Our most holy and sacred mission. Forces that started the band protected us so we can be here at this stage in the Earth's development. This is absolutely true.

It's only now that the wider public are beginning to appreciate the precognitive nature of Killing Joke's work. If you want to see what's coming on the planet, it's probably a good idea to have a look at the complete lyrics of Killing Joke.

When I think about our unblemished record – lyrically, thematically – from the first album to where we are now, all we could ever do is be honest and say: "You call me mad, but this is coming. You don't realise – this is coming." And now we're here.

You could say, figuratively speaking, we've been privileged to be kept alive so we can hold the world's hand as we walk through the transition from one world to a new world.

Suddenly, Killing Joke is everywhere and we now are, indisputably, the most influential band in the world.

Shepherd's Bush Empire, London – February 2005 © Tony Woolliscroft

ACKNOWLEDGEMENTS

I am deeply indebted to everyone who took the time to contribute to this project. No people, no book. Simple as.

But I need to express special thanks to certain individuals. Frank Jenkinson, for opening up his unrivalled archive of images from those early, heady days of the band. He even dusted off folders I don't believe he himself had looked at in almost 40 years in a successful search for images to illustrate the making of *What's THIS for...!* Visit his Killing Joke Picture Book Facebook page and look out for more physical releases from Frank. Mont Sherar allowed me use of previously unseen images, including what he calls 'The Last Supper'. His *Sex Wax N Rock N Roll and Other Foolish Explorations* is coming your way in 2021. Mike Coles went way above and beyond to send me a choice selection from his book *Forty Years in the Wilderness*, a thing of genuine beauty. And thanks to Michael Dent for permission to use extracts from his unpublished autobiography *Fanboy – Stories of My Life in Music.*

On the networking front, Matt Tibbits was a constant source of encouragement and good guidance, bringing up names and lines of investigation that turned up trumps. Rob Moss suggested I contact Brian James, which resulted in a tale and a link with Killing Joke that I had no idea even existed. And, late in the project, Ron Synovitz in Prague put together a series of superb interviews that form the bedrock for the band's timeline from the mid-2000s to the present day.

None of the above needed to do what they did. And I know they didn't do it because of me. They did it because they all love this unique band, this force of nature, these geniuses we have been privileged to experience – KILLING JOKE.

Chris Bryans ***October 2020***

The publishers would like to say a special thanks to Paula Flack for the idea and the introduction. Nick Lawrence for all his help in pulling this book together. And thanks to Mike Coles, Frank Jenkinson, Ian Robertson, Adrian Wason and Tony Woolliscroft for all the photos.